Principles of Fi
Services and Products

LOMA (Life Office Management Association, Inc.) is an international association founded in 1924. LOMA is committed to a business partnership with its worldwide members in the insurance and financial services industry to improve their management and operations through quality employee development, research, information sharing, and related products and services. Among LOMA's activities is the sponsorship of several self-study education programs leading to professional designations. These programs include the Fellow, Life Management Institute (FLMI) program and the Fellow, Financial Services Institute (FFSI) program. For more information on all of LOMA's education programs, please visit www.loma.org.

Statement of Purpose: LOMA Educational Programs Testing and Designations
Examinations described in the *LOMA Education and Training Catalog* are designed solely to measure whether students have successfully completed the relevant assigned curriculum, and the attainment of the FFSI and other LOMA designations indicates only that all examinations in the given curriculum have been successfully completed. In no way shall a student's completion of a given LOMA course or attainment of the FFSI or other LOMA designation be construed to mean that LOMA in any way certifies that student's competence, training, or ability to perform any given task. LOMA's examinations are to be used solely for general educational purposes, and no other use of the examinations or programs is authorized or intended by LOMA. Furthermore, it is in no way the intention of the LOMA Curriculum and Examinations staff to describe the standard of appropriate conduct in any field of the insurance and financial services industry, and LOMA expressly repudiates any attempt to so use the curriculum and examinations. Any such assessment of student competence or industry standards of conduct should instead be based on independent professional inquiry and the advice of competent professional counsel.

Principles of Financial Services and Products

Mary C. Bickley

LOMA

Information That Works®

LOMA Education and Training
Financial Services Institute
Atlanta, Georgia
www.loma.org

Information in this text may have been changed or updated since its publication date. For current updates, visit www.loma.org.

LOMA 286 TEXT — PRINCIPLES OF FINANCIAL SERVICES AND PRODUCTS

Author:	Mary C. Bickley, J.D., FLMI, CLU, AIRC, ACS, AIAA, PAHM, AAPA
Contributing Authors:	Susan Conant, FLMI, CEBS, HIA, PAHM
	Patsy Leeuwenburg, Ph.D., FLMI, ACS, ALHC, ARA, AIRC, AAPA, AIAA, PAHM
Manuscript Editor:	Nicholas L. Desoutter, FLMI, AAPA, PCS
Exam Editor:	Sean Schaeffer Gilley, FLMI, ACS, HIA, CEBS, AIAA, PAHM, MHP, AIRC, AAPA, ARA, FLHC
Project Manager:	Gene Stone, FLMI, ACS, CLU
Production Manager:	Stephen J. Bollinger, ACS
Copyeditor:	Eastman Communications
Indexer:	Mary Rusch
Typesetters:	Stephen J. Bollinger, ACS
	Kathleen Ryan, FLMI, FAHM, PCS, AIAA, AIRC, ARA
	Amy Souwan
Production Coordinator:	Amy Souwan
Print Buyer:	Audrey H. Gregory, ACS
Permissions Coordinator:	Iris F. Hartley, FLMI, ALHC
Administrative Support:	Mamunah Carter
Cover Design:	Stephen J. Bollinger, ACS
	Kathleen Ryan, FLMI, FAHM, PCS, AIAA, AIRC, ARA

12 11 10 09 08 07 06 05 04 10 9 8 7 6 5 4 3 2 1

Library of Congress Cataloging-in-Publication Data

Bickley, Mary C.
Principles of financial services and products / Mary C. Bickley.
p. cm.
Includes index.
ISBN 1-57974-205-X
1. Financial services industry--United States. 2. Finance, Personal--United States. 3. Investments--United States. 4. Insurance--United States. I. Title.

HG181.B435 2004
332.1'0973--dc22

ISBN 1-57974-205-X

Printed in the United States of America

Contents

Preface

Principles of Financial Services and Products is the textbook for the initial course of LOMA's new Fellow, Financial Services Institute education program. The major categories of financial services—cash management, credit, asset protection, asset accumulation and management, and asset distribution—form the framework for this text, which surveys banking, insurance, and investment products.

Acknowledgments

LOMA's Education and Training Division has assembled a team of writers, editors, and production staff who work together closely to create educational publications such as this textbook. This staff team, however, depends on the work of industry professionals who devote countless hours to help ensure that LOMA's educational publications are as accurate and complete as possible.

Textbook Review Panel

Writing this text would not have been possible without the efforts of the review panel, who care enough about the educational needs of current and future industry employees to volunteer their time and expertise to this project. These individuals read and commented on the outline and the manuscript, answered many author questions, and provided ideas and documents for supporting materials. LOMA is grateful to the following individuals:

- Thomas Burdg, CPA, Senior Financial Consultant, Thrivent Financial
- Marcelo Ruben Crespo, UBA, Chief Financial Officer and Chief Compliance Officer, MassLife Seguros de Vida S.A.
- Steve Degnan-Schmidt, Director, Six Sigma, Allstate Insurance Company
- Alan L. Fry, CLU, ChFC, CFP, FLMI/M, AAPA, PCS, President and Chief Executive Officer, e-Consulting Services, Inc., Retirement Planning Consulting
- Stéphane Goyer, FSA, MAAA, Vice President, Variable Product Development Actuary, Protective Life Insurance Company
- Michael D. Kaska, CLU, CFP, Vice President, Agency Sales Management and Development, John Hancock International, Inc.

- Alun D. G. Masterton, CGA, Director of Finance, Manulife Bank of Canada
- Carolann V. Mathews, FLMI, CLU, ChFC, MSM, Vice President, AXA Financial
- Luu Ky Nam, FLMI, Assistant Director, Agency Support and Administration, Prudential (U.K.) Vietnam
- Douglas A. Pennington, FLMI, ACS, AIAA, AIRC, ARA, AAI, CISR, I-Net+, Product Trainer, Chubb Group of Insurance Companies
- Richard A. Reger, FLMI/M, CLU, ChFC, Career Agent, Farm Bureau Financial Services
- Stephanie L. Riva, CFA, FLMI/M, CCIM, Managing Director, Principal Global Investors
- Eric T. Sondergeld, ASA, CFA, MAAA, Corporate Vice President and Director, Retirement Research Center, LIMRA International
- Steven N. Weisbart, Ph.D., CLU, Vice President, Financial Communications, TIAA-CREF
- Berry Wilson, CPA, CISA, FLMI, Head of Operational Risk Management, ING Americas

We also wish to thank the following individuals who reviewed portions of the text:

- Marc E. Cavadel, J.D., FLMI, AIRC, AAPA, ACS, PCS, ARA, AIAA, ASF, CSF, Assistant Vice President – Product Development, Protective Life Insurance Company
- Elizabeth E. Friberg, RN, MSN, PAHM, Healthcare Consultant
- Jason M. Gibson, Compliance Manager, Lincoln Financial Advisors
- Thomas F. Grillo, Vice President and Director of Regulatory Oversight, Chase Insurance Agency, Inc.
- Scott Herchenbach, FSA, MAAA, FLMI, Vice President and Actuary, Mutual of Omaha Insurance Company
- William C. Huff, FSA, MAAA, Assistant Vice President and Managing Actuary, Safeco Life Insurance Company
- William R. Keller, Jr., CLU, FLMI, CRA, CRC, Vice President, Annuity Product Strategy, AIG VALIC

- Lucian J. Lombardi, ASA, Vice President, Product and Distribution Research, LIMRA International
- Anita Potter, Research Manager, LIMRA International
- Steven A. Rohrig, ChFC, CRPS, Individual Retirement Plans Consultant, Mutual of Omaha
- Steven I. Silberberg, FSA, EA, MAAA, Principal, Mercer Human Resource Consulting
- Bethany Spurrier, Manager, Retirement and Savings Plans, Dynegy, Inc.
- John W. Stinnett, Underwriting Specialist, St. Paul Fire and Marine Insurance Company
- Mary M. Swanson, CLU, Associate Scientist, Retirement Research, LIMRA International
- David A. Ueeck, CPCU, ChFC, CLU, ARM, AU, Director, Learning & Development, Sate Farm
- Charles F. Vickery, Investment Advisor Representative, Thrivent Financial
- Christine L. Washington, FLMI, AAPA, ACS, IRA/Annuity Administrator, ING Institutional Markets, ING
- Bruce H. Wynn, J.D., P.C., Partner, Employee Benefits and Executive Compensation, Morris, Manning & Martin, LLP

LOMA Staff

Writing a text at LOMA is a collaborative effort not only with our industry reviewers, but with other LOMA staff members who lend their time and expertise so unselfishly. These individuals from Education and Training Products include Nicholas L. Desoutter, FLMI, AAPA, PCS, Senior Associate, who served as Manuscript Editor; Gene Stone, FLMI, ACS, CLU, Senior Associate, who served as Project Manager; Joyce R. Abrams, J.D., FLMI, PCS, AAPA, AIRC, ARA, AIAA, PAHM, ALHC, HIA, MHP, Assistant Vice President, who reviewed the entire text in her capacity as Department Manager; Susan Conant, FLMI, CEBS, HIA, PAHM, Senior Associate, who wrote two of the chapters; Patsy Leeuwenburg, Ph.D., FLMI, ACS, ALHC, ARA, AIRC, AAPA, AIAA, PAHM, Senior Associate, who wrote two chapters; Harriett E. Jones, J.D., FLMI, AIRC, ACS, Senior Associate; Jena L. Kennedy, FLMI, ALHC, ACS, PAHM, CLU,

Assistant Vice President; Monica R. Maxwell, J.D., FLMI, AIRC, ACS, ARA, AIAA, Senior Associate; and Miriam A. Orsina, FLMI, PCS, ARA, PAHM, Senior Associate. Thanks go to Mark Adel, FLMI, PCS, AAPA, AIRC, PAHM, Senior Associate, who developed the *LOMA 286 Quick Review—Principles of Financial Services and Products* CD-ROM that accompanies this text. Also to be thanked is Mamunah Carter, Administrative Assistant III, who provided administrative support.

Individuals in the Examinations Department who contributed to the text include Sean Schaeffer Gilley, FLMI, ACS, HIA, CEBS, AIAA, PAHM, MHP, AIRC, AAPA, ARA, FLHC, Senior Associate, who served as Exam Editor; Julia K. Wooley, FLMI, ACS, ALHC, HIA, MHP, Assistant Vice President; Melanie R. Green, FLMI, ACS, AIAA, Senior Associate; Vivian Heeden, FLMI, CLU, FLHC, PCS, AIAA, AIRC, ARA, AAPA, PAHM, Senior Associate; Cynthia Mathis Henry, FLMI, ALHC, ACS, PAHM, Senior Associate; and Kelly W. Neeley, FLMI, ALHC, ACS, AIAA, PAHM, Senior Associate.

Other LOMA staff members who lent their assistance to the development of this text include Todd A. Blandin, Director, Product Marketing; Scott Cipinko, J.D., Executive Director of Life Insurers Council and Vice President of LOMA; Steve Forbes, Ph.D., FLMI, Senior Vice President, Research; Jean C. Gora, Manager of Research; Michele LaBouff, Second Vice President, Human Resources; Stephanie McDonald, Senior Human Resources Associate, Human Resources; and E. Allison Middleton, FLMI, PCS, FAHM, AIAA, Assistant Vice President, International Division.

In LOMA's Production Department, thanks go to Stephen J. Bollinger, ACS, Production Manager, who oversaw the production of the text and handled the technical development of the *Quick Review*; Kathleen Ryan, FLMI, FAHM, PCS, AIAA, AIRC, ARA, Production Coordinator II; and Amy Souwan, Production Coordinator II/Scheduling Coordinator. Also to be thanked are Eastman Communications for copyediting the manuscript and Iris F. Hartley, FLMI, ALHC, a LOMA consultant, who secured the necessary permissions.

Also deserving of thanks are the individuals in LOMA's Information Center who provided valuable research services: Patricia Ann Touchstone Toups, Librarian; Olivia Blakemore, ACS, Technical Administrator; Mallory Eldridge, Research Analyst/Writer; and Janet Smith, Researcher.

Special thanks go to Katherine C. Milligan, FLMI, ACS, ALHC, Vice President, and William H. Rabel, Ph.D., FLMI, CLU, Senior Vice President, both of the Education and Training Division, who provided guidance, support, and encouragement for this project.

Mary C. Bickley, J.D., FLMI, CLU, AIRC, ACS, AIAA, PAHM, AAPA
Atlanta, Georgia
2004

Introduction

The purpose of *Principles of Financial Services and Products* is to provide an overview of the services and products provided by the financial services industry. LOMA has designed this book for students who are preparing to take the examination for LOMA 286—Principles of Financial Services and Products—which is part of the Fellow, Financial Services Institute (FFSI) and other LOMA designation programs. Each chapter includes several features to help you organize your studies, reinforce your understanding of the materials, and prepare for the examination. As we describe each of these features, we give you suggestions for studying the material.

- **Learning Objectives.** The first page of each chapter contains a list of learning objectives to help you focus your studies. Before reading each chapter, review these learning objectives. Then, as you read the chapter, look for material that will help you meet the learning objectives.

- **Chapter Outline.** The first page of each chapter contains an outline of the chapter. Review this outline to gain an overview of the major topics that will be covered; then scan through the chapter to familiarize yourself with the presentation of the information. Looking at the headings and figures will give you a preview of how the various subjects relate to each other.

- **Key Terms.** This text reviews the key terms associated with the services and products of the financial services industry. All of the important terminology introduced in this text is defined or explained when it is first used. Important terminology is highlighted with ***bold italic type*** when the term is first defined, and a list of these key terms appears at the end of each chapter. All key terms also appear in a comprehensive glossary at the end of the book. As you read each chapter, pay special attention to those key terms.

- **Figures.** Figures that appear throughout the text illustrate the text's discussions of selected important topics. Note that information contained in figures may be tested on the examination for this course.

- **Insights.** Insights that appear throughout the text amplify the text's descriptions of certain topics. These insights should help you get a better feel for the financial services industry's services and products. Note that information contained in insights may be tested on the examination for this course.

- **Glossary.** A comprehensive glossary containing definitions of all key terms appears at the end of the book. Following each glossary entry is a number in brackets that indicates the chapter in which the key term is defined. The glossary includes references to important equivalent terms, acronyms, and contrasting terms.

The text and study aids for LOMA courses may be revised periodically. To ensure that you are studying from the correct materials, check the current *LOMA Education and Training Catalog* for a description of the texts and study aids assigned for the examination for which you are preparing.

Using LOMA Study Aids

LOMA has prepared study aids designed to help students prepare for the LOMA 286 examination. LOMA recommends that you use all of the study aids available for this course. **Studies indicate that students who use LOMA study aids consistently perform significantly better on LOMA examinations than students who do not use these study aids.**

Test Preparation Guide and Instructor's Kit

In addition to this book, LOMA's *Test Preparation Guide for LOMA 286* is assigned reading for students preparing for the LOMA 286 examination. Used along with this textbook, the Test Preparation Guide will help you master the course material. The Test Preparation Guide includes case studies, practice exam questions, a full-scale sample examination in both paper and electronic format, and answers to every question in the Test Preparation Guide.

LOMA also has prepared an *Instructor's Kit for LOMA 286*, designed to help company instructors prepare to teach preparatory classes for the LOMA 286 examination.

Using the *Quick Review* CD-ROM Accompanying This Text

The CD-ROM found on the inside back cover of this text contains the *LOMA 286 Quick Review—Principles of Financial Services and Products*, which gives you an overview of the materials found in this text. The *Quick Review* is designed for instructors and students studying for the LOMA 286 examination.

Suggested Additional Reading

Some students may find it helpful to read the following LOMA *StepOne Series* publication that is related to this course: *Intro to Financial Services* (2001).

Principles of Financial Services and Products

chapter 1

The Financial Services Industry

outline

Financial Services

- Categories of Financial Services and the Needs They Fulfill
- Advice as a Financial Service

Traditional Financial Institutions

- Depository Institutions
- Finance Companies
- Insurance Companies
- Mutual Funds
- Securities Firms

Government's Role in the Financial Services Industry

- Social Insurance
- Taxation

Evolution of the Financial Services Industry

- Convergence
- Consolidation
- Globalization

objectives

After reading this chapter, you should be able to

- Describe the categories of financial services and the needs they fulfill
- Discuss the emergence of the financial planning profession
- Distinguish among the various financial services institutions
- Discuss government's role in the financial services industry
- Describe the evolution of the financial services industry's competitive landscape

Many people have some or all of the following financial products: a checking account, a debit card, a credit card, a mortgage, homeowners insurance, life insurance, health insurance, automobile insurance, and a brokerage account. In addition, many people participate in an employer-sponsored retirement plan. All of these financial products help people achieve their goals in life. Financial products can help people manage income and debt, improve their lifestyles, accumulate resources to enjoy retirement, and protect themselves and their families from financial losses due to unexpected occurrences such as natural disasters, disability, or premature death. The financial services industry offers a vast array of products to serve these purposes.

The ***financial services industry*** is the industry consisting of financial institutions that offer products and services to help people, businesses, and governments meet their financial goals. A ***financial institution*** is a business that owns primarily financial assets, such as stocks and bonds, rather than fixed assets, such as equipment and raw materials. Financial institutions include banks, finance companies, insurance companies, mutual fund companies, and securities firms.

Financial institutions play an important role in the economy as financial intermediaries. A ***financial intermediary*** is an organization that channels funds from those people, businesses, and governments who have a surplus of funds (savers) to those who have a shortage of funds (borrowers). For example, a bank is a financial intermediary because it accepts deposits from its customers who are saving their funds, pools these funds, and then lends them to other customers who need the funds to make purchases.

The transfer of funds from savers to borrowers through the services of a financial intermediary is known as ***intermediation***. Moving funds through intermediation helps savers, borrowers, and the economy as a whole. Through intermediation, savers can protect or increase their wealth in anticipation of future financial needs. In addition, borrowers can secure funds to buy goods and services or make investments in new businesses or equipment, leading to growth in the economy.

The financial services industry is one of the most important sectors of the economy of many developed countries. For example, the financial services sector contributed 9 percent to the United States gross domestic product in 2001.[1] The gross domestic product (GDP) is the value of all goods and services produced in the economy.

The purpose of this text is to provide an understanding of the services and products offered by the financial services industry. We focus on the services and products rather than the institutions that offer them because the industry is undergoing changes that tend to obscure the distinctions among institutions. We also focus more on the individual customer than on the business customer.

In this text, you will learn some fundamental financial concepts, such as the time value of money and the risk-return tradeoff, knowledge of which is necessary for a thorough understanding of financial services. The majority of the text is devoted to the characteristics of financial products and how the products can satisfy certain financial needs. Note, though, that this is not a financial planning text.

We begin in this chapter with a general overview of the services and products offered by the financial services industry, the traditional types of financial institutions, government's role in the financial services industry, and the evolution of the financial services industry.

Financial Services

The financial services industry does not provide tangible goods to its customers. Instead, the industry offers services. A ***service*** is a primarily intangible activity that one party performs for another. Services can be experienced only as they are performed, used, or consumed. Although financial services may be evidenced by pieces of paper (the "products"), they have no other physical manifestation. For example, although insurance is evidenced by a written document, insurance is actually an insurer's intangible promise to pay benefits upon the occurrence of an insured event.

Categories of Financial Services and the Needs They Fulfill

The categories of financial services reflect the customer needs they are designed to fulfill. These categories are illustrated in Figure 1.1.

In this section, we describe these categories of financial services, which provide the framework for our discussion of financial products in this text.

Cash Management

Cash management is the allocation of readily available funds among various living expenses as well as among savings and investment opportunities. People need cash management products that enable them to pay bills, make purchases, and store money for short periods with little cost or risk.

FIGURE 1.1 Categories of Financial Services

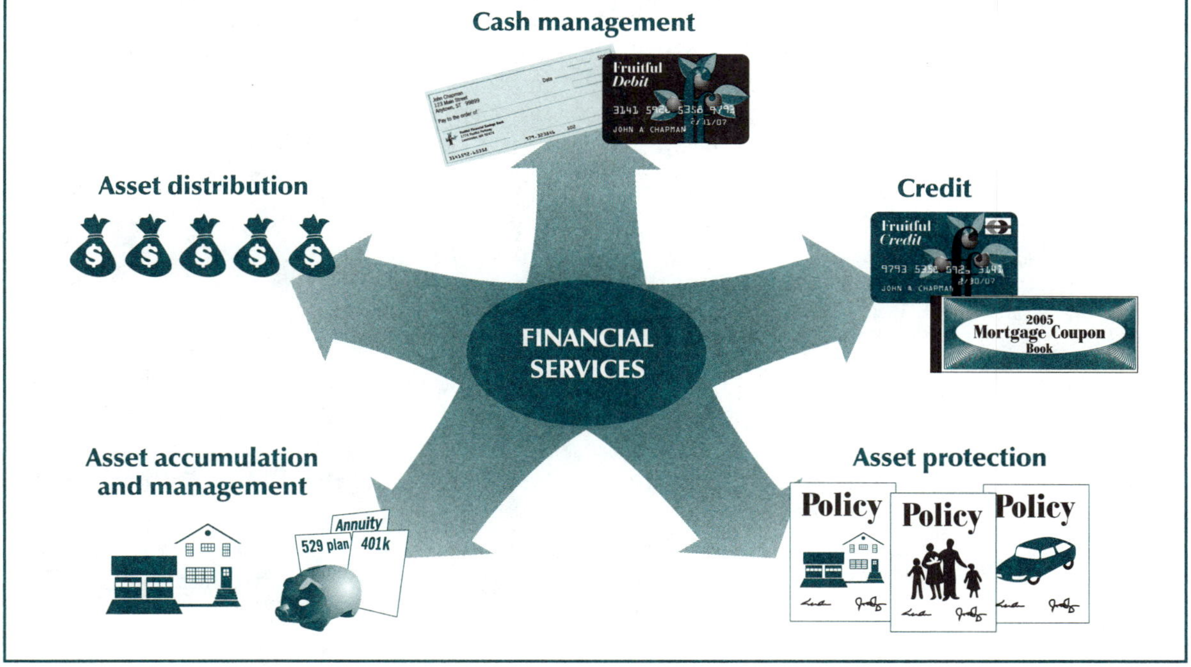

Example: Harold Schmidt has just graduated from college. He has obtained employment and is looking for an apartment. When Harold receives his first paycheck, he will need a place to keep his money and a way to distribute funds to his creditors.

Analysis: A cash management product will enable Harold to pay his bills, purchase goods and services, and store money. A common cash management product that Harold can use is a checking account, which provides the account holder with check-writing privileges. When he receives his first paycheck, Harold can open a checking account and deposit his paycheck into the account. Harold can then easily pay for typical living expenses such as rent and utilities, and he has a convenient method of making purchases for items such as groceries and clothing. Harold also can choose to transfer money from his checking account to longer-term savings and investment products.

Typical cash management products that we will discuss in Chapter 3 include checking accounts, money market accounts, savings accounts, and savings instruments. We also discuss electronic funds transfer.

Credit

Credit is a financial service that enables people to purchase now by giving a promise to pay in the future. Credit products can serve as convenient substitutes for cash. In addition, they enable people to pay for services or make purchases they otherwise would not be able to afford using their current savings and income. Thus, credit products may mean the solution to an emergency (such as a hospital bill or home repair) or an improvement in lifestyle (such as a new home or auto). In Chapter 4, we discuss typical credit products, including credit cards, installment loans, mortgages, and home-equity lines of credit.

Asset Protection

As a person acquires and manages his money and property, the possibility, or risk, of financial loss is ever present. A natural disaster or fire could destroy his home, a reckless driver could demolish his car and disable him, his child could be diagnosed with a serious illness, or his spouse could die prematurely. Although a person cannot guard against the emotional losses that accompany these events, he can protect himself financially through proper risk management. In Chapter 2, we discuss the concept of risk and ways to manage risk.

One of the most popular means of managing risk and protecting assets is ***insurance***, which is a mechanism for transferring the risk of financial loss from a person or entity to an insurance company. The basic premise of insurance is that a person can pay a predictable amount of money before he suffers a financial loss to protect himself from paying a less predictable and possibly much larger amount in the event a financial loss occurs. Insurance products exist to protect people and organizations from financial loss caused by premature death, illness, accident, disability, property loss or damage, and liability. These types of insurance are introduced in Chapter 2 and will be discussed more fully in Chapters 5 through 10.

Asset Accumulation and Management

People accumulate money for a variety of reasons, such as to fund a child's education or to leave an estate—all the assets accumulated during a lifetime—for their heirs. One of the most important reasons people accumulate assets is so they will have funds to live on when they retire. People need financial products that allow them to accumulate and manage their assets. In this text, asset accumulation refers to the accumulation of financial assets.

In most countries, funding for retirement comes from three sources, or three pillars as this trilogy is commonly called: the government, personal savings, and employers. Insight 1.1 explains the three pillars of retirement savings and how some experts are adding a fourth pillar.

INSIGHT 1.1 The Three Pillars Become Four Pillars

People in most countries rely on some or all of the three pillars of funding to support them when they retire:

- A government-provided retirement program that gives a basic level of support
- Personal savings
- An employer-sponsored retirement plan that promises employees a certain level of benefits upon retirement or that ties benefits to what has been paid into the plan on their behalf

Because of the inadequacy of these three pillars, most experts are adding a fourth pillar of support:

- Continuation of income, particularly from part-time employment, after the traditional retirement age

Industry experts foresee people working longer or taking part-time jobs after retirement to supplement income from the government, personal savings, and employers. However, this continuation of employment is not driven solely by the need for adequate income. Rather, as people live longer, they will want to remain active, productive members of society.

Later in this chapter, we discuss government's role as a provider of retirement funds. We discuss personal asset accumulation products, such as securities and annuities, as well as asset management products, such as brokerage accounts, in Chapters 11 and 12. We discuss tax-advantaged savings plans in Chapter 13 and employer-sponsored retirement plans in Chapter 14.

Asset Distribution

People purchase some asset accumulation products with the purpose of eventually having those assets distributed in some fashion, such as in the form of retirement income. Thus, these asset accumulation products have a secondary purpose of asset distribution. As we discuss asset accumulation in Chapters 12, 13, and 14, we also will discuss asset distribution.

Advice as a Financial Service

In addition to providing customers with the types of services and products we have just discussed, the financial services industry provides customers with advice to help meet their goals. The advice given by employees, representatives, and agents of financial institutions may be as simple as suggesting to a customer an appropriate checking account or as complex as assisting a customer with her financial planning.

"Early Retiree, endangered species"
www.CartoonStock.com

Financial planning is the process of consciously determining how to spend, finance, protect, accumulate, and distribute assets to meet financial goals.

In recognition of the emerging need for comprehensive financial planning services, a new profession has developed. A ***financial planner*** is a professional who analyzes a customer's personal financial circumstances and goals and prepares a plan, usually in writing, to meet the customer's financial goals. Some financial planners are also stockbrokers, insurance agents, certified professional accountants (CPAs), or other types of financial advisers. Insight 1.2 describes the services provided by a financial planner.

The financial planning profession is evolving in two areas in particular—compensation and services. Financial planners traditionally have charged commissions based on sales of financial products, an hourly fee, or a flat fee. The flat fee is becoming increasingly prevalent as a method of compensation. In terms of services, some foresee financial planners becoming one-stop financial shops, providing planning, asset management, tax return preparation, and more.

As the average customer's level of financial sophistication increases and the number of independent financial planners swells, financial institutions increasingly are aware of the need for their employees, agents, and representatives to offer financial planning services to their customers. Thus, education and training have taken on a new importance in the financial services industry.

INSIGHT 1.2 Services of a Financial Planner

A financial planner begins by meeting with the client to collect personal data, determine the client's general attitude toward risk, discuss the client's goals, and clarify the services the client expects to receive from the financial planner. Personal data includes age, marital status, number of dependents and their ages, annual income, and net worth. The client's attitude toward risk influences the types of asset protection and asset accumulation products that the financial planner recommends. The client's goals may be short term (a European vacation) and/or long term (a comfortable retirement). In terms of expectations, the client may want only retirement planning services, or she may want the entire spectrum of financial planning services—from cash management planning to estate planning.

The client then provides the financial planner with copies of relevant financial documents, which may include her current bank statements, insurance policies, and investment portfolio statements. The client also informs the financial planner of any outstanding or foreseeable debts or liabilities, including mortgages, car loans, and charitable pledges.

The planner analyzes the information provided in light of the client's needs and goals. Depending on the services requested by the client, the planner may examine insurance coverages to determine where the client is vulnerable to loss. He may scrutinize the client's investments and risk tolerance to determine whether a different allocation of assets may be more suitable to achieve the client's goals. He may project the client's needs at retirement, determine the number of years the client's current income and savings will support her during retirement, and calculate the additional savings necessary to make up any shortfall. He may review all potential assets of the client's estate to determine if the estate is being properly structured to achieve the client's final wishes.

Having fully analyzed all pertinent financial information, while always considering the impact of inflation and taxes on various transactions and events, the financial planner creates a financial plan with suitable cash management, credit, asset protection, asset accumulation and management, and asset distribution recommendations. The financial planner also may consult with other advisers, such as the client's attorney, accountant, and investment adviser, in developing a comprehensive financial plan.

Financial institutions also are aware of and promote the need for their employees, agents, and representatives to act in an ethical manner toward clients. ***Ethics*** is a system of accepted standards of conduct and moral judgment that combines the elements of honesty, integrity, and fair treatment. Making ethical business decisions involves behaving in accordance with accepted legal and moral principles of right and wrong.

Many companies and industry associations have developed codes of ethics, and many of the organizations that have these codes require their employees or members to sign a statement that they have read and understood the code. LOMA's Code of Professional Ethics for those people who have earned a fellowship designation is reprinted in Insight 1.3.

INSIGHT 1.3 Code of Professional Ethics for LOMA Fellowship Designees

Individuals earning LOMA fellowship designations shall adhere to LOMA's Code of Professional Ethics, which consists of the following canons:

- The Designee shall discharge all duties with honesty, integrity, objectivity, fairness, and professionalism.
- The Designee shall deal with others in a manner in which he or she would want to be dealt with by others.
- The Designee shall place the public interest above his or her own interest.
- The Designee shall continually strive to master all aspects of his or her business and to improve his or her professional knowledge and skills.
- The Designee shall diligently strive to ascertain clients' best interests and seek to ensure that these interests are met.
- The Designee shall respect clients' privacy and the confidentiality of information they provide, within the constraints of the law.
- The Designee shall comply with the spirit and letter of the law in all his or her activities.
- The Designee shall hold his or her professional designation proudly and seek to enhance the reputation of the designation, as well as the financial services industry, in every way.

Traditional Financial Institutions

The traditional types of financial institutions are as follows:

- Depository institutions
- Finance companies
- Insurance companies
- Mutual fund companies
- Securities firms

Depository Institutions

A ***depository institution*** is a financial institution that specializes in accepting deposits and making loans. In the United States, depository institutions include commercial banks, savings and loan associations, savings banks, and credit unions.

- A ***commercial bank*** is a depository institution that accepts deposits from people, businesses, and government agencies and uses these deposits to make loans to people, businesses, and government agencies.

- A ***savings and loan association (S&L)*** is a depository institution that principally pools the savings of people and makes residential mortgage loans.

- A ***savings bank (SB)*** is a depository institution similar to a savings and loan association in that it accepts deposits—primarily savings account deposits—mainly from people rather than businesses and makes primarily mortgage loans; but SBs are legally permissible only in certain states, primarily in the northeast.

- A ***credit union*** is a nonprofit depository institution that does business only with its depositors—called *members*—who traditionally shared a common bond, such as their employer or their industry.

Savings and loan associations and savings banks are sometimes referred to as ***thrifts*** because they were established to encourage the careful management of money and to help finance home building. In addition, commercial banks, savings and loan associations, and savings banks are now allowed to merge, resulting in the public's use of the term *bank* to refer to all three institutions.

In the past, these depository institutions were readily distinguishable from one another, but the distinctions between these institutions have blurred as each has expanded its product offerings. However, commercial banks in the United States still tend to make more loans to businesses—known as *commercial loans*—than do the other depository institutions, and commercial banks serve both the public and private sectors. Loans made to people, other than mortgage loans, are known as *consumer loans*. Credit unions focus on consumer loans, whereas thrifts focus on mortgages. In Canada, the large national banks provide a full range of products for both commercial clients and consumers, while some smaller banks specialize in either commercial or consumer services.

Figure 1.2 lists the typical products and services offered by a traditional commercial bank. Today, many commercial banks also distribute insurance and annuity products, as well as mutual funds. In the United States, banks are not allowed to issue—that is, accept the risk on—insurance and annuity products. However, banks can serve in the role of marketing intermediary for these products.

Finance Companies

A ***finance company*** is a financial institution that specializes in making short- and medium-term loans to businesses and to people. Three types of finance companies are commercial finance companies, consumer finance companies, and sales finance companies.

FIGURE 1.2 Typical Products and Services of a Traditional Commercial Bank

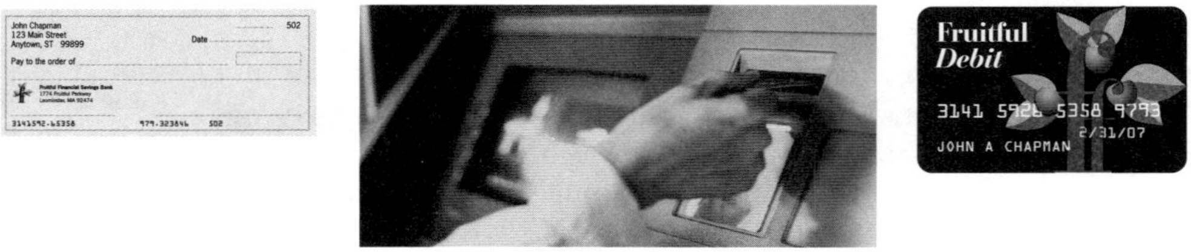

- Checking accounts
- Savings accounts
- Consumer loans
- Commercial loans
- Credit cards
- Debit cards
- Mortgages
- Safety-deposit boxes
- Financial counseling
- Electronic banking services
- Automatic bill payment
- Trust services

- A ***commercial finance company***, also called a *business finance company*, extends loans and leases equipment to businesses.
- A ***consumer finance company*** makes loans to people so that they can buy items such as furniture and appliances, make home improvements, and pay off small debts. Some consumer finance companies specialize in making loans to people who cannot obtain credit from other sources.
- A ***sales finance company*** is owned by a retail company as a means of assisting customers in purchasing the retail company's goods. For example, numerous automobile manufacturers own finance companies to help customers obtain credit to purchase the manufacturer's cars and trucks.

Insurance Companies

An ***insurance company*** is a financial institution that provides protection against the risk of financial loss caused by specified events. Insurance companies receive payments from customers in exchange for providing insurance policies that protect against insured events. Insurers can be categorized by the type of coverage they provide and by how they are organized. In terms of coverage, the two major types of insurance companies are the life and health insurance company and the property/casualty insurance company.

- A ***life and health insurance company*** insures a person against financial loss from death, disability, illness, and accident by providing life and health insurance. Some life insurers also protect against the risk of outliving financial resources by issuing annuities. Note that in some countries, such as Canada, basic health insurance is provided to all citizens and residents by government-sponsored programs, although many people also are covered by private plans that supplement the government programs. In addition, note that in some countries, such as many of those in Europe, health insurance is classified as nonlife insurance.

- A ***property/casualty insurance company***, or simply *nonlife insurance company* or *general insurance company*, insures against financial loss from property damage and theft by providing property insurance, such as homeowners insurance and automobile insurance, and from being held responsible for harming others or their property by providing liability insurance.

Insurance companies are organized as stock companies, mutual companies, or fraternal organizations.

- A ***stock insurance company*** is an insurance company that is owned by the people and organizations that purchase shares of the company's stock.

- A ***mutual insurance company*** is an insurance company that is owned by its policyowners.

- A ***fraternal benefit society*** is an organization formed to provide social and insurance benefits to its members. The members of such societies often share a common ethnic, religious, or vocational background, although membership in some societies is open to the general public.

Insight 1.4 explains how some insurance companies have been moving from a mutual form of ownership to a stock form of ownership.

Mutual Funds

A ***mutual fund company*** is an investment company that operates a number of mutual funds. A ***mutual fund***, known as a *unit trust* in the United Kingdom and many other countries, is an investment vehicle that pools the funds of investors and uses these funds to buy a number of stocks,

INSIGHT 1.4 Demutualization

The majority of life and health insurers are organized as stock companies, and the numbers continue to grow as mutual companies reorganize as stock companies through the process of ***demutualization***. Typically in a demutualization, the insurer's policyowners surrender their rights in the mutual corporation in exchange for shares of stock in the new stock corporation. The policyowners' policies remain in force and are simply transferred to the new corporate entity.

The primary reason a mutual company decides to demutualize is that raising funds is easier to do as a stock company because a stock company can issue additional shares of stock to the public. However, many companies also find compelling reasons to retain the mutual form of ownership.

bonds, and other financial instruments to create a diversified portfolio of financial investments. Mutual fund investors own shares in these funds. The value of a share varies in proportion with the value of the investments owned by the fund. Mutual funds give individual investors the opportunity to hold a diversified portfolio of investments that otherwise would be unavailable to them because of the high costs involved in purchasing the investments individually.

Securities Firms

A ***securities broker-dealer*** is a financial institution that specializes in the purchase and sale of investment instruments, such as stocks and bonds, which are known as ***securities***. A ***broker*** is a "middleman" institution that matches buyers of securities with sellers of those securities. A ***dealer*** is an institution that holds an inventory of securities and is always ready to buy and sell securities from its own account. Because most of these institutions fulfill the functions of both brokers and dealers, they commonly are referred to as *broker-dealers*, *brokerage firms*, or *brokerages*. The largest national and international brokerages often are referred to as *wire houses*.

A broker-dealer can be classified as either full service or discount. Both types execute orders to buy and sell securities, but full-service firms also provide investment advice and planning services. As a result, customers typically pay more for the services of full-service firms than for discount firms.

An *investment bank* is another type of financial institution that facilitates the purchase and sale of securities. Whereas a securities broker-dealer assists in the resale of securities among members of the public, an investment bank primarily assists corporations and governments with the initial sale of securities to the public. However, some firms engage in both investment banking and broker-dealer activities.

Government's Role in the Financial Services Industry

Around the world, government regulates the financial services industry. In addition to acting as a regulator, government typically performs three other functions in the financial services industry:

- Provides social insurance programs
- Influences spending and savings through taxation
- Influences spending and savings through control of the money supply

In these three functions, government affects the supply and demand for financial services in the private sector. In this section, we describe various government plans of social insurance and explain government's use of taxation to influence spending and savings. Government's influence over spending and savings through control of the money supply is beyond the scope of this text.

Social Insurance

A ***social insurance program*** is a welfare plan established by law and administered by a government that provides the population with income security. Although we will not survey all social insurance programs, we will discuss retirement income benefit programs because they are such important financial products to many people worldwide and because financial services institutions offer products that complement or compete with these government-provided programs.

Social Insurance Fundamentals

Social insurance may provide cash payments to replace income lost because of old age, disability (nonoccupational sickness or injury), death (survivor benefits), occupational injuries, and unemployment. Alternatively, social insurance may provide services such as medical care. Figure 1.3 shows the number of countries with various types of social insurance programs.[2]

In some countries, social insurance coverage is *universal*, meaning that it includes the entire population, although citizenship and residency requirements may need to be met. The United Kingdom's national health care system, which covers all citizens, is an example of universal coverage. Other coverage is employment related, such as Social Security in

FIGURE 1.3 Social Insurance Programs by Type of Program

Type of Program	Number of Countries with Type of Program		
	1940	1995	1999
Old age, disability, survivor	33	158	167
Sickness and maternity	24	105	112
Work injury	57	159	164
Unemployment	21	63	69
Family allowances	7	81	88

Source: Social Security Administration (1995), as quoted in Harold D. Skipper, Jr., *International Risk and Insurance: An Environmental-Managerial Approach* (Boston: Irwin/McGraw-Hill, 1998), 534. Social Security Administration, *Social Security Programs Throughout the World—1999* (Washington, DC: U.S. Government Printing Office, 1999), xxviii–xxxiii.

the United States. Yet another type of coverage is means-tested, with eligibility for benefits based on a person's income or financial resources. The Medicaid system in the United States, which provides health care to those with limited financial resources, is an example of means-tested coverage.

In some countries, social insurance programs may be financed by payroll taxes, out of the government's general revenues, or both. In other countries, citizens must participate in private plans that provide social benefits.

Another important point about social insurance programs is that neither the amount a person pays nor the amount she receives is based on the risk that the particular person poses. In other words, if the government provides a disability insurance program, the amounts a person pays to or receives from the program will not be based on the person's likelihood of becoming disabled.

Retirement Income

In the United States, government retirement income benefits are provided under several programs, including (1) the Civil Service Retirement Act, (2) the Railroad Retirement Act, and (3) the Old Age, Survivors, Disability and Health Insurance (OASDHI) Act, or, as it is better known, Social Security. ***Social Security*** is a federal program that provides specified benefits, including monthly retirement income benefits, to people who have contributed to the plan during their income-earning years. The program also provides a benefit to qualified disabled individuals, as well as to the surviving spouses and dependent children of qualified deceased workers.

Social Security is the predominant public pension plan in the United States. A ***pension plan*** is a plan that accumulates assets and provides a retirement income benefit for people participating in the plan. A public pension is sponsored by a government, whereas a private pension is usually sponsored by an employer.

Nearly all people employed in the United States, including those employed by the armed forces, are covered under Social Security, which is an employment-related social insurance program. The only sizable groups not covered are federal civil service workers who are covered by the Civil Service Retirement Act, railroad workers who are covered by the Railroad Retirement Act, and some state and municipal civil service workers. Because Social Security covers far more people than do the other U.S. public retirement income plans, we limit our discussion to the benefits provided through Social Security.

Social Security provides a monthly income benefit to people who have contributed to the system during their income-earning years. Social Security retirement benefits are available to covered persons who are age 62 or older, although people retiring before their full retirement age of 65 or older, as specified by law, typically receive a lesser monthly benefit amount than they would receive if they retired at their full retirement age.

Social Security is essentially a pay-as-you-go system, which means that current workers fund the benefits paid to current retirees. During working years, each covered worker must contribute a stated percentage of her earned income, up to a specified maximum yearly contribution amount. The worker's employer must contribute an amount equal to that contributed by the employee. A self-employed person must contribute a higher percentage of earnings than does an employee because a self-employed person's contributions are not matched by any employer contributions.

The amount of monthly benefit a person receives depends on the wages earned during the contribution period and also is subject to a specified maximum amount. However, the amount of the retirement benefit is increased periodically to reflect increases in the cost of living, as measured by the Consumer Price Index (CPI) in the United States.[3]

In Canada, retirement income benefits are provided to retirees through three separate government plans, which are discussed in Figure 1.4.

In the United States, concern exists that the Social Security system will not be adequately funded in the years to come because of the aging of the population. As the average age of the population rises and these people begin to retire, the ratio of active workers to retirees narrows. For

FIGURE 1.4 Canadian Government Pension Plans

Pensions are provided to Canadian retirees through three separate government plans: (1) the Old Age Security Act, which is in effect throughout Canada; (2) the Canada Pension Plan, which operates in all Canadian provinces except Quebec; and (3) the Quebec Pension Plan, which operates only in Quebec.

The Old Age Security Act

The federal ***Old Age Security (OAS) Act*** is a universal public pension plan that provides a pension to virtually all Canadian residents who are age 65 or older, whether or not they have been employed. The right to receive a pension under the OAS Act is not dependent on a person's preretirement wages or current employment. Each person who has reached age 65 and has met certain residency requirements receives the same pension amount, which is tied to the Canadian Consumer Price Index. The money to fund these pensions is taken from federal government general tax revenues.

Canada Pension Plan and Quebec Pension Plan

The ***Canada Pension Plan (CPP)*** is a federal program that provides a pension for wage earners who have contributed money into the plan during their working years. The CPP covers workers in all provinces except Quebec, which has elected to establish its own provincial plan. The ***Quebec Pension Plan (QPP)*** is a plan that functions in the same manner as the CPP except that the QPP applies only to wage earners in Quebec. The CPP and QPP are closely coordinated and tend to operate as one plan. For example, contributions made into one of these plans can be transferred to the other plan if a person moves into or out of Quebec. In addition to pension benefits, the CPP and the QPP provide survivorship benefits, lump-sum death benefits, benefits for orphans, and long-term disability income benefits.

Participation in these plans is mandatory for employees covered by the plans, and virtually all employees and self-employed persons in Canada are covered. Benefits are funded through compulsory contributions from employees, their employers, and self-employed persons. The amount of the monthly benefit paid following retirement is related to the amount contributed to the plan by or on behalf of the person; the amount is also limited to a legislatively established maximum amount. Benefit amounts are adjusted annually to reflect cost-of-living increases.

example, in the United States the ratio of workers to retired persons was approximately 5:1 in 2001, but this ratio could reach approximately 2.5:1 by 2040.[4] As the ratio constricts, contributions to Social Security from current workers will not keep up with the benefits needed to pay retirees. Thus, some current workers are worried that Social Security benefits may be eliminated by the time they retire. On the other hand, some demographers believe that the impact of the aging population will be offset by the influx of new immigrant workers.

INSIGHT 1.5 The Privatization of Mexico's Public Pension System

In 1997, Mexico was the fourth Latin American country to privatize its pension insurance system, after Chile (1981), Colombia (1994), and Argentina (1994). Today, employers must contribute 2 percent of an employee's salary toward a retirement pension. Employees may contribute, on a voluntary basis, up to 10 percent of their salary on a tax-free basis. Pension sector participants are

- Administradoras de Fondos para el Retiro (AFOREs), which collect employer and employee contributions. Employees may change their AFORE every six months and are free to withdraw funds contributed voluntarily after they have been held in the AFORE for a minimum of six months.
- Sistemas de Inversion Especializada en Fondos para el Retiro (SIEFOREs), which invest the AFORE funds.
- The Social Security Institute—Instituto Mexicano del Seguro Social (IMSS)—which pays a set amount for the pension to a private annuity company chosen by the beneficiary.

Pensions take the form of immediate life annuities. Also provided by the system are

- Lifetime annuities for disability
- Lifetime annuities payable to widows and widowers
- Annuities to orphans until they become 18 or, if they continue studying, to age 25

Source: Adapted from Jennifer C. Rankin, "A Silver Lining," *Resource* (© October 2002): 10. Used with permission; all rights reserved.

Other nations share the United States' concern over the future of their retirement income programs. Many nations worldwide are engaging in pension reform. Insight 1.5 describes the privatization of Mexico's pension system.

Taxation

Many governments use taxation as a mechanism for accomplishing social, in addition to economic, goals. Through taxation, governments can influence populations to act or refrain from acting in certain ways. For example, governments tax tobacco heavily not only to raise revenue, but also to discourage use of the product. Governments also offer people reductions on taxable income for contributions made to qualified charities.

With concern growing about public retirement systems, governments are increasingly using tax policies to encourage people to invest in and employers to provide retirement savings plans. Such tax incentives can be quite effective because they maximize the time value of money, a concept we shall discuss in Chapter 2. Such governmental incentives benefit the financial services industry because of the increased demand for private retirement savings products.

Evolution of the Financial Services Industry

The financial services industry is one of the most rapidly evolving industries worldwide. Increasingly, the various financial institutions are entering each other's traditional core businesses, obscuring the distinctions among institutions and creating an intensely competitive and integrated financial services industry. Figure 1.5 summarizes some of the competitive opportunities among financial institutions.

The evolution of the financial services industry is characterized by convergence, consolidation, and globalization, all of which have resulted in significant upheaval in the competitive environment of the financial services industry. We discuss these forces of change in the following sections.

FIGURE 1.5 New Opportunities for Traditional Financial Institutions

- Insurance companies enter the banking arena by acquiring or creating their own thrifts.
- Banks enter the insurance arena by distributing property/casualty insurance products.
- Insurers and banks distribute mutual funds, which in the past were the domain of mutual fund companies and securities firms.
- Commercial banks, securities firms, and mutual fund companies distribute life insurance and annuities.
- Mutual fund companies, banks, and securities firms compete with insurance companies for employer-sponsored retirement plans and management of people's retirement savings.
- Brokerage firms and mutual fund companies offer money market mutual funds to compete with commercial banks for consumer deposits.
- Insurance companies compete with banks for the management of trusts.

Source: Adapted from Gene Stone, *Insurance Company Operations* (Atlanta: LOMA, © 2000), 33. Used with permission; all rights reserved.

Convergence

Convergence is the movement toward a single financial institution being able to serve a customer's banking, insurance, and securities needs. Convergence is occurring not only in the industry's structure, but also in distribution and products.

Structural Convergence

Historically, the institutions composing the financial services industry were distinctly segmented. Numerous laws and regulations clearly defined each segment's business and prevented affiliations among firms from different segments. Now, however, a move is underway worldwide whereby traditionally separate components of the financial services industry—banks, insurance companies, and securities firms—can structurally converge. For example, the segmentation characterizing the U.S. financial services industry officially changed with the passage of a federal law in 1999. The ***Gramm-Leach-Bliley (GLB) Act*** removed many of the regulatory barriers that prevented affiliations among different types of financial institutions.

The primary impact of the GLB Act is that the traditionally separate components of the financial services industry now can enter into structural affiliations under the umbrella of a financial holding company. A ***holding company system*** is a corporate ownership structure in which one company—known as the ***holding company***, or *parent company*—owns and controls another company (or companies)—known as a ***subsidiary*** of the holding company. A company is an ***affiliate*** of another company if the two companies are under the common control of a holding company. A ***financial holding company*** is a holding company that conducts activities that are financial in nature or incidental to financial activities, such as insurance, banking, investment, and financial advisory services. Figure 1.6 illustrates a financial holding company structure.

FIGURE 1.6 Financial Holding Company

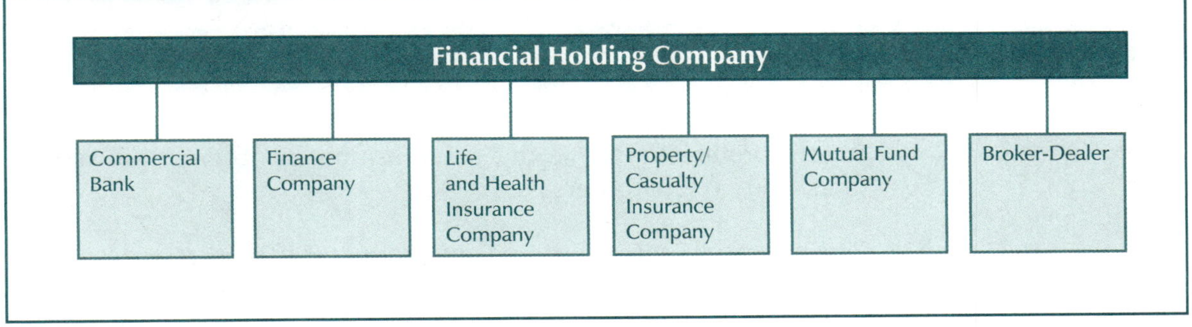

FAST FACT

Of 8,321 commercial and federally insured savings banks, 3,833 or 46.1 percent participated in insurance activities in the first six months of 2003.[5]

Bank insurance companies, also known as *bancassurance companies*, which are companies that offer both banking and insurance services, have been commonplace in Europe for decades. Banks and insurers in the United States now are able to affiliate under the financial holding company structure. This option is still not open to banks and insurers under Canadian law.

As mentioned earlier, banks cannot issue insurance policies directly in the United States. However, under the financial holding company structure, an insurance company affiliate of a bank may underwrite insurance policies that the bank then may distribute.

Distribution Convergence

Distribution convergence is the ability of financial institutions to distribute each other's products. Although the distribution of one financial services sector's products by another sector is not new, such intermingling of distribution channels is intensifying. For example, banks and brokerage companies in the United States now distribute insurance and annuity products issued by unaffiliated insurers.

Product Convergence

Product convergence is the development of products bearing the characteristics of more than one type of financial product. Merrill Lynch paved the way for the combination of cash management and securities products in the late 1970s with the introduction of its Cash Management Account™ (CMA). The CMA provided for the transfer of customer account balances into money market mutual funds and permitted customers to write checks against these funds. Other examples of product convergence are variable life insurance and variable annuities, which combine aspects of insurance and investment products.

Results of Convergence

Financial institutions benefit from convergence by gaining the ability to offer a more complete selection of financial products to their existing customers, as well as gaining new customers and distribution channels for their products. Although convergence offers many benefits to financial institutions, it also poses challenges.

- Financial services products are complex. Those selling and servicing the products must be able to communicate product information effectively to customers.

- The potential for misrepresenting products will increase as employees are called on to become familiar with a wide range of products from various sectors.

- Regulations governing each sector of the financial services industry and its products are complex.
- Corporate cultures in the various sectors are dissimilar, and working in a new culture can be unsettling for employees.

Consolidation

Consolidation, as the term is frequently used in the industry, is the combination of financial services institutions within or across sectors. The *Report of Consolidation in the Financial Sector*, which studied 13 developed economies, identified 7,300 transactions during the 1990s involving the acquisition of a financial institution. The aggregate value of these transactions was US$1.6 trillion.[6]

Consolidation is largely the result of companies trying to take advantage of the economic principles of economies of scale and economies of scope. ***Economies of scale*** is the economic principle that holds that as production volume increases, the cost per unit of production decreases. In other words, as the number of units produced increases, the costs of producing those units will be increasingly spread out such that the per unit cost of production decreases. ***Economies of scope*** is the economic principle that holds that as the types of products sold through one outlet increase, the cost per unit of production will be lower than if each product were sold separately. Bank insurance is a prime example of economies of scope in action.

The legal definition of *consolidation* is a transaction in which two or more corporations are extinguished and a new corporate entity is formed that assumes the assets and liabilities of the former corporations. This form of consolidation is rare. Instead, consolidation in the financial services industry occurs primarily through mergers and acquisitions.

- A ***merger*** is a transaction in which one corporation absorbs another corporation, with the absorbed corporation ceasing to exist.
- An ***acquisition*** is a transaction in which one corporation purchases a controlling interest in another corporation, typically resulting in a parent/subsidiary relationship between formerly independent corporations; after the transaction, both corporations survive.

Consolidation has resulted in a decreasing number of traditional financial services institutions within each sector. For example, the number of commercial banks in the United States declined from approximately 25,000 before World War I to 8,096 in 2001.[7] However, as the number of financial institutions has decreased, the remaining institutions have grown in size. The financial services industry is now charac-

FAST FACT

The proportion of life insurance companies operating in the United States that are foreign-owned has climbed in recent years from 4 percent of all U.S. life insurers in 1996 to 11 percent in 2002.[8]

terized by a growing number of huge financial conglomerates that provide everything to everyone through numerous distribution channels. Some small- and medium-sized institutions survive and thrive, but the trend is toward fewer, larger companies.

Globalization

The financial services industry is evolving into a globally competitive environment. Giant financial services enterprises, particularly those from Western Europe and North America, are seizing new opportunities to expand their customer bases in nations outside their countries of origin. As an example of the extent of international business conducted, Canadian life and health insurers generated 58 percent of their premiums abroad in 2002.[9]

Asia and Latin America are particularly attractive regions for expansion of these multinational financial institutions. China is developing into one of the world's most attractive financial services markets because of its move toward a market economy and its huge population. Russia and Eastern European countries also are promising financial services markets as they evolve into market economies.

Large corporations must strategically address international expansion to determine if it is right for them or if they are possible targets of another company's expansion efforts. Small- and medium-sized companies cannot ignore globalization because the domestic markets for their products are facing increasing competition from international companies. The competitive playing field is evolving, and all companies must respond accordingly.

Key Terms

financial services industry
financial institution
financial intermediary
intermediation
service
cash management
credit
insurance
financial planning
financial planner
ethics
depository institution
commercial bank
savings and loan association (S&L)
savings bank (SB)
credit union
thrift
finance company
commercial finance company
consumer finance company
sales finance company
insurance company
life and health insurance company

property/casualty insurance company
stock insurance company
mutual insurance company
fraternal benefit society
mutual fund company
mutual fund
demutualization
securities broker-dealer
security
broker
dealer
social insurance program
Social Security
pension plan
Old Age Security (OAS) Act
Canada Pension Plan (CPP)
Quebec Pension Plan (QPP)
convergence
Gramm-Leach-Bliley (GLB) Act
holding company system
holding company
subsidiary
affiliate
financial holding company
bank insurance company
consolidation
economies of scale
economies of scope
merger
acquisition

Endnotes

1. Insurance Information Institute, *Financial Services Fact Book 2003*, http://www.financialservicesfacts.org/financial2/today/gdp (5 November 2003).
2. Much of the information in this section came from William S. Custer, "Social Insurance," in *International Risk and Insurance: An Environmental-Managerial Approach*, ed. Harold D. Skipper, Jr. (Boston: Irwin/McGraw-Hill, 1998), 530–531.
3. The *Consumer Price Index (CPI)* measures the change in the price of a fixed basket of goods and services bought by a typical consumer. The goods and services included in the CPI include food, transportation, housing, utilities, clothing, and medical care.
4. Stephen W. Forbes, *International Issues in the Financial Services Industry* (Atlanta: LOMA, 2002), 89.
5. BankInsurance.com, Michael White Associates, (6 October 2003).
6. "Group of Ten, Report on Consolidation in the Financial Sector," January 2001, as summarized in *World Financial Centers: New Horizons in Insurance and Banking*, sigma No. 7/2001, Swiss Re, 16, as reported in Stephen W. Forbes, *International Issues in the Financial Services Industry* (Atlanta: LOMA, 2002), 102.
7. *Financial Services Fact Book 2003.*
8. ACLI, *Life Insurers Fact Book: 2003* (Washington, DC: American Council of Life Insurers, 2003), 5.
9. Canadian Life and Health Insurance Association, Inc., *Canadian Life and Health Insurance Facts*, 2003 ed., http://www.clhia.ca/e3i_FactBook.htm (5 November 2003).

chapter

2

Financial Services Concepts

outline

The Time Value of Money

- Interest
- Inflation

Basic Tax Concepts

- Effect of Taxes on the Time Value of Money
- Exclusions, Credits, Deductions, and Deferrals

The Risk-Return Tradeoff

- Risk
- Return

Managing Risk Through Insurance

- Characteristics of Insurable Risks
- Insurability of Specific Risks

Diversification

Opportunity Cost

objectives

After reading this chapter, you should be able to

- Explain the concept of the time value of money
- Explain the differences between simple interest and compound interest
- Discuss how compounding, the number of compounding periods, and the length of time an investment is held affect the earnings on an investment
- Discuss how inflation and taxes affect the value of money
- Explain the concept of the risk-return tradeoff
- Define the following types of risk: *business risk, default risk, inflation risk, interest rate risk, liquidity risk, market risk, political risk,* and *reinvestment risk*
- Discuss the characteristics of insurable risks
- Explain the concepts of diversification and opportunity cost

Drew Stewart receives a $1,500 bonus check and wonders what he should do with this unexpected bounty. The options that immediately come to mind are paying off a loan, taking a vacation, and investing the money. Drew is extremely busy at work as well as indecisive about how to use the money, and the check stays in his wallet for six months. During that time, world and economic events cause grocery and gas prices to increase 10 percent and interest rates to decrease 3 percentage points. At the end of that six-month period when Drew finally deposits the check in his checking account, the $1,500 is actually able to buy less than it could when he received it.

Having deposited the check, Drew decides to invest the money. However, he cannot decide between investing in a mutual fund or in his cousin's new company, which his cousin promises will do exceptionally well. Drew is unsure how to analyze his options.

Had Drew understood some basic financial concepts, he could have made money from his bonus during the six months that the check was in his wallet. In addition, he would know how to analyze the potential risks and rewards presented by each investment option. He would appreciate the value of and employ diversification, perhaps by investing a portion of his money in his cousin's company and the remainder in a mutual fund. He would understand opportunity cost—the cost of giving up one activity to engage in another.

In this chapter, we explain the following financial concepts:

- The time value of money
- The risk-return tradeoff
- Managing risk through insurance
- Diversification
- Opportunity cost

Knowledge of these concepts will help you to better understand the financial products and services we discuss in later chapters.

The Time Value of Money

The ***time value of money*** is the concept that the value of a sum of money will change over time as the result of the effect of interest. ***Interest*** is a fee an institution or a person pays for the use of someone else's money. Generally, a sum of money invested today will have a present value that is less than its future value because of the effect of interest. The ***present value*** of a sum of money is the amount that must be invested today at a specified interest rate to accumulate a specified amount by a certain future date. The ***future value*** is the value at the end of a given period of time of a sum of money invested at a specified interest rate. In other words, the future value of a sum of money is the amount that you have invested plus what you will earn in interest over a certain period of time.

Example: Latisha Ervine deposits $100 in an interest-bearing savings account, and her account is worth $110 a year from now without her making any more deposits.

Analysis: At the time Latisha deposited the money, its present value was $100 and its future value was $110.

Financial institutions use the concept of the time value of money to perform such functions as pricing products and comparing investment alternatives. People, too, rely on the concept of the time value of money. An understanding of this concept equips them to determine the true cost of purchases, compare the value of alternative uses of money, and make informed decisions about household finances.

"ONE FINAL QUESTION: IS THERE AN OBSERVATION ROOM WHERE I CAN WATCH MY MONEY GROW?"

www.CartoonStock.com

If you understand the time value of money, you also understand how your money can work for you. For example, a person who keeps his paycheck in his wallet earns nothing, while a person who deposits his paycheck in an interest-bearing account earns additional income.

Interest

Understanding interest and how it is calculated is the key to understanding the time value of money. As mentioned earlier, interest is a fee paid for the use of someone else's money. Lenders earn interest from lending money, and borrowers pay interest as the price of borrowing money. From an investor's perspective, an investment can be thought of as a loan made by the investor, because the investor is lending money with the expectation of earning additional money in interest.

Financial institutions usually express interest in terms of an ***interest rate***, which is interest stated as a percent of the principal. A ***principal*** is a sum of money originally borrowed or lent. Interest rates are frequently shown in decimal form because they are used in calculations. For example, a 5 percent interest rate may be expressed as 0.05 and a 10 percent interest rate may be expressed as 0.10.

Interest Calculations

To find the dollar amount of interest earned, we multiply the principal by the interest rate expressed in decimal form:

Principal × Interest Rate = Interest Earned

For example, we can find the amount of interest earned on a principal of $1,000 invested at a 5 percent interest rate for a year as follows:

$1,000 × 0.05 = $50

Interest rates are measured in terms of a specified period of time, usually one year. For example, if you deposit $1,000 in a savings account that pays an annual interest rate of 3 percent, then at the end of the year your earnings on that $1,000 will be $30 ($1,000 × 0.03 = $30).

You can use the relationship between the principal, the interest rate, and interest earned to solve for any one of these terms if you know the other two, as demonstrated in Figure 2.1.

Simple and Compound Interest

Interest can be calculated as simple or compound interest. ***Simple interest*** is a type of interest that is calculated only on the original principal

FIGURE 2.1 The Principal, Interest Rate, and Interest Earned Relationship

Solving for:

Principal (P)	Interest Rate (R)	Interest Earned (I)
P = I ÷ R	R = I ÷ P	I = P × R
P = $25 ÷ 0.05	R = $25 ÷ $500	I = $500 × 0.05
P = $500	R = 0.05	I = $25

Source: Adapted from Mary C. Bickley and David F. Johnson, *Intro to Financial Services* (Atlanta: LOMA, © 2001), 17. Used with permission; all rights reserved.

amount. For each interest period, the original principal amount is multiplied by the interest rate to determine the interest paid by a borrower or earned by a lender. None of the interest earned in one period earns interest on itself in future periods. Thus, the interest paid or earned is the same for each successive period.

Example: Ruben Ochoa deposits $1,000 in an interest-earning account for two years at a 5 percent annual simple interest rate.

Analysis: At the end of the second year, Ruben will have $1,100 in the account. The $1,000 deposit generated $50 in interest each year ($1,000 × 0.05 = $50) for a total of $100 in interest that Ruben has in addition to the $1,000 principal.

In contrast, ***compound interest*** is interest payable both on the principal and on all accumulated interest. ***Compounding*** is the process of determining a future value when compound interest is applied. When interest is compounded, the interest earned during one period is added to the principal so that in future periods the accumulated interest earnings themselves earn interest.

Example: Ruben Ochoa deposits $1,000 in an interest-earning account for two years at a 5 percent interest rate compounded annually.

Analysis: At the end of the second year, Ruben will have $1,102.50 in the account. The $1,000 deposit generated a total of $102.50 in interest calculated as follows:

First year's interest = $1,000 × 0.05 = $50

Principal and accrued interest = $1,000 + $50 = $1,050

Second year's interest = $1,050 × 0.05 = $52.50

Total interest = $50 (first year's interest) + $52.50 (second year's interest) = $102.50

Figure 2.2 demonstrates that, as time progresses, the amount of interest earned each year with compound interest grows while the amount earned with simple interest remains the same each year. The figure also

FIGURE 2.2 Comparison of Simple and Compound Interest

The following figure reflects how $1,000 accumulates at 10 percent simple interest and at 10 percent interest compounded annually.

Simple Interest

Year	P Amount Subject to Interest (Principal — does not change)	I Interest Earned (P × 0.10)	T Total = Principal + Interest (prior year's T + current I)
1	$1,000	$100	$1,100
2	$1,000	$100	$1,200
3	$1,000	$100	$1,300
4	$1,000	$100	$1,400
5	$1,000	$100	$1,500

Compound Interest

Year	P Amount Subject to Interest (Principal — prior year's T)	I Interest Earned (P × 0.10)	T Total = Principal + Interest (P + I)
1	$1,000	$100	$1,100
2	$1,100	$110	$1,210
3	$1,210	$121	$1,331
4	$1,331	$133	$1,464
5	$1,464	$146	$1,610

Source: Adapted from Mary C. Bickley and David F. Johnson, *Intro to Financial Services* (Atlanta: LOMA, © 2001), 18. Used with permission; all rights reserved.

shows that the gap between compound interest earned and simple interest earned widens the longer you invest, given the same principal amount and interest rate.

The amount of interest earned through compounding is a function of three factors:

- The interest rate
- The frequency of compounding
- The number of periods in which compounding occurs

The formula for calculating compound interest is beyond the scope of this text. However, a simple rule of thumb known as the *rule of 72* can help estimate how fast an investment doubles at a specified compound interest rate. The rule of 72 states that the approximate number of years needed for an investment to double in value is calculated as 72 divided by the interest rate of the investment. The rule of 72 also demonstrates how increasing the interest rate increases the amount of interest earned. Insight 2.1 explains the rule of 72 in more detail.

Interest can be compounded at any interval, but typical intervals are annually, quarterly, monthly, or daily. Thus, a one-year investment that has an annual interest rate of 4 percent and that is compounded quarterly (that is, four times per year) is said to pay "4 percent interest compounded quarterly." The more frequently interest is compounded, the greater the amount of interest that will be earned.

The total amount of interest earned under compounding also increases dramatically the longer an investment is held. For this reason, many financial advisers stress the advantages of funding long-term investment programs early, even if a client can budget only relatively small amounts of money for such investments.

Figure 2.3 demonstrates that the more frequent the compounding intervals and the longer a principal sum remains invested, the more powerful are the effects of compounding.

Today, virtually all interest charged on loans and paid on investments is calculated as compound interest. The interest you pay on a credit card debt or a mortgage is compound interest. So, too, is the interest you earn from savings accounts, most certificates of deposit, and many other types of investments.

Effective Interest Rates

The interest rates we have discussed so far to demonstrate interest rate calculations have been examples of the ***nominal interest rate***, also known as the *stated interest rate*, which can be defined as an interest rate that is quoted without the effects of compounding. *Nominal* means "in name only."

INSIGHT 2.1 Rule of 72

To find the approximate number of years for an investment to double at a given rate of interest compounded annually, you can use the following formula:

Years to double = 72 ÷ interest rate

For example, suppose you want to know how many years it will take for an investment to double at an interest rate of 10 percent. You divide 72 by 10, which gives you 7.2 years. Suppose the interest rate on your investment is 6 percent. In that case, 72 ÷ 6 = 12 years. Although these are only approximations, they are relatively close to the results of an exact calculation.

The rule of 72 also can help you determine the rate of interest an investment must have to double in a certain number of years. For example, suppose a friend tells you he doubled his money in nine years by investing in a certain investment. What interest rate did he receive on his investment? You can use the following rule of 72 formula:

Interest rate = 72 ÷ Y

In this formula, "Y" is the number of years the investment was held. In your friend's case, Y = 9 years, and his interest rate was approximately 8 percent.

One fact that the rule of 72 demonstrates is that the interest rate an investment earns makes a big difference in how quickly your investment will double. The following chart gives you some examples of rule of 72 approximations:

Interest Rate	Years to Double an Investment
1%	72.0
2%	36.0
3%	24.0
4%	18.0
5%	14.4
6%	12.0
7%	10.3
8%	9.0
9%	8.0
10%	7.2
15%	4.8
20%	3.6

Although the rule of 72 is an approximation, it does show that doubling the rate of interest on an investment decreases by one-half the amount of time it takes to double the investment. Thus, at 3 percent interest, an investment doubles in 24 years; but at 6 percent interest, the investment doubles in 12 years.

Source: Adapted from Mary C. Bickley and David F. Johnson, *Intro to Financial Services* (Atlanta: LOMA, © 2001), 19. Used with permission; all rights reserved.

FIGURE 2.3 How Compounding Affects Investments

The following figure reflects how $1,000 accumulates at 10 percent interest compounded at different intervals and for different time periods.

Intervals	Time Periods: 1 year	10 years	20 years	30 years
Compounded annually	$1,100.00	$2,593.74	$6,727.50	$17,449.40
Compounded quarterly	1,103.81	2,685.06	7,209.57	19.358.15
Compounded monthly	1,104.71	2,707.03	7,328.02	19,837.38
Compounded daily	1,105.16	2,717.90	7,386.99	20,077.15

Source: Adapted from Mary C. Bickley and David F. Johnson, *Intro to Financial Services* (Atlanta: LOMA, © 2001), 20. Used with permission; all rights reserved.

The interest rate that includes the effects of compounding is known as the ***effective interest rate***. Stated simply, the effective interest rate is the interest rate that is actually paid or earned. The effective interest rate is greater than the nominal interest rate because of the effects of compounding. For example, if a bank quotes you an interest rate of 10 percent compounded quarterly, the nominal interest rate is 10 percent. The effective rate, however, is 10.38 percent. For the remainder of this text, when we refer to a given percentage rate, we mean a nominal rate, unless otherwise stated.

Inflation

Up to this point, we have discussed the time value of money as a function of interest. However, the value of money over time also is influenced by inflation. ***Inflation*** is a rise in the average price level of goods and services in an economy. The opposite—a decrease in the average level of prices for goods and services—is ***deflation***. During periods of inflation, the purchasing power of money erodes. In other words, other factors being equal, inflation leads to goods and services costing more money to purchase than they did previously. The ***inflation rate*** is the percentage increase in the prices for goods and services during a specific period.

Inflation is far more common than deflation, as shown in Figure 2.4. Some inflation is considered normal in a growing economy. However, inflation is a concern to investors and lenders because inflation decreases the purchasing power of future earnings and principal.

FIGURE 2.4 U.S. Average Annual Inflation by Decade

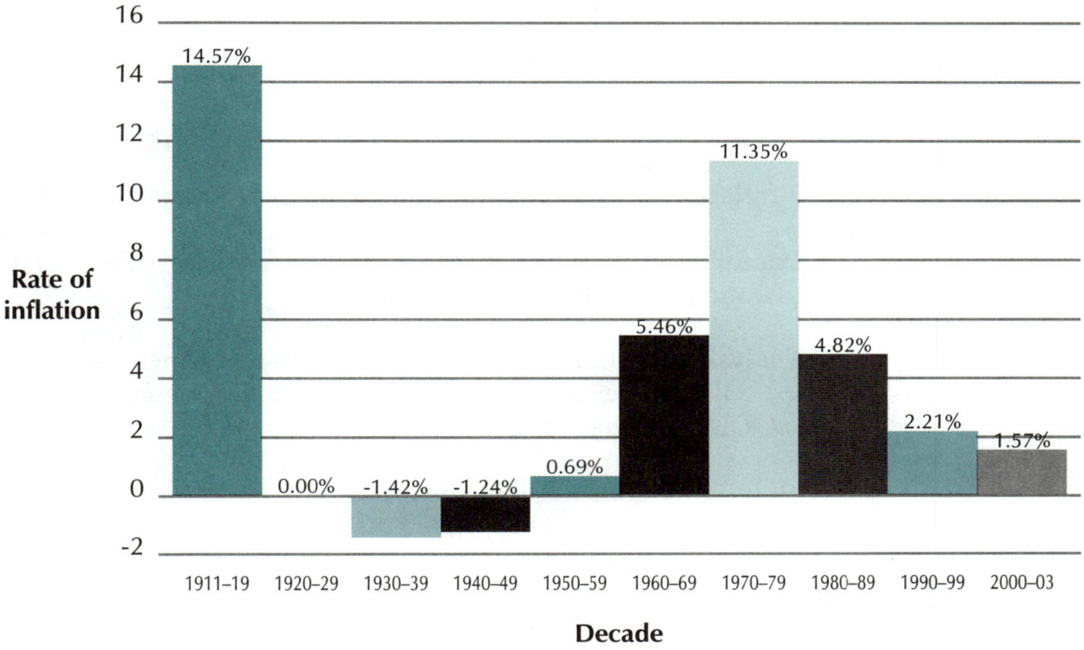

Source: Excerpted from "Inflation by Decade," InflationData.com, http://inflationdata.com/Inflation/Inflation_Rate/DecadeInflation.asp (3 November 2003). Used with permission.

Example: Trisha Glering invests $1,000 in an investment that promises a 10 percent annual interest rate. The inflation rate is 5 percent.

Analysis: After one year, Trisha's return will be $100, and her principal and interest will total $1,100. But because of the effect of inflation, her principal and interest ($1,100) one year from now will be worth 5 percent less (in this case, $55 less) in terms of purchasing power than her principal plus interest would be worth today. In today's money, her principal and interest one year from now is calculated as $1,100 – $55 and thus is worth $1,045 in terms of purchasing power.

Rates of inflation vary over time, and no one knows what the future rate of inflation will be. Because inflation inevitably reduces the purchasing power of money, investors, lenders, and borrowers are motivated to estimate future inflation rates as accurately as possible and to plan their financial activities to compensate for the effects of inflation.

Basic Tax Concepts

In this section, we discuss the effect of taxes on the value of money over time. We also discuss how governments use tax exclusions, credits, deductions, and deferrals to encourage certain behavior.

Effect of Taxes on the Time Value of Money

Just as inflation affects the time value of money, so too does taxation.

Example: Joel Lavista places $5,000 in an investment that guarantees a 10 percent annual return.

Analysis: At the end of the first year, Joel's investment is worth $5,500. However, if he owes taxes on that investment, the after-tax value of the investment is less.

As with inflation, taxes reduce the interest earnings that the investor or lender actually retains. Thus, investments that generate earnings that are taxed at a relatively low rate tend to be attractive to investors because the actual earnings on these investments are higher than the earnings would be if the investments were taxed at a high rate.

Generally, in the United States, interest income is taxed as ordinary income, which typically bears a higher rate than the taxes on capital gains on investments. ***Capital gains*** are profits made when an asset is sold for a price that is higher than the price paid to purchase the asset. For example, if you purchase a share of stock for $90 and sell it for $110, you have realized a capital gain of $20 on your investment. Typically, that $20 would be subject to taxation. ***Capital losses*** are losses taken when an asset is sold for a price that is lower than the price paid to purchase the asset.

Exclusions, Credits, Deductions, and Deferrals

As we discussed in Chapter 1, governments can use their taxing powers to influence the actions of people and businesses. Four primary tax mechanisms that governments use to influence social policy are exclusions, credits, deductions, and deferrals. Each of these mechanisms may increase the value of a sum of money relative to alternate uses of that money.

An ***exclusion*** is funds received that are not taxed. For example, many governments exclude the death benefits of life insurance policies from taxation to encourage the purchase of life insurance to protect survivors in the event of a breadwinner's premature death. This exclusion thus furthers the social purpose of preventing survivors from requiring governmental support. Furthermore, life insurance benefits, like property insurance benefits, are designed to reimburse beneficiaries for a loss, so the benefits are not considered income.

A ***credit*** is a reduction from tax liability. The full amount of a credit is offset against taxes owed. For example, in the United States, eligible taxpayers may take a child tax credit, which allows the taxpayer to subtract a specified amount each year from the tax he owes the government for each child under 17 years of age.

A ***deduction*** is an expense that is subtracted from adjusted gross income in computing taxable income.[1] For example, in the United States, charitable donations are deductions, and the amount of the deduction may be subtracted from an individual's adjusted gross income to determine taxable income. The fact that taxable income will be reduced because of making charitable contributions encourages people to make such contributions.

A ***deferral*** is a postponement of payment of taxes from the current year to a later year.

Many governments allow deductions and deferrals from current taxable income to encourage the use of certain savings plans, as we will discuss in Chapter 13.

The Risk-Return Tradeoff

When faced with two or more options, people usually weigh the potential negative outcomes against the potential positive outcomes of each option. For example, Drew Stewart, from our example at the beginning of this chapter, must weigh the chance of losing all his money in his cousin's new company against the possibility of becoming rich through this investment. He must go through the same analysis with the option of investing in a mutual fund. Drew is balancing the risks and returns of his choices.

A fundamental concept in financial services is the relationship between risk and return. ***Risk*** is the possibility of an unexpected outcome, which is typically a loss. ***Return*** is the compensation that results from investing or lending money. The ***risk-return tradeoff*** is the concept that a direct relationship exists between the risk of an investment and the level of return the investment potentially will provide. That is, the higher the risk associated with an investment, the greater the potential return on the investment. Likewise, the lower the risk associated with an investment, the lower its potential return.

The risk-return tradeoff does not mean that riskier investments always will produce higher returns than safer investments. Instead, it means that the potential returns of an investment tend to correlate with the risk of that investment.

FIGURE 2.5 Risk and Return

Lower Risks and Lower Potential Returns	Higher Risks and Higher Potential Returns
Short-term investments	Long-term investments
Loans to borrowers with good credit	Loans to borrowers with poor credit
Highly liquid assets	Generally illiquid assets
Loans to businesses that have adequate financial resources	Loans to businesses that have inadequate financial resources
Loans backed by a pledge of specific property	Loans not backed by a pledge of specific property
Products that are inexpensive to develop and break even quickly	Products that are expensive to develop and are slow to break even
Products that are familiar	Products that are new and unfamiliar

Source: Adapted from Susan Conant, *Capital Management for Insurance Companies* (Atlanta: LOMA, © 2001), 11. Used with permission; all rights reserved.

Some financial products carry greater risk than others. For example, the stock of a new company typically is high risk because the company might fail, rendering its stock worthless. On the other hand, a U.S. federally insured savings account is low risk because it is backed by the full faith and credit—which means the further borrowing and taxing power—of the U.S. government up to a limit. However, stocks typically have the potential to provide greater returns than do savings accounts.

Virtually every financial decision is subject to the risk-return tradeoff. Examples of investment characteristics that typically have lower or higher levels of risk and return—all other characteristics held constant—are set forth in Figure 2.5.

Some people are not comfortable accepting higher risks even if potential returns are higher. Other people are comfortable accepting a very high level of risk. The degree to which a person is willing to accept financial risk is known as that person's ***risk tolerance***. When a financial adviser begins working with a new client, one of the adviser's first tasks (after identifying the client's goals) is to assess the client's risk tolerance, because the level of risk that a person will accept determines which financial services and products are best suited to help meet that person's needs.

Figure 2.6 presents the risk-return pyramid, which illustrates the relationship between risk and return for a variety of investments.

FIGURE 2.6 Risk-Return Pyramid

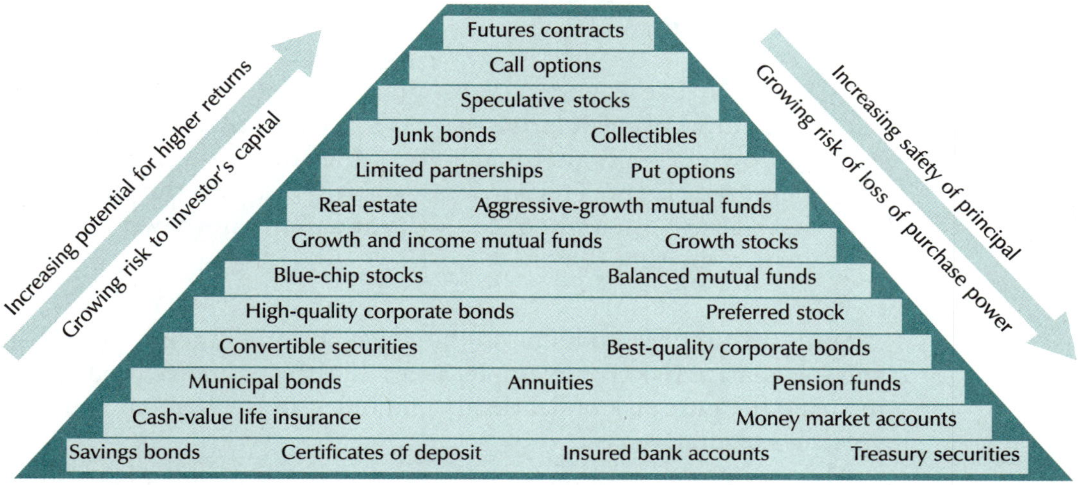

Source: Reprinted from E. Thomas Garman and Raymond E. Forgue, *Personal Finance,* Seventh Edition, 394. Copyright © 2003 by Houghton Mifflin Company. Used with permission.

Risk

We all face risks every day. We take risks when we drive, do chores at home, and make decisions at work. Personal financial decisions also involve risk because typically such decisions rely on assumptions about an uncertain future. For example, when you invest money, you make assumptions about the rate of inflation, the rate of taxation, other future economic conditions, and how specific investment products will perform. When you borrow money, you assume that you will continue making sufficient income to repay the loan. When you save for retirement, you assume that you will live for a certain period after you stop working and that your expenses will fall within a certain range.

Both people and businesses experience two basic kinds of risk—speculative risk and pure risk. ***Speculative risk*** involves three possible outcomes: loss, gain, or no change. For example, the value of stock that you purchase may increase, decrease, or remain the same.

Pure risk involves no possibility of gain; either a loss occurs or no loss occurs. An example of pure risk is driving a car. Either you will have an accident that will cause financial loss or you will be accident-free and no loss will occur. This possibility of financial loss without the possibility of gain—pure risk—is the only kind of risk that can be insured. Insurance exists to compensate for financial loss and not to provide an opportunity for financial gain.

Example: Henry and Janet Fowler are both employed full time. They have used $10,000 of their savings to purchase stock in a growing software company. They believe that the software company is strong and that their investment will soon be worth a lot more than $10,000.

Analysis: The Fowlers' investment in a software company is an example of speculative risk. As a result of their investment, the Fowlers may gain financially or they may lose part or all of their investment. The Fowlers also are faced with the pure risk that one or both of them could die and their family would lose the income that they now earn.

Some insurance products do, however, have elements of both pure and speculative risk. For example, a variable life insurance product, while insuring the pure risk of death, also includes an investment element involving speculative risk.

Risk is an important factor to be considered as people make financial decisions. In this section, we discuss the types of risks and different ways to manage them.

Types of Risk

The following types of risk affect financial services and products:

- ***Business risk*** is the risk that the business itself will fail. Some businesses are inherently more risky to invest in than others. For example, investing in a new technology company generally carries more business risk than does investing in an established financial services company.

- ***Default risk*** is the risk that a borrower will not make scheduled payments of principal and interest to the lender.

- ***Inflation risk,*** also known as *purchasing power risk*, is the risk that the real value of the returns on an investment will be less than anticipated because of higher-than-expected inflation.

- ***Interest rate risk*** is the risk that the value of an investment will decline in the future because of changes in the market interest rate, which is the prevailing interest rate for a similar type of investment. Market interest rates rise and fall depending on forces in the economy.

Example: First Safety Bank lends Toucan Corporation $100,000 for 10 years at 5 percent interest. Two years into the loan, the market interest rate available on similar loans has increased to 8 percent.

Analysis: An increase in market interest rates causes previous fixed-rate loans to be less valuable to a lender or investor. In effect, First Safety's principal is invested at a lower rate than the interest rate currently available. Therefore, First Safety is receiving a lower return on that principal than it would if it were able to invest or lend the principal at the new, higher market interest rate.

- ***Liquidity risk*** is the risk that an investor will not be able to sell an asset or investment quickly at its market value. ***Liquidity*** is the ease with which an asset can be converted into cash for an approximation of its true value. Cash is the most liquid of all investments. Real estate investments and investments in companies that are not actively traded in stock markets are examples of assets that are generally not liquid. In some cases, selling an asset that is not liquid earlier than originally planned can result in a loss of principal.

- ***Market risk*** is the possibility of losses or reduced returns simply because of the tendency of prices to move together.

- ***Political risk*** is the possibility of losses or reduced returns because of changes in laws, regulations, or taxes. For example, an increase in tax rates decreases the real return on the underlying investments. Alternatively, a decrease in tax rates increases the real return on investments. Another example of political risk is the risk that, in some countries, the government may seize private businesses.

- ***Reinvestment risk*** is the risk that after the principal and interest on a loan or other investment have been returned, the lender or investor may have difficulty finding another investment that offers returns as high as the previous investment. Reinvestment risk increases when interest rates are falling. Reinvestment risk may also affect people who have had money in retirement funds and are required to withdraw those funds upon retirement or upon reaching a certain age specified by law. These investors may find reinvesting their funds at attractive rates difficult.

Example: Maya Kincaid has two investment opportunities:

(1) Purchase a $1,000 two-year bond with an interest rate of 10 percent

(2) Purchase a $1,000 one-year bond with an interest rate of 10 percent

Analysis: If Maya purchases the two-year bond, she will earn $100 at the end of the first year and $100 at the end of the second year, for a total of $200.

If Maya purchases the one-year bond with an interest rate of 10 percent, she will have earned $100 in interest at the end of the year. At that time, she may choose to purchase another one-year bond. If the interest rate has decreased to 8 percent, the second bond will earn only $80 in interest and Maya will have earned only a total of $180. However, if the interest rate has increased to 12 percent, the second bond will earn $120 in interest and Maya will have earned a total of $220.

These types of risks will be mentioned throughout this text in conjunction with various financial products.

Managing Risk

The practice of ***risk management*** involves identifying, assessing, and dealing with risk. Each person is his own personal risk manager every day. Four risk management strategies are

- **Avoiding the risk.** Avoiding the risk is a risk management strategy that involves declining to take a risk. For example, a person may avoid the risk of a fall from a horse by not getting on the horse. Sometimes, however, avoiding risk is not effective, practical, or desirable.

- **Controlling the risk.** Controlling the risk is a risk management strategy that entails taking steps to prevent or reduce losses. Installing smoke detectors and sprinkler systems in a building is a way to control risk by reducing the likelihood of fire damage and lessening the severity of fire damage should it occur.

- **Accepting the risk.** Accepting the risk is a risk management strategy that involves deciding to take a risk and assuming all financial responsibility for that risk. For example, people who invest in stocks

INSIGHT 2.2 Self-Insurance

Self-insurance is a risk-management strategy by which a person or business accepts financial responsibility for losses associated with specific risks. For example, many employers provide medical expense benefits to their employees. An employer can self-insure such a benefit plan by either setting aside money to pay employees' medical expenses or paying those expenses out of its current income rather than purchasing coverage from an insurance company.

When a person selects a high deductible on his automobile insurance, he is partially self-insuring. For example, if Latonda Purt has a $500 deductible on her car insurance and she gets in an accident that causes only $450 of damage, she will not submit an insurance claim. Rather, she will pay the $450 out of savings or current income because this amount is less than her deductible.

risk losing their principal, but they accept the risk because stock investments provide the opportunity to increase wealth. Insight 2.2 describes a method of accepting risk known as self-insurance.

- **Transferring the risk.** Transferring the risk is a risk management strategy that involves shifting some or all of the financial responsibility associated with a risk to another party, generally in exchange for a fee charged by the other party. People often transfer risk when the risk is either unavoidable or the costs of accepting that risk are unacceptably high. Individuals and businesses typically transfer risk by purchasing insurance coverage. We discuss the management of risk through insurance in more detail later in this chapter.

Return

People who invest money hope to receive a positive return on their investment. As mentioned earlier, in the context of financial services, return is the compensation that results from investing or lending money. A return can come in many forms, such as interest earned, capital gains realized, and dividends received. The return on stocks, for example, is composed of capital gains (the price appreciation) and dividends. A ***dividend*** is a distribution of a business' earnings to its shareholders.

Frequently, return is expressed as a percentage of the amount of money invested. Thus, the ***rate of return*** is the profit that results from investing money, expressed as a percentage of the amount invested.

Example: Rhonda Richardson invests $100 for one year, and at the end of the year she sells her investment for $110.

Analysis: Rhonda's return is $10 and her rate of return is 10 percent ($10 ÷ $100 = 0.10 or 10 percent).

Typically, rates of return are expressed in terms of a specific period of time because the amount of time an investment takes to generate a given return is important to investors. Measuring rates of return in terms of a standard unit of time helps investors understand how their investments are performing and compare investment options. One important measure for investors is the annual rate of return, which is the rate of return measured over a one-year period of time.

Some types of investments offer a rate of return that is known in advance, while other investments generate returns that are not known in advance. The interest rates paid on certificates of deposit, for example, are set in advance. The rates of return that an investor receives on stocks and real estate are not known in advance, however, because the rates of return are partly dependent on the market value of these investments at the future date when the investor sells them.

Managing Risk Through Insurance

In the previous section, we introduced the concept of risk management and explained that a popular risk management strategy is to transfer risk through the mechanism of insurance. When we speak of asset protection in this text, we are referring to the transfer of risk through the purchase of insurance.

When an insurance company agrees to provide a person or a business with insurance coverage, the insurer issues an insurance policy. The ***policy*** is a written document that contains the terms of the agreement between the insurance company and the owner of the policy. The agreement is a legally enforceable contract under which the insurance company agrees to pay a certain benefit amount when a specific loss occurs, provided the insurer has received a specified amount of money it charges for the coverage, called the ***premium***.

The ***applicant*** is the person or business that applies for an insurance policy. In most cases, the applicant owns the policy issued by the insurance company. However, the applicant may name someone else to be the ***policyowner***—the person or business that actually owns an individual insurance policy. The policyowner and the ***insured***—the person whose life, health, or property is insured under the policy—typically are the same person. The insured under a life insurance policy is known as the *life insured* in Canada, which is just one instance of terminology differences found in the financial services industry worldwide.

If the event insured against occurs while the insurance policy is effective—or *in force*—the insurer pays the policy benefit. Life insurance policy benefits usually are paid to the policy's ***beneficiary***—the person or legal entity named to receive the policy benefits when the insured dies. Health insurance policy benefits usually are paid either to the insured or the medical care provider that rendered medical services. Property insurance policy benefits typically are paid to the insured, and liability insurance policy benefits may be paid to the insured or the person or entity to whom the insured is liable.

Insurance can cover three basic types of risk:

- ***Personal risk*** is the risk of economic loss associated with death, poor health, injury, and outliving one's economic resources. Life and health insurance and annuities are insurance products designed to cover personal risks.

- ***Property damage risk*** is the risk of economic loss resulting from damage to or loss of a person's property. Property insurance provides a benefit if insured items are damaged or lost because of specified causes of loss, such as accident, theft, fire, or natural disaster.

- ***Liability risk*** is the risk of economic loss resulting from a person being held responsible for harming others or their property. For example, a person may be held liable for the payment of medical bills if someone comes into his home, slips, falls, and must be hospitalized. Liability insurance provides a benefit payable on behalf of a covered party who is legally responsible for unintentionally harming others or their property.

Insurance is based on the concept of risk pooling. By issuing policies and collecting premiums on many individuals facing the same risk of loss, an insurer is able to spread the cost of the few losses that actually occur among all the insured persons. Insurance, then, provides protection against the risk of economic loss by applying a simple principle:

> If the economic losses that actually result from a given peril can be shared by large numbers of people who are all subject to the risk of such losses, and the probability of loss is relatively small for each person, then the cost to each person will be relatively small.

Characteristics of Insurable Risks

For a risk—a potential loss—to be insurable, it must occur by chance, be definite, be significant, be predictable, and not be catastrophic to the insurer. These five basic characteristics, which are illustrated in Figure 2.7, define an insurable risk and are basic principles underlying the business of insurance. A potential loss that does not have these characteristics generally is not considered an insurable risk.

FIGURE 2.7 Characteristics of Insurable Risks

The Loss Must Occur by Chance

The loss must be caused either by an unexpected event or by an event that is not intentionally caused by the person covered by the insurance. In the case of life insurance, although the event itself—death—is certain to occur, the timing of the event typically is unexpected.

The Loss Must Be Definite

For most types of insurance, a loss must be definite in time and amount to be insurable. In other words, the insurer must be able to determine when to pay policy benefits and how much those benefits should be. The timing of a loss typically is easily determined. For example, death and property damage are obvious events occurring at a moment in time.

The amount of benefits payable if a covered loss occurs while the policy is in force is set forth in the insurance policy. Depending on the manner in which a policy states the amount of the policy benefit, every insurance policy can be classified as being either a contract of indemnity or a valued contract.

Contract of Indemnity

A ***contract of indemnity*** is an insurance policy under which the amount of the policy benefit payable for a covered loss is based on the actual amount of financial loss as determined at the time of loss. The policy states that the amount of the benefit is equal to the amount of the covered financial loss or a maximum amount stated in the contract, whichever is less. When the owner of the policy submits a ***claim***—a request for payment under the terms of an insurance policy—the benefit paid by the insurance company will not be greater than the actual amount of the financial loss. Many types of health insurance policies, as well as property and liability policies, are contracts of indemnity.

> **Example:** Alon Dumont is admitted to the hospital when he complains of chest pains. Alon's health insurance policy states the maximum amount payable to cover Alon's medical expenses if he is hospitalized.
>
> **Analysis:** The insurer will pay a sum based on the actual amount of Alon's hospital bill, up to the stated maximum.

Valued Contract

A ***valued contract*** specifies the amount of the benefit that will be payable when a covered loss occurs, regardless of the actual amount of the loss that is incurred. Life insurance contracts are valued contracts.

> **Example:** Patricia Herling bought a $100,000 life insurance policy covering her own life.
>
> **Analysis:** Upon Patricia's death, the insurance company will pay a benefit of $100,000. No analysis will be made of the actual loss caused by Patricia's death.

Some life insurance policies provide that the benefit paid will vary over the life of the policy. These policies still are considered valued contracts because changes in the amount of the benefit are based on factors that are not directly related to the amount of the actual loss that will result from the insured's death.

The Loss Must Be Significant

If a loss is trivial in amount, the administrative expenses of paying benefits would drive the cost of such protection so high in relation to the amount of the potential loss that most people would not find purchasing the coverage worthwhile. The result would be that insurance companies would discontinue offering such coverage. Thus, losses must be significant enough to make protection of such losses economically feasible.

The Loss Rate Must Be Predictable

An insurance company must be able to predict the probable rate of loss—the loss rate—that the people insured by the coverage will experience. Predicting the loss rate involves determining the probable number and timing of covered losses that will occur in a group of insureds. Although insurers cannot predict the losses that a specific person will experience, they can predict with a reasonable degree of certainty the number of people in a given large group who will suffer a particular loss. This ability to accurately predict loss occurrences is based on the concept of the law of large numbers.

> The ***law of large numbers*** states that, typically, the more times we observe a particular event, the more likely our observed results will approximate the true probability that the event will occur.

The classic example of how the law of large numbers operates is the coin toss. If you toss a coin, the probability is 50-50 that it will land heads up. If you tossed the coin a dozen times, you would not necessarily get an equal number of heads and tails. However, if you tossed it 1,000 times, you could expect a result of approximately 50 percent heads and 50 percent tails to occur.

Insurance companies rely on the law of large numbers to predict the probability of losses that a given group of insureds is likely to experience during a given time period. Insurance companies collect specific information about large numbers of people in order to identify the patterns of losses that those people experience. Such information allows insurers to properly price insurance products.

The Loss Must Not Be Catastrophic to the Insurer

If a potential loss is likely to result in catastrophic financial damage to the insurer, the loss is not insurable because the insurer could not responsibly promise to pay benefits for the loss. One method insurers use to reduce the possibility of catastrophic loss is to spread the risks they choose to insure. Thus, for example, a prudent property insurer would not insure homes only in a region prone to tornadoes, but would spread its coverage zone across more regions or nationwide.

Another method insurers use to reduce the possibility of catastrophic risk is to transfer risks to another insurer by reinsuring those risks, as explained in Insight 2.3.

Insurability of Specific Risks

The five characteristics we described in the preceding section are useful in identifying the general kinds of losses that are insurable and provide a helpful framework for the study of insurance principles and products. However, insurance is sold on a case-by-case basis, and insurers consider a number of factors to determine whether a specific risk is insurable.

INSIGHT 2.3 Reinsurance

Reinsurance is insurance that one insurance company—known as the ***ceding company***—purchases from another insurance company—known as the ***reinsurer***, *reinsurance company*, or *assuming company*—to transfer risks on insurance policies the ceding company issued. To ***cede*** insurance business is to obtain reinsurance on that business by transferring all or part of the risk to a reinsurer.

The ceding company typically sets a maximum amount of insurance—known as its ***retention limit***—on which it is willing to retain the risk before transferring some of the risk to a reinsurer. The ceding company collects the premiums and pays the policy benefits to the proper recipient when due. In fact, the owners of policies that have been reinsured typically are unaware of the reinsurance agreement.

Some insurance companies act only as reinsurers. Other insurance companies issue policies directly to people and businesses as well as act as reinsurers for other insurance companies. Sometimes a reinsurer transfers risk to another reinsurer in a transaction known as ***retrocession***. The reinsurance company that accepts the risk in a retrocession is known as a ***retrocessionaire***.

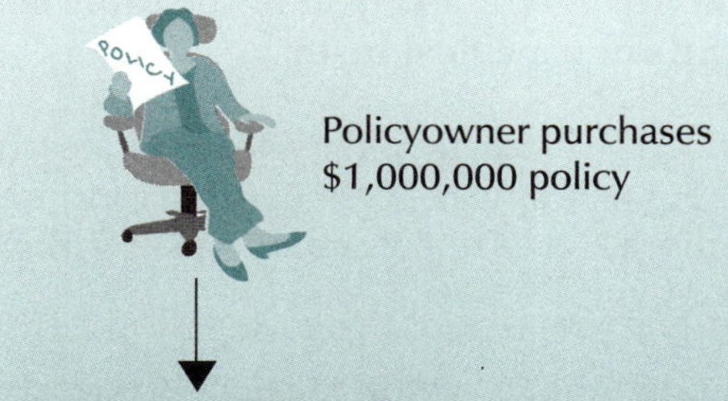

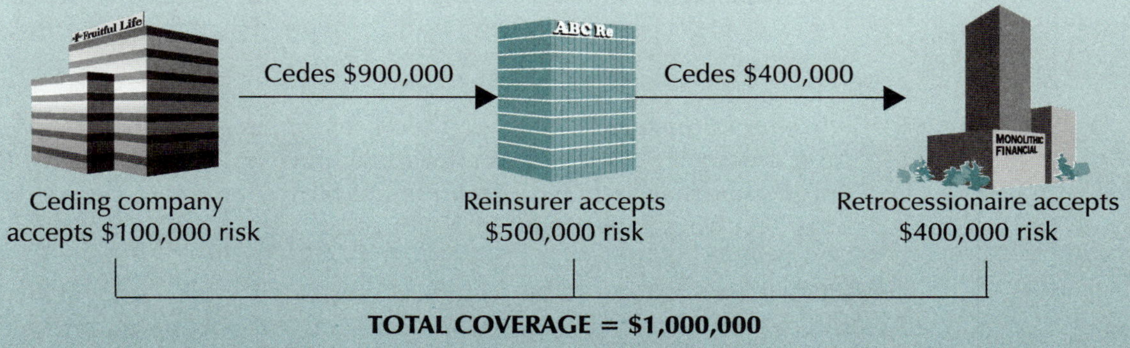

Assessing the Degree of Risk

An insurance company must assess the degree of risk it will assume with each application it receives because not every application presents an average likelihood of loss. In addition, those individuals who believe they have a greater-than-average likelihood of loss tend to seek insurance protection to a greater extent than do those who believe they have an average or a less-than-average likelihood of loss. This tendency, called ***antiselection***, *adverse selection*, or *selection against the insurer*, is a primary reason that insurers carefully review each application to assess the degree of risk it presents.

The process of identifying and classifying the degree of risk represented by a proposed insured is called ***underwriting*** or *selection of risks*, and the insurance company employees who are responsible for evaluating proposed risks are called *underwriters*. As noted earlier, although insurers cannot predict when a specific insured will suffer a loss, they have identified factors associated with an increased or decreased likelihood that an insured will suffer a loss. The most important of these factors that increase the possibility of loss are physical hazards, moral hazards, morale hazards, and financial hazards.

- A ***physical hazard*** is a physical characteristic that may increase the likelihood of loss. For example, a person with a history of heart attacks possesses a physical hazard that will increase the likelihood that the person will die sooner than will a person of the same age and sex who does not have the same medical history.

- A ***moral hazard*** is the likelihood that a person may act dishonestly in the insurance transaction. For example, a person with a criminal record for fraudulent acts is more likely to defraud an insurer than is a person with no such record.

- A ***morale hazard*** is the likelihood that a person may act carelessly. For example, a person who knows he is insured may not lock his car at night.

- A ***financial hazard*** is the likelihood that a person who purchases more insurance than he can afford may have an ulterior motive in doing so or that he may ultimately not be able to afford the premiums, resulting in the insured discontinuing his coverage.

After the risks presented by a proposed insured have been identified, the underwriter classifies the proposed insured into an appropriate risk category to determine the equitable premium rate to charge for the requested coverage.

Insurable Interest Requirement

As noted earlier, only pure risks are insurable. The purpose of insurance is to compensate an individual or business for a financial loss, not to provide an opportunity for gain. At one time, people used insurance as a wagering device by purchasing policies on people or property in which they had no interest so that they could profit from a loss if one were to occur.

Purchasing insurance policies for wagering purposes is now considered to be against public policy. Laws require that when a policy is issued, the policyowner must have an insurable interest in the risk that is insured. An ***insurable interest*** is the interest a person has in the risk that is insured such that the person will suffer a genuine economic loss if the event insured against occurs. For example, the owner of a life insurance policy has an insurable interest in the insured when the policyowner is likely to benefit if the insured continues to live and is likely to suffer some loss or detriment if the insured dies. Part of the insurer's underwriting process is determining whether the proposed policyowner has an insurable interest in the insured risk.

Diversification

As we have noted, insurance operates through the principle of risk pooling. The investment principle of diversification is based on a similar principle. ***Diversification*** is the process of investing in a number of financial instruments to minimize the impact of risk associated with any one investment or type of investment. Through diversification, positive returns earned from some investments within an investment portfolio may offset the negative impact of one or more poorly performing investments. In investments, a ***portfolio*** is a collection of various securities usually assembled by an investor for the purpose of meeting a defined set of financial goals. As we shall discuss in Chapter 11, one of the greatest benefits of mutual funds is that they provide a relatively easy and economical means of diversification.

At the beginning of this chapter, you saw that Drew Stewart could diversify his investments by placing part of his money in his cousin's new business and part in a mutual fund. Such action would spread his risk between different investment vehicles. In addition, we mentioned diversification of risks when we pointed out that property insurers typically will spread their coverage across regions or entire countries so as not to limit their risks to one physical location. Diversification of risks

"MY FIRST PIECE OF ADVICE IS NOT TO PUT ALL YOUR EGGS IN ONE BASKET."

www.CartoonStock.com

is also one of the attractions for a financial services company that wishes to expand internationally. The risks it faces domestically may be completely different than those it faces in other countries. Proper diversification of risks should decrease the company's overall risk exposure. The same concept is true if the company wishes to broaden its product offerings, thus reducing the negative impact on the company if one product performs poorly.

Opportunity Cost

Opportunity cost is the alternative benefit that is given up when limited resources are used in choosing one alternative over another. The opportunity cost of choosing to achieve one goal is the alternative benefit you chose not to enjoy in order to achieve your goal.

> **Example:** Drew Stewart decides to take the vacation rather than invest in a mutual fund.
>
> **Analysis:** Drew's opportunity cost of taking the vacation is losing the potential investment returns provided by the mutual fund.

People make choices that involve opportunity costs every time they allocate scarce resources among financial services products. For example, a decision to purchase disability insurance results in an opportunity cost equal to the lost potential return the premium dollars could have earned if invested. While opportunity cost is a concept that is more relevant in a financial planning text, you should keep it in mind as you learn about the costs and benefits of financial products covered in this text.

Key Terms

time value of money
interest
present value
future value
interest rate
principal
simple interest
compound interest
compounding
nominal interest rate
effective interest rate
inflation
deflation
inflation rate
capital gains
capital losses
exclusion
credit
deduction
deferral

risk
return
risk-return tradeoff
risk tolerance
speculative risk
pure risk
business risk
default risk
inflation risk
interest rate risk
liquidity risk
liquidity
market risk
political risk
reinvestment risk
risk management
self-insurance
dividend
rate of return
policy
premium
applicant
policyowner
insured
beneficiary
personal risk
property damage risk
liability risk
contract of indemnity
claim
valued contract
law of large numbers
reinsurance
ceding company
reinsurer
cede
retention limit
retrocession
retrocessionaire
antiselection
underwriting
physical hazard
moral hazard
morale hazard
financial hazard
insurable interest
diversification
portfolio
opportunity cost

Endnote

1. A "deduction" is technically an expense subtracted from adjusted gross income. However, in this text, we use the term "deduction" also to refer to what is technically an "adjustment to income" because this terminology is commonly used in the financial services industry. Both deductions and adjustments to income are expenses that are subtracted from income in computing taxable income.

chapter 3

Cash Management

outline

objectives

After reading this chapter, you should be able to

- Discuss the needs that cash management products fulfill
- Describe the Federal Deposit Insurance Corporation and the National Credit Union Share Insurance Fund
- Define and distinguish between a demand deposit account and a time deposit account
- Discuss and distinguish among types of checking accounts and money market accounts
- Explain the purposes and operations of traveler's checks, money orders, and cashier's checks
- Discuss certificates of deposit and savings bonds
- Describe the most common forms of electronic funds transfer

As we learned in Chapter 1, cash management is the allocation of readily available funds among various living expenses as well as among savings and investment opportunities. Cash management services and products typically are the first exposure most people have to the financial services industry. When a young adult enters the working world, she will need help in managing cash inflows and outflows. Cash management typically entails storing income in one or more liquid accounts from which funds are distributed to pay bills and make purchases, while maintaining the safety of the funds and sometimes earning at least a modest rate of interest. Recall from Chapter 2 that liquidity is the ease with which an asset can be converted into cash for an approximation of its true value. Cash management also involves storing income in short-term savings instruments for purposes such as emergencies.

In this chapter, we explore various cash management services and products, including checking accounts, money market accounts, savings accounts and instruments, and electronic funds transfer. We begin, though, with a discussion of the needs cash management products fulfill.

Needs Fulfilled by Cash Management Products

Cash management products fulfill people's needs for ready access to funds, safety of funds, adequate return, low transaction costs, and wide acceptance as a substitute for cash. The products we discuss in this chapter meet some or all of these needs to varying degrees.

Ready Access to Funds

Because people predominantly use cash management products to pay bills and to transfer money to other savings and investment vehicles, they need relatively quick and easy access to their funds and the ability to convert these funds to cash quickly. Thus, cash management products must offer a high degree of liquidity. Note, though, that maintaining more liquid funds than necessary involves an opportunity cost. These funds could have been invested elsewhere to earn a greater return.

A further benefit of cash management products is that they allow people to avoid carrying large amounts of cash and paying bills in person. Thus, access to funds is convenient, and the risk of theft is substantially decreased.

Safety of Funds

People typically deposit their incomes into cash management products, and they need these products to offer safety of principal and freedom from financial risk. In the United States, the federal or a state government insures most of the financial products we discuss in this chapter. Products that are not insured are considered riskier than insured products. As you might expect from our discussion of the risk-return tradeoff in Chapter 2, products without government protection typically offer higher interest rates than protected products offer. Insight 3.1 discusses the governmental agencies that insure deposit accounts in the United States.

In Canada, the Canadian Deposit Insurance Corporation (CDIC) insures eligible deposits. The maximum basic coverage that is available for all eligible deposits that are held in the name of a depositor at a single member institution is Canadian $60,000, although separate coverage is available for certain types of deposits.

Return

The return on a cash management product is the interest earned on the product. Cash management products do not appreciate in value, but most of them pay interest. The interest rates for all the products we discuss in this chapter, with the exception of certificates of deposit, fluctuate with market forces.

Typically, the more liquidity a cash management product offers, the lower its interest rate and therefore its return. For example, cash kept in a regular checking account is extremely liquid, but it earns no interest. On the other hand, a 10-year certificate of deposit has limited liquidity but offers a greater interest rate than most other cash management products. Figure 3.1 shows a comparison of interest rates offered on the cash management products we discuss in this chapter.

Low Cost

People who place their incomes into cash management products that earn only minimal returns typically expect no fee structure other than perhaps minimum balance requirements and certain low transaction costs. The less money people pay in fees and charges, the more money they retain for their own use.

INSIGHT 3.1 U.S. Agencies That Insure Deposits

In the United States, the practice of providing people with insurance on the funds placed in depository institutions began after a large number of banks failed during the late 1920s and the 1930s. These failures wiped out many people's savings. Because people could not determine which banks were financially sound and which were not, these failures also caused people to lose faith in the security of their deposits in all banks. A system of deposit insurance backed by the full faith and credit of the government helps to maintain consumer confidence in the safety of the banking system. Two federal agencies insure funds in accounts offered by most commercial banks, savings and loan associations, savings banks, and credit unions.

- The ***Federal Deposit Insurance Corporation (FDIC)*** is a federal agency that insures deposits made in member commercial banks and thrifts. The FDIC administers the Bank Insurance Fund (BIF), which is responsible for insuring commercial banks, and the Savings Association Insurance Fund (SAIF), which is responsible for insuring savings and loan associations and mutual savings banks. The FDIC and its associated funds insure up to $100,000 per person/per institution. As long as a consumer has $100,000 or less in total on deposit in all of his FDIC-insured accounts at an FDIC-insured institution, the consumer bears essentially no risk that he will lose his funds, no matter what the financial condition or performance of the institution servicing the product.*

  Not all depository institutions are FDIC insured. One means of determining if an institution is FDIC insured is to look for an official sign, which must be displayed at each teller window or teller station of insured institutions. Insured thrifts typically display the official savings association (eagle) symbol, while insured commercial banks typically display the official bank (FDIC) symbol.

  Each Depositor Insured to $100,000
  FDIC
  FEDERAL DEPOSIT INSURANCE CORPORATION

  Deposits Federally Insured to $100,000
  Backed by the Full Faith and Credit of the United States Government

  In addition, not all accounts at FDIC-insured institutions are covered. To help people and bankers learn about deposit insurance and to provide information about the insurance coverage of specific groups of accounts, the FDIC has developed the Electronic Deposit Insurance Estimator (EDIE) system. EDIE, which is located on the FDIC's Web site (www.fdic.gov), allows consumers or bankers to enter information about an account or group of accounts at an FDIC-insured institution and receive a report that states whether the funds are fully insured. If any funds are uninsured, EDIE will identify them and explain why the funds are not covered.

- The National Credit Union Administration (NCUA) is a federal agency whose insurance arm, the ***National Credit Union Share Insurance Fund (NCUSIF)***, insures credit union accounts up to $100,000.

Programs sponsored by individual states insure deposit accounts in some depository institutions that are chartered by the state government (rather than the federal government). In many cases, a state contracts for private insurance for accounts at these institutions. Whether the federal or a state government manages deposit insurance, the goal is the same—to provide owners of deposit accounts with protection against the loss of funds in those accounts and with confidence in depository institutions.

* A consumer may have insured accounts in excess of $100,000 under certain conditions, an explanation of which is beyond the scope of this text.

Source: "FDIC: Your Insured Deposit—General Insurance Page," Federal Deposit Insurance Corporation, 10 June 1999, http://www.fdic.gov/deposit/deposits/insured/general.html (16 November 2003); "Frequently Asked Questions about the NCUSIF," National Credit Union Administration, http://webapps.ncua.gov/ins/InsuredFunds/FAQ.htm (16 November 2003). Also, adapted from Mary C. Bickley and David F. Johnson, *Intro to Financial Services* (Atlanta: LOMA, © 2001), 33. Used with permission; all rights reserved.

FIGURE 3.1 Comparison of Interest Rates Offered on Cash Management Products

Type of Account	Interest Rate*
NOW checking account	0.1%
Savings account	0.25
Money market deposit account	0.35
Money market mutual fund	0.35
Three-month certificate of deposit	0.6
One-year certificate of deposit	0.75
Series EE savings bond	2.61
Five-year certificate of deposit	3.2
Ten-year certificate of deposit	3.2

*Rates as of November 18, 2003

Wide Acceptance

To pay bills and make purchases, a person needs a product that transfers money in a form that is widely accepted. The accounts we discuss in this chapter typically offer at least a couple of ways of transferring cash in a widely acceptable manner.

Checking Accounts

A ***checking account*** is a demand deposit account that allows the account owner to write checks for specified amounts against funds he has deposited into the account. A ***demand deposit account*** is an account under which the financial institution must give the account holder access to his funds upon the account holder's demand. A ***check*** is a signed, written order by which the owner of the account instructs the financial institution to pay a stated sum from the account to another party. Depository institutions are the primary source of checking accounts.

Features of Checking Accounts

The features of checking accounts include

- **Ready access to funds.** Checking accounts are known as *demand deposits* because the depository institution must honor checks and other withdrawals up to the balance of the account on demand of the account holder. The owner of a checking account does not have to notify the depository institution of a withdrawal in advance, so the funds in the account are accessible at any time. Furthermore, in addition to writing checks, checking account holders can access their funds by electronic funds transfer, which we discuss later in this chapter.

- **Safety of funds.** The Federal Deposit Insurance Corporation (FDIC) typically insures checking accounts up to $100,000.

- **Low cost.** People can open checking accounts with small amounts of money, and depository institutions typically charge very low fees or no fees to maintain these accounts. We discuss costs and fees later in this section.

- **Wide acceptance.** Most businesses accept checks and electronic funds transfers as a means of payment. Common check substitutes are explained in Figure 3.2.

All types of checking accounts offer the added benefit of providing the account holder with a written record of deposits into and withdrawals from the account. These records are useful for budgeting, tax, and other legal purposes. For example, a canceled check can provide proof of a payment that the account holder made to another party.

Types of Checking Accounts

Depository institutions offer several types of checking accounts; some pay interest to the account holder, while others do not. Interest earned on a checking account is taxed annually at the account holder's ordinary income tax rate.

- A ***regular checking account***, also called a *non-interest-earning checking account*, is a checking account that does not pay interest. Some people prefer a regular checking account to an interest-earning account because typically depository institutions offer either lower fees or no minimum balance requirement on regular checking accounts to differentiate them from interest-earning accounts.

FIGURE 3.2 Check Substitutes

Traveler's checks, money orders, and cashier's checks are check substitutes that are widely accepted and offer liquidity and safety at a low cost. Like checks, check substitutes enable a person to avoid carrying large amounts of cash. A person does not need to have a checking account in order to obtain and use these check substitutes.

Traveler's Checks

A ***traveler's check*** is a check bought by a person from a financial institution, typically to use as a substitute for cash while traveling. A person usually buys a number of traveler's checks in different denominations ($10, $20, $50, and $100) for which he pays the financial institution the face amount of the checks, plus a low fee—typically 1 percent of the amount of the checks. At the time he buys the traveler's checks, the person signs each check in the presence of the financial institution's representative. When the person is ready to make a purchase using the traveler's checks, he fills in the name of the retailer. He then countersigns the traveler's checks in the presence of the retailer, who compares the countersignature with the original signature as a means of verifying the person's identity.

Traveler's checks are highly liquid and function like cash in that when they are presented to a retailer for the purchase of an item that costs less than the face amount of the traveler's check, the retailer will give the person cash as change. However, traveler's checks are safer than cash, because traveler's checks offered by most institutions generally are replaceable if they are lost or stolen on the condition that the owner has a record of their serial numbers.

Traveler's checks are issued by well known financial institutions and sold through a wide variety of financial institutions. The issuer guarantees the checks, thus making them widely accepted worldwide. Note, though, that not all retailers accept traveler's checks.

Money Order

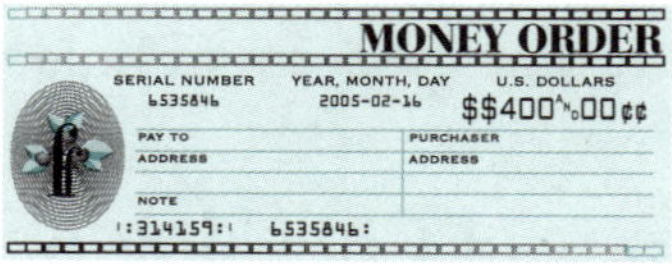

A ***money order*** is a type of check issued by a financial institution, the U.S. Postal Service, and some retail stores that allows the party named on the order to receive the face amount in cash on demand. A person buys a money order for a specific, typically small, amount and then the name of the party to whom the money is to be paid is written on the money order. A person who does not have a checking account may prefer to purchase money orders for a small fee each based on the amount of the money order (typically less than $10 per money order) several times a month than to open a checking account.

Cashier's Check

A ***cashier's check*** is a check issued on a financial institution's own account and backed by the creditworthiness of the institution. A person pays the issuing institution the face amount of the check and a small fee at the time of purchase. The cashier's check is made out to a specific party for a specific amount. Cashier's checks typically are used for large transactions, such as a real estate sale, between a person and a third party when the third party demands cash or its equivalent and the person does not want to carry a large amount of cash.

Commercial banks, savings and loans, and savings banks offer regular checking accounts.

- A *negotiable order of withdrawal account*, usually called a ***NOW account***, is a checking account that earns interest. Commercial banks, savings and loans, and savings banks offer NOW accounts. Typically, these institutions require that a NOW account holder maintain a pre-set minimum balance or average monthly balance before the financial institution pays interest on the account. Some NOW accounts pay ***tiered interest rates***, also called *graduated interest rates*, which are interest rates that vary according to the amount on deposit in the account. Lower account balances earn lower interest rates than do higher balances.

- A ***share draft account*** is a checking account that is offered by credit unions. A share draft account is similar to a NOW account. Share draft accounts pay dividends (rather than interest) based on the amount of money the credit union member has on deposit. For practical purposes, however, share draft dividends are treated the same as interest earned on a checking account.

Different individuals have different cash management needs. Thus, depository institutions have created variations on each of the three types of checking accounts with differences in minimum balance requirements, the number of checks that may be written each month without a fee being charged, and the type and amount of service fees. For example, a bank may offer one regular checking account that charges a fee if more than a certain number of checks are written each month, but charges a low monthly fee to maintain the account. A second regular checking account may allow the owner to write an unlimited number of checks without a fee, but will charge a high monthly fee to maintain the account. A third regular checking account may charge a flat fee per check, regardless of the number of checks written. A fourth regular checking account may charge no fees and allow unlimited checking if the account owner maintains an agreed-upon minimum balance, such as $1,000, in the account. A fifth regular checking account may offer unlimited free checking without a minimum balance if the account holder is part of a certain group.

Some depository institutions waive fees associated with certain accounts under certain conditions. For example, most banks charge a fee to print new checks for account owners. However, a bank may waive this fee if the account holder maintains at least a specified minimum balance.

Money Market Accounts

A ***money market account*** is a category of interest-earning accounts that offers higher interest rates than most NOW accounts and savings accounts and allows a limited number of checks to be written on the account. The four major types of money market accounts are super NOW accounts, money market deposit accounts, money market mutual funds, and asset management accounts. Interest earned on money market accounts is taxed annually at a person's ordinary income tax rate, with the exception of some tax-free money market mutual funds.

Super NOW Accounts

A ***super NOW account*** is a high-interest NOW account that offers only limited check-writing privileges. For example, a super NOW account may allow the account holder to write only six checks a month. However, the account holder may withdraw his funds by other means at any time. This type of account is offered by depository institutions and is government insured.

The initial minimum deposit is typically at least $1,000 for a super NOW account. If the account balance falls below this amount at any time, the interest rate will fall to that offered on a traditional NOW account.

Money Market Deposit Accounts

A ***money market deposit account (MMDA)*** is a deposit account offered by a depository institution that invests amounts on deposit in short-term, low-risk investments and then pays an interest rate according to the performance of these investments. MMDAs offer check-writing privileges, but they are not as liquid as checking accounts because usually the number of transactions is limited to six per month.

MMDAs typically require an initial deposit that is higher than that required to open a checking account. The initial deposit requirement typically is $1,000. In addition, MMDAs typically require maintenance of a minimum balance to avoid an account fee.

As with checking accounts, MMDAs also may be subject to transaction fees. One advantage of MMDAs is that they generally pay a higher interest rate than interest-earning checking accounts and even super NOW accounts and still present essentially no risk because they typically are government insured.

Money Market Mutual Funds

A ***money market mutual fund (MMMF)*** is a mutual fund that pools the funds of customers and uses the funds to invest in short-term, low-risk investments and then pays customers interest rates that fluctuate according to the performance of these investments. MMMFs typically offer limited check-writing privileges and sometimes minimum check amount limits. One disadvantage of MMMFs is that funds held in an MMMF account are not accessible through an automated teller machine (ATM). Money market mutual funds are offered by depository institutions, brokerage firms, and mutual fund companies.

MMMFs are similar to MMDAs in that they typically have relatively high initial deposit minimums. Some MMMFs charge an account fee. MMMFs pay higher interest rates than interest-earning checking accounts and savings accounts, but they are not government insured. Nonetheless, MMMFs are considered relatively safe because the funds are typically invested in extremely low-risk securities, such as some of those issued by the government.

Asset Management Accounts

An ***asset management account (AMA)***, also called a *sweep account*, is an account that offers checking services as part of a package of financial services, including a money market account—an MMDA or MMMF—securities brokerage services (such as the buying and selling of mutual funds, stocks, and bonds), credit and debit cards, loans, and unified record keeping. Depository institutions, mutual fund companies, and securities brokerage firms offer AMAs. AMAs usually require an initial deposit of between $1,000 and $25,000 to open the account. Account holders typically must pay an annual service fee and maintain total assets above a specified amount.

The typical AMA includes at least three subaccounts—a checking account, a money market account—an MMDA or MMMF, and a brokerage account. AMAs are not insured by the FDIC or a similar organization, but the checking account and any MMDA within the AMA typically are insured.

AMAs are called sweep accounts because money in the AMA is moved, or swept, automatically in and out of the money market account as needed to cover checks and to ensure that excess funds are earning the money market interest rate. For example, when the AMA needs funds to pay a check, money is swept from the money market account into the checking account. When additional cash comes into the AMA, such as when the account holder deposits a paycheck, the majority of the deposit is automatically swept into the money market account until it is needed in the checking account. When the account holder makes brokerage transactions, cash used for or received from the transaction is swept automatically out of or into the money market account. If the AMA includes a loan account, the loan proceeds are swept into the money market account, and periodic loan repayments are swept automatically out of the money market account. The goal of sweeping funds in and out of the money market account is to generate the highest possible return on the consumer's deposits. Figure 3.3 illustrates how an AMA operates.

The previous paragraph gives examples of sweeps triggered by specific events. A financial institution also may sweep AMAs monthly, weekly, or even daily to maximize returns. The financial institution provides the customer with a record of all of these transactions. Many consumers who frequently move funds in and out of investments find the record-keeping function of AMAs to be a valuable service.

FIGURE 3.3 Operation of an Asset Management Account

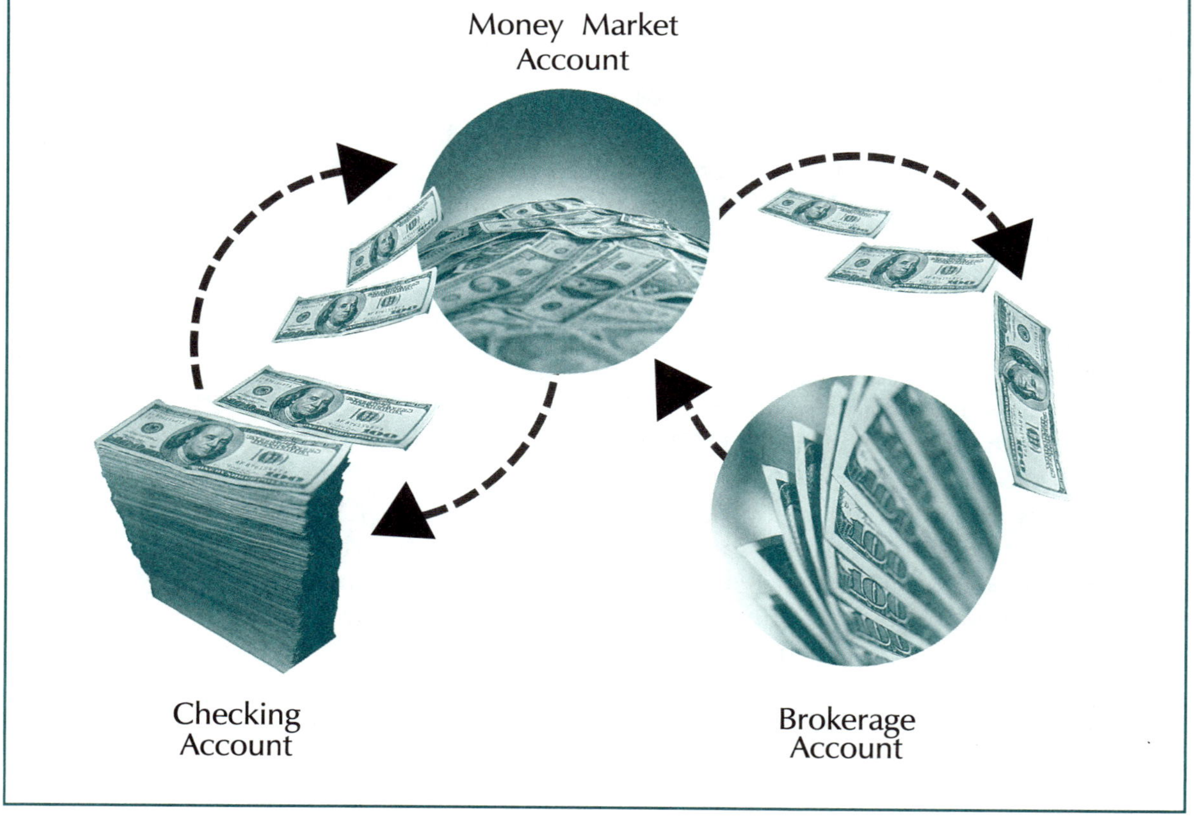

Savings Accounts and Instruments

When a person's income exceeds his daily living expenses, he may want to store the excess funds in a savings account or savings instrument for a short time to earn a higher return than he could by placing the funds in an interest-earning checking account. In this section, we discuss savings accounts and short-term savings instruments, which offer liquidity and safety at a low cost. Note, though, that with savings instruments—CDs and savings bonds—a person gives up some liquidity for a higher return than that paid on checking accounts and money market accounts.

Savings Accounts

A ***savings account*** is a time deposit account that pays interest on deposited funds, typically from the day of deposit to the day of withdrawal. A ***time deposit account*** is an account into which funds are deposited with the expectation that they will remain on deposit for a period of time. Despite this expectation, financial institutions usually allow withdrawals from savings accounts at any time with no advance notice and with no penalty. Savings accounts are highly liquid because account holders may make an unlimited number of deposits and withdrawals at any time. Consumers typically use savings accounts as a repository for emergency funds and for funds to be invested in the future.

Commercial banks, savings and loan associations, and savings banks offer savings accounts. Credit unions also offer savings accounts, called *share accounts*. Because the Federal Deposit Insurance Corporation (FDIC) and the National Credit Union Share Insurance Fund (NCUSIF) insure most savings and share accounts, these accounts are considered extremely safe. However, interest rates on savings and share accounts, while typically higher than those on NOW accounts, are lower than those on money market deposit accounts and money market mutual funds.

Depository institutions typically do not charge fees on savings and share accounts, although some depository institutions charge a fee if a minimum balance is not maintained or if no activity takes place in the account for a specified period. Interest earned on savings and share accounts is taxed annually at a person's ordinary income tax rate.

Certificates of Deposit

A ***certificate of deposit (CD)*** is an interest-earning time deposit held in a depository institution for a specified period of time. At the end of the specified period, the CD matures. Upon maturity, the depository institution pays the principal and interest to the CD owner. The Canadian equivalent of a certificate of deposit is a guaranteed investment certificate.

Depository institutions issue CDs in various amounts—$100 to $100,000 or more—and various maturities—1 week to 10 years. In exchange for the customer agreeing to leave funds on deposit for a specified time period, the depository institution pays an interest rate that is higher than the rate paid on NOW accounts, savings accounts, MMDAs, and MMMFs. Typically, the longer the maturity of a CD, the higher its interest rate. In addition, higher amount CDs may pay higher interest rates than lower amount CDs, except in times of extreme market volatility. Interest earned on a CD is taxed annually at the person's ordinary income tax rate even though the interest is not paid until the CD matures.

The interest rate on most CDs is locked in for the term of the CD, but some CDs have variable rates. ***Variable rate certificates of deposit***, also known as *adjustable rate CDs*, are certificates of deposit that pay an interest rate that rises and falls in accordance with a benchmark rate. (We discuss the determination of variable rates in more detail in Chapter 4.) Some of these variable rate CDs allow the holder to lock in a rate at any time before the CD matures, and some variable rate CDs have a minimum guaranteed rate.

Depository institutions charge a penalty—for example, a portion of the interest earned—for redeeming a CD prior to its maturity date. Because of this penalty for early redemption, CDs are not considered as liquid as savings accounts. In fact, an early redemption could result in a loss of principal.

In most cases, CDs of $100,000 or less are FDIC or NCUSIF insured. However, if a consumer purchases a CD in an amount greater than $100,000, the amount over $100,000 will not be insured. In this case, the consumer has an even greater need to evaluate the financial stability of the depository institution than if the amount was less than $100,000.

CDs are a good short- to medium-term investment choice for consumers seeking safety of principal and guaranteed interest. However, consumers face reinvestment risk when the CD reaches maturity. As we discussed in Chapter 2, reinvestment risk is the risk that after the principal and interest on an investment have been returned, the investor may have difficulty finding another investment that offers returns as high as the previous investment.

FAST FACT

Beginning December 11, 2001, the Series EE savings bonds have been inscribed with the special legend "Patriot Bond" as a means of allowing Americans to express their support of the nation's anti-terrorism efforts.[1]

Savings Bonds

The United States government issues savings bonds, which are debt instruments of the government. In other words, a person who buys a savings bond is loaning the government money. The government promises to repay the principal and to pay interest on the funds borrowed. Savings bonds are backed by the full faith and credit of the U.S. government. In addition, if a savings bond is lost or stolen, it can be replaced.

The most popular savings bond is the ***series EE savings bond***, which is a U.S. government bond purchased for 50 percent of its face value that earns interest at rates based on the yields of Treasury notes and bonds, which we discuss in Chapter 11. Series EE bonds do not pay periodic interest. Rather, the interest is reinvested every month and compounded semiannually. In this manner, the interest earned on a series EE bond accumulates until it equals the difference between the bond's purchase price and its face value, at which point the bond is said to mature. A series EE savings bond is illustrated in Figure 3.4.

Series EE savings bonds are issued in denominations ranging from $25 to $10,000. They are available for purchase at various financial institutions, through some employers by means of payroll deduction, or over the Internet through TreasuryDirect. Series EE bonds have a maximum purchase limit of $30,000 per person annually.

Because series EE bonds earn market interest rates and do not mature until their purchase price has grown to equal their face value, a person cannot accurately predict when a savings bond will mature. However, the government guarantees that the bond will mature in no more than 17 years, even if the government has to add funds to the bond to bring its value up to its face value. Series EE savings bonds can be held beyond maturity, and their value will continue to increase. However, series EE savings bonds stop earning interest 30 years after their issue date.

If a person cashes in, or *redeems*, a series EE bond within six months of issue, she will earn no interest. Bonds redeemed after six months but before five years incur a three-month interest penalty.

Series EE savings bond interest earned is exempt from state and local taxes. At the bondholder's option, federal income tax on interest earned may be paid each year or it may be deferred until the bond is redeemed or until 30 years from its issue date. If certain conditions are met, interest earned on series EE savings bonds may be excluded from income if the proceeds of the bond are used for higher education expenses.

FIGURE 3.4 Series EE Savings Bond

A ***series HH savings bond*** is a U.S. government bond that is purchased at face value not by paying cash but by exchanging series EE bonds. Series HH savings bonds pay interest semiannually at a fixed rate for 10 years, which is when they reach maturity, but they can be held for an additional 10 years. Thus, people who purchased series EE savings bonds to accumulate funds for retirement may choose to exchange those savings bonds for series HH savings bonds that can provide an income stream during retirement.

Series HH savings bonds are issued in denominations of $500, $1,000, $5,000, and $10,000. Bondholders who redeem series HH savings bonds prior to maturity are penalized for doing so because they receive less than face value. Interest earned on series HH savings bonds is exempt from state and local income taxes but federal income tax on the interest earned must be paid each year. Federal income tax on the interest that accrued on the series EE savings bonds exchanged for the series HH savings bonds continues to be deferred for the maximum 20-year life of the series HH savings bond or until the series HH savings bond is redeemed.

Electronic Funds Transfer Services

Advances in technology have revolutionized cash management services. People now can access and transfer cash without carrying cash, writing checks, or using check substitutes. Financial institutions provide these new access and transfer services by ***electronic funds transfer (EFT)***, which is the transfer of funds electronically among accounts. The most common forms of EFT involve debit cards, automated teller machines, point-of-sale terminals, smart cards, stored-value cards, preauthorized deposits and payments, and online home banking services.

Debit Cards

A ***debit card*** is a plastic card with coded account information that allows an account holder to access his funds in an account electronically. Some debit cards may be used only at automated teller machines (ATMs) and may be known as *ATM cards*. Some debit cards may be used only at retail establishments and may be known as *check cards*. Some debit cards are used at both ATMs and retail establishments.

An ***automated teller machine (ATM)*** is a computer terminal that allows electronic access to a person's account and various transactions, including cash withdrawals, 24 hours a day, 7 days a week. Using a debit card and a personal identification number (PIN) or other identification, a person can perform a number of functions electronically at an ATM, including viewing account balances; making loan repayments; moving funds among accounts; and depositing, withdrawing, or transferring funds. The cardholder simply inserts his card in the ATM, enters his PIN number to identify himself, and follows the instructions on the screen for the desired transaction.

"Nothing is wrong with the machine. Press the buttons harder. You need to work on your people skills."

www.CartoonStock.com

ATMs typically belong to a particular bank and are located outside that bank's offices, as well as in numerous other locations, including shopping malls, grocery stores, and airports. Many banks belong to an EFT network that allows their account holders to access their accounts worldwide via the ATMs of any other bank that is a member of that network. However, most banks that allow such network access charge either a per-transaction fee or a flat fee per month for a certain number of transactions.

People use debit cards to make purchases electronically from retailers using a ***point-of-sale terminal***, which is a computer terminal at a retail location that allows a person to use his debit card to take funds from his account and transfer them directly to the retailer's account. The person's account is debited virtually immediately for any amount withdrawn. Thus, a cardholder has no means of stopping payment, as he could do with a check.

A debit card looks like a credit card, but it differs from a credit card in that a debit card provides access to one's own funds rather than to borrowed funds. However, some debit cards double as credit cards. The cardholder selects how he wants to use the card—as a debit card or a credit card—by selecting certain functions at the ATM or point-of-sale terminal. We discuss credit cards in Chapter 4.

Smart Cards and Stored-Value Cards

Other types of cards that can replace the need to carry cash are smart cards and stored-value cards, both of which are plastic cards that contain a computer chip. These chips are programmed to represent a certain amount of cash. Every time the card is used, the cash amount decreases. With a ***smart card***, money can be added to the card again when the stored value is depleted. With a ***stored-value card***, the cardholder must get a new card when the stored value is expended.

Unlike debit cards, smart cards and stored-value cards are not tied to an account at a financial institution. Instead, these cards must be paid for before they are used. However, these cards can be used to make purchases in many of the same ways as debit cards. In addition, some businesses issue their own smart cards or stored-value cards that can be used only at that business. For example, Kinko's issues smart cards to its customers to use for copying. In addition, many universities issue smart cards to students to use to pay for meals, books, and other expenses.

Preauthorized Deposits and Payments

A person who has an account at a financial institution often can authorize certain institutions to deposit money to or withdraw money from that account. The funds will be transferred electronically from one account to another. For example, an employee typically can preauthorize her employer to deposit her paychecks to her checking account and authorize her mortgage company to withdraw her monthly mortgage payments from the account. A person also can authorize her financial institution to make regular bill payments of irregular amounts (for example, water and electric bills) on her behalf.

Online Banking Services

In addition to being able to access their accounts by means of the telephone, many people now are able to bank online. Using a personal computer, a person can access her account 24 hours a day, 7 days a week. The account the person accesses may be that of a traditional "bricks and mortar" depository institution or of a purely online bank—one that exists only on the Internet.

Online banking allows an account holder to view her balance, find out which checks have cleared, and balance her checkbook electronically. As we discussed in the preceding section, most depository institutions also offer account holders electronic deposits of payroll checks or other periodic income, as well as preauthorized bill payments. Furthermore, some depository institutions allow online mortgage and other loan applications. Depending on the other financial products offered by the institution or the institution's partners, a person also could use these electronic services to buy and sell investments and purchase insurance.

Although depository institutions traditionally have charged a monthly fee for account holders to use online banking services, many depository institutions are now providing these services at no charge.

Key Terms

Federal Deposit Insurance Corporation (FDIC)
National Credit Union Share Insurance Fund (NCUSIF)
checking account
demand deposit account
check
regular checking account
traveler's check
money order
cashier's check
NOW account
tiered interest rates
share draft account
money market account
super NOW account
money market deposit account (MMDA)
money market mutual fund (MMMF)
asset management account (AMA)
savings account
time deposit account
certificate of deposit (CD)
variable rate certificate of deposit
series EE savings bond
series HH savings bond
electronic funds transfer (EFT)
debit card
automated teller machine (ATM)
point-of-sale terminal
smart card
stored-value card

Endnote

1. TreasuryDirect, "Patriot Bond" (6 March 2003), http://www.publicdebt.treas.gov/sav/savpatriotbond.htm (11 December 2003).

chapter

4

Credit Services

outline

objectives

After reading this chapter, you should be able to

- Explain the advantages and disadvantages of credit for lenders and borrowers
- List common methods lenders use to limit the risk of default
- Define the terms *finance charge* and *annual percentage rate*
- Explain the differences between installment loans and noninstallment loans
- Distinguish a mortgage from other installment loans
- Explain how a reverse mortgage operates

As we discussed in Chapter 1, credit is a financial service that enables people to purchase now by giving a promise to pay in the future. Credit services play an important role in the economy by helping people finance purchases, thereby increasing sales for manufacturers and service providers and providing financial institutions with profitable lines of business.

Depository institutions and finance companies are the primary providers of credit. These financial institutions have developed many products and services that enable a person to borrow money to make purchases or for other purposes. Examples of these products and services include credit cards, personal loans, auto loans, student loans, mortgages, and home-equity lines of credit.

People also can obtain loans from other financial products. Examples include life insurance policy loans, margin loans on brokerage accounts, and loans from employer-sponsored retirement plans. We discuss these types of loans in later chapters.

We begin this chapter with a discussion of the advantages and disadvantages of credit for both lenders and borrowers, how lenders can reduce default risk, and the cost of credit. We then examine the two major categories of credit—noninstallment credit and installment credit—and the primary subcategories of each.

Advantages and Disadvantages of Credit

Credit arrangements are advantageous to lenders and borrowers. For lending institutions, the benefit of providing credit is the ability to earn a profit by charging interest on the funds they lend.

For borrowers, the benefits of obtaining credit include

- **An improved standard of living.** By borrowing money, a person is able to finance purchases that would otherwise have to be delayed or foregone.
- **Assistance in times of need.** In emergencies, people can use borrowed funds to cover necessary expenses.
- **Convenience.** Using credit relieves people of the need to obtain and carry cash. In addition, some transactions are difficult to complete without using a credit card as a security deposit. For example, many car rental agencies and hotels require a credit card to make a reservation.

- **Record keeping.** Credit services provide borrowers with a record of purchases and payments made. Borrowers use these records for budgeting, legal, and tax purposes.

- **Budgeting tool.** Regular payments on loans serve as a budgeting tool for some people. For example, the need to make scheduled payments on a loan can provide a person with discipline in financing a purchase.

- **Tax advantages.** In the United States, people may lower their income tax liability by deducting from their income the interest paid on certain loans, such as mortgages and student loans.

Credit services, however, have some potential disadvantages for lending institutions and borrowers. For lenders, the chief risk in lending money is default risk—that is, the risk that the borrower will fail to repay the loan. A loan default causes the lender to lose some or all of the principal, to lose the income stream generated by interest payments, and possibly to fail to recover the expenses of issuing and servicing the loan. We discuss how lenders reduce the default risk in the next section of this chapter.

The principal disadvantage of credit services for the borrower is that borrowing money costs money because the borrower must pay interest and fees to the lender. In the long run, purchases made on credit are more expensive than purchases made with cash unless the borrower pays the balance before interest is charged to the account.

In addition, because of the convenience of credit, a borrower may be tempted to borrow more than she can repay. Borrowers who are unable to repay loans may have purchases repossessed by the lender or even may have to file for bankruptcy. ***Bankruptcy*** is a state of insolvency that occurs when a court finds that the debts of a borrower exceed her assets, and her income is not sufficient to provide a reasonable expectation that the debts will be repaid in full in the future. If a court declares a borrower to be bankrupt, the borrower may find that obtaining credit at an affordable rate in the future is difficult.

"But I can't take early retirement - I haven't paid off my student loan yet."

Managing Default Risk

A lender evaluates default risk by careful evaluation of the borrower's ability to repay the loan. Figure 4.1 explains how lenders determine whether to grant credit to a person.

In some situations, a lender decides that it can agree to a loan only if the borrower accepts certain conditions intended to reduce the risk of default. The three primary means available to a lender of reducing default risk, as well as the potential losses in the event of a default, are

- **Requiring collateral.** ***Collateral*** is property that serves as security for the repayment of a loan. A loan backed by collateral is a ***secured loan***, and a loan that is not backed by collateral is an ***unsecured loan***. For example, a mortgage is a loan secured by the value of a specified piece of property.

- **Requiring the loan to be co-signed.** A ***co-signer*** is a person who agrees to repay a loan if the borrower defaults on that loan, but who has no ownership rights to the property being financed by the loan.

FIGURE 4.1 Criteria for Granting Credit

Lenders take into account a number of factors when determining whether to grant credit to a person. The most prominent factor is the credit score, which is a numerical value that reflects the credit risk posed by a person. Credit scores are calculated based on factors found in a person's credit report. A ***credit report*** is a document that provides information on a person's credit history and on the amount of unused credit the person may have available from other sources. Some of the items detailed in a credit report include

- The type and amount of credit used
- The length of time accounts have been open
- Repayment history
- Other sources of credit the borrower has sought
- Public records on bankruptcy and other legal actions affecting credit

A credit score is not the only factor upon which lenders make their decisions. They also take into account a person's net worth, income, liabilities, and employment history, among other items.

- **Requiring credit life insurance and mortgage life insurance.** These types of life insurance, which we discuss in Chapter 5, pay the amount of unpaid debt on a loan if the borrower dies.

Interest and the Cost of Credit

The concepts of interest and interest rates that we explained in Chapter 2 are particularly important in credit services because interest is a substantial cost of borrowing money for borrowers, as well as a principal source of income for the financial institutions that provide loans.

The interest rate charged by lending institutions varies depending on several factors, including the rates charged by competing institutions, the type and amount of credit sought by the borrower, and the degree of risk the institution assumes by extending the credit. The greater the risk to the lender, the higher the interest rate charged. For example, a lender generally charges a higher rate on an unsecured loan than on a secured loan. Similarly, a lender may charge a borrower with a poor credit history a higher interest rate on a loan than the lender would charge a borrower with an excellent credit record for the same loan type and amount. However, in the United States, lenders cannot charge interest rates that are higher than the maximum prescribed by state law. In addition, lenders tend not to charge interest rates too much higher than competitors' rates for similar products because people typically shop around for the best rate.

Fixed and Variable Interest Rates

The interest rate on a loan or other credit arrangement may be either fixed or variable. A ***fixed interest rate*** does not change over the stated repayment schedule of the loan. A ***variable interest rate*** fluctuates according to the rise and fall of interest rates in the marketplace. A variable rate is determined by adding a certain number of percentage points to a benchmark interest rate. For example, some interest rates are stated as "the prime interest rate plus x percent." The ***prime interest rate*** is the interest rate banks charge their best and most creditworthy customers. The credit agreement specifies which benchmark rate is used and how frequently the variable rate charged on the balance of the loan is adjusted to rise and fall as that benchmark rate rises and falls. The degree to which the variable rate on a loan exceeds the specified benchmark rate reflects the type of loan and the creditworthiness of the borrower.

Typically, a fixed interest rate is slightly higher than an initial variable rate on an otherwise identical loan because the lender faces greater interest rate risk on a fixed-rate loan than on a variable rate loan. As we explained in Chapter 2, if a lender makes a fixed rate loan and then the benchmark interest rate increases before the loan is paid off, the lender is accepting a lower interest rate on the unpaid principal than it could earn if it loaned the principal based on the new benchmark rate. Conversely, if interest rates fall during the term, the borrower is more likely to pay off the loan early using proceeds from a new loan with a lower rate, thus depriving the lender of anticipated interest income.

However, lenders face greater default risk with variable rate loans than with fixed-rate loans. If the variable rate increases, the borrower may not be able to make the higher payments, resulting in default.

Finance Charges and Annual Percentage Rates

The U.S. Truth in Lending Act requires lenders to disclose to borrowers the finance charge and annual percentage rate of a loan. The ***finance charge*** is the total cost of credit paid by a borrower for a loan, expressed as a dollar amount. Many people use the term *finance charge* to refer only to late fees or special charges. However, in financial services terminology, the finance charge is the sum of all costs for credit, including interest, all applicable fees, and the cost of any insurance that is required as a condition of the loan.

The ***annual percentage rate (APR)*** is the total cost of credit expressed as a yearly rate of interest. Borrowers can evaluate loans with different finance charges and other terms by comparing the APRs, as illustrated in Figure 4.2.

The lender also must disclose the ***periodic rate***, which is the APR divided by the number of billing periods per year.

Noninstallment Credit

Noninstallment credit is any loan or credit arrangement that does not require the borrower to make a series of periodic payments on the loan or credit balance. Noninstallment credit takes two forms: single-payment loans and open-end credit.

Single-Payment Loans

A ***single-payment loan*** is a loan in which the borrower receives the entire principal at one time and agrees to pay the principal and any interest in a single payment on a specified future date. The single-payment loan is commonly used between people, such as family members and friends.

FIGURE 4.2 Comparison of Annual Percentage Rates

Trudy Hoyt needed a one-year $5,000 loan to pay some medical bills. She applied for a loan with three banks, which quoted different interest rates and different loan fees. The interest rates and fees quoted by these banks, as well as the APRs, are set forth in the table below.

	Interest Rate	Interest Expense	Loan Fee	Total Loan Expense	Average Annual Loan Expense	APR*
Bank A	10%	$500	$0	$500	$500	10%
Bank B	8%	$400	$250	$650	$650	13%
Bank C	6%	$300	$500	$800	$800	16%

Based on interest rates alone, it may appear that Bank A's loan is the most expensive. However, the comparison of the loans' APRs reveals that Bank A's loan is actually the least expensive.

* The APR is calculated by dividing the average annual loan expenses by the average annual loan balance. This example is greatly simplified because the loan is for just one year.

Source: Jeff Madura, *Personal Finance* (Boston: Addison Wesley, 2002), 219.

Financial institutions typically make single-payment loans only to businesses in anticipation of the sale of a product or service. The assets of the business serve as collateral for the loan. For example, a farmer who needs to fund operating expenses or capital improvements for a period of time before a crop is harvested and who is willing to have his land or machinery serve as collateral is a typical applicant for a single-payment loan.

Open-End Credit

A much more common type of noninstallment credit is open-end credit. ***Open-end credit***, also called *revolving credit*, is a credit arrangement that allows a person to borrow money repeatedly up to a pre-arranged limit and to make at least minimum payments, allowing the credit balance to continue to accrue interest. Open-end credit therefore gives a person the option of borrowing any amount of money up to the pre-arranged limit and paying the balance in unequal payments over time. The borrower can borrow additional money (up to the pre-arranged limit) before completely repaying previous balances.

Credit card accounts are the most common form of open-end noninstallment credit. A ***credit card*** is a plastic card that entitles the cardholder to access an open-end line of credit. Two characteristics of most credit card accounts make them an extremely convenient means for consumers to finance purchases:

- Collateral is not required.
- A separate loan application for each purchase is not required.

However, these two characteristics also increase the default risk for the financial institution issuing the credit card because this type of credit is so easy for the borrower to use.

The default risk on credit card accounts is high relative to the default risk associated with most other types of credit. The increased risk and the relatively high costs of servicing open-end credit typically result in relatively high interest rates charged on credit card balances when compared to other types of loans.

Credit card accounts fall into two broad categories:

- A **retail credit card account** is an open-end credit account offered by a specific business, often a retailer. Retail credit cards usually are honored only by the business that issued the card or affiliated businesses. Examples of retail credit cards include cards issued by department stores and oil companies. Typically, a finance company affiliated with the retailer is the source of funds for the credit.
- A **bank credit card account** is an open-end credit account offered by a specific financial institution. Although the financial institution is the source of the loan funds, the electronic network for these credit cards is provided by businesses such as Visa, MasterCard, and Discover. Unlike cards issued by retail merchants, bank credit cards are designed to be accepted by a large number of businesses.

Credit card issuers do not limit the number of transactions that a cardholder can make using the card, but each credit card account contains a ***credit limit***, which is the maximum amount of credit available to the cardholder. The credit limit varies based on the card issuer's assessment of the creditworthiness of the cardholder. Typical limits range from $5,000 to $25,000, but limits can be much lower or much higher.

Most bank credit card agreements allow cardholders to borrow cash as well as make purchases. A ***cash advance*** is cash borrowed from the issuer of the credit card. The ***cash advance limit*** is the maximum amount of cash available to a cardholder and can be less than or equal to the credit limit. Most financial institutions charge a higher interest rate to cardholders on cash advances than on purchases.

Financial institutions generally assess interest charges and account fees on credit card accounts. Account fees may include any or all of the following: application fees, monthly billing fees, transaction fees, late payment fees, and annual service fees. Lenders generally do not charge a per-transaction fee on purchases. However, some lenders do apply fees to cash advances on a per-transaction basis, usually using either a flat amount or a percentage of the cash advance, whichever is greater.

At the end of each billing period—typically 21 to 30 days—the lender sends the cardholder a statement of account. The statement lists the balance carried forward from the previous billing period, payments received from the cardholder, new charges made on the card, finance charges, the periodic rate, and the annual percentage rate.

Lenders must inform credit card holders when finance charges will be applied to the account balance. Some lenders give cardholders a ***grace period***, which is a period of time between the date of a purchase and the date the lender begins to charge interest during which no interest accrues.

Lenders also must disclose to borrowers the method used to calculate the amount of the outstanding balance, which will affect the amount of the finance charge. These methods include:

- ***Average daily balance method***—Determined by adding together each day's balance during the billing period and then dividing this total by the number of days in the billing period. Payments made during the billing period are taken into account when calculating the balances, and purchases may or may not be included.

- ***Previous balance method***—Determined by using the balance due on the account at the end of the previous billing period as the current billing period's outstanding balance without including payments or new purchases made in the current billing period.

- ***Adjusted balance method***—Determined by subtracting any payments made during the current billing period from the balance at the end of the previous billing period, but does not add new purchases to the balance.

Figure 4.3 illustrates these different methods of calculating the amount of the outstanding loan balance and how they affect the amount of the finance charge.

Installment Credit

Installment credit is a credit arrangement that requires the borrower to make periodic repayments on the loan amount according to a prearranged schedule. Typically, an installment loan requires monthly repayments in equal amounts. Installment credit is frequently referred to as a *personal loan* and is used to finance a wide variety of purchases, including motor vehicles (car loans), furniture, and home improvement projects (home-equity loans). Installment credit used to purchase a home is known

FIGURE 4.3 Methods of Calculating Outstanding Loan Balance

	Average Daily Balance (including new purchases)	Average Daily Balance (excluding new purchases)	Previous Balance	Adjusted Balance
Periodic rate	1½%	1½%	1½%	1½%
APR	18%	18%	18%	18%
Previous balance	$400	$400	$400	$400
Payments	$300 on 15th day (new balance=$100)	$300 on 15th day (new balance=$100)	$300	$300
New purchases	$50 on 18th day	$50 on 18th day	n/a	n/a
Average daily balance	$270*	$250**	n/a	n/a
Interest portion of finance charge	$4.05 (1½% × $270)	$3.75 (1½% × $250)	$6.00 (1½% × $400)	$1.50 (1½% × $100)

* To calculate average daily balance (including new purchases):

$$\frac{(\$400 \times 15 \text{ days}) + (\$100 \times 3 \text{ days}) + (\$150 \times 12 \text{ days})}{30 \text{ days}} = \$270$$

** To calculate average daily balance (excluding new purchases):

$$\frac{(\$400 \times 15 \text{ days}) + (\$100 \times 15 \text{ days})}{30 \text{ days}} = \$250$$

Source: Federal Trade Commission, "Choosing and Using Credit Cards: Fast Facts," Facts for Consumers, February 1993, http://www.pueblo.gsa.gov/cic_text/money/credit-card/credcard.htm (13 November 2003).

as a mortgage, which we will discuss in the next section. A popular type of installment credit is the student loan, which we discuss in Insight 4.1.

The following differences exist between installment loans and noninstallment loans:

- A borrower obtaining an installment loan typically receives the entire loan amount when the loan is taken out, whereas noninstallment loans allow the borrower to draw on the credit line repeatedly up to the credit limit.

- Installment loans are repaid according to a schedule of periodic payments that is defined at the time the loan is approved, whereas noninstallment loans require only that the account holder make a minimum payment each billing period.

INSIGHT 4.1 Student Loans

With the cost of attending college escalating, many people have taken advantage of student loan programs offered by the United States federal government and financial institutions. To encourage education, the federal government typically subsidizes the interest rates on these loans. Repayment is deferred until after the student has completed his studies. In addition, interest paid on a U.S. student loan is tax deductible up to $2,500 a year.

Installment Loan Payments

Installment loans typically are repaid through ***amortization***, which is the process of eliminating a debt through periodic payments. A portion of each payment is applied to payment of interest on the outstanding principal balance, and the remainder is applied to repayment of the principal. Over time, the portion of each payment applied to interest decreases and the portion applied to principal increases.

The following factors affect the amount of each periodic payment:

- **The amount borrowed.** The higher the loan amount, the higher the periodic payment, assuming other loan provisions are the same.

- **The amortization period.** The loan's ***amortization period*** is the period of time during which the loan is paid off through periodic payments. The longer the amortization period of the loan, the lower each periodic payment, assuming other loan provisions are the same. Note that the amortization period is not the same as the loan's ***term***, which is the period of time during which the loan is outstanding and the interest rate is guaranteed. A loan's term may be shorter than its amortization period, in which case a balloon payment may be due at the end of the term. A ***balloon payment*** is a final debt payment that is much larger than the preceding payments.

- **The loan interest rate.** The higher the interest rate, the higher the periodic payment, assuming other loan provisions are the same.

Amortization Period of the Loan

For any two installment loans that have the same principal amounts and interest rates, the loan with a longer amortization period requires lower periodic payments and results in greater total interest charges. The total interest paid is higher on the loan with a longer amortization period because the interest rate is applied to the principal for a longer period of

FIGURE 4.4 Influence of Length of Amortization Period on Monthly Payments and Total Cost of a Loan

Monthly Payment and Total Principal and Interest Paid on a $200,000 Loan at 7% Interest Based on Different Amortization Periods		
Amortization Period (Years)	**Monthly Payment**	**Total Principal and Interest Paid**
15	$1,797.66	$323,578.18
20	$1,550.60	$372,143.49
25	$1,413.56	$424,067.52
30	$1,330.60	$479,017.80

Source: Adapted from Mary C. Bickley and David F. Johnson, *Intro to Financial Services* (Atlanta: LOMA, © 2001), 54. Used with permission; all rights reserved.

time—that is, the borrower is borrowing the money and paying interest on that money for a longer period. The periodic payments are lower because generally the amount of each periodic payment is derived by dividing the total cost of the loan by the number of periodic payments scheduled for the amortization period of the loan.

Figure 4.4 illustrates how differences in a loan's amortization period can affect the periodic payment amounts and the total amount paid by the borrower over the entire loan.

Although a borrower faces higher total interest costs on a loan with a long amortization period than a comparable loan with a shorter amortization period, some borrowers prefer longer amortization periods because of the lower monthly payments. In addition, by lengthening the amortization period, the borrower can afford a larger loan amount.

On some installment loans, lenders charge borrowers a fee for prepaying a loan—that is, repaying the loan before the final due date. Such loans are said to include a prepayment penalty. Other installment loans—particularly most mortgages—do not include prepayment penalties.

Loan Interest Rates

As we have mentioned, the higher the loan interest rate, the higher the periodic payments, assuming the other loan conditions are the same. Figure 4.5 illustrates how different interest rates can affect the periodic payments and total amount paid by the borrower over a 30-year loan.

FIGURE 4.5 Influence of Interest Rate on Monthly Payments and Total Cost of a Loan

Monthly Payment and Total Principal and Interest Paid at Different Interest Rates on a $200,000 30-Year Loan		
Interest Rate	Monthly Payment	Total Principal and Interest Paid
6.00%	$1,199.10	$431,676.38
7.00%	$1,330.60	$479,017.80
8.00%	$1,467.53	$528,310.49
9.00%	$1,609.25	$579,328.28

Source: Adapted from Mary C. Bickley and David F. Johnson, *Intro to Financial Services* (Atlanta: LOMA, © 2001), 54. Used with permission; all rights reserved.

FAST FACT

In the United States in 2001, 67.3 percent of a home's purchase price was being borrowed by the average home buyer, versus 41.3 percent 20 years ago.[1]

Mortgages

An important category of installment loans is the ***mortgage***, a real estate loan in which property being financed is pledged as collateral for the loan. Although businesses take out mortgages to purchase commercial property, such as office buildings and apartment complexes, in this text we will limit our discussion to residential mortgages taken out by individuals.

Like most installment loans, mortgages are repaid according to an amortization schedule. However, mortgages have several characteristics that distinguish them from other installment loans:

- In issuing a mortgage loan, the lender places a lien on that property to secure the loan. A ***lien*** is a legal claim on property for payment of a debt. The legal proceeding by which a lender acquires the title to a mortgaged property from a borrower in default of its loan terms is called ***foreclosure***.

- In many cases, the real estate securing a mortgage increases in value over the duration of the mortgage. By contrast, property that secures other installment loans typically declines in value after the purchase is made.

- The term of a mortgage loan is usually 15 to 30 years—far longer than the 1 to 5 or 6 years of most other installment loans.

INSIGHT 4.2 Fannie Mae and Freddie Mac

FannieMae

Freddie Mac

Fannie Mae (Federal National Mortgage Association) and Freddie Mac (Federal Home Loan Mortgage Corporation) are two private, shareholder-owned corporations created by the U.S. federal government to increase the opportunities for affordable home ownership. Neither organization makes loans to homebuyers. Instead, both organizations buy loans from mortgage lenders. The proceeds of these sales allow mortgage lenders to make even more mortgage loans to homebuyers.

Fannie Mae and Freddie Mac also issue securities to investors and use the proceeds they receive from the sale of these securities to buy more mortgage loans.

Through the work of Fannie Mae and Freddie Mac, the flow of funds for mortgage loans is increased, thereby increasing the ability of potential homebuyers to obtain mortgage loans.

Source: "About Fannie Mae," Fannie Mae, http://www.fanniemae.com/aboutfm (16 November 2003). "Who We Are," Freddie Mac, http://www.freddiemac.com/corporate/whoweare/ (16 November 2003).

- The loan amount on most mortgages is typically much greater than the loan amount on most other types of installment loans.

Depository institutions and finance companies offer mortgages. In Insight 4.2, we discuss two government-sponsored enterprises—Fannie Mae and Freddie Mac—that increase the flow of mortgage funds available to borrowers.

Types of Mortgages

Lenders typically offer two types of mortgages—conventional and adjustable rate. A ***conventional mortgage*** is a mortgage in which the interest rate, term, and periodic payment amount are all fixed in advance. The advantage of a conventional mortgage is that all costs are known in advance by both the borrower and the lender.

An ***adjustable rate mortgage (ARM)***, also called a *variable rate mortgage*, is a mortgage in which the interest rate fluctuates according to a benchmark rate specified in the mortgage agreement. Because the interest rate on an ARM can change over time, the periodic payment amount also can change over time. If the interest rate increases, the periodic payment amount increases as well. Conversely, the periodic payment on an ARM decreases if the interest rate decreases. Regardless of whether the payments increase or decrease, amortization occurs throughout the amortization period, and the amortization period remains the same.

Most mortgage interest rates are closely related to, yet somewhat higher than, the prime interest rate at the time of the loan. Over time, the prime rate can change. If the prime rate decreases, the fixed interest rate on a mortgage obtained in the past may be greater than the interest rates on currently available mortgages. Borrowers in this situation may seek ***mortgage refinancing***, the process of obtaining a new mortgage and using some or all of the new mortgage loan to pay off the old mortgage.

By refinancing, the borrower may be able to choose a new amortization period and new periodic payment amounts. The borrower also may seek a new mortgage for an amount greater than the amount due on the old mortgage—in effect, borrowing extra money against the ***equity***, or ownership interest, the borrower has built up in a mortgaged property. Equity in a home is determined by subtracting the amount of the outstanding mortgage loan balance from the market value of the home. For example, if the home's market value is $200,000 and the outstanding loan balance is $150,000, the homeowner has $50,000 in equity.

Mortgage Risks

Lenders face less interest rate risk with ARMs than with conventional mortgages, just as they do with other variable rate loans as compared to fixed rate loans. Thus, lenders typically offer ARMs at initial interest rates that are below the interest rates for conventional mortgages.

However, lenders face greater default risk with ARMs than with conventional mortgages. A rising interest rate could result in the periodic payment on the mortgage increasing to the point that the borrower is unable to make those payments and has to default on the mortgage. To reduce this risk, a lender may include either of two options in an ARM:

- A ***payment cap*** is a loan provision that sets a maximum on the periodic payment amount on an ARM.
- An ***interest-rate cap*** is a loan provision that sets a maximum limit on the interest rate that will be charged on an ARM, even if the benchmark interest rate exceeds that cap in the future.

Mortgage lenders also attempt to reduce default risk by requiring down payments because the risk of default is lower if the borrower has his own money at stake. A ***down payment*** is a portion of the purchase price paid by a borrower at the time of purchase. The higher the down payment, the lower the mortgage loan amount and the lower the periodic payments on the loan, all other factors being equal. In addition, some lenders will charge a lower interest rate with high down payments.

A mortgage applicant typically must meet the lender's loan-to-value ratio requirement. The ***loan-to-value ratio*** is a ratio of the amount of the mortgage loan to the value of the property. For example, suppose a person applies for a mortgage loan on a $150,000 residence, and the lender's loan-to-value ratio is 80 percent. In this case, the maximum amount that the lender will loan is $120,000, which is $150,000 multiplied by 0.80. To obtain this loan, the borrower must make a down payment of $30,000, which is the difference between the $150,000 cost of the residence and the $120,000 maximum amount the lender will loan on that residence.

A large down payment may take a borrower years to save, however. One mechanism that allows lenders to make loans to creditworthy borrowers without requiring large down payments is private mortgage insurance. ***Private mortgage insurance*** is a form of insurance that protects the lender by insuring the gap between the required down payment—typically 20 percent of the home purchase price—and the actual down payment made by the borrower.

Usually, the cost of the private mortgage insurance is included in the borrower's periodic loan payments. Lenders require borrowers to maintain private mortgage insurance until the loan-to-value ratio meets the lender's minimum requirement. Borrowers bear the responsibility of determining when the ratio is met and then asking the lender to drop the private mortgage insurance.

Closing Costs

The fees that a borrower incurs in taking out a mortgage are referred to as ***closing costs***. These closing costs are in addition to the loan application fee some lenders charge just to review a mortgage application submitted by a potential borrower. This loan application fee typically ranges from $100 to $500.

The most significant closing costs are described in Figure 4.6. In Canada, points are rarely charged, and the lender pays most closing costs.

Second Mortgages

The mortgage obtained for the initial purchase of a house is known as a first mortgage. Over the course of a first mortgage's term, borrowers build equity in the house being financed by the mortgage. Equity can build in two ways:

- **Cash equity.** Cash equity results from amounts paid by the borrower that reduce the principal of the mortgage. At the time of purchase, the down payment represents cash equity. Thereafter, part of each periodic payment the borrower makes reduces the principal owed on the mortgage. Assuming the house retains its market value, any reduction in principal owed to the lender represents an increase in the borrower's cash equity in the house.

- **Value equity.** The house can increase in market value over time. As the owner of the house, the borrower owns this increase in value.

FIGURE 4.6 Major Closing Costs

- **Points.** A ***point*** is a fee charged at the time a mortgage is taken out and is equal to one percent of the loan amount. Paying points typically allows the borrower to receive a lower interest rate than if no points were paid.

  Example: Fred Blaine buys a $150,000 home by paying a $15,000 down payment and taking out a $135,000 mortgage. The lender charged 2 points.

  Analysis: Each point equals $1,350 for a total of $2,700 that either will be added to the total mortgage or paid in cash by Mr. Blaine.

- **Origination Fee.** An origination fee is an administrative fee charged by the lender and is typically equal to 0.5 to 2.0 percent of the loan amount. The origination fee can be charged in addition to points.
- **Title Search and Insurance.** A person buying a home wants to be sure that when the transaction is complete, he will hold a clear title, or legal right of ownership, to the property. Thus, the borrower typically must hire an attorney to complete a title search, which is a history of the property ownership. In addition, the lender may require that the borrower purchase title insurance, which protects the lender by covering the loan amount should the title later be found defective. The homeowner can purchase additional title insurance to cover the amount of his down payment. Typically, title insurance does not cover the homeowner as his equity in the property builds.
- **Appraisal Fee.** Some lenders require that a professional appraiser provide a valuation of the property, and the charge typically is passed on to the borrower.
- **Recording Fees.** Certain documents must be filed with the local government, and typically the borrower pays these recording fees.

Borrowers who have equity in their homes but have not completely paid off their first mortgage may be able to secure another loan using the equity as collateral. A ***second mortgage*** is a mortgage loan secured by the borrower's equity in real estate that is already collateral for a first mortgage. At any given time, the interest rate charged on a second mortgage is slightly higher than the interest rate on the first mortgage because 1) as the amount of debt on the collateral increases, the probability of borrower default increases and 2) in case of default on either mortgage, the claim of the first mortgage lender is given preference over the claim of the second mortgage lender.

Second mortgages allow homeowners to convert equity in their homes to cash without selling the house. Second mortgage borrowers often use the funds from the second mortgage to make improvements to the house, pay debts, pay for education expenses, start a business, or make other purchases that require substantial funds.

Traditionally, lenders have limited the amounts of second mortgage loans to less than the total value of the equity owned by the borrower. Traditional second-mortgage lenders might, for example, lend up to 80 percent of the borrower's equity. Lenders loan less than the equity as a means of reducing the risk that they would not recover the balance due on a second mortgage in the event of default.

Lenders may structure second mortgages as home-equity lines of credit or home-equity installment loans. A ***home-equity line of credit*** is an agreement giving the borrower a line of credit equal to a specified amount of the borrower's equity. The borrower can use this amount as needed, and she pays interest only on the funds actually borrowed. A home-equity line of credit is a type of noninstallment loan. The interest rates on home-equity lines of credit typically are variable.

A ***home-equity installment loan*** is a second mortgage in which the borrower receives a specified amount of the equity and then repays this loan with fixed or variable periodic payments of principal and interest over a fixed period. Home-equity lines of credit and home-equity installment loans are popular credit mechanisms among borrowers in the United States because interest paid on a home-equity loan is tax deductible up to a limit.

Reverse Mortgages

A ***reverse mortgage*** is a special type of loan by means of which older people can convert the equity in their homes into cash. A reverse mortgage is indeed the reverse of a mortgage. Instead of the homeowner making regular payments to the lender, the lender makes payments to the homeowner, who continues to own the home. Depository institutions and finance companies offer reverse mortgages.

Only those people over age 62 who own their own home can qualify for a reverse mortgage. A homeowner does not have to meet credit or income requirements. Even homeowners with outstanding mortgages are eligible. However, federal regulations specify the type of home that is eligible and require that a home be free of structural defects and comply with safety codes for a reverse mortgage to be granted. Thus, the homeowner must pay for repairs, although the cost can be financed with the reverse mortgage and the repairs can be completed after the reverse mortgage is approved.

To protect consumers, the U.S. federal government requires that a homeowner contemplating a reverse mortgage must meet with a reverse mortgage counselor. The counselor educates the homeowner about reverse mortgages and about the homeowner's other options for obtaining needed funds. The federal government provides the counseling free of charge.

The size of the reverse mortgage depends on many factors, including the homeowner's age, the value of the home, the amount outstanding on an existing mortgage, and current interest rates. Typically, the older the homeowner and the higher the value of the home, the higher the loan amount will be.

Fees and charges similar to those imposed on typical mortgages are imposed on reverse mortgages. These fees include an origination fee, a mortgage insurance premium, and an appraisal fee. Many of these fees can be financed as part of the loan.

The proceeds of a reverse mortgage can be received in a lump sum, fixed monthly payments (up to life), a line of credit, or a combination of any of these options. Proceeds are tax free and can be used for any purpose.

The homeowner must pay off the reverse mortgage only when the homeowner ceases to reside in the home as his primary residence due to moving out, selling the home, or death. However, the homeowner or his heirs can continue to own the home as long as the reverse mortgage is paid off. No payments are due while the loan is outstanding.

Key Terms

bankruptcy
collateral
secured loan
unsecured loan
co-signer
credit report
fixed interest rate
variable interest rate
prime interest rate
finance charge
annual percentage rate (APR)
periodic rate
noninstallment credit
single-payment loan
open-end credit
credit card
credit limit
cash advance
cash advance limit
grace period
average daily balance method
previous balance method
adjusted balance method
installment credit
amortization
amortization period
term
balloon payment
mortgage
lien
foreclosure
conventional mortgage
adjustable rate mortgage (ARM)
mortgage refinancing
equity
payment cap
interest-rate cap
down payment

loan-to-value ratio
private mortgage insurance
closing costs
point
second mortgage
home-equity line of credit
home-equity installment loan
reverse mortgage

Endnote

1. "Stat Bank," *Journal of Financial Planning* (July 2003), 21.

chapter

5

Individual Life Insurance and Supplemental Benefits

outline

Needs Met by Life Insurance

- Personal Needs
- Business Needs

Types of Individual Life Insurance

- Term Life Insurance
- Cash Value Life Insurance
- Endowment Insurance

Supplemental Benefits for Individual Life Insurance Policies

- Disability Benefits
- Accident Benefits
- Accelerated Death Benefits
- Benefits for Additional Insureds
- Insurability Benefits

Finished on-
Done

objectives

After reading this chapter, you should be able to

- Identify the personal and business needs that life insurance can meet
- Describe the basic types of life insurance
- Distinguish between renewable term life and convertible term life insurance
- Identify three different types of term life insurance coverage and give an example of each
- Identify and describe three different types of whole life insurance coverage
- Distinguish among universal life, variable life, and variable universal life insurance
- Identify and describe the various types of supplemental disability benefits, accident benefits, accelerated death benefits, benefits for additional insureds, and insurability benefits

Life insurance is insurance that provides protection against the economic loss caused by the death of the person whose life is insured. This economic loss can take many forms. For example, family members may need the insurance benefits to pay funeral expenses, medical bills, debts, and estate taxes and/or to replace the income of the person who has died. Businesses may need the benefits to continue the operations of the company after the death of an owner.

Only life insurance companies may issue life insurance. They may do so on an individual or group basis. An ***individual life insurance policy*** is an insurance policy that is issued to insure the life of a named person. A ***group life insurance policy***, which is also known as a *master group insurance contract*, is an insurance policy that is issued to a party that is purchasing life insurance coverage for a specific group of people. For example, many employers purchase group life insurance to provide life insurance coverage to their employees.

The primary types of life insurance policies are term, cash value, and endowment.

- ***Term life insurance*** provides coverage only if the insured dies during the period specified in the policy.

- ***Cash value life insurance***, also known as *permanent life insurance*, provides coverage throughout the insured's lifetime and contains a savings element. The savings element of a cash value life insurance policy is known as the ***cash value***.

- ***Endowment insurance*** provides a policy benefit payable either when the insured dies or on a stated date if the insured is still alive on that date. Although endowment insurance is rarely written any more in the United States, this type of insurance is popular in some countries, particularly those in Southeast Asia.

In Chapter 2, we introduced some basic insurance concepts and terminology. In this chapter, we explain the needs that life insurance fulfills and describe in more detail the basic types of individual life insurance policies and supplemental benefits. In Chapter 6, we discuss individual life insurance policy provisions and pricing. In Chapter 7, we cover group life insurance.

Needs Met by Life Insurance

As the examples we mentioned earlier in this chapter illustrate, life insurance can meet personal and business needs.

Personal Needs

Many people who purchase life insurance do so to leave their survivors with no debts and with adequate means of support. Some view life insurance as a means of accumulating funds for their retirement. In this section, we explore some of the many personal needs that life insurance fulfills.

Debts, Final Expenses, and Taxes

When a person dies, he may leave behind debts, such as a mortgage, credit card debt, and an automobile loan. He may also have final expenses, such as hospital bills and funeral expenses. In addition, many countries impose an estate tax on the assets left by a person upon his death. To raise money to pay these obligations, the deceased's survivors may be forced to sell estate assets or even their own property. Such a forced sale of assets can garner less than true market value. The proceeds of a life insurance policy can alleviate the need for a forced sale.

Example: Kathleen Marshall is a 50-year-old widow who owns her own home and has recently purchased a new automobile. Kathleen has both a mortgage and an automobile loan. She wants to ensure that when she dies, her son will inherit her assets, including the house, and will have enough cash on hand to pay the mortgage, the automobile loan, any of her other outstanding debts, and taxes.

Analysis: As part of an estate plan, Kathleen should consider purchasing insurance on her life and naming her son as the beneficiary. In deciding what amount of insurance to purchase, Kathleen should try to determine the amount of cash that her son might need to pay her debts and estate taxes and to maintain the house as his residence.

Dependents' Support and Education

Perhaps more important than immediate debt relief is the need for life insurance proceeds to support the survivors who depended on the deceased person. When someone whose income supports or helps support a family dies and the income stops, expenses continue. In some cases, the death may create additional expenses, such as childcare. Another possible consequence of a parent's premature death is the lack of tuition when children reach college age. Life insurance proceeds can be used to meet the survivors' current and future needs.

To encourage people to provide for their dependents' financial needs, some countries have given life insurance favorable tax treatment. Generally, in the United States, Canada, and many other countries, when the proceeds of a life insurance policy are paid in a lump sum to a named beneficiary following the death of the insured, those proceeds are not considered taxable income to the beneficiary.

Access to Cash Values for Retirement and Other Needs

As people age, their need to provide for the support of their dependents after their death decreases while their need to provide for their own support upon retirement increases. Life insurance policies that accumulate a cash value can meet both needs.

A cash value policy serves the original purpose of providing insurance coverage while it is needed during the working years; and later, the policy's cash value can be used to provide retirement income or for other needs. For example, the policy's owner can use the cash value to purchase an annuity that will make periodic payments for the remainder of his life. Alternatively, the policy's owner can use the cash value to pay off his home mortgage or buy a retirement home.

Example: Conrad and Esther Cerwinski are approaching retirement age. Their house is paid for, but Conrad and Esther are concerned that their government-provided retirement benefit and Conrad's pension benefit will not be sufficient to support them after they both retire. When he was 25 years old, Conrad purchased a cash value life insurance policy that has accumulated a considerable cash value.

Analysis: If Conrad no longer needs life insurance coverage, he can use the cash value of his life insurance policy to purchase a single-premium annuity, which will provide a periodic income throughout the remainder of Esther's and his lifetimes.

People may use their cash value policies for many other purposes. For example, some people use these policies as a source of emergency funds.

Business Needs

Two of the most popular reasons for which businesses typically purchase life insurance are

- To ensure that the business continues in the event of the death of an owner, partner, or other important person
- To provide an employee benefit

Business Continuation Insurance

While large corporations typically have the financial resources to ensure the continuation of business after the death of an individual who is important to the organization, smaller businesses may need to establish a business continuation plan for such an event. A ***business continuation plan*** is a plan designed to enable a business to continue operations upon the death of an owner or other person important to the business. Business continuation plans can involve buy-sell agreements or key person life insurance.

Buy-Sell Agreements

A ***buy-sell agreement*** is an agreement in which (1) one party agrees to purchase the financial interest that a second party has in a business following the second party's death and (2) the second party agrees to direct his estate to sell his interest in the business to the purchasing party. Typically, a second integral part of a business continuation plan involving a buy-sell agreement is life insurance. For example, in a sole proprietorship situation (a business owned by a single person), the sole proprietor and his most trusted employee may enter into a buy-sell agreement that provides for the purchase of the business by the employee upon the employer's death. The employee then may purchase a life insurance policy on the life of the owner and name himself the beneficiary to receive the proceeds when the owner dies. The proceeds fund the purchase of the owner's financial interest in the business under the terms of the buy-sell agreement.

> **Example:** Indira Patel owns a bookstore and wants the business to continue in the event of her death. Her only child, Anish, is not interested in owning the store. Indira's only employee, Warren Richter, has agreed to purchase the bookstore if Indira should die. Warren and Indira enter into a buy-sell agreement. Warren, however, will not have enough cash to purchase the store from Indira's estate if Indira should die within the next 10 years.

Analysis: Warren can purchase an insurance policy on Indira's life and name himself as the policy beneficiary. The proceeds of the policy should be high enough to allow him to purchase the business from Indira's estate if Indira should die within the next 10 years.

Note that the life insurance policy is not a part of the buy-sell agreement. The insurance is simply the funding instrument for the agreement. The party buying the deceased's interest in the business could have other sources of funds, but life insurance proceeds are the typical funding vehicle.

Key Person Life Insurance

A ***key person*** is any person or employee whose continued participation in a business is necessary to the success of the business and whose death would cause the business a significant financial loss. A key person can be almost anyone who is of importance to the business, including an owner, a top salesperson, or an employee possessing unique technical skills. ***Key person life insurance*** is insurance that a business purchases on the life of a key person. The business owns, pays the premiums on, and is the beneficiary of a key person life insurance policy, which can be any type of life insurance.

Whereas the proceeds of life policies purchased in connection with buy-sell agreements go toward buying a deceased owner's share of the business, the proceeds of a key person life insurance policy compensate the business for the financial losses it will suffer because of the key person's death. Potential uses of the proceeds include replacing the revenue generated by the deceased, paying for finding and training a replacement, and serving as assurance to creditors and suppliers that the business will continue operating.

Employee Benefits

Employers have found that offering life insurance as an ***employee benefit***—an item of nonwage compensation—can help them attract and retain quality employees. Thus, employers often offer eligible employees group life insurance, group health insurance, and retirement plans, all of which we shall discuss in this text.

Insight 5.1 discusses two popular types of individual life insurance employee benefit plans. The examples given are general, as the features of these plans may vary from company to company. An employer always should confirm the tax treatment of these plans, especially split-dollar plans, prior to offering them because of changes to the tax laws.

INSIGHT 5.1 Individual Life Insurance Employee Benefit Plans

Split-Dollar Life Insurance Plan. A ***split-dollar life insurance plan*** is an agreement under which a business provides individual life insurance policies for certain employees, who share in paying the cost of the policies. Typically, the policy is a form of cash value insurance, and the employer pays the portion of each annual premium that is equal to the amount by which the policy's cash value will increase that year. The employee pays the remainder of each annual premium. Either the employer or the employee may own the policy.

If the employee dies while the policy is in force, the employer receives proceeds in an amount equal to its premium payments and interest, which also equal the policy's cash value. The beneficiary named by the employee receives the remainder of the proceeds. If the employee retires or leaves the company, the employer typically gives him ownership of the policy on the condition that he reimburse the employer for the premiums it paid.

Deferred Compensation Plan. A ***deferred compensation plan*** is a plan established by an employer to provide income benefits to an employee at a date later than the income was earned, such as after the employee's retirement, if the employee does not voluntarily terminate employment before that date. To fund a deferred compensation plan, the employee usually agrees to defer a portion of her salary or current compensation—such as a percentage of her regular pay, the amount of an annual salary increase, or the amount of a bonus—until some future date. The employer uses this deferred compensation to purchase an insurance policy on the employee's life.

In a deferred compensation plan, the employer owns, pays the premiums for, and is the named beneficiary of the policy insuring the employee's life. The policy is typically one that builds cash value. At the time of the employee's retirement, the employer uses the policy's cash value to fund an annuity, which will provide the employee with retirement income. The employer also usually agrees that if the employee dies before reaching retirement, the policy proceeds will fund an annuity that will provide income benefits to the employee's spouse and family.

Most deferred compensation agreements state that if the employee voluntarily terminates employment before a date specified in the agreement, she is entitled to receive only the total amount of compensation that she has deferred to date. Thus, the deferred compensation plan serves as an incentive for the employee to remain with the company.

Types of Individual Life Insurance

All life insurance policies provide for the payment of a benefit if the insured dies while the policy is in force. However, as we have discussed, life insurance fills many different needs. The features of policies vary to reflect these needs. Some people need a policy to provide only life insurance protection, while others need protection plus a savings element. Still other people feel the need for protection, savings, and the ability to direct the investment of the policy's funds. In this section, we describe various types of individual life insurance policies.

Term Life Insurance

FAST FACT

Of new individual life policies purchased in the United States in 2002, 49 percent, or 7 million, were term insurance, totaling $1.2 trillion, or 69 percent, of the individual life face amount issued.[1]

Term life insurance provides a benefit only if the insured dies during a finite period specified in the policy. The ***policy term***—the specified period of time during which a term life insurance policy provides coverage—can vary in length according to the policy. If a person buys traveler's insurance to insure her life during an airplane flight, she has bought term insurance that will last only as long as the flight itself. Typically, though, a person buys term life insurance for a specified number of years or for a period until he reaches a certain age. For example, a term insurance policy that covers an insured until age 65 is referred to as *term to age 65*, and the policy's coverage expires on the policy anniversary that falls either closest to or, in some policies, immediately following the insured person's 65th birthday. The ***policy anniversary*** generally is the anniversary of the date on which coverage under an insurance policy became effective.

Term policies do not build cash values. If the policyowner stops paying premiums for a term policy, then the policy terminates and the parties have no further liability to each other unless the policy is subsequently *reinstated*, or put back in force.

Some term policies offer the policyowner the option to continue coverage beyond the original term, change the coverage to a plan of cash value insurance, or both. A ***renewable term insurance policy*** gives the policyowner the option to renew the coverage at the end of the policy term without presenting evidence of insurability. ***Evidence of insurability*** is proof that an insurance underwriter requires to determine that a proposed insured meets the insurer's health and lifestyle requirements and is an insurable risk. In other words, when renewing a renewable term insurance policy, the insured is not required to undergo a physical examination or provide the insurer with an updated health history. However, many policies limit the number of times or the insured's age to which coverage may be renewed.

Typically, the renewal is for the same term and face amount that were provided originally by the policy. The ***face amount*** of a life insurance policy is the monetary value of the benefit applied for by the applicant. However, the premium usually increases to an amount based on the insured's *attained age*—or current age—on the renewal date.

Example: Tamar Rashad, age 30, just purchased a $100,000 five-year term life insurance policy on her own life. The policy's annual premium is $126. The policy contains a renewal provision that gives Tamar the option to renew her policy without having to submit evidence of her insurability.

Analysis: During the five-year policy term, Tamar will pay $126 each year for her coverage. On the policy anniversary at the end of the five-year term, Tamar has the right to renew her coverage, even if she has developed serious health problems. The coverage will be for the same $100,000 face amount as the original policy and for the same five-year term. The new premium amount, however, will be $155 per year to reflect Tamar's attained age of 35 at the time of renewal. Tamar will pay this higher premium during the five-year renewal period. At the end of the second five-year period, Tamar will again have the option to renew the policy at a premium rate based on her attained age of 40 without providing evidence of her insurability. The policy allows Tamar to continue to renew her coverage until the policy anniversary date in the year of her 65th birthday.

Yearly renewable term (YRT) insurance is one-year term life insurance that is renewable at the end of each policy year. This type of coverage is especially popular as group insurance, as we shall discuss in Chapter 7.

A ***convertible term insurance policy*** gives the policyowner the right to convert the term policy to a cash value life insurance policy without providing evidence of insurability. The premium for the cash value coverage can be based on an increase in the insured's age but not on any changes in the insured person's health. Some policies do not permit conversion after the insured has attained a specific age, such as 55 or 65, or after the term policy has been in force for a specified time. In addition, the face amount of the converted policy may be limited to a certain percentage of the original face amount.

Example: Frank DeLucca, age 35, purchased a $100,000 ten-year convertible term life insurance policy on his own life with an annual premium of $140.

Analysis: At the end of the ten-year policy term, Frank would be permitted to change the policy to a cash value life insurance policy without providing additional evidence of his insurability. The insurer may base the premium for the cash value life policy on Frank's attained age of 45, but not on any changes in Frank's health.

As we discuss in the following sections, term life insurance policies may be categorized by whether the face amount payable remains level, decreases, or increases throughout the policy term. Any of these types of policies may be renewable, convertible, or both.

Level Term Life Insurance

The most common type of term insurance is ***level term life insurance***, which provides a face amount that remains the same over the policy term. For example, under a five-year level term policy that provides $50,000 of coverage, the insurer agrees to pay $50,000 if the insured dies at any time during the five-year period that the policy is in force. The amount of each annual premium usually remains the same throughout the stated term.

Note that "level term" can mean level premium term or level face amount term, although level face amount is the standard meaning. Always verify whether premiums or the face amount remain level during the entire coverage period to determine which is the correct meaning.

Decreasing Term Life Insurance

Decreasing term life insurance provides a face amount that decreases in amount over the policy term. For example, a five-year decreasing term policy may have a face amount of $50,000 during the first year, with the face amount to be decreased by $10,000 each year until the policy expires at the end of the fifth year. Typically, the amount of each annual premium stays constant throughout the term.

Decreasing term life insurance is a good example of how specific types of insurance coverage can be adapted to meet specific needs. Variations of decreasing term coverage include (1) mortgage life insurance, (2) credit life insurance, and (3) family income insurance. We describe these types of term insurance in Figure 5.1.

Increasing Term Life Insurance

Increasing term life insurance provides a face amount that starts at one amount and increases by some specified amount or percentage at stated intervals over the policy term. For example, coverage may start at $100,000 and then increase by 5 percent on each policy anniversary date throughout the policy term. Alternatively, the face amount may increase according to increases in the cost of living, as measured by a standard index, such as the Consumer Price Index (CPI).[2] Increasing term insurance frequently is used to provide a policy benefit that matches the growing financial needs associated with raising children and providing funds for college if an insured parent were to die. The premium generally increases as the amount of coverage increases.

FIGURE 5.1 Types of Decreasing Term Life Insurance

Mortgage Life Insurance

Mortgage life insurance is a plan of decreasing term life insurance designed to provide a face amount that corresponds to the decreasing amount owed on a mortgage loan. The term of a mortgage life policy is based on the length of the mortgage, which is usually 15 or 30 years. Premiums generally are level throughout the term. A beneficiary may use the proceeds to pay off the mortgage, but he is not required to do so. Mortgage lenders sometimes require borrowers to obtain mortgage life insurance and to name the lender as beneficiary.

Credit Life Insurance

Credit life insurance is a type of term life insurance designed to pay the balance due on a loan other than a mortgage if the borrower dies before the loan is repaid. Like mortgage life insurance, credit life insurance is usually decreasing term insurance, with the benefit payable equal to the amount of the unpaid debt. If credit life covers credit card debt, the benefit payment may increase or decrease depending on the outstanding loan balance. Premiums may be level over the term or may increase or decrease along with the loan balance. Unlike mortgage life insurance, credit life insurance policies always provide that the proceeds are payable directly to the lender, and the loan typically must be of a type that can be repaid in ten years or less.

Family Income Insurance

Family income insurance is a plan of decreasing term life insurance that provides a stated monthly income benefit amount to the insured's beneficiary—typically the surviving spouse—if the insured dies during the term of coverage. Monthly income benefits continue until the end of the term specified when the coverage was purchased. Most family income coverage is a form of decreasing term insurance because the longer the insured remains alive during the term of coverage, the shorter the length of time over which the insurer may be required to pay monthly income benefits; the shorter the length of the benefit period, the smaller the total amount of benefits the insurer will pay out.

Example: Karen Lepkowicz has purchased 10-year family income insurance that provides for a $1,000 monthly income benefit. Her coverage specifies that the income benefit will be paid for at least 3 years if she dies during the 10-year term of coverage.

Analysis: If Karen dies 2 years after buying the family income policy, the insurer will pay a total of $96,000 in monthly income benefits ($1,000 per month x 12 months x 8 years) to Karen's husband, who is her beneficiary. If she dies 6 years after buying the coverage, the monthly income benefit will be paid for 4 years; thus, the insurer will pay Karen's husband a total of $48,000 ($1,000 per month x 12 months x 4 years). If, however, Karen dies 9 years after purchasing the coverage, then the income benefit will continue for the specified 3-year minimum, for a total of $36,000 ($1,000 per month x 12 months x 3 years).

Cash Value Life Insurance

As we have discussed, cash value life insurance is designed to provide coverage throughout the insured's lifetime, as well as a savings element known as the cash value. As we will learn in Chapter 6, before the insured's death, a policyowner has the right to *surrender*—or terminate—a cash value life insurance policy for its net cash surrender value or to take out part of the cash value in the form of a policy loan or in some cases a withdrawal. However, while the policy remains in force, the cash value can earn interest.

Although the interest rate earned on a life insurance policy's cash value may be less than the rate available on savings accounts or other investments, using life insurance as a savings vehicle offers certain advantages. Many cash value policies, for example, guarantee that the policyowner will earn at least a specified interest rate and that the cash value will not be reduced regardless of the economic situation. In addition, the policyowner usually is not required to pay income taxes each year on the interest earned on the policy's accumulated cash value as he must on interest earned from most savings and investment vehicles. Note, however, that when a policyowner actually receives the cash value, he may owe income taxes if he receives more from the policy than he paid for it, although in some countries the values received are entirely tax free.

Cash value life insurance has evolved along with the needs of customers. In this section, we discuss the major types of cash value insurance. As we have pointed out, terminology used to describe insurance products is not consistent throughout the insurance industry. You may see two or more different terms used to identify the same product, and sometimes one term can be used in several contexts. The term *whole life* is perhaps the best example of an insurance term that is employed in several contexts. In one context, whole life refers to the broad classification of insurance products that are considered to be permanent insurance in that they insure you for the whole of your life; thus, in this context, some of the newer products such as universal life insurance and variable life insurance, are forms of whole life insurance. Whole life is also used to refer to a specific type of cash value insurance product, which is how we will use the term in this text.

Whole Life Insurance

Whole life insurance, also known as *traditional whole life insurance*, remains in effect, if the premiums are current, until the insured dies. This type of coverage is called whole life because the policyowner does not need to renew the policy or provide evidence of insurability after policy issue. As long as the policyowner pays the premiums, the policy will provide coverage for the insured's entire lifetime.

Whole life policies can be classified on the basis of the length of the policy's premium payment period. Figure 5.2 describes continuous-premium, limited-payment, and single-premium whole life insurance policies.

Specialized types of whole life insurance are described in Figure 5.3.

FIGURE 5.2 Whole Life Insurance Premium Payment Periods

Continuous-Premium Policies

A ***continuous-premium whole life policy***, also known as a *straight life insurance policy* or an *ordinary life insurance policy*, is a whole life policy for which premiums are payable until the insured's death. Because premiums are payable over the life of the policy, the amount of each premium payment is lower than the premium amount required under any other premium payment schedule.

Limited Payment Policies

A ***limited-payment whole life policy*** is a whole life policy for which premiums are payable only until some stated period expires or until the insured's death, whichever occurs first. The stated period may be a specific number of years or the insured's attainment of a specified age. For example, a paid-up-at-age-65 policy provides that premiums are payable until the insured reaches the policy anniversary closest to or immediately following her 65th birthday, at which time the premium payments cease but the coverage continues.

Because fewer annual premium payments are expected to be made for a limited-payment policy than for a comparable continuous-premium policy, the annual premium for the limited payment policy is larger than the annual premium for the continuous-premium policy. Likewise, cash values generally build more rapidly under limited-payment policies than they do under continuous-premium policies, with a cash value sometimes being available at the end of the first year for a limited-payment policy but not until the third policy year for a continuous-premium whole life policy.

Example: Boris Vatutin, who has just turned 45, plans to retire at age 65, at which time his income will be reduced considerably. Boris wishes to obtain permanent life insurance, but he is concerned that he will not be able to pay the premiums from his retirement income. He has, therefore, purchased a 20-payment whole life policy.

Analysis: Boris will make his last premium payment at age 65, at which time he will have a paid-up policy that will require no further premium payments but which will provide life insurance coverage for the rest of his life.

Single-Premium Policies

A ***single-premium whole life policy*** is a type of limited-payment policy that requires only one premium payment. A sizable cash value is available immediately after paying the premium on any single-premium policy, and the cash value increases over time as interest earnings are credited to the policy.

FIGURE 5.3 Specialized Types of Whole Life Insurance

Joint Whole Life Insurance

Joint whole life insurance has the same features and benefits as individual whole life insurance, except that it insures two or more lives under the same policy. Joint whole life insurance is often referred to as *first-to-die life insurance* because, upon the death of one of the insureds, the policy benefit is paid to the surviving insured and the coverage ends.

Last Survivor Life Insurance

Last survivor life insurance, also known as *second-to-die life insurance*, is a variation of joint whole life insurance under which the policy benefit is paid only after both people insured by the policy have died. Premiums may be payable only until the first insured dies or until the death of both insureds. Premiums are typically less than those of either two individual whole life policies or a joint whole life policy. Last survivor life insurance was designed primarily to insure married couples who want to provide funds to pay estate taxes upon their deaths.

Family Policy

A ***family policy*** is a type of life insurance policy that covers all the members of a family under one contract. The primary insured is issued a whole life insurance policy, and the insured's spouse and children receive term life insurance coverage. Some insurers issue the spouse limited-payment whole life. The term coverage is a fraction—generally one-fourth or one-fifth—of the amount of the insured's whole life coverage. Typically, the family members must provide evidence of insurability before issuance of the policy, after which each child born to or adopted by the family is covered automatically.

Example: Henry and Kathy Kwan want to purchase a family policy to cover themselves and their two children, Peter and Jennifer. Henry will be covered by $100,000 of whole life insurance and his wife and children will each be covered by ¼ of the face amount of Henry's coverage.

Analysis: The total amount of life insurance provided by Henry's family policy is $175,000, which is summarized as follows:

$100,000 of whole life coverage on Henry
$25,000 of term life coverage on Kathy
$25,000 of term life coverage on Peter
$25,000 of term life coverage on Jennifer

If Henry and Kathy have a third child, then the family policy will also provide $25,000 of term life coverage on that child without any evidence of insurability or change in premium.

(continued on next page)

FIGURE 5.3 *(continued)* Specialized Types of Whole Life Insurance

Monthly Debit Ordinary (MDO) Insurance

Monthly debit ordinary (MDO) insurance, also known as *debit insurance*, is whole life insurance that is marketed through the home service distribution system and is paid for by monthly premium payments. The ***home service distribution system*** is a method of selling and servicing insurance policies through commissioned sales agents who sell a range of products and provide specified policyowner services, including the collection of renewal premiums, within a specified geographic area. MDO policies are similar to, although sold in smaller face amounts than, traditional whole life insurance policies.

Pre-need Funeral Insurance

Pre-need funeral insurance, also known as *pre-need insurance*, is whole life insurance that provides funds to pay for the insured's funeral and burial. In most cases, the policyowner makes an assignment of the policy benefit to a funeral home in consideration for a guarantee by the funeral home that it will provide specified funeral services and merchandise. The face amount of the whole life insurance policy is usually designed to increase over the life of the insured so that it keeps pace with the increases in the cost of providing the selected funeral. Pre-need funeral insurance tends to be sold in relatively small face amounts, and some insurers market this type of coverage through funeral home employees who are licensed insurance agents.

Universal Life Insurance

Universal life insurance is a form of cash value life insurance characterized by flexible premiums, flexible face amounts and death benefits, and unbundled product structures. An ***unbundled product structure*** is a life insurance and annuity product design in which an insurer explicitly discloses various expense and benefit charges to customers and specifies the rate of investment return being credited to customers. A ***bundled product structure*** is a life insurance and annuity product design in which an insurer presents a product to customers as a package of benefits provided in exchange for a given payment. In other words, with a bundled product structure, the insurer reveals to the policyowner only the lump sum amount of money the insurer actually charges for a policy—the ***gross premium***—without breaking it down into its component parts.

Whereas term and whole life insurance policies, which are bundled products, state the gross premium that the policyowner must pay to keep the policy in force, universal life insurance policies, which are unbundled products, list each of the three pricing factors that we will discuss in Chapter 6—operating expenses, cost of benefits, and investment earnings—separately. This unbundling allows customers to compare charges and interest rates when selecting among competing policies.

At the time of purchasing a universal life insurance policy and subject to certain limitations, the policyowner selects a face amount and decides whether the policy will be an Option A or an Option B plan. An ***Option A plan***, also known as an *Option 1 plan*, is a universal life insurance policy that provides a level death benefit amount, which is always equal to the policy's face amount. An ***Option B plan***, also known as an *Option 2 plan*, is a universal life insurance policy that provides a death benefit amount that, at any given time, is equal to the policy's face amount plus the amount of the policy's cash value. Some companies use the terms *Option A plan* and *Option B plan* but switch the meanings.

Note the difference between a policy's face amount—the amount of benefits applied for—and the ***death benefit***, also known as *policy proceeds*—the amount of money actually paid by an insurer to the beneficiary when the insured dies. As we just discussed, the death benefit will exceed the face amount by the amount of the cash value under an Option B plan of universal life insurance. In addition, the death benefit may exceed the face amount if policy dividends are earned but not yet paid or if dividends are used to purchase additional paid-up life insurance. The death benefit may be less than the face amount if the insured of a cash value policy dies with a policy loan outstanding. We explain dividends and policy loans in Chapter 6.

Variable Life Insurance

Variable life (VL) insurance is a form of cash value life insurance in which premiums are fixed, but the face amount and other values may vary, reflecting the performance of the investment subaccounts selected by the policyowner. A ***subaccount*** is one of several alternative pools of investments to which a policyowner allocates premiums paid and accumulated cash values. Variable life is similar to what is called *unit-linked life insurance* in the United Kingdom.

The subaccounts in which premiums and cash values are invested are part of an insurer's ***separate account***, also known as a *segregated account*, which is an investment account maintained separately from an insurer's general account to isolate and help manage the funds placed in variable products. The ***general account*** is an undivided investment account in which an insurer maintains funds that support contractual obligations for guaranteed insurance products such as whole life insurance or fixed annuities. The funds in the general account are placed in relatively secure investments so that the insurer is assured of having funds available to pay the benefits guaranteed to policyowners.

Insurers are able to give investment control to VL policyowners because they do not guarantee investment earnings or the cash value of variable products as they do for guaranteed insurance products. Policyowners accept the investment risk of variable products because they hope that the investment performance of the subaccounts will outperform any guaranteed benefits they could have received under a guaranteed product.

The insurer follows a different investment strategy for each subaccount, and the policyowner selects from among the available subaccounts according to her investment objectives. For example, some subaccounts may seek growth and consequently invest in blue chip stocks, while others may seek current income and invest in bonds. The policyowner typically may change her selection of subaccounts at least annually.

Variable life insurance policies are subject to regulation as securities because the policyowner, not the insurer, assumes the investment risk. Although the death benefit and cash value are not guaranteed, most variable life policies guarantee that the face amount will not fall below the amount that was initially purchased, regardless of the subaccounts' performance.

Variable Universal Life Insurance

Variable universal life (VUL) insurance, also referred to as *flexible variable life*, is a form of cash value life insurance that combines the premium and death benefit amount flexibility of universal life insurance with the investment flexibility and risk of variable life insurance. Like a universal life policy, a variable universal life policy allows the policyowner to choose the premium amount, the face amount, and an Option A plan or an Option B plan. Like a variable life policy, premiums and cash values are placed in subaccounts selected by the policyowner. Variable universal policies do not guarantee investment earnings or cash values. In the United States, they are considered securities and must comply with securities laws.

Figure 5.4 illustrates how VUL products combine the features of UL and VL products.

Endowment Insurance

Endowment insurance provides a policy benefit payable either when the insured dies or on a stated date if the insured is still alive on that date. Each endowment policy specifies a ***maturity date***, which is the date on which the insurer will pay the policy's face amount to the policyowner if the insured is still living. The maturity date is either 1) the end of a stated term, such as 20 years, or 2) the insured's attainment of a stated age, such as age 65. If the insured dies before the maturity date, the insurer pays the face amount to the beneficiary. Thus, an endowment insurance policy pays a benefit whether the insured survives to the policy's maturity date or dies before the maturity date.

As with most whole life policies, a policyowner can purchase an endowment policy with a single premium or with a series of premiums

FIGURE 5.4 How VUL Products Combine Features of UL and VL Products

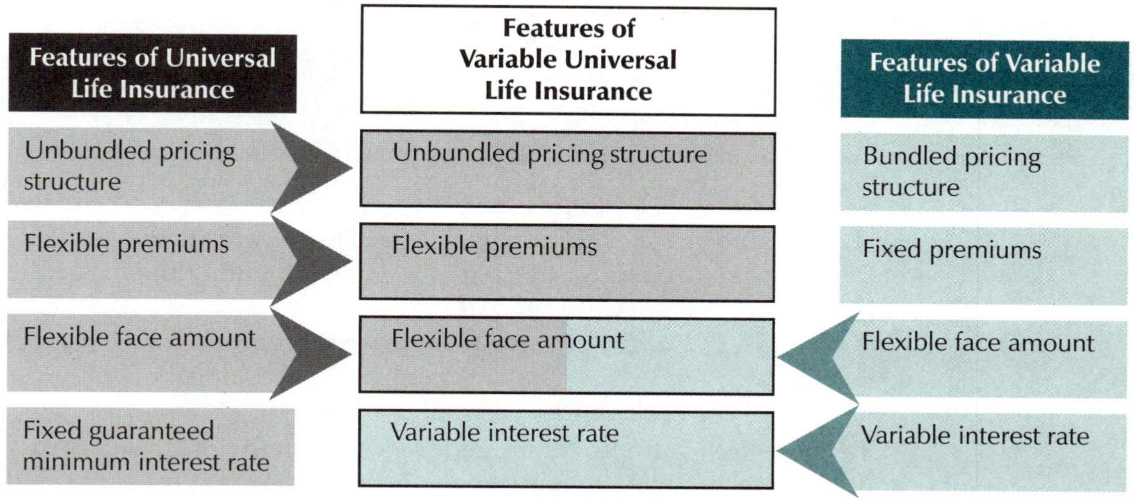

Source: Adapted from Deborah Bellange and Dani L. Long, *Intro to Variable Universal Life Insurance* (Atlanta: LOMA, © 2000), 11. Used with permission; all rights reserved.

over a limited period. If the endowment policyowner pays a series of premiums, they typically are level while the policy is in force. In addition, endowment policies also build cash values.

Sales of endowment insurance in the United States and Canada have fallen steadily, primarily because of the unfavorable income tax treatment afforded it. Endowment insurance, however, remains a popular product in many other countries where tax laws treat it more favorably. Insight 5.2 describes the popularity of endowment insurance in Vietnam.

Supplemental Benefits for Individual Life Insurance Policies

The dominant benefit of any life insurance policy is the benefit paid upon the death of the insured. However, a number of other benefits may be added to all types of life insurance policies. These additional, or supplemental, benefits may be provided through standard policy provisions, but typically they are provided by adding a rider to the policy. A ***rider***, also known as an *endorsement*, is an amendment or addition to a contract that either expands or limits the benefits payable under or otherwise modifies the contract. In addition to providing supplemental benefits,

INSIGHT 5.2 Popularity of Endowment Insurance in Vietnam

The life insurance industry in Vietnam came into existence in the late 1990s. As of 2003, endowment insurance is overwhelmingly the most popular type of life insurance in this country, making up 94.1 percent of the market. The average face amount is US$1,420. Premiums are not tax deductible, but proceeds are received tax free.

riders may be used to increase the amount of the policy's benefits or otherwise modify the policy's coverage. Riders may be included with the policy at issue or added or deleted later, thus providing the insurer and policyowner with maximum flexibility.

The insurer typically charges an additional premium for each supplemental benefit while the benefit is in force. These additional premiums do not affect the cash value, if any, of the basic policy.

Term insurance riders can be added to most cash value life insurance policies to increase the amount of the benefit payable if the insured dies while the coverage is in force. In this section, we describe other common supplemental benefits, which fall into five categories: disability benefits, accident benefits, accelerated death benefits, benefits for additional insureds, and insurability benefits.

Disability Benefits

Disability benefits generally are classified as a type of health insurance coverage because such benefits are paid to cover financial losses that result from a sickness or injury rather than those that result from the insured's death. However, some disability benefits can be added to a life insurance policy by means of a policy provision or rider.

Waiver of Premium for Disability Benefit

A ***waiver of premium for disability (WP) benefit*** is a supplemental life insurance policy benefit under which the insurer promises to give up its right to collect premiums that become due while the insured is disabled according to the policy or rider's definition of disability. The insurer actually pays the fees and expenses. Under the terms of some policies, the insurer also continues to contribute to the cash value as if the policyowner were paying premiums. As long as the insured is totally disabled, as defined by the policy, she does not pay premiums. Most WP riders define *total disability* as the insured's inability to perform the essential acts of her own occupation or any other occupation for which she is reasonably suited by education, training, or experience.

The WP benefit typically contains the limitations and exclusions listed in Figure 5.5.

FAST FACT

Of individual life policies in force in 2002, 22 percent, or 42 million, allowed the premium to be waived during disability, representing $3 trillion, or 32 percent, of the individual life face amount in force.[3]

FIGURE 5.5 Limitations on the Waiver of Premium for Disability Benefit

■ **Most WP benefits contain a three- to six-month waiting period after the insured becomes disabled before the insurer will waive the payment of the premiums.** The policyowner must continue to pay premiums that come due during the waiting period, although some WP benefits provide that these premiums will be refunded should the insured still be disabled when the waiting period ends.

■ **The WP benefit usually only covers disabilities that begin up to a specified age.** Chances of disability increase significantly as an insured ages, so the cost of providing the WP benefit would be quite high if it were to cover disabilities that begin after a certain age, such as age 65.

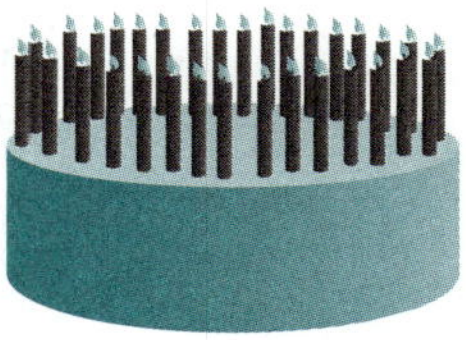

■ **When a disability begins, the interval at which premium payments are due cannot be changed.** This limitation prevents a policyowner from changing to a more frequent premium payment schedule. For example, if renewal premiums are paid annually, the policyowner may not change to a monthly premium payment mode. Doing so could result in some of the premiums being waived even if the disability were to end before the annual premiums became due.

■ **Disabilities resulting from the following causes typically are excluded from coverage:**

- Intentionally self-inflicted injuries
- Injuries the insured suffered while committing a crime
- ***Pre-existing condition***—an injury or sickness that occurred or manifested itself within a specified period—usually two years—before the policy was issued and that was not disclosed on the application for insurance
- Injuries resulting from any act of war while the insured is in military service

The WP benefit may be added to almost all types of life insurance policies, including renewable and convertible term insurance policies. If a renewable term policy's premium is being waived on a renewal date, the insurer typically renews the policy automatically and continues to waive renewal premiums until either the insured is no longer totally disabled or the policy is no longer renewable. If a convertible term insurance policy's premiums are being waived when the policy becomes convertible to whole life insurance, the policyowner usually may convert to a whole life policy; but the WP benefit may or may not be included in the new policy, subject to the terms of the original policy.

Because universal life insurance policies have variable premiums, the standard WP rider usually is not offered. Instead, universal life policies may have a *waiver of costs of insurance* rider that simply waives most of the internal costs of the policy if the insured meets the definition of disability.

Waiver of Premium for Payor Benefit

Whereas a WP benefit provides a waiver of premium if the *insured* becomes disabled, a ***waiver of premium for payor benefit*** is a supplemental life insurance policy benefit that provides that the insurance company will waive its right to collect a policy's premiums if the payor—the person responsible for paying premiums—dies or becomes totally disabled. The waiver of premium for payor benefit was designed for third-party policies, such as juvenile insurance policies. A ***juvenile insurance policy*** is a policy that is issued on the life of a child but is owned and paid for by an adult, usually the child's parent or legal guardian.

Waiver of premium for payor benefit riders typically have a two-part definition of total disability. The payor is considered totally disabled during the first two years of disability if he is unable to perform the essential acts of his own occupation. After that two-year period, the payor is considered totally disabled if he is unable to perform the essential acts of any occupation for which he is reasonably suited by education, training, or experience.

Disability Income Benefit

A ***disability income benefit*** is a supplemental life insurance policy benefit that provides a monthly income benefit if the insured becomes totally disabled while the policy is in force. Typically, the amount of the monthly disability income benefit is a stated dollar amount—such as $10—per $1,000 of life coverage. Disability income benefits usually include a three- to six-month waiting period before payment of benefits begin.

Example: Ernesto Valdez was the policyowner-insured of a $150,000 life insurance policy that included a disability income benefit rider. The rider stated that, if Ernesto became totally disabled, then the insurance company would pay him a monthly benefit of $10 per $1,000 of life insurance coverage during the period of disability; the rider includes a three-month waiting period. While the policy was in force, Ernesto became disabled as defined in the disability income benefit rider. Two years later, he died as a result of his disability.

Analysis: Three months after he became disabled, Ernesto became eligible to receive a disability income benefit of $1,500 per month.

$ 10	Monthly benefit per unit
× 150	Number of units ($150,000/$1,000)
$1,500	Monthly disability income

This monthly disability income benefit was payable as long as Ernesto remained disabled. Upon Ernesto's death, the policy's entire death benefit became payable to the named beneficiary.

Policies issued with a disability income benefit generally include a WP benefit as well. In such a case, the insurer waives the life policy premiums, the additional premiums charged for the disability income benefit, and the WP premiums during the total disability of the insured.

Accident Benefits

Accident benefits may be added to any type of individual life insurance policy. The two most commonly offered accident benefits are accidental death benefits and dismemberment benefits.

Accidental Death Benefit

An ***accidental death benefit*** is a supplemental life insurance policy benefit that provides a death benefit in addition to the policy's basic death benefit if the insured's death occurs as the result of an accident. When the amount of the accidental death benefit is equal to the face amount of the life insurance policy, which it often is, the benefit is referred to as a ***double indemnity benefit*** because the total death benefit payable if the insured dies in an accident is double the policy's face amount. The accidental death benefit may be some other multiple of the policy's face amount, or it may be totally unrelated to the face amount. Most accidental death benefits expire when the insured reaches age 65 or 70.

Generally, for the accidental death benefit to be payable, the insured's death must have been caused, directly and independently of all other causes, by an accidental bodily injury. Because determining the precise cause of an insured's death sometimes can be quite difficult, some accidental death benefits include a limitation stating that the insured's death must occur within a stated time, for example, 90 days, after the accident for the benefit to be payable.

Example: An insured with a history of heart problems died in an automobile accident. Her policy provides a $50,000 death benefit and includes an accidental death benefit rider that provides an accidental death benefit of $50,000.

Analysis: The accident itself may have caused the insured's death. In that case, the accidental death benefit is payable in addition to the policy's basic death benefit: $100,000 in benefits. On the other hand, she may have died from a heart attack while driving her automobile. If so, then the death did not result from an accident, and only the policy's basic death benefit is payable to the named beneficiary: $50,000 in benefits.

Accidental death benefits typically have the following exclusions that state that the insurer will not be required to pay the benefit if the insured's death results from certain stated causes, including

- Self-inflicted injuries (suicide)
- War-related accidents
- Accidents resulting from aviation activities if, during the flight, the insured acted in any capacity other than as a passenger
- Accidents resulting from the insured's committing a crime

Dismemberment Benefits

If an accidental death benefit provides an additional benefit for dismemberment as the result of an accident, it is known as an ***accidental death and dismemberment (AD&D) benefit.*** Typically, dismemberment entails the loss of, or loss of use of, any two limbs or the sight in both eyes; and the dismemberment benefit is equal to the amount of the accidental death benefit. In many cases, however, a smaller amount is payable if the insured loses one limb or sight in one eye. AD&D riders usually state that the insurer will not pay both accidental death benefits and dismemberment benefits for injuries suffered in the same accident.

"And we guarantee if you lose an arm or leg we'll help you find it."

www.CartoonStock.com

Accelerated Death Benefits

An ***accelerated death benefit***, also known as a *living benefit*, is a supplemental life insurance policy benefit that provides that a policyowner may elect to receive all or part of the policy's death benefit before the insured's death if certain conditions are met. The death benefit payable to the beneficiary at the insured's death is then reduced by the amount of the accelerated death benefit paid to the policyowner.

The conditions that trigger the policyowner's right to collect accelerated death benefits differ according to the type of benefit and its wording. In this section, we describe three commonly offered types of accelerated death benefits—the terminal illness benefit, the dread disease benefit, and the long-term care benefit.

Terminal Illness Benefit

The ***terminal illness (TI) benefit*** is an accelerated death benefit under which the insurer pays some or all of the policy's death benefit to a policyowner if the insured suffers from a terminal illness and has a physician-certified life expectancy of 12 months or less. Some TI benefits pay the full face amount of the policy prior to the insured's death, but generally the maximum TI benefit is a stated percentage—usually between 25 and 75 percent—of the policy's face amount up to a specified maximum dollar limit, such as $250,000. Whereas insurers may impose additional premium charges for other supplementary benefits, they typically assess an administrative charge for the TI benefit when the policyowner elects to exercise the benefit.

Dread Disease Benefit

A ***dread disease (DD) benefit***, also known as a *critical illness benefit*, is an accelerated death benefit under which the insurer agrees to pay a portion of the policy's face amount to a policyowner if the insured suffers from one of a number of specified diseases. Another form of dread disease coverage can be purchased as a stand-alone health insurance policy. We will discuss that type of coverage in Chapter 8.

Most insurers provide DD coverage only to insureds who are under the age of 70 and who have no serious health problems. An insured becomes eligible for DD benefits when he contracts certain diseases or undergoes certain medical procedures specified in the policy or rider, which are known as *insurable events* and which usually include

- Life-threatening cancer
- AIDS
- End-stage renal (kidney) failure
- Myocardial infarction (heart attack)
- Stroke
- Coronary bypass surgery

Some DD benefits also include vital organ transplants and Alzheimer's disease as insurable events.

Most insurers pay the DD benefit in a lump sum, but others pay the benefit in monthly installments over a period of 6 to 12 months. Some insurers do not make payments for multiple or recurring events.

Some DD benefits come with a premium waiver option under which the insurer agrees to waive all premiums payable after the accelerated death benefit payment. However, sometimes the premium waiver option applies only to premiums payable while the insured is disabled; if the insured recovers, then subsequent premiums are no longer waived.

Long-Term Care Insurance Benefit

A ***long-term care (LTC) insurance benefit*** is an accelerated death benefit under which the insurer agrees to pay a monthly benefit to the policyowner if the insured requires constant care for a medical condition. The types of care given and medical condition required to qualify for the LTC benefit are specified in the LTC policy provision or rider. The insurer typically waives premiums on both the LTC benefit and the basic life insurance policy during the period that the insured receives LTC benefits.

The amount of each monthly LTC benefit typically is equal to a stated percentage of the policy's death benefit. For example, the benefit may provide that the insurer will pay 2 percent of the policy's death benefit each month if the insured requires nursing home care and 1 percent of the death benefit if the insured requires home health care. The insurer generally pays monthly benefits until a specified percentage of the policy's basic death benefit—usually between 50 and 100 percent of the face amount—has been paid. Any remaining death benefit is paid to the beneficiary after the insured's death.

Long-term care benefits also are provided as a stand-alone health insurance product. We will discuss LTC in more detail in Chapter 8.

Benefits for Additional Insureds

As we mentioned earlier, term insurance riders can be added to most cash value life insurance policies to increase the amount payable upon the death of the insured. In addition, term insurance riders can be added to cash value life insurance policies, and in some cases to term policies, to provide benefits if someone other than the basic policy's insured dies. The most common of these riders are the spouse and children's insurance rider, the children's insurance rider, and the second insured rider.

Spouse and Children's Insurance Rider

A ***spouse and children's insurance rider*** is a supplemental life insurance policy benefit that provides term coverage on the insured's spouse and children. The coverage provided by such a rider is typically sold on the basis of coverage units unlike the coverage provided under a family insurance policy, which is typically a percentage of the face amount provided on the life of the primary insured. Typically, an insurer offers no more than 5 or 10 coverage units, with each coverage unit providing $5,000 of term insurance coverage on the spouse and $1,000 of term insurance coverage on each child.

Example: Wallace Groom purchased a $100,000 whole life insurance policy. He also purchased 10 coverage units under a spouse and children's insurance rider to cover his wife, Elizabeth, his 16-year-old daughter, Felicity, and his 6-year-old son, Fred.

Analysis: The following coverages are provided under Wallace's spouse and children's insurance rider:

$50,000 of term insurance coverage on Elizabeth
$10,000 of term insurance coverage on Felicity
$10,000 of term insurance coverage on Fred

If Wallace and Elizabeth have a third child, the rider also automatically will provide $10,000 of term insurance coverage on that child at no extra premium charge.

The premium for the children's coverage is a specified, flat amount. So that the insurer does not have to revise the premium amount upon the birth or adoption of each child, additional children are covered automatically at no extra premium charge, although the coverage typically does not become effective until the child is 15 days old. The coverage on each child expires when that child reaches a specified age, which is typically 21 or 25. Spouse and children's insurance riders usually include a conversion privilege that allows each child to convert his term insurance coverage to an individual life insurance policy of up to a certain multiple of his term coverage without providing evidence of insurability.

Children's Insurance Rider

A ***children's insurance rider*** is a supplemental life insurance policy benefit that provides term coverage on the insured's children. Insurers developed this form of coverage largely in recognition of the growing number of single-parent households. The rider operates in the same manner as does a spouse and children's rider, except that no spousal coverage is included. The premium charged for each coverage unit is a stated amount regardless of the number of children covered, the ages of those children, or the age and sex of the insured parent. For example, a single father of three children could purchase a children's insurance rider for the same amount as a single mother of one child.

Second Insured Rider

A ***second insured rider***, also known as an *optional insured rider* or an *additional insured rider*, is a supplemental life insurance policy benefit that provides term insurance coverage on the life of a person other than the policy's insured. The person insured under the rider is known as the *second insured* and may be the spouse of the insured, another relative, or an unrelated person, such as a business partner of the insured. Typically, the amount of coverage a second insured rider provides is unrelated to the amount of coverage the basic policy provides. The premium rate required for the second insured rider is based on the risk characteristics of the second insured. A second insured rider typically provides more coverage in years when it is needed most at a lower premium than a separate policy, but only up to a point.

Insurability Benefits

Insurers offer two types of supplemental benefits that allow policyowners to purchase additional insurance without the insured providing evidence of insurability at the time of purchase. These benefits are the guaranteed insurability benefit and the paid-up additions option benefit.

Guaranteed Insurability Benefit

The ***guaranteed insurability (GI) benefit***, also known as the *guaranteed insurability option (GIO)*, is a supplemental life insurance policy benefit that gives the policyowner the right to purchase additional insurance of the same type as the basic life insurance policy for an additional premium amount on specified option dates or upon specified events (for example, the marriage of the insured or the birth of the insured's child) during the life of the policy without providing evidence of the insured's insurability. Typically, the amount of coverage provided on an option date is limited to the policy's face amount or to an amount specified by the GI benefit, whichever is less. Most GI benefits terminate when the insured reaches age 40.

Most GI benefits specify that if the policyowner does not take positive action to purchase additional coverage on the option dates or events, he loses the right to do so until the next option date or event. However, some GI benefits provide automatic temporary term insurance coverage for the 60- or 90-day period during which the policyowner has the right to exercise the option. The insurer also will issue the additional coverage automatically if the basic policy included a WP rider and the insured is disabled at the time an option to purchase additional insurance goes into effect.

Paid-Up Additions Option Benefit

The ***paid-up additions option benefit*** is a supplemental life insurance policy benefit that allows the owner of a whole life insurance policy to purchase single-premium paid-up additions to the policy on stated dates, such as each policy anniversary, and thus to increase the amount of coverage provided under the basic policy. Typically, the additions for which the policyowner may apply must fall between the minimum and maximum amounts established by the terms of the benefit. Because the additions are whole life insurance, the paid-up additions also have their own cash values. Premiums for the paid-up additions are based on the insured's attained age at the time the paid-up additions are purchased.

A policyowner must provide evidence of the insured's insurability to add a paid-up additions option rider to an in-force policy. However, no additional evidence of insurability is required to purchase each paid-up addition when the rider is in force.

Most paid-up additions option benefits state that if the policyowner does not exercise the purchase option for a stated number of years, then the benefit will terminate. The paid-up additions already purchased remain in force, but the policyowner can no longer exercise the option to purchase new paid-up additions.

Key Terms

- life insurance
- individual life insurance policy
- group life insurance policy
- term life insurance
- cash value life insurance
- cash value
- endowment insurance
- business continuation plan
- buy-sell agreement
- key person
- key person life insurance
- employee benefit
- split-dollar life insurance plan
- deferred compensation plan
- policy term
- policy anniversary
- renewable term insurance policy
- evidence of insurability
- face amount
- yearly renewable term (YRT) insurance
- convertible term insurance policy
- level term life insurance
- decreasing term life insurance
- increasing term life insurance
- mortgage life insurance
- credit life insurance
- family income insurance
- whole life insurance
- continuous-premium whole life policy
- limited-payment whole life policy
- single-premium whole life policy
- joint whole life insurance
- last survivor life insurance
- family policy
- monthly debit ordinary (MDO) insurance
- home service distribution system
- pre-need funeral insurance
- universal life insurance
- unbundled product structure
- bundled product structure
- gross premium
- Option A plan
- Option B plan
- death benefit
- variable life (VL) insurance
- subaccount
- separate account
- general account
- variable universal life (VUL) insurance
- maturity date
- rider
- waiver of premium for disability (WP) benefit
- pre-existing condition
- waiver of premium for payor benefit
- juvenile insurance policy
- disability income benefit
- accidental death benefit
- double indemnity benefit

accidental death and dismemberment (AD&D) benefit
accelerated death benefit
terminal illness (TI) benefit
dread disease (DD) benefit
long-term care (LTC) insurance benefit
spouse and children's insurance rider
children's insurance rider
second insured rider
guaranteed insurability (GI) benefit
paid-up additions option benefit

Endnotes

1. ACLI, *Life Insurers Fact Book: 2003* (Washington, DC: American Council of Life Insurers, 2003), 94.
2. An index provides a mathematical measure that indicates the relative changes in a specific factor—such as costs, production, or prices—at a given point in time as compared to a specific time in the past. As we learned in Chapter 1, the *Consumer Price Index* (CPI) measures the change in the price of a fixed basket of goods and services bought by a typical consumer. The goods and services included in the CPI include food, transportation, housing, utilities, clothing, and medical care.
3. ACLI, *Life Insurers Fact Book: 2003* (Washington, DC: American Council of Life Insurers, 2003), 98.

chapter

6

Individual Life Insurance Policy Provisions and Pricing

outline

Individual Life Insurance Policy Provisions

- Provisions Typical of All Types of Policies
- Provisions Unique to Cash Value Policies

Individual Life Insurance Pricing

- Premium Rates
- Premium Amounts
- Level Premium Pricing System

Finished on.
Done.

objectives

After reading this chapter, you should be able to

- Describe the typical individual life insurance policy provisions that deal with the validity and operation of the insurance policy as a legal document and those provisions concerning the policyowner's rights
- Identify the three factors insurance companies use to calculate life insurance premiums and recognize how each factor affects premium rate calculations
- Explain the level premium pricing system

As we noted in Chapter 2, an insurance policy is a legal contract between the insurance company and the policyowner. The policy is composed of provisions setting forth the parties' agreement, as well as their rights and duties. Many of these provisions are standard in principle—though not in exact wording—throughout the life insurance industry worldwide.

In return for an insurer's promise to pay benefits under the terms of the policy, the policyowner agrees to pay premiums. Premiums are the price of coverage, and ***pricing*** is the process of determining the amount to charge a customer for a product.

In this chapter, we discuss the provisions found in individual life insurance policies and the pricing of these policies.

Individual Life Insurance Policy Provisions

Some policy provisions are typical of all types of individual life insurance policies, while some are found in only cash value life insurance policies.

Provisions Typical of All Types of Policies

In Figure 6.1, we explain the typical provisions that deal with the validity and operation of the insurance policy as a legal document. In the body of this section, we describe the typical provisions concerning the policyowner's rights under an individual life insurance policy.

Beneficiary Provision

As we noted in Chapter 2, the beneficiary is the person or legal entity named to receive the policy benefits when the insured dies. A policyowner who insures his own life has the right to designate anyone he wishes as the beneficiary when the policy is issued and to change the beneficiary designation at any time while the policy is in force. However, a policyowner who insures someone else's life must provide evidence of his own insurable interest and that of any third-party beneficiary. As we also learned in Chapter 2, an insurable interest is the interest a person has in the risk that is insured such that the person will suffer a genuine economic loss if the event insured against occurs.

Insurers routinely review beneficiary designations to be sure that the insurable interest requirement is met when the application is received. However, typically insurers do not review beneficiary changes because the insurable interest requirement applies only at policy issue.

FIGURE 6.1 Typical Individual Life Insurance Policy Provisions

Free-Look Provision

A ***free-look provision***, also known as a *free-examination provision*, allows the policyowner a specified period, usually at least 10 days, following policy delivery within which to cancel the policy and receive a refund of all premiums paid.

Entire Contract Provision

An ***entire contract provision*** defines which documents—typically the policy itself, the application if it is attached to the policy, and any attached riders—constitute the entire contract between the insurer and the policyowner.

Incontestability Provision

An insurer has the right to contest, or challenge, the validity of a policy on the basis that the applicant misrepresented material facts in the application for insurance. A ***misrepresentation*** is a false or misleading statement. A ***material misrepresentation*** is a misrepresentation of the facts by an insurance applicant that is relevant to the insurer's evaluation of a proposed insured. A misrepresentation is considered material when, if the truth had been known, the insurer would not have issued the policy or would have issued the policy on a different basis, such as for a higher premium or for a lower face amount.

Life insurance policies contain an ***incontestability provision*** that limits the time within which an insurer has the right to avoid the contract due to material misrepresentation in the application for the policy. This time limit is typically two years from the date of policy issue.

Grace Period Provision

A ***grace period provision*** specifies a length of time following each premium due date within which the premium due may be paid without loss of coverage. This length of time—the ***grace period***—is typically 30 or 31 days, and the policy remains in force throughout this period. If a renewal premium is not paid by the end of the grace period, the policy is said to ***lapse***. Some insurers, however, do not consider a policy as having lapsed if that policy has a cash value; the owner of a policy that provides a cash value has the right to continue the coverage under a nonforfeiture option. We describe nonforfeiture options later in the chapter.

Reinstatement Provision

A ***reinstatement provision*** describes the conditions a policyowner must meet for the insurer to reinstate—or put back into force—a policy that has either lapsed or been continued under the extended term or reduced paid-up insurance nonforfeiture options.

(continued on next page)

FIGURE 6.1 *(continued)* Typical Individual Life Insurance Policy Provisions

Misstatement of Age or Sex Provision

The ***misstatement of age or sex provision*** describes the action the insurer will take to adjust the amount of the policy benefit in the event that the age or sex of the insured is incorrectly stated in the insurance application. If the misstatement is discovered after the insured's death, the insurer will pay the benefits that the premiums paid would have purchased for the correct age or sex. If the misstatement is discovered before the insured's death, the insurer may give the policyowner the option of paying—or receiving as a refund—any difference in premium amount caused by the misstatement instead of having the insurer adjust the policy's benefits to reflect the premiums actually paid.

Example: While processing a death claim, the insurance company discovered that when Peter Sharp applied for insurance on his life, he mistakenly listed his age as 35, when in fact he was then age 40.

Analysis: The insurer will reduce the policy's benefit to the amount that the premiums paid would have purchased for Peter at age 40. If Peter had mistakenly listed his age as 45, then the insurer would have increased the benefit to the amount that the premiums paid would have purchased at age 40.

Example: Connie Liu purchased an insurance policy on her mentor, Lisa, who was supporting her financially, and named herself beneficiary. Connie and Lisa had an argument, and Lisa quit supporting Connie; but Connie did not cancel the policy or change the policy beneficiary designation. After Lisa's death, Connie filed a claim for the policy proceeds.

Analysis: The insurable interest requirement was met when Connie purchased the policy because she had an insurable interest in Lisa's life at that time. As a result, the coverage is valid. Connie was no longer required to have an insurance interest in Lisa's life in order to receive the policy proceeds following her death.

The beneficiary may be referred to as the *primary beneficiary* to distinguish him from the contingent beneficiary. The policyowner may name a ***contingent beneficiary***, also known as a *secondary beneficiary*, who is the party designated to receive the proceeds of a life insurance policy following the insured's death if the primary beneficiary dies before the insured. The policyowner has the right to name any number of primary beneficiaries and contingent beneficiaries and to indicate how the proceeds are to be divided among them.

Example: Oscar Costanza owned a $50,000 insurance policy on his life. He named his sons, John and Steven, as equal primary beneficiaries and his wife, Carla, as contingent beneficiary. Steven died several years before Oscar, who was survived by John and Carla.

Analysis: As the sole surviving primary beneficiary, John is entitled to receive the $50,000 policy proceeds.

If no primary beneficiary or contingent beneficiary survives the insured, then the insurer pays the proceeds to the policyowner if he is not the insured or the policyowner's estate if he is the insured.

A life insurance policy beneficiary whose right to the policy's proceeds can be cancelled or reduced by the policyowner at any time before the insured's death is known as a ***revocable beneficiary***. The vast majority of beneficiaries are revocable. However, the policyowner may designate an ***irrevocable beneficiary***—a life insurance policy beneficiary who has a vested interest in the policy proceeds even during the insured's lifetime because the policyowner has the right to change the beneficiary designation only after obtaining the beneficiary's consent. A vested interest is a property right that has taken effect and cannot be altered or changed without the consent of the person who owns the right. Because the irrevocable beneficiary has a vested interest, the policyowner cannot exercise some of her ownership rights—for example, to obtain a policy loan, surrender the policy for cash, or assign ownership of the policy—without the irrevocable beneficiary's consent.

Example: When Srini Mukundun purchased an insurance policy on his life, he named his sister Binta as the irrevocable beneficiary. Several years later, Srini married and wanted to change the beneficiary designation to his wife. At that time, however, Binta was terminally ill and unable to provide a written consent to the beneficiary change.

Analysis: Without the consent of the irrevocable beneficiary—or a person who qualifies to represent her—Srini cannot change the policy's beneficiary designation. If Binta dies, Srini can then change the beneficiary designation.

Policy Ownership Provisions

A policyowner has the right to transfer ownership of the policy to another person or entity. The transfer of ownership does not result in a change in the beneficiary unless the new owner takes further action.

An ***assignment*** is an agreement under which one party transfers some or all of his ownership rights in a particular property, such as a life insurance policy, to another party. Note that the insurance company is not a party to the assignment; nor is the insurer obligated to act in accordance with the terms of the assignment until it has written notice of the assignment. However, most individual life insurance policies include an ***assignment provision***, which describes the duties of the insurer and the policyowner when the policy is assigned. Policies typically state that an assignment will not be binding on the insurer unless the insurer is notified in writing of the assignment.

Example: McKenzie Abbott was the policyowner-insured of a life insurance policy issued by the Bloom Insurance Company and naming her husband, Julian, as the policy beneficiary. McKenzie made an assignment of her policy to her father, Edward Cochran, and sent a written notification of the assignment to Bloom. Edward then notified Bloom that he wished to change the beneficiary of the policy to McKenzie's daughter, Phyllis.

Analysis: Because McKenzie provided Bloom with written notification of her policy assignment, Bloom is obligated to name Edward as the new policyowner and then change the beneficiary of the policy from Julian to Phyllis.

Many life insurance policies currently being issued include a ***change of ownership provision***, which specifies a simple, direct method of transferring all the policy's ownership rights. Under this method, policy ownership can be transferred without requiring the policyowner to enter into a separate assignment agreement. According to a typical change of ownership policy provision, the policyowner can change ownership of the policy by notifying the insurer, in writing, of the change. When the insurer records the ownership change in its records, the change becomes effective as of the date the policyowner signed the written notification.

Example: Bertie Holloman purchased a $30,000 whole life insurance policy on the life of her daughter, Allison, shortly after Allison's second birthday. When Allison turned 21, Bertie decided to transfer ownership of the policy to Allison as a gift. Bertie notified her insurer, in writing, of the change in ownership.

Analysis: Upon receipt of the written notice from Bertie, the insurer changed its policy records to indicate that Allison was the owner of the policy.

The change of ownership provision typically gives the insurer the right to require that the ownership change be endorsed in the policy. In such a case, the policyowner must send the policy to the insurer, which adds an endorsement to the policy stating the name of the new owner.

Premium Payment Provision

Typically, a life insurance policy grants a policyowner the right to determine the premium payment mode. The ***premium payment mode*** is the frequency (monthly, quarterly, semiannually, or annually) at which renewal premiums are payable. More frequent premium payment modes often result in higher premium costs to offset the insurer's higher administrative costs to handle the more frequent payments.

In addition, policyowners use a number of methods to pay premiums, including

- **Check or money order delivered by mail or in person.**
- **Credit/debit card.**
- **Electronic funds transfer.** The policyowner authorizes the insurer to deduct premiums automatically from his bank account on premium due dates.
- **Payroll deduction.** The policyowner's employer deducts insurance premiums directly from the policyowner's paycheck and sends them to the insurer.

Exclusions

An ***exclusion*** is an insurance policy provision that describes circumstances under which the insurer will not pay benefits that otherwise would be payable. For example, insurance policies issued during periods of war or threats of war in the past sometimes included a *war exclusion clause*, which stated that the insurer would not pay the policy proceeds if the insured's death was connected with war. Today in Argentina, life insurance companies typically include a terrorism exclusion that states that the insurer will not pay the policy benefits if the insured's death was caused by the insured's active participation in terrorist activities, but death as the result of being a victim of those acts is not excluded. However, at this time, most insurers are not including terrorism exclusions in their life insurance policies.

Most policies issued now include a ***suicide exclusion provision***, which states that policy proceeds will not be paid if the insured dies as the result of suicide as defined within the policy within a specified period following the date of policy issue. The period of the exclusion is typically one or two years. Insurers include such a provision in the hopes of dissuading people who intend to commit suicide from purchasing life insurance policies. If the insured does commit suicide during the exclusion period, the insurer typically returns the premiums paid less the amount of any unpaid policy loan.

Policy Dividends Provision

In the United States, life insurance policies can be issued on either a participating or nonparticipating basis. A ***participating policy*** is simply a form of life insurance policy under which the policyowner shares in the insurance company's divisible surplus. A ***nonparticipating policy*** is exactly the opposite—a form of life insurance policy under which the policyowner does not share in the insurance company's divisible surplus. Surplus is the amount by which a company's assets exceed its liabilities and capital. Surplus results from a company's profitable operations. The amount of surplus available for distribution to owners of participating policies is called the ***divisible surplus***, and a policyowner's share of this divisible surplus is called a ***policy dividend***. Policy dividends are considered premium refunds, and, unlike dividends earned on shares of stock, they usually are not considered taxable income to the policyowner unless policy dividends received exceed premiums paid.

FAST FACT

Three-quarters of individual life policies purchased in the United States in 2002 were nonparticipating.[1]

Each cost element involved in setting premium rates, which we will discuss in more detail later in this chapter, is a potential source of surplus. If the people insured by a company experience a more favorable mortality rate than the company expected, fewer claims will be paid. If a company earns a higher rate of return on investments than anticipated, the investment income will be greater than needed to maintain the reserves at the required levels. If a company spends less money on administrative expense than was planned, additional funds will be available. An insurer that issues participating policies can distribute a portion of this surplus to the owners of those participating policies in the form of policy dividends.

In the United Kingdom and other countries that follow its system, such as many nations in Southeast Asia, participating policies are known as *with profits policies* and nonparticipating policies are known as *without profit policies*. In addition, in these countries, policy dividends are known as *reversionary bonuses* and *compounding reversionary bonuses*.

Any type of life insurance policy—term, cash value, and endowment—may be a participating or a nonparticipating policy. In addition, annuities may be issued on a participating and nonparticipating basis. Policy dividends are not guaranteed, but most insurers pay policy dividends on participating policies that are expected to remain in force over a long term. The insurer's board of directors generally approves annually the amount of policy dividends to be paid.

Participating life insurance policies contain a ***policy dividends provision*** that describes the ***dividend options***—the ways in which the policyowner may receive the policy dividends. Figure 6.2 describes the typical dividend options. The policyowner selects a dividend option when he completes the application; and he may change the option at any time, although a change to the additional term insurance option is subject to certain restrictions. Each participating policy specifies an ***automatic dividend option***, which is the dividend option that an insurer will apply if the policyowner does not choose an option. Typically, policies state that the paid-up additional insurance dividend option is the automatic dividend option.

Settlement Options Provision

Typically, the insurer pays the proceeds of a life insurance policy to the beneficiary in a lump sum following the insured's death. The insurer also may place the policy proceeds in an interest-bearing account established in the beneficiary's name. Because the beneficiary may withdraw funds from this account by check at any time and in any amount, such an account also is considered a lump-sum settlement.

FIGURE 6.2 Typical Dividend Options

- ***Cash Dividend Option.*** The insurer sends the policyowner a check in the amount of the policy dividend.
- ***Premium Reduction Dividend Option.*** The insurer applies policy dividends toward the payment of renewal premiums.
- ***Accumulation at Interest Dividend Option.*** The insurer retains the policy dividends on deposit to accumulate at interest. While the policy is in force, the policyowner may withdraw all or part of any accumulated dividends. Dividends on deposit when the insured dies usually are payable to the named beneficiary.
- ***Paid-Up Additional Insurance Dividend Option.*** The insurer uses each policy dividend as a net single premium to purchase additional insurance on the insured's life; the paid-up additional insurance is issued on the same plan as the basic policy and in whatever face amount the policy dividend can provide at the insured's age at the time of purchase. A ***net single premium*** is the lump sum of money the insurer needs to provide benefits for the policy.
- ***Additional Term Insurance Dividend Option.*** The insurer uses the dividend as a net single premium to purchase one-year term insurance on the insured's life.

A ***settlement options provision*** grants the policyowner or beneficiary several choices—***settlement options***—as to how the insurer will distribute a policy's proceeds. The policyowner may select a settlement option at the time of application or at any time while the policy is in force. Unless he has made the option irrevocable, the policyowner may change the option at any time during the insured's lifetime. When the policyowner selects an optional mode of settlement while the policy is in force, the terms of the settlement usually are incorporated into a *settlement agreement*, which is a contractual agreement that governs the rights and obligations of the parties after the insured's death.

If the policyowner has not chosen a settlement option at the time of the insured's death, then the beneficiary has the right to do so. The beneficiary also typically has the right to change the settlement option selected by the policyowner when the policy proceeds become available, unless the settlement option is irrevocable. When the beneficiary selects a settlement mode, the insurance company and the beneficiary usually enter into a settlement agreement that is sometimes referred to as a *supplementary contract*.

The typical settlement options are described in Figure 6.3.

Provisions Unique to Cash Value Policies

Cash value life insurance policies typically contain several provisions that are unique to this kind of insurance, including a policy loan provision, nonforfeiture provision, and—in the case of universal life insurance—policy withdrawal provision.

FIGURE 6.3 Settlement Options

- ***Interest Option.*** The insurer invests the policy proceeds for the policy beneficiary or policy ***payee***—the person or party who is to receive insurance policy proceeds in accordance with the terms of a settlement agreement—and the interest earned is paid out annually, semi-annually, quarterly, or monthly.
- ***Fixed Period Option.*** The insurer pays the policy proceeds and interest in a series of annual or more frequent installments for a preselected period.
- ***Fixed Amount Option.*** The insurer pays equal installments of a preselected amount until the policy proceeds, plus the interest earned, are exhausted.
- ***Life Income Option.*** The insurer pays the policy proceeds in periodic installments over the payee's lifetime.

Policy Loan Provision

A ***policy loan provision*** specifies the terms on which a policyowner may obtain a policy loan. A ***policy loan*** is a loan secured by a policy's cash value that an insurer makes to the owner of a cash value life insurance policy. A policy loan is actually an advance payment of part of the death benefit. Thus, a policyowner is not legally obligated to repay a policy loan or the interest that insurers typically charge. If the amount of a policy loan plus unpaid interest grows above the amount of the cash value while the insured is still living, the policy will lapse. If the insured dies while the loan is outstanding, the insurer deducts the amount of the loan, plus outstanding interest, from the death benefit.

Nonforfeiture Provision

Life insurance policyowners may choose to *surrender*—or terminate—their coverage at any time during the insured's lifetime. If a cash value policy is surrendered or lapses, the policyowner does not forfeit his interest in the policy's cash value. A ***nonforfeiture provision*** sets forth the options available to the owner of a cash value policy if the policy lapses or if the policyowner decides to surrender the policy. These nonforfeiture options include the cash payment nonforfeiture option and two continued insurance coverage nonforfeiture options—reduced paid-up insurance and extended term insurance. We discuss these options below along with the automatic nonforfeiture benefit.

Cash Payment Nonforfeiture Option

The ***cash payment nonforfeiture option*** gives the policyowner the right to receive the net cash surrender value in a lump-sum payment upon discontinuation of premium payments as a result of surrender or lapse. Cash value policies include a chart that lists the cash values available at various times. However, the amount of cash value actually available to a policyowner upon surrender or lapse of a policy may not be the exact cash value amount listed in the policy. The ***net cash surrender value*** is the actual cash value available to a policyowner upon policy surrender or lapse; it equals the cash value shown in the policy increased by any cash values of paid-up additions, policy dividend accumulations, and advance premium payments and decreased by outstanding policy loans and any charges imposed on the surrender.

> **Example:** Lise Andersen wants to surrender her whole life insurance policy for its net cash surrender value. The cash value amount shown in her policy is $5,000, and the cash value of the paid-up additions purchased by Lise is $150. Lise also has accumulated $250 in policy dividends, has made an advance premium payment of $200, and has an outstanding policy loan plus interest of $1,000.

Analysis: The net cash surrender value that the insurance company paid to Lise was $4,600. That amount was calculated as follows:

$5,000	Cash value shown in policy
+ 150	Cash value of paid-up additions
+ 250	Amount of policy dividend accumulations
+ 200	Amount of advance premium payment
–1,000	Outstanding policy loan plus interest
$4,600	Amount insurer paid to Lise

Continued Insurance Coverage Nonforfeiture Option—
Reduced Paid-Up Insurance

The ***reduced paid-up insurance nonforfeiture option*** allows the owner of a policy with a cash value to discontinue premium payments and to use the policy's net cash surrender value to purchase paid-up insurance of the same plan as the original policy. Under this nonforfeiture option, the policy's net cash surrender value is used as a single premium to buy a policy with the same duration as the original policy but a lower face amount (hence the term *reduced*). The coverage issued under this option builds a cash value, and the policyowner continues to have the right to surrender the policy for its cash value and the right to receive policy dividends if the original policy was issued on a participating basis. However, supplemental benefits that were available on the original policy usually are not available on the paid-up policy.

Continued Insurance Coverage Nonforfeiture Option—
Extended Term Insurance

The ***extended term insurance nonforfeiture option*** allows the owner of a policy with a cash value to discontinue premium payments and to use the policy's net cash surrender value as a net single premium to purchase term insurance for the full face amount of the original policy for as long as the net cash surrender value can provide. The length of the term depends on the policy's face amount, the amount of the net cash surrender value, the sex of the insured, and the insured's age when the policyowner exercises the extended term option. Typically, a policyowner who elects the extended term nonforfeiture option loses his rights to policy loans, policy dividends, and supplemental benefits. However, the policyowner does retain the right to cancel the extended term insurance before the end of its term and receive the remaining original cash value.

Automatic Nonforfeiture Benefit

The ***automatic nonforfeiture benefit*** is the specified nonforfeiture benefit that becomes effective automatically when a premium for a cash value life insurance policy is not paid by the end of the grace period and the policyowner has not elected another nonforfeiture option. While the extended term insurance benefit is the most typical automatic nonforfeiture benefit, laws in a few jurisdictions require that policies include an automatic premium loan (APL) provision and specify that the automatic nonforfeiture option is the automatic premium loan. An ***automatic premium loan (APL) provision*** allows an insurer automatically to pay an overdue premium for a policyowner by making a loan against the policy's cash value as long as the cash value equals or exceeds the amount of the premium due. The use of an automatic premium loan keeps the original policy in force for the full amount of coverage, net of the loan, including all supplemental benefits. The APL provision also is widely used in policies issued in jurisdictions where it is not required by law.

Policy Withdrawal Provision

Universal life insurance policies typically allow policyowners to make withdrawals. A ***withdrawal*** is a payment of a portion of the cash value of a universal life policy to the policyowner while the policy is in force. A ***policy withdrawal provision*** permits the universal life policyowner to reduce the amount in the policy's cash value by withdrawing up to the amount of the cash value. Insurers do not charge interest on these withdrawals; rather, the amount of the cash value is reduced by the amount of the withdrawal. Many policies impose a charge for each withdrawal and limit the number of withdrawals allowed each year. In addition, in Option B universal life policies that have an increasing death benefit, a withdrawal also will reduce the death benefit by the amount of the withdrawal.

Individual Life Insurance Pricing

Insurers are in the business of accepting someone else's risk in return for a price. As we mentioned at the beginning of the chapter, pricing is the process of determining the amount to charge a customer for a product. In this section, we discuss how insurance companies price individual life insurance policies.

Premium Rates

Actuaries establish the premium rates that an insurance company will charge for its products. An ***actuary*** is a technical expert in insurance, annuities, and financial instruments who applies mathematical knowledge to industry and company statistics and performs all of the calculations needed to ensure that an insurance company's products are financially sound. The three most important factors that actuaries consider as they establish premium rates for life insurance policies are

- Operating expenses
- Cost of benefits
- Investment earnings

A simplified formula for premium rate calculations is shown below.

Premium rate	=	Operating expenses	+	Cost of benefits	−	Investment earnings

When calculating premium rates, actuaries make assumptions about these three primary factors, as well as many others. ***Actuarial assumptions*** are the estimated values on which an insurer bases its product pricing calculations. In this section, we discuss the three major factors that affect product pricing, or premium rate, calculations.[2]

Operating Expenses

The amount of company operating expenses that an actuary includes in a product's pricing design is based on an estimate of the costs—other than the costs of benefits—associated with developing and supporting the product. Such costs include maintenance of the company's offices, personnel costs, systems costs, taxes, and product development, distribution, and promotion costs.

Cost of Benefits

A product's ***cost of benefits*** is the value of all contractually required benefits that a product promises to pay. The cost of benefits equals all of the insurer's potential payments of benefit obligations to customers times the expected probability that each benefit will be payable. ***Mortality***—the incidence of death in a specified group of people—is an important element of the cost of benefits for all life insurance products because the mortality rate determines the probability that benefits involving mortality risk will be payable. A ***mortality rate*** is the percentage rate at which death occurs among a defined group of people of a specified age and sometimes of a specified gender. The cost of benefits for life insurance products depends in part upon the mortality rate times the death benefit amount.

www.CartoonStock.com

Although an insurer cannot predict when a specific person will die, it can predict with a fair amount of accuracy the rate at which a great number of people die each year. The ability to make this prediction stems largely from the fact that life insurers accumulate and share statistical information on mortality. The information is organized into ***mortality tables***, which are charts that show the expected death rates among a particular group at each age—that is, how many people in each age group may be expected to die in a given year.

Mortality tables show that, on average, women live longer than men. Recognizing this difference in expected life spans, most insurers price equivalent life insurance policies at a lower rate for women than for men of the same age.

Life insurance policies with cash values have additional contractual benefits—cash surrender values and withdrawals—that must be taken into consideration when pricing the product.

Investment Earnings

Premiums are the primary source of funds that insurers use to pay policy claims, and investment earnings are the secondary source. Because most policies are in force for some time before claims become payable, insurers invest the premiums. The earnings from these investments provide additional funds that insurers can use to pay claims. The availability of investment earnings enables insurers to charge lower premium rates than they could if they relied on premiums alone to fund claims. To illustrate the importance of investment earnings, 25 percent of the total income of U.S. life insurance companies in 2002 resulted from investment earnings.[3]

Premium Amounts

Keep in mind that actuaries do not set the premium amount that each policyowner pays for coverage. Rather, they establish premium rates for blocks of policies. A ***block of policies*** is a group of policies issued to insureds who are all the same age, the same sex, and in the same risk classification. For example, an insurer may classify into one block all term policies issued to males age 35 who are nonsmokers and have no significant medical history. In most cases, premium rates for a block of policies are based on a $1,000 life insurance coverage amount, known as a *coverage unit*. Consequently, the premium rate typically is expressed as the rate per thousand; and the annual premium amount is calculated by multiplying the premium rate by the number of coverage units.

Example: The annual premium rate for a $50,000 life insurance policy might be expressed as $3.50 per thousand.

Analysis: The annual premium amount for that policy would be $175. That amount is calculated as follows:

$3.50	Price per coverage unit ($1,000 of coverage)
× 50	Number of coverage units ($50,000 ÷ $1,000)
$175	Annual premium amount

Other factors, such as the application of policy fees and policy dividends, may affect the premium amount actually charged to a policyowner.

Level Premium Pricing System

If insurers always charged policyowners the amount it cost to provide coverage at the insured's current age, then the mortality expense would be low when the insured was young and increase as the insured grew older. Most people would not be able to pay for the cost of insurance in their later years when mortality rates and expenses are high. Thus, insurers developed the ***level premium pricing system***, which is a life insurance pricing system that allows the policyowner to pay the same premium amount each year the policy is in force. This pricing system is used to price many types of cash value life insurance, term insurance that provides coverage for more than one year, and endowment insurance. Figure 6.4 shows the difference between the premium rate of one-year term policies issued at various ages compared with the premium rate of a level premium policy.

Insurers are able to charge the same premium (a level premium) throughout the premium-paying period (whether that period is the duration of life, a limited-payment period, or a policy term) because premium rates charged for these level premium policies are higher than necessary to pay claims and expenses during the early years of coverage when the mortality rate is low. During these early years, the premiums paid in excess of that needed to cover the costs of claims and expenses

FIGURE 6.4 Comparison of Monthly Premium Rates for One-Year Term Policies Issued at Various Ages and Level Premium Policy

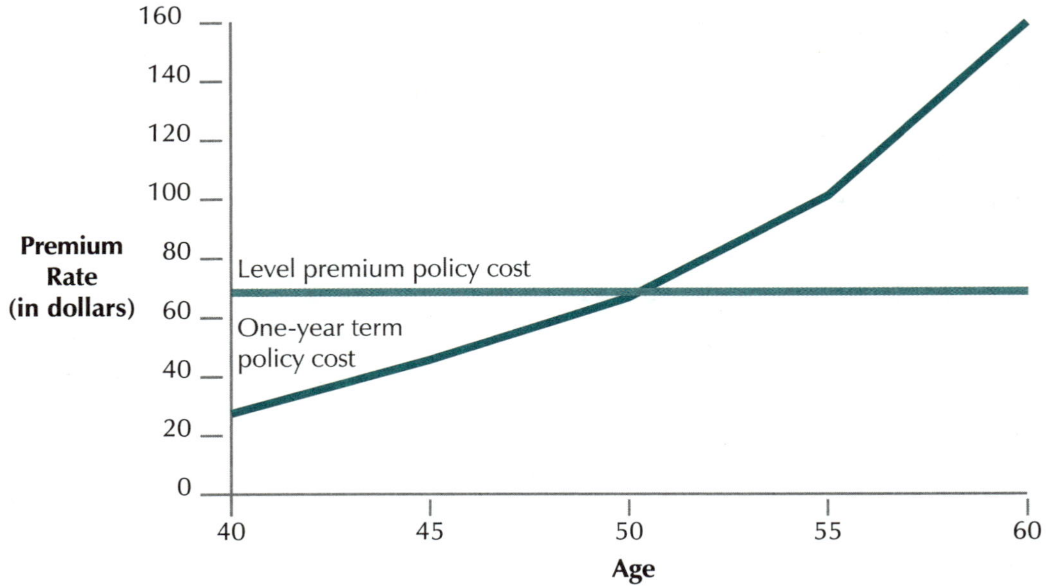

Source: Excerpted from Harriett E. Jones and Dani L. Long, *Principles of Insurance: Life, Health, and Annuities,* 2nd ed. (Atlanta: LOMA, © 1999), 97. Used with permission; all rights reserved.

are invested by the insurance company. As the insureds in a block of level premium policies age and the mortality rate increases, the insurer uses these excess premiums, plus investment earnings, to pay the increasing claims. Thus, the premium rate on these level premium policies can remain the same throughout the duration of the policy.

Key Terms

pricing
free-look provision
entire contract provision
misrepresentation
material misrepresentation
incontestability provision
grace period provision
grace period
lapse
reinstatement provision
misstatement of age or sex provision
contingent beneficiary
revocable beneficiary
irrevocable beneficiary
assignment
assignment provision
change of ownership provision

premium payment mode
exclusion
suicide exclusion provision
participating policy
nonparticipating policy
divisible surplus
policy dividend
policy dividends provision
dividend options
automatic dividend option
cash dividend option
premium reduction dividend option
accumulation at interest dividend option
paid-up additional insurance dividend option
net single premium
additional term insurance dividend option
settlement options provision
settlement options
interest option
payee
fixed period option
fixed amount option
life income option
policy loan provision
policy loan
nonforfeiture provision
cash payment nonforfeiture option
net cash surrender value
reduced paid-up insurance nonforfeiture option
extended term insurance nonforfeiture option
automatic nonforfeiture benefit
automatic premium loan (APL) provision
withdrawal
policy withdrawal provision
actuary
actuarial assumptions
cost of benefits
mortality
mortality rate
mortality table
block of policies
level premium pricing system

Endnotes

1. ACLI, *Life Insurers Fact Book: 2003* (Washington, DC: American Council of Life Insurers, 2003), 97.
2. Much of the information in this section is from Susan Conant, *Product Design for Life Insurance and Annuities* (Atlanta: LOMA, 2001)
3. ACLI, *Life Insurers Fact Book: 2003* (Washington, DC: American Council of Life Insurers, 2003), 64.

chapter

7

Group Life Insurance

Finished on 11/26/08
Done:

outline

Fundamentals of Group Life Insurance

Types of Group Life Insurance

- Group Term Life Insurance
- Group Accidental Death and Dismemberment
- Group Cash Value Life Insurance
- Group Creditor Life Insurance

Supplemental Benefits for Group Life Insurance Policies

Group Insurance Policy Provisions

- Group Life and Health Insurance Policy Provisions
- Group Life Insurance Policy Provisions

Group Insurance Pricing

- Premium Rates
- Premium Amounts
- Premium Refunds

objectives

After reading this chapter, you should be able to

- Describe the parties to and the basic operations of a group life insurance policy
- Describe group term life, accidental death and dismemberment, cash value life insurance, and creditor life insurance
- Identify and describe three types of group supplemental benefits
- Describe the typical group life insurance policy provisions
- Distinguish among experience rating, manual rating, and blended rating

As we explained in Chapter 5, the primary difference between an individual life insurance policy and a group life insurance policy is that while the former insures one person, the latter insures a number of people. In some countries, the amount of group life insurance in force almost equals that of individual life insurance in force. For example, in 2002, group life insurance represented 42 percent of the life insurance in force in the United States and 48 percent of the life insurance in force in Canada.[1] The popularity of group life insurance in these countries stems largely from the fact that the product is often offered by employers to employees as an employee benefit.

In this chapter, we begin with an explanation of the fundamentals of group life insurance. We then discuss the types of group life insurance as well as group supplemental benefits. We conclude with a discussion of typical policy provisions and pricing.

Fundamentals of Group Life Insurance

The group life insurance policy is a written contract, and the parties to the contract are the insurance company and the policyholder. The ***policyholder*** is the employer or other type of organization that decides what kind of coverage to purchase for the group, negotiates the terms of and enters into the group insurance contract with the insurer, and usually administers part or all of the coverage.

Note that we use the term *policyholder* rather than *policyowner* because the party that enters into a group insurance contract does not have the same ownership rights as the owner of an individual insurance policy. Instead, some of these rights, such as the right to designate a beneficiary, are granted to the ***group insureds***, or the *group life insureds*, who are the group members insured by a group insurance policy. Group insureds often are referred to as *certificate holders* because they receive a ***certificate of insurance***, which is a document that a group policyholder delivers to each group insured that describes the coverage provided and the group insureds' rights under the contract.

Some group insurance policies cover group insureds and their dependents, but dependents do not have the same policy rights as do group insureds. For example, a covered dependent typically cannot designate his beneficiary; instead, the policy may grant the group insured the right to name the dependent's beneficiary or may specify that the dependent's beneficiary is the group insured.

Group insurance differs from individual insurance primarily in the area of underwriting. Group insurance underwriting focuses on the characteristics of the group and typically does not require the proposed individual group insureds to present evidence of insurability. The group characteristics taken into consideration by the insurer include the size, stability, and activities of the group.

When underwriting a group policy, the insurer also will determine whether the group was formed for a reason other than obtaining insurance. People who think they would not qualify for individual insurance would be more likely to join a group formed solely to obtain group insurance coverage than would individuals who can obtain individual insurance. Thus, claims would be higher for a group formed solely to obtain group insurance coverage than they would be with a group formed for purposes other than to obtain insurance coverage. Figure 7.1 explains the types of groups that typically are eligible for purchasing group insurance. Because most group insurance policies insure a group of employees, our discussions of group insurance in this text will concentrate on single-employer group policies.

The policyholder is responsible for making premium payments, although group insureds may contribute a portion or all of the premium amount. In employee benefit plans, such as group insurance, a premium payment is sometimes referred to as a ***contribution***, which is a payment from any source to fund the plan's benefits. A ***contributory plan*** is an employee benefit plan under which participating employees must contribute all or a portion of the cost to be covered under the plan. A ***noncontributory plan*** is an employee benefit plan under which participating employees are not required to contribute any part of the cost for coverage.

The amount of life insurance that a group policy provides for each group insured is specified in a schedule found in the group policy known

FIGURE 7.1 Types of Groups

- Single-employer groups
- Labor union groups
- Multiple-employer groups
- Association groups
- Debtor-creditor groups
- Credit union groups
- Discretionary groups

FIGURE 7.2 Examples of Group Life Insurance Policy Benefit Schedules

Benefit Schedule Based on Annual Salary

Salary	Amount of Life Insurance
Less than $60,000	1 × salary
$60,000 to $100,000	2 × salary

Benefit Schedule Based on Standard Amount

Salary	Amount of Life Insurance
Any	$50,000 per group insured

Benefit Schedule Based on Job Classification

Job Classification	Amount of Life Insurance
Nonmanagement personnel	$30,000
Supervisors	$50,000
Managers	$100,000
Officers	$200,000

as a ***benefit schedule***. One type of benefit schedule bases the amount of coverage on a specified formula, such as a multiple of each employee's salary. A second type of benefit schedule specifies the same amount of coverage for all group insureds. A third type of benefit schedule specifies a different amount of coverage for each class of group insureds. Figure 7.2 illustrates these benefit schedules.

Types of Group Life Insurance

The majority of group life insurance policies issued are yearly renewable term (YRT) policies. Group accidental death and dismemberment coverage also is popular. Groups apply for cash value policies infrequently.

In this section, we discuss group term life insurance, group accidental death and dismemberment insurance, and group cash value policies. We also discuss group creditor life insurance, which differs from other group insurance in that the policyholder is also the beneficiary.

Group Term Life Insurance

The YRT insurance coverage under group life policies is similar to YRT coverage under individual policies. Group insureds do not have to present evidence of insurability each year at time of renewal, and the insurer may change the premium rate each year.

If an employer pays for part or all of an employee's group term insurance coverage, income tax laws sometimes consider the cost of such coverage provided by the employer as taxable income to the employee. For example, in the United States, an employee can receive up to \$50,000 of noncontributory group term insurance coverage without incurring an income tax liability. However, an employee must pay income taxes on the employer's cost of providing group term life insurance over \$50,000. The cost of this coverage, which is not the same as the premium paid by the employer, is determined by reference to a government table.

Example: Laurel Martin and Erik Stein are employed by the Atrium Corporation and are enrolled in Atrium's noncontributory group term insurance plan. Laurel has \$75,000 of coverage and Erik has \$45,000 of coverage.

Analysis: Laurel and Erik are each entitled to receive \$50,000 of noncontributory group term insurance coverage without incurring an income tax liability. Erik has \$45,000 of coverage, so he is not required to pay income tax on this benefit. Laurel, however, has \$75,000 of coverage, and she must pay income tax on the employer's cost to provide her with the additional \$25,000 of coverage.

Employers sometimes fund other employee benefit plans with group YRT insurance. For example, an employer may have established a ***survivor income plan***, which is an employee benefit plan that provides periodic income payments to specified dependents who survive a covered group member. Survivor income benefits typically are funded by group YRT insurance. In other words, when a group insured dies, the proceeds of his YRT insurance pay the benefits promised his surviving dependents under the survivor income plan.

Group Accidental Death and Dismemberment

Groups also apply for accidental death and dismemberment (AD&D) policies and for AD&D supplemental benefits attached to a group term life policy. When the accidental death benefit is added to a group term life policy, the accidental death benefit amount typically is equal to the amount of the death benefit provided under the term policy. Many AD&D policies and supplemental benefits issued to employer groups provide an additional

"How are you fixed for group insurance?"

www.CartoonStock.com

travel accident benefit for accidents that occur while the employee is traveling for the employer. In other words, an employee may die as the result of an accident that occurs while he is traveling. If he is simply on vacation, his beneficiary receives benefits under the AD&D coverage; if he is on a business trip, his beneficiary receives benefits under the AD&D coverage plus an additional benefit because he was traveling for the employer.

Example: Daisy Fitzpatrick is covered under the group insurance coverage provided by the Sycamore Company. Sycamore provides $100,000 of group term life insurance, $50,000 of group accidental death and dismemberment (AD&D) insurance, and $25,000 of business travel accident insurance.

Analysis: If Daisy dies in an accident while she is traveling on business for Sycamore, then her beneficiary is entitled to receive $175,000 in benefits ($100,000 + $50,000 + $25,000). If Daisy dies in an accident while she is on vacation, then her beneficiary is entitled to receive $150,000 in benefits ($100,000 + $50,000).

Group Cash Value Life Insurance

Group cash value life insurance is not as popular as group term life in the United States primarily because it does not receive the same favorable income tax treatment that group term life receives. However, some employers offer group cash value life insurance because they want their employees to have coverage that will continue after retirement, when group term insurance typically ends. Many employers that offer group cash value coverage do so as an optional, supplemental coverage that employees may purchase in addition to their group term life insurance.

The characteristics of group cash value insurance vary depending on the type of policy selected by the group policyholder. The three most common group cash value life insurance policies are group paid-up, level premium whole life, and group universal life. Some employers offer group variable universal life.

Group Paid-Up Plans

Group paid-up plans combine paid-up whole life insurance with decreasing amounts of term insurance in a contributory plan under which

- The employee's premium contribution is used as a net single premium to purchase paid-up whole life insurance

- The employer's premium contribution is used to purchase the amount of group term insurance required to bring the employee's total coverage up to a predetermined amount

The total amount of paid-up insurance on each group insured increases each year, and the amount of group term insurance that the employer must purchase for participating employees decreases each year.

The paid-up whole life stays in force after the employee retires or otherwise terminates his membership in the group, while the term life ends on these occasions. The premium paid by the employer is eligible for the favorable tax treatment that group YRT premiums receive.

Level Premium Whole Life Plans

Level premium whole life plans issued to groups typically are of the limited-payment type, such as paid-up-at-age-65 whole life. If the group whole life plan is noncontributory, the employee typically has no right to the cash value. Thus, if the employee leaves the group, his coverage terminates and any accumulated cash value belongs to the employer. If the group whole life plan is contributory, the employee has a right to the cash value up to the amount of the employee's premium contributions.

Group Universal Life Plans

Group universal life plans function much like individual universal life plans. The group insured typically pays the entire premium, and she chooses the premium amount she wants to pay. Thus, the size of the cash value depends on the size of the group insured's premium payments, and the cash value belongs entirely to the group insured. In addition, group insureds may change their coverage amounts under a group universal life plan, but they may be required to provide evidence of insurability to do so.

Group universal life plans differ from most other group life insurance plans in that under a group universal life plan, an individual's coverage is ***portable***, which means that a group insured who leaves the group can continue his coverage under the group plan. In most other types of group life insurance plans, an individual who leaves the group and wishes to retain the coverage can do so only by converting her group insurance coverage to an individual insurance policy.

Group Variable Universal Life Plans

Group variable universal life plans are similar to group universal life plans. However, as with individual variable universal life insurance, the participants are given a choice of different options for investing their cash value.

Group Creditor Life Insurance

Group creditor life insurance is insurance issued to a creditor, such as a bank, to insure the lives of the creditor's current and future borrowers. Unlike other group life insurance policies, group creditor life policies designate the policyholder—the creditor—as the beneficiary to receive the benefit payable when a group insured dies. The amount of coverage on each group insured always is equal to the amount of debt that person owes to the policyholder-creditor.

Typically, the debtor pays the premium for group creditor life insurance, subject to maximums set by law. However, the creditor may pay all or a portion of the premium.

Although a creditor may require a borrower to purchase insurance to secure a loan, the creditor may not require a borrower to purchase that insurance from the creditor. In other words, the borrower has the right to purchase coverage from any source he chooses.

Supplemental Benefits for Group Life Insurance Policies

Supplemental benefits for group life insurance policies may be added as riders or written as separate contracts. The most typical group supplemental benefits are accidental death and dismemberment insurance, survivor income benefits, waiver of premium for disability, and dependent life insurance. We discussed AD&D insurance and survivor income benefits in the previous section. Waiver of premium for disability, which we

FAST FACT

Of group life policies in force in the United States in 2002, 26 percent provided for waiver of premium for disability, comprising 52 percent of the group life face amount in force at $3.6 trillion.[2]

covered in Chapter 5, also can be found as a policy provision in large group plans. Group supplemental dependent life insurance operates in basically the same manner as a spouse and children's insurance rider, which we discussed in the section on individual life insurance supplemental benefits. Group long-term care insurance is becoming increasingly popular.

Group Insurance Policy Provisions

Just as individual life insurance policies are contracts composed of contract provisions, so too are group life insurance policies. These provisions are also somewhat standard throughout the industry. Some of these provisions also are found in group health insurance policies.

Group Life and Health Insurance Policy Provisions

The four provisions we discuss in this section—eligibility, incontestability, grace period, and termination—are included in both life and health group insurance policies.

Eligibility Provisions

Each group policy describes who is eligible for coverage under the policy. For example, in an employer group, eligible employees are those who fall in a specified class based on conditions of employment, such as salary, occupation, or length of employment. For example, an eligible employee class may be all full-time employees.

The following two provisions are the most common eligibility requirements for an employer group insurance policy:

- ***Actively-at-work provision.*** This provision states that to be eligible for coverage, an employee must be actively at work—rather than ill or on leave—on the day the coverage is to take effect. If the employee is not actively at work on that day, coverage for that group insured does not become effective until the next day that the employee is actively at work. An employee may not claim that he is actively at work on a weekend, holiday, or vacation.

- ***Probationary period.*** This provision specifies the length of time—typically from one to six months—that a new group member must wait before becoming eligible to enroll in an employee benefit plan. Under a noncontributory plan, the group member's coverage will begin automatically at the end of the probationary period. Under a contributory plan, the probationary period is followed by an ***enrollment period***, which is a specified time, usually 31 days, during which a new group member who is eligible for group insurance coverage may first enroll for that coverage, usually without having to provide evidence of insurability.

Example: Arthur and Winnie Crawford recently relocated to a different city and will begin working at new jobs on June 1. They both will be eligible for coverage under group life insurance policies provided by their employers. Both policies provide similar coverage, and both include a 30-day probationary period, the last day of which is June 30. The primary difference is that Arthur's coverage is contributory, whereas Winnie's coverage is noncontributory. They want to determine when their group insurance coverages will become effective.

Analysis: Because Arthur's coverage is contributory, his 30-day probationary period will be followed by a 31 day enrollment period. At any time during the enrollment period, he may enroll for the coverage without having to provide evidence of insurability. Thus, Arthur's coverage will become effective as soon as he enrolls within the enrollment period—anytime between July 1 and July 31.

Winnie's noncontributory coverage will automatically become effective on the first day following the end of the 30-day probationary period—July 1.

Incontestability Provision

The incontestability provision in a group insurance policy limits to two years from the date of issue the period during which the insurer may use statements in the group insurance application to contest the validity of the master group insurance contract. Insurers rarely contest the validity of group insurance contracts, though, because material misrepresentation is a rare occurrence with these contracts.

However, the incontestability provision in a group insurance policy also allows the insurer to contest an individual group insured's coverage without contesting the validity of the master group contract itself. If a group insured is required to provide evidence of insurability in an application for group coverage (which is rare) and he makes a material misrepresentation, the insurer has the right to contest the individual's coverage for one or two years, depending on the policy provision, after the date of the group insured's application.

Example: Joseph Carmichael was required to fill out a medical questionnaire in order to be eligible for group medical expense coverage. In completing the questionnaire, Joseph made material misrepresentations about his health. Eleven months later,

Joseph filed a claim for medical expense benefits. While investigating the claim, the insurance company discovered Joseph's material misrepresentation. The group policy contained a typical two-year incontestability provision.

Analysis: The insurer discovered the material misrepresentation within two years after Joseph's coverage became effective. As a result, the insurer had the right to contest Joseph's coverage on the basis of those material misrepresentations. The validity of the master group insurance contract was not affected by Joseph's material misrepresentations.

Grace Period Provision

Group life and health insurance policies typically contain a grace period provision that specifies a length of time—usually 31 days—following a premium due date within which the policyholder may pay the renewal premium without penalty and during which coverage will be continued despite nonpayment of the premium. If the group policyholder does not pay the premium by the end of this period, the group policy will terminate. Unlike an individual policy, a group life policy's grace period provision specifies that if the policy terminates for nonpayment of premium, the policyholder is legally obligated to pay the premium for the coverage provided during the grace period.

Termination Provisions

Termination provisions in group insurance policies must cover two situations: (1) the termination of the group insurance policy and (2) the termination of a group insured's coverage. Typically, a group policyholder may terminate a policy at any time by notifying the insurer in writing. Subject to certain conditions stated in the group policy, the insurer has a similar right to terminate the policy on any premium due date. For example, if the insurer had established a requirement that a certain number of group members obtain coverage and that requirement is not met, the insurer may notify the policyholder in writing that the coverage will terminate upon a specified premium due date.

Most group insurance policies provide that a group insured's coverage will terminate if the group insured

- Ceases to be a member of a class of persons eligible for coverage
- Terminates her employment or group membership
- Fails to make a required contribution to the premium

FIGURE 7.3 Application of Incontestability, Grace Period, and Termination Provisions in Group Life and Health Insurance Policies

	As Applied to a Group Contract	As Applied to Individuals Covered Under a Group Contract
Incontestability provision	The insurer can contest the validity of the group contract for two years following policy issue on the grounds of material misrepresentation in the application.	The insurer can contest the validity of an individual insured's coverage for one or two years, depending on the policy provision, following the insured's application for coverage. Termination of the insured's coverage does not terminate the group contract.
Grace period provision	The grace period for the group contract is usually 31 days. The group policyholder is responsible for paying premiums for any coverage provided during the grace period.	The grace period for individual insureds is usually 10 days if premiums are paid monthly and 31 days if premiums are paid less often than monthly. Termination of the insured's coverage does not terminate the group contract.
Termination provision	The group contract terminates if (1) the policyholder elects to cancel the coverage or (2) the insurer determines that the group no longer satisfies conditions specified in the policy.	A group insured's coverage generally terminates if the insured (1) ceases to be eligible for coverage, (2) terminates employment or group membership, or (3) fails to make a required contribution to premium.

Figure 7.3 summarizes the incontestability, grace period, and termination provisions as they apply to a group master life or health insurance policy and as they apply to an individual covered under the policy.

Group Life Insurance Policy Provisions

The final four provisions we discuss in this section—misstatement of age, conversion, beneficiary, and settlement options—are typical of group life insurance policies but not of group health insurance policies.

Misstatement of Age

As we have learned, individual life insurance policies typically specify that the insurer will adjust the death benefit in the event of a misstatement of age or sex. By contrast and because the group insured's death benefit is specified in the benefit schedule, group life insurance policies provide that the insurer will adjust retroactively the amount of premium required for the coverage if the age is misstated. Group life insurance is rated on a unisex basis, so policies do not have a misstatement of sex provision.

Conversion Privilege

A ***conversion privilege*** allows a group insured whose coverage terminates for certain reasons to convert the group life coverage to an individual life insurance policy. Typically, a group insured does not have to present evidence of insurability to convert if she purchases the new individual policy within a specified conversion period, which is usually 31 days after the group coverage terminates. If a group insured dies within the conversion period without exercising her conversion privilege, insurers will pay a death benefit, which is the largest amount that the insurer would have issued as an individual policy to the group insured.

Beneficiary Provision

Each group insured, rather than the group policyholder, has the right to name her own beneficiary under the terms of a group life insurance policy, with the restriction that she not designate the group policyholder as the beneficiary. The only exception is with creditor group life in which, as mentioned earlier, the group policyholder—the creditor—is always the beneficiary.

Settlement Options

When a group insured dies while his coverage is in force, the beneficiary usually receives the death benefit in a lump sum. If a group policy does offer optional modes of settlement such as those offered under individual life insurance policies that we discussed in Chapter 6, the group insured and/or the beneficiary has the right to select an option. However, they may select the life income option only if the death benefit is at least a stated minimum.

Group Insurance Pricing

Because of the expense savings inherent in the operation of group insurance policies, insurers can provide coverage for a number of people at a cost that is relatively low compared to the cost of individual insurance. For example, policy issue costs and sales costs are generally lower for group insurance than for individual insurance. In the following sections, we explain how the insurer establishes the premium rates to charge for a group's coverage, how specific premium amounts are calculated, and how excess premiums can be refunded. Note that the general principles of pricing explained in this section can apply to group health insurance policies as well as group life insurance policies.

Premium Rates

Insurance companies typically establish group insurance premium rates on a case-by-case basis; that is, an insurer evaluates each group and establishes a premium rate that will be adequate to pay the group's claims and equitable to the policyholder. Insurers usually guarantee the group's premium rate for only one year and may change the rate at the beginning of each policy year or on any premium due date, as long as changes do not occur more than once in any 12-month period.

To calculate group premium rates, insurers must determine what costs they will incur in (1) providing the benefits promised by the group policy and (2) administering the group policy. Insurers use experience rating, manual rating, or a blend of both to estimate these costs. Figure 7.4 contains explanations of these group premium rating methodologies.

FIGURE 7.4 Group Premium Rating Methodologies

- ***Experience rating*** is a method of calculating group insurance premium rates by which the insurer bases the premium rate on the particular group's prior claims and expense experience. Insurers typically use experience rating for setting renewal premiums for large groups.
- ***Manual rating*** is a method of calculating group insurance premium rates for broad classes of groups, especially for groups with no credible claims and expense experience. The insurer often uses its own past experience with incurred claims and expenses to develop manual rates. However, an insurer may use industry studies on mortality and expenses when the insurer has limited data on a new product or market or wants to evaluate its own data. Insurers typically use manual rating for (1) groups that have not been insured previously and therefore don't have experience of their own and (2) small groups whose experience is unreliable because of their small size.
- ***Blended rating*** is a method of calculating premium rates for group insurance that combines manual rating and experience rating. Insurers use blended rating for groups that are too small to rely fully on experience rating yet large enough to consider their claims and expense experience to be significant.

In addition to determining whether or to what extent a group's own experience can be used, an insurer must consider a number of other factors when setting group premium rates. For example, benefit costs depend not only on the claims experience (that is, the mortality rates), but also on the actual benefits provided by the policy.

In addition, the administrative costs incurred will depend not only on the insurer's or policyholder's expense experience but on how much of the administrative functions the group policyholder will handle. The administration of a group insurance policy is largely a matter of record keeping—for example, maintaining the names, benefit amounts, and beneficiaries of the group insureds and updating the records as members join or leave the group. If the policyholder maintains the records, the administrative expenses will be lower than if the insurer is responsible for record maintenance.

Premium Amounts

A premium rate typically is calculated on the basis of a stated benefit unit of $1,000. In other words, the premium rate is stated as a rate per $1,000 of death benefit provided by the group life insurance policy. Although the premium rate generally is guaranteed for one year, the premium amount, which is typically payable monthly, varies depending on the amount of insurance in force that month. Thus, a group life insurance policy requires a monthly premium amount that is equal to the premium rate per $1,000 of coverage multiplied by the number of benefit units ($1,000 of coverage) in force that month. If an employer hires several new employees one month, the premium amount the employer pays to the insurer will increase; the premium rate per $1,000 of coverage, though, does not change during the year.

Example: The Hillside Company provides $25,000 of noncontributory group life insurance coverage for each of its full-time employees. The current monthly premium rate for this coverage is $0.35 per $1,000 of coverage. In January, Hillside had 10 full-time employees. In March, Hillside hired two new full-time employees, who became eligible for group life insurance coverage in April.

Analysis: In January, February, and March, Hillside provided $25,000 of group life insurance coverage to 10 employees. Thus, the premium amount payable in each of those three months was $87.50.

$ 25,000	Coverage per employee
× 10	Number of employees
$250,000	**Total group coverage**

$ 0.35	Monthly premium rate
× 250	Number of coverage units ($250,000÷$1,000)
$ 87.50	**Monthly premium payments**

In April, Hillside provided $25,000 of group life insurance coverage to 12 employees. Thus, the premium amount payable in April was $105.

$ 25,000	Coverage per employee
× 12	Number of employees
$300,000	**Total group coverage**

$ 0.35	Monthly premium rate
× 300	Number of coverage units ($300,000 ÷ $1,000)
$ 105	**Monthly premium payment**

Premium Refunds

The insurer may refund a portion of the group insurance premium to the policyholder at the end of each policy year if warranted by claims and expense experience. All premium refunds are payable to the group policyholder, even if the plan is contributory. If the amount of the refund to the policyholder of a contributory plan is greater than the portion of the group premium that was paid out of the policyholder's funds, the excess must be used for the benefit of the group insureds, for example by paying a portion of the group insureds' contributions during the next year.

Key Terms

policyholder
group insured
certificate of insurance
contribution
contributory plan
noncontributory plan
benefit schedule
survivor income plan
portable
group creditor life insurance
actively-at-work provision
probationary period
enrollment period
conversion privilege
experience rating
manual rating
blended rating

Endnotes

1. ACLI, *Life Insurers Fact Book: 2003* (Washington, DC: American Council of Life Insurers, 2003), 103; Canadian Life and Health Insurance Association, Inc., *Canadian Life and Health Insurance Facts,* 2003 ed., (Toronto: Canadian Life and Health Insurance Association, 2003), 6
2. ACLI, *Life Insurers Fact Book: 2003* (Washington, DC: American Council of Life Insurers, 2003), 100.

chapter

8

Types of Health Insurance

outline

Medical Expense Coverage

- Traditional Medical Expense Insurance
- Government-Sponsored Medical Expense Coverage
- Managed Care Plans
- Consumer-Driven Health Care

Disability Income Coverage

- Government-Provided Disability Income Coverage
- Disability Income Insurance

Started on 11/26/08
finished on

objectives

After reading this chapter, you should be able to

- Describe the two basic types of health insurance
- Describe the services typically covered and the services typically excluded from coverage under major medical expense insurance policies
- Identify the most common expense participation features included in major medical policies and describe their purpose
- Describe the most common types of supplemental medical expense coverage
- Explain the differences between Medicare and Medicaid
- Describe the primary types of managed care organizations (MCOs) and the techniques they use to manage the costs, utilization, and quality of health care services
- Describe the three primary forms of consumer-driven health plans
- Identify the common definitions of total disability included in disability income insurance policies
- Describe the methods insurers use to calculate benefit amounts under individual and group disability income insurance policies
- Identify some of the supplemental and specialized disability coverage options that are available to individuals, groups, and businesses

Most people cannot afford to pay the full costs of their medical treatment if they become seriously ill or suffer a serious injury. They also cannot afford to lose income if they are unable to work because of a prolonged illness or injury. ***Health insurance*** is insurance that provides protection against the risk of financial loss that may result from illness, injury, or disability.

Health insurance includes two basic types of coverage:

- ***Medical expense coverage***, which provides benefits to pay for the treatment of an insured's illnesses and injuries
- ***Disability income coverage***, which provides income replacement benefits to an insured who is unable to work because of illness or injury

Health insurance can be purchased by individuals to provide coverage for themselves and their dependents or by organizations—usually employers as a type of employee benefit—to provide coverage for group participants and their dependents.

In this chapter, we describe the various types of medical expense coverage available to individuals and groups. We then describe the benefits provided by disability income insurance products.

Medical Expense Coverage

Medical expense coverage in the United States is available in three basic forms: (1) traditional medical expense insurance policies, which offer indemnity benefits, (2) government-sponsored health care programs, and (3) private managed care plans. Medical expense coverage also is available in the form of consumer-driven health plans.

Traditional Medical Expense Insurance

Traditional medical expense insurance products provide ***indemnity benefits,*** or *reimbursement benefits*, which are contractual benefits that are based on the actual amount of financial loss. In traditional medical expense insurance policies, insureds are reimbursed for the covered medical expenses they incur up to a maximum dollar amount. Under this arrangement, when an insured receives medical treatment for an illness or injury from any licensed provider of recognized medical services, the insured is responsible for paying all charges by the medical care provider. The insured then files a claim with the insurance company for policy benefits. If the insurer determines that the charges are covered under the policy, the insurer reimburses the insured for the expenses according to the terms of the contract. Alternatively, the provider can file a claim with the insurer for the total cost of treatment and then bill the insured for any amount that remains after the insurer pays its share.

Traditional medical expense insurance provides three types of coverage: (1) basic medical expense coverage, (2) major medical expense coverage, and (3) supplemental medical expense coverage. These coverage options can be offered under separate policies or combined under a single policy.

Basic Medical Expense Coverage

When insurance companies first offered medical expense policies, they offered ***basic medical expense coverage***, which consisted of separate benefits for each of the following types of medical expenses:

- ***Hospital expenses,*** which include charges for specific inpatient and outpatient hospital services, such as room and board, medications, laboratory services, and other fees associated with a hospital stay

- ***Surgical expenses,*** which include charges for inpatient and outpatient surgical procedures

- ***Physician expenses,*** which include charges associated with physicians' visits both in and out of the hospital

Coverage for these expenses could be provided in separate policies or combined under a single policy.

Basic medical expense coverage typically provides ***first-dollar coverage***—that is, the insurer begins to reimburse the insured for eligible medical expenses without first requiring an out-of-pocket contribution from the insured. However, benefits under basic medical expense policies typically are limited, and many types of medical expenses are not covered.

Major Medical Expense Coverage

Today, rather than offering basic medical expense coverage, most insurers offer ***major medical expense coverage***, which provides substantial benefits for (1) basic hospital, surgical, and physician expenses, (2) additional medical services related to illness or injuries, and (3) preventive care. Figure 8.1 lists some of the specific services commonly included under major medical expense coverage.

Major medical expense coverage typically is available in two forms:

- A ***supplemental major medical policy*** is a separate policy issued in conjunction with an underlying basic medical expense insurance

Figure 8.1 Services Covered Under Major Medical Expense Policies

- Hospital room and board in a semi-private room
- Miscellaneous inpatient hospital services, such as laboratory tests, X-rays, medications, and the use of an operating room
- Surgical supplies and services
- Anethesia and oxygen
- Physical, occupational, and speech therapy
- Surgeons' and physicians' services
- Registered nurses' services
- Specified outpatient services, such as laboratory tests, X-rays, and prescription drugs
- Preventive services, such as childhood immunizations and periodic screening and diagnostic tests

policy. The supplemental policy is designed to provide payment for expenses that exceed the benefit levels of the underlying basic plan and, often, for expenses that are not covered by the underlying plan.

- A ***comprehensive major medical policy*** is a single policy that combines coverages provided by both a supplemental major medical policy and an underlying basic medical expense policy. A comprehensive major medical policy provides substantial medical expenses coverage under one policy, and that policy covers most of the medical expenses the insured may incur.

Today, the majority of major medical expense coverage in the United States is issued in the form of comprehensive major medical policies.

Benefit Amounts

Major medical policies, like all health insurance policies, pay benefits only for allowable expenses—that is, those expenses the insured incurs that are covered under the policy. Most policies specify a maximum benefit amount that the insurer will reimburse for any allowable expense. In most cases, the maximum benefit amount for a particular service is based on the usual, customary, and reasonable fee for that service. The ***usual, customary, and reasonable (UCR) fee*** is the amount that physicians within a particular geographic region commonly charge for a particular medical service. For example, an insurer might set its maximum benefit amount for an appendectomy in a given state at 90 percent of the UCR fee for the procedure in that state. If an insured files a claim for an amount that is equal to or less than the maximum benefit for the treatment received, the insurer will allow the entire amount of the claim. If the amount of the claim is greater than the maximum benefit, the insurer will allow expenses up to the maximum and the insured will be responsible for paying fees that exceed the maximum benefit amount.

Most major medical expense policies also include a maximum lifetime benefit amount, such as $1 million. Under these policies, benefit payments cease after the insured person has received the maximum amount in medical care benefits specified in the contract.

Expense Participation Requirements

Under most major medical expense policies, allowable expenses are subject to expense participation, or cost-sharing, requirements designed to encourage insureds to control medical expenses. The two most common forms of expense participation are deductibles and coinsurance. A ***deductible*** is usually a flat dollar amount of allowable expenses that the insured must pay before the insurer will begin making benefit payments under a medical expense insurance policy. ***Coinsurance*** is generally a specified percentage of all allowable expenses that remain after the deductible has been paid under a medical expense insurance policy and that must be paid by the insured.

The deductible in most major medical policies is expressed as a ***calendar-year deductible***, which is a deductible that applies to the total of all allowable expenses an insured incurs during a given calendar year. An insured's payments toward the deductible are calculated separately for each year and partial deductibles generally are not carried forward. In other words, an insured is required to pay the deductible specified in the policy each year in which he submits claims.

Example: Michael DuPont is covered by a comprehensive major medical policy that specifies a $500 calendar-year deductible. During 2004, Mr. DuPont incurred a total of $400 in allowable expenses. In 2005, he incurred a total of $800 in allowable expenses.

Analysis: Because Mr. DuPont's allowable expenses for 2004 did not meet the $500 calendar-year deductible specified in his policy, he was required to pay the entire $400 in expenses he incurred that year. In 2005, he was required to pay $500 of the $800 in allowable expenses he incurred to satisfy the policy deductible, but he was eligible to receive reimbursement from the insurer for the remaining $300.

The coinsurance requirement in major medical policies applies to amounts remaining after the deductible is paid. Most major medical policies set the coinsurance amount at 10, 20, or 30 percent of remaining allowable expenses.

Example: Suppose that, in addition to a $500 calendar-year deductible, Mr. DuPont's policy included a 20 percent coinsurance requirement.

Analysis: Of the $800 he incurred in allowable expenses for 2005, Mr. DuPont was responsible for paying the $500 deductible and coinsurance equal to $60 (0.20 × $300). His total out-of-pocket costs, therefore, were $560 ($500 + $60). The insurer paid the remaining $240.

Most major medical policies limit the amount of money the insured must pay under the coinsurance provision by including a stop-loss provision. The ***stop-loss provision*** specifies that the policy will cover 100 percent of allowable medical expenses after the insured has paid a specified amount out-of-pocket to satisfy deductible and coinsurance requirements.

Example: Maria Alvarez is covered under a comprehensive major medical policy that includes a $500 calendar-year deductible, a 20 percent coinsurance requirement and a $5,000 stop-loss provision. Ms. Alvarez incurred a total of $2,500 in allowable expenses in January when she was hospitalized for treatment of an illness. In May of that same year, Ms. Alvarez incurred an additional $30,000 in allowable expenses when she underwent surgery.

Analysis: Of the $2,500 in allowable expenses Ms. Alvarez incurred in January, she was required to pay $500 to meet the policy's calendar-year deductible and an additional $400 (0.20 × $2,000) in coinsurance. The insurer paid the remaining $1,600. Because she had satisfied her deductible in January, Ms. Alvarez was required to pay only coinsurance on the allowable expenses she incurred in May. The amount of this coinsurance was $6,000 (0.20 × $30,000). However, the stop-loss provision in her policy requires Ms. Alvarez to pay only $5,000 of her expenses for the year. Because she had already paid $900 in deductible and coinsurance amounts in January, she paid only $4,100 of her May expenses ($5,000 - $900). The insurer paid the remaining $25,900.

Exclusions

Although major medical policies cover most medical expenses, they commonly exclude from coverage any medical expenses that result from the treatments listed in Figure 8.2.

FIGURE 8.2 Major Medical Policy Exclusions

Most major medical expense policies exclude coverage for

- Cosmetic surgery other than corrective surgery required as a result of an accidental injury or other medical reasons
- Treatment of an illness or injury that occurs while the insured is in military service or that results from an act of war
- Treatment of intentionally self-inflicted injuries
- Treatment that is provided free-of-charge in a government facility or that is paid for by other organizations
- Routine dental treatments, routine eye examinations, and corrective lenses

An insured who incurs expenses for excluded services or for services not covered under the policy is required to pay the full amount of those expenses. In addition, excluded or non-allowable expenses are not counted toward the insured's deductible.

Supplemental Medical Expense Coverage

Insurers also offer supplemental coverage to provide benefits for expenses that exceed the benefit levels of major medical policies or for expenses that are not covered under the policies. The supplemental coverages most often provided include dental care, prescription drugs, vision care, treatment of dread diseases and critical illnesses, and long-term care. Insurers also offer a variety of Medicare supplemental expense coverages. (We will discuss Medicare supplements in the next section of this chapter.) Most types of supplemental coverage are provided in stand-alone policies.

Dental Expense Coverage

Basic and major medical expense policies typically do not provide benefits for expenses incurred in obtaining routine dental work and dental treatments. As a result, ***dental expense coverage***—which provides benefits for routine dental examinations, preventive work, and dental procedures needed to treat tooth decay and diseases of the teeth and jaw—typically is provided under a separate supplemental dental expense policy.

Most dental expense policies include both a deductible and a coinsurance feature. Most policies also provide different levels of coverage for different types of treatment. For example, because early detection and treatment of dental problems can result in significantly lower expenses overall, most dental policies provide full coverage for routine examinations and other preventive services. Policies provide lower amounts of coverage for basic services, such as fillings, and major services, such as root canals or crowns. Deductibles typically also are required for basic and major services. A common benefit structure used in dental expense policies is a "100–80–50" structure, in which the insurer pays 100 percent of expenses incurred for preventive services, 80 percent of expenses for basic services, and 50 percent of expenses for major services.

Prescription Drug Coverage

Another common supplemental benefit is ***prescription drug coverage***, which provides benefits for the purchase of drugs and medicines that are prescribed by a physician and are not available over-the-counter. Most prescription drug policies require the insured to pay part of the cost of the prescription out-of-pocket at the time of purchase. The insured, or in some cases the pharmacy, then submits a claim for the remainder of the cost of the prescription to the insurer or an organization that administers the prescription benefits. To encourage physicians and patients to help control costs, some policies now provide benefits for over-the-counter drugs, as long as they are prescribed by a physician for treatment of a specific condition.

Benefit levels and expense participation requirements under prescription drug policies usually vary according to the type of drug. For example, some policies require insureds to pay one out-of-pocket amount for generic drugs and a higher amount for brand-name drugs. As an alternative, some medical expense policies and most managed care plans include a formulary—a listing of drugs by therapeutic category or disease class, that are considered preferred therapy and that are to be used by providers in prescribing medications—and the insured's out-of-pocket expenses depend on whether or not a prescribed drug is included in the formulary. Some policies and plans provide no benefits for non-formulary drugs; others cover drugs not included in the formulary, but at a lower level than for formulary drugs. Coverage also can be structured to include three expense-participation tiers: one for generic drugs in the formulary, a higher one for brand-name drugs in the formulary, and a still higher one for non-formulary drugs.

Vision Care Coverage

Vision care coverage provides the insured with benefits for expenses incurred in obtaining eye examinations and corrective lenses. Most policies that provide vision care coverage allow benefits for one routine eye examination per year for each person covered under the plan. Policies also specify the maximum benefit amount the insurer will pay for eyeglass lenses and frames or contact lenses.

Dread Disease Coverage

In some states in the United States, insurers offer ***dread disease coverage*** to provide benefits for medical expenses incurred by an insured who has contracted a specified disease. The most commonly offered form of coverage is cancer insurance. Supplemental dread disease coverage typically is issued in combination with basic medical expense coverage and serves the same purpose as major medical coverage if the insured should incur medical expenses as a result of having the disease named in the policy.

Critical Illness Coverage

As an alternative to dread disease coverage, some insurers offer ***critical illness (CI) coverage*** that pays a lump-sum benefit if the insured is diagnosed with a critical illness while the policy is in force. The conditions that are considered critical illnesses are specified in the policy and usually include heart attack, stroke, and life-threatening cancer. The specific conditions covered vary from insurer to insurer. CI coverage typically includes a return-of-premium benefit that is payable if the insured dies without having a critical illness.

Long-Term Care Insurance Coverage

An increasing number of insurers also offer long-term care insurance coverage. ***Long-term care (LTC) insurance coverage*** provides benefits for medical and other services to insureds who, because of their advanced age or the effects of a serious illness or injury, need constant care in their own homes or in a qualified nursing facility. To encourage taxpayers to purchase LTC coverage, U.S. federal income tax laws now allow taxpayers to deduct premiums paid for LTC coverage as a medical expense, subject to certain limitations. In addition, benefits received from an LTC policy are nontaxable. Long-term care insurance also has become an important component of retirement planning, financial planning, and estate planning.

FAST FACT

The total number of long-term care insurance policies sold in the United States has grown from 815,000 in 1987 to 8.3 million in 2001.[1]

The specific benefits provided by long-term care policies vary widely depending on the policy, but most policies offer coverage for both skilled nursing home care and in-home custodial care to help insureds perform normal daily activities. Benefit levels also vary depending on the policy, but most policies give insureds the option to add an inflation protection feature that allows benefit levels to increase with increases in the cost of living. Figure 8.3 lists some of the typical features of LTC policies.

Government-Sponsored Medical Expense Coverage

In many countries, governments or public agencies provide citizens with comprehensive medical expense coverage of core health care services, including hospital care and physician services. In the United States, medical expense insurance benefits are provided to qualified individuals through a variety of government programs. In this section, we describe the two most important of these government-sponsored medical expense programs—Medicare and Medicaid.

FIGURE 8.3 Typical Features of Long-Term Care Insurance Policies

Feature	Details
Basic services	Nursing home care (includes skilled, intermediate, and custodial care) Home health care Assisted living
Optional services/benefits	Alternate care Hospice care Respite care Care coordination/case management Homemaker/chore assistance Bed reservation Medical equipment coverage Spousal discount
Daily benefit	Nursing home care: $75–$250/day Home health care: Percentage of nursing home rate or specified amount/day
Benefit eligibility	Medical necessity, cannot perform activities of daily living, or cognitive impairment
Benefit period	1 year–lifetime
Deductible period	0–100 days
Pre-existing condition exclusion	0–6 months, for condition disclosed during application
Renewability	Guaranteed renewable
Alzheimer's disease coverage	Yes
Age limits for purchasing	18–99 years
Waiver of premium	Yes
Free-look period	30 days
Inflation protection	Yes
Nonforfeiture benefits	Shortened benefit period, return of premium, or reduced paid-up coverage

Medicare

Medicare is a federal government program established by the Old Age, Survivors, Disability and Health Insurance (OASDHI) Act that provides medical expense benefits to elderly and disabled persons. Medicare benefits are available to the following groups:

- Persons age 65 or older and eligible for Social Security or Railroad Retirement benefits
- Persons with qualifying disabilities (regardless of age)
- Persons with end-stage renal disease (ESRD) or their dependents

Certain persons not meeting these requirements can purchase benefits.

Medicare consists of three components: Medicare Part A and Medicare Part B, which describe the services and benefits available to program enrollees, and Medicare Advantage, which addresses delivery of services and program administration.

Medicare Part A provides basic hospital insurance that covers the costs of inpatient hospital services, confinement in nursing facilities or other extended care facilities after hospitalization, home care services following hospitalization, and hospice care. Individuals who satisfy Medicare eligibility requirements are automatically enrolled in Medicare Part A and pay no premiums for coverage. However, Medicare Part A has deductible and coinsurance requirements, which are reviewed annually.

Medicare Part B provides benefits to cover the costs of physicians' professional services, whether the services are provided in a hospital, a physician's office, an extended-care facility, a nursing home, or an insured's home. Benefits under Medicare Part B also cover ambulance services, medical supplies and equipment, hospital outpatient services, diagnostic tests, and other services necessary for the diagnosis or treatment of illness or injury. Unlike Medicare Part A, Medicare Part B is a voluntary program and enrollment is not automatic; eligible beneficiaries must enroll for Part B coverage. Participants in Medicare Part B pay monthly premiums deducted from their Social Security benefits plus an annual deductible and coinsurance.

Funding for Medicare Part A comes primarily from a payroll tax imposed on employees and employers. Funding for Medicare Part B comes primarily from premiums paid by enrollees. Additional funding for Part B benefits comes from the federal government's general tax revenues.

Medicare Advantage describes how and by whom covered services are delivered to enrollees. Figure 8.4 lists the service delivery options that Medicare Advantage offers to enrollees.

All Medicare Advantage plans, except the high-deductible MSA plans, must cover at least Medicare Part A and Medicare Part B benefits. Addi-

FIGURE 8.4 Medicare Advantage Service Delivery Options

- **Traditional fee-for-service**, under which the federal government reimburses providers for the actual services they deliver to enrollees.
- **Private fee-for-service (PFFS) plans**, under which coverage is provided by private insurance carriers rather than by the federal government.
- **Coordinated care plans (CCPs)**, which are managed care plans and include (1) health maintenance organizations (HMOs), with or without an out-of-network benefit component, (2) preferred provider organizations (PPOs), and (3) provider-sponsored organizations (PSOs).
- **Medicare medical savings account (MSA) plans**, which consist of a high-deductible catastrophic insurance policy and a tax-advantaged medical savings account established for individual Medicare beneficiaries. Very few individuals enrolled in these plans, and new enrollments were suspended on January 1, 2003.

tional services may be offered as part of the benefit package or as a supplement for which enrollees may be required to pay extra. Medicare Advantage plans have federal preemption from state-mandated benefit and provider requirements.

In December of 2003, the Medicare Prescription Drug, Improvement, and Modernization Act was signed into law. The Act calls for prescription drug plans to be available to Medicare recipients in 2006. In the meantime, Medicare will contract with private companies to offer drug discount cards that can help Medicare recipients save 10 to 25 percent on prescription drugs beginning in 2004.

Because Medicare Part A and Part B cover only a portion of enrollees' expenses, Medicare recipients frequently purchase supplemental Medicare coverage. These supplements are private medical expense insurance policies designed to reimburse insureds for out-of-pocket expenses, such as deductibles and coinsurance payments, or to provide benefits for medical expenses excluded from Medicare coverage.

Medicare supplements are available in two major forms: Medigap insurance policies and Medicare SELECT plans. A ***Medigap policy*** is an individual medical expense insurance policy sold by an insurance company to supplement Medicare Part A and Part B coverage. A ***Medicare SELECT plan*** is a managed care plan that supplements Medicare Part B coverage. Medicare SELECT does not apply to Part A benefits.

Federal laws contain extensive rules to prevent overlap or duplication of benefits provided by Medicare and Medicare supplements. These rules define the individuals for whom Medicare will be the primary payer and secondary payer of benefits. Private insurance plans include similar provisions to integrate their medical benefits with those provided by Medicare and prevent insureds from receiving more in benefits than the actual expenses incurred.

Medicaid

Medicaid is a joint federal and state program that provides basic medical expense and nursing home coverage to the low-income population and certain aged and disabled individuals. The federal government establishes broad guidelines for Medicaid programs, provides partial funding for states, and sets minimum standards for eligibility, benefits, and provider participation and reimbursement. Individual states provide additional funds and administer the programs.

Each state is free to customize its Medicaid program as long as the program satisfies minimum federal requirements. For example, states can expand benefits beyond federal guidelines by offering coverage for services such as prescription drugs, dental care, or vision care. States also can expand eligibility to include certain other groups. In all cases, Medicaid is considered the secondary payer of benefits. This means that Medicaid benefits are paid only after benefits from all other available sources have been exhausted.

Managed Care Plans

Over the last several decades, medical expense coverage in the United States has changed dramatically. In the past, most medical expense coverage was provided by traditional medical expense insurance, which dealt only with financing health care services. In other words, traditional medical expense insurance was concerned only with an individual's medical bills.

Today, most insureds in the United States are covered by some type of managed care plan. ***Managed care*** is a method of integrating the financing and delivery of health care services within a system that manages the cost, accessibility, and quality of care. The organizations that operate within the managed care system are referred to as managed care organizations (MCOs).

Types of Managed Care Plans

A variety of managed care plans have been developed in response to consumer needs and rising health care costs, and employers may offer their employees a choice of plans. The distinctions among the plans often hinge in part on how they manage plan members' access to health care services. MCOs manage access through the use of provider networks. A ***network*** is the group of physicians, hospitals, and ancillary services providers that a specific managed care plan has contracted with to deliver health care services to its members. Ancillary, or supplemental, services providers include laboratories, radiologists, home health care providers, and physical, speech, and occupational therapists.

Although classifying managed care plans is not easy, they generally fall into one of the following basic categories:

- A ***health maintenance organization (HMO)*** is a health care financing and delivery system that provides comprehensive health care services to plan members—often referred to as *subscribers*—in a particular geographic area; it typically requires subscribers to gain access to services through a primary care provider and use in-network providers. Subscribers are required to pay a small ***copayment***—a specified, fixed amount for specified services—out of pocket at the time of service, but they do not pay deductibles or coinsurance and do not file claims for benefits. We will discuss copayments in more detail later in this chapter.

- A ***preferred provider organization (PPO)*** is a health care benefit arrangement that provides incentives for members to use network providers, but also provides at least some coverage for services rendered by non-network providers. PPOs do not provide health care directly to plan members; instead, they act as brokers or middlemen by contracting with health care providers to deliver medical services to a specific group of covered individuals at a discounted cost. More than half of the PPOs in the United States are owned by insurance companies. The remainder are owned by physician or hospital groups, Blue Cross and Blue Shield Plans, third-party administrators, or employers. A ***third-party administrator (TPA)*** is an organization other than an insurance company that provides administrative services to the sponsors of group benefit plans.

- A ***point-of-service (POS) product*** is a managed care option under which plan members in need of medical care can choose, at the point of service, whether to seek care in-network or out-of-network. A POS option or product may be offered by a network-based plan or by an insurer. Point-of-service products, which combine aspects of traditional group medical expense insurance and aspects of managed care, are among the fastest growing forms of managed care today.

- A ***managed indemnity plan*** is organized and administered like a traditional indemnity plan, but uses managed care techniques, such as precertification and utilization review, to control costs. Plans allow insured members to use the providers of their choice and do not offer provider networks.

These basic plan types are part of a health care coverage continuum, shown in Figure 8.5, that is anchored at one end by traditional indemnity medical expense insurance and at the other by pure managed care.

Principles of Managed Care

Managed care plans differ from traditional medical expense insurance plans in a number of ways, including the way in which health care services, access, utilization, and costs are managed.

Medical Management

MCOs manage the types of health care services they offer to ensure that plan members receive medically necessary and medically appropriate services and that resources are not used for unnecessary or excessive services. This process is referred to as medical management. Most MCOs define ***medically necessary services*** as those services that are considered to be

- Consistent with the symptoms, diagnosis, and treatment of the member's condition
- In accordance with the standards of good medical practice
- Not solely for the convenience of the member, member's family, physician, or other health care provider
- Furnished in the least intensive type of medical care setting required by the member's condition[2]

Medically appropriate services are diagnostic or treatment measures for which the expected health benefits exceed the expected risks by a margin wide enough to justify the measures.[3] In general, questions of

FIGURE 8.5 Health Care Coverage Continuum

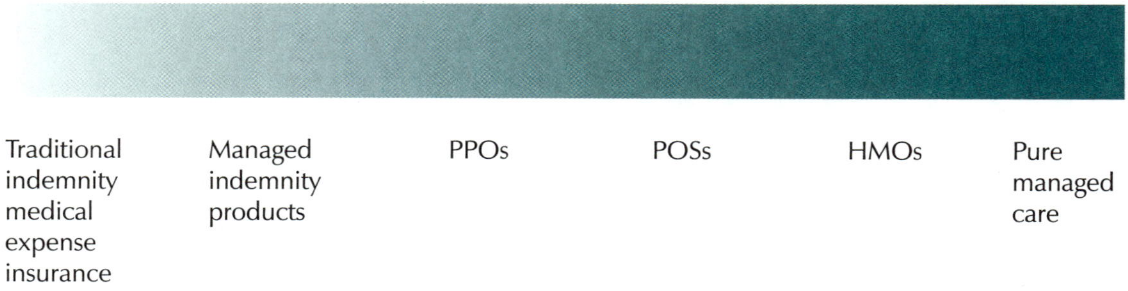

"IT APPEARS YOUR HMO WILL ONLY ALLOW YOU 2 REPRESSED MEMORIES, 1 CHILDHOOD TRAUMA, AND 3 FLASHBACKS PER VISIT."

www.CartoonStock.com

medical necessity apply to the needs of particular plan members and drive case-by-case decisions. Questions of medical appropriateness apply to a plan's member population and drive decisions that affect segments of that population.

Within the framework of medically necessary and appropriate services, MCOs offer a menu of basic medical benefits, many of which are mandated by federal and state laws. In addition, MCOs typically offer

- Extensive preventive care programs, including pre-natal and well-baby care, routine physical examinations, screening programs, 24-hour telephone line access to a nurse, and childhood immunizations

- Access to wellness programs, including smoking cessation, weight management, and stress management programs

- Patient education programs, including seminars, newsletters, and medical self-help booklets.

Most HMOs also provide supplemental medical services, such as vision care, dental care, mental health care, and prescription drugs.

Network Management

In most health care delivery systems, health care costs are directly related to access to services. One of the most effective ways of managing costs, therefore, is to manage access. As we mentioned earlier, MCOs accomplish this through the use of provider networks.

HMOs generally require plan members to choose providers from the network in order to receive benefits. PPOs and POS options allow members to use both in-network and out-of-network providers, but offer financial incentives to members who choose network providers. For example, a PPO or POS might require members to pay a minimal copayment for services received from network providers and a higher copayment—or additional deductible and coinsurance amounts—for services received from providers outside the network.

Some MCOs (usually HMOs and POS plans) also manage access to health care services through the use of primary care providers (PCPs) who coordinate members' medical care and treatment. In a PCP-based system, a plan member can receive basic medical care, preventive care, and wellness care directly from the PCP, without obtaining authorization from the plan. To receive specialized care, however, the plan member may need to obtain authorization or a referral from the PCP. The PCP thus serves as a plan member's point of entry into the system and as a gatekeeper to additional services. Plans encourage members to obtain services through PCPs by requiring little or no out-of-pocket cost for PCP-based care.

Utilization and Quality Management

Managed care plans also manage costs by managing the use and quality of health care services. ***Utilization management*** is a process designed to help ensure that plan members receive the most appropriate care from the most appropriate provider in the most appropriate and most cost-effective setting. In most managed care plans, utilization review, case management, and disease management are important components of the utilization management process. These components are described in Figure 8.6.

Quality management and improvement programs are designed to ensure that plan members receive high-quality care. These quality management and improvement programs include peer review for PCPs and specialists, accreditation standards for hospitals and ancillary services providers, overall plan accreditation standards, and performance evaluation.

Cost Sharing

Another way MCOs can manage health care costs is by requiring plan members and providers to share the cost of health care services. In most managed care plans, plan members receive comprehensive health care in exchange for payment of a fixed, periodic—usually monthly—premium. This premium covers most health care services, no matter how often the member uses those services. In addition, at the time in-network services are rendered, plan members generally pay a copayment, which as we mentioned earlier is a specified, fixed amount for specified services.

FIGURE 8.6 Components of the Utilization Management Process

Utilization review (UR) is a process managed care plans use to evaluate the medical necessity, appropriateness, and cost-effectiveness of health care services and treatment plans. Although the specific details of utilization review vary from plan to plan, most UR programs include the following components:

- ***Prospective review***, which is the review and possible authorization of proposed treatment plans for a patient before the treatment is implemented
- ***Concurrent review***, which is the review of treatment plans and services that takes place while the patient is in the hospital or receiving ongoing treatment
- ***Retrospective review***, which involves evaluating the treatment and services a plan member received

Case management is a process by which a plan (1) identifies plan members who require extensive, complex health care, (2) develops an appropriate treatment strategy based on medical necessity and appropriateness and the availability of alternative care solutions, and (3) coordinates and monitors patient care. Case management is most often used in situations in which the patient has an illness or injury that is likely to require very expensive treatment.

Disease management is a coordinated system of preventive, diagnostic, and therapeutic measures intended to provide cost-effective, quality health care for a patient population who have or are at risk for a specific chronic illness or medical condition. Disease management programs focus on specific conditions and coordinate care for those conditions across different providers and health care delivery settings.

Example: Vincent Morgan is a member of a managed care plan that requires a $15 copayment for physician office visits and a $20 copayment for prescription drugs. On February 1, Mr. Morgan visited his PCP for treatment of a sprained ankle. During the office visit, the PCP ordered X-rays to confirm the sprain. The PCP also wrote Mr. Morgan a prescription for pain medication.

Analysis: Before leaving the PCP's office Mr. Morgan paid a $15 copayment to cover the office visit. The remaining charges for the office visit and the X-rays were covered by the health plan. When Mr. Morgan took his prescription to the pharmacy, he paid a $20 prescription copayment. The pharmacy billed the health plan for the remaining cost of the prescription.

Although copayments generally are significantly lower than deductibles and coinsurance requirements included in traditional medical expense insurance policies and managed care plans, they provide an incentive for plan members to manage the utilization, and therefore the cost, of health care services.

Managed care plans also require providers to share in the financial risk of providing medical care. This requirement is designed to encourage providers to deliver necessary care in a cost-effective way. Managed care plans achieve risk sharing by negotiating fee arrangements with health care providers and making other contractual agreements that encourage cost-effective care. Negotiated fee arrangements for in-network providers generally include salaries, fee schedules, fee caps, and capitation payments. A ***capitation payment*** is a flat amount a provider receives each month for each patient under the provider's care, regardless of the number or cost of services provided. If the costs of medical services exceed the provider's negotiated fee, the provider must absorb the loss. Out-of-network providers typically are reimbursed on a fee-for-service basis.

Consumer-Driven Health Care

Although the methods used by managed care organizations have helped reduce some of the costs of providing health care coverage, they also have drawn complaints from employers, employees, providers, and insurance companies. In response to these complaints, a variety of alternative health care options have been proposed. The most promising alternative falls under the general heading of consumer-driven health plans. A ***consumer-driven health plan*** is an employer-sponsored health benefit plan that gives individuals freedom to choose health care providers and benefits, but also requires them to assume financial risk for their choices. In 2002, 1.5 million U.S. workers—less than 1 percent of the employer coverage market—participated in consumer-driven health care plans. Health plans and benefit consultants predict that as many as 50 percent of employers will offer consumer-driven health plans by 2007.[4]

The two key components of consumer-driven health care are (1) financial incentives for individuals to manage health care costs and utilization and (2) information—usually in the form of Internet-based medical information tools—to enable individuals to make informed decisions about basic health care.

Financial incentives for managing health care costs are built into plan funding mechanisms. Most consumer-driven health plans are structured as defined-contribution plans. In general terms, a defined-contribution plan is an employer-sponsored employee benefit plan under which the employer contributes a fixed dollar amount (a defined contribution) toward provision of benefits rather than promising to pay whatever it costs to provide a given package of benefits (a defined benefit). In the context of health care, a defined-contribution consumer-driven health care plan is an employer-sponsored health benefit plan under which the employer allocates a fixed dollar amount toward health care coverage for each participating employee and the employee then uses that amount to pay for selected medical services. In Chapter 14, we discuss defined contribution plans in the context of employer-sponsored retirement plans.

Because the amount of funding is defined in advance, employees assume the financial risk if the costs of their health care selections exceed the employer's contribution. As a result, employees have a considerable incentive to manage their use of medical services and to make sure they have a complete and accurate picture of the quality and cost of those services.

Internet sites allow customers to (1) track and manage health care bills, (2) manage and improve their health through health education and preventative services, (3) gather information about provider quality and services, and (4) get group-rate prices from providers. As providers upgrade to electronic medical records (EMR), information to support consumer decision making will increase.

Consumer-driven health plans take one of three basic forms: tax-advantaged personal health spending accounts, individually designed network and benefit plans, and customized package plans.

Tax-Advantaged Personal Health Spending Accounts

A tax-advantaged personal health spending account is an account established with contributions from an employer and/or employee. Employer contributions to the account are exempt from employee state and federal income taxes and Social Security taxes. Employee contributions are exempt from income taxes, but are subject to Social Security taxes. Withdrawals used to pay substantiated medical expenses also are tax exempt. Withdrawals for non-medical purposes are allowed, but such withdrawals are subject to income taxes and a 15 percent penalty tax.

Most personal health spending accounts are accompanied by a high-deductible medical expense insurance policy and the amount contributed to the account is linked to the amount of the policy deductible. For example, most plans limit contributions to a percentage of the policy deductible. If the account is employer-funded, the employer also can include the amount of the premium for the policy in the employee's account. Alternatively, the employer can pay the policy premium separately. If the account is employee-funded, the employee is responsible for paying the policy premium. In plans that don't require an accompanying insurance policy, account contributions typically are subject to specified maximums.

If an employee's medical expenses exceed the amount in the account, the employee is required to pay excess costs out-of-pocket. In plans accompanied by a high-deductible medical expense policy, out-of-pocket payments are required until the policy deductible is satisfied, After the deductible is paid, the medical expense policy pays benefits according to the terms of the contract. In plans not accompanied by a high-deductible insurance policy, out-of-pocket expenses are not limited. If the account has remaining funds at the end of the year, those funds "roll over" to future years. In addition, accounts generally move with employees who change employment.

Currently, three basic types of tax-advantaged personal health spending accounts are available: medical savings accounts (MSAs), health reimbursement arrangements (HRAs), and health savings accounts. The basic features of these personal health spending accounts are described in Figure 8.7. Some employers offer flexible spending accounts that allow employees to set aside a pre-determined amount of pre-tax wages for qualified, mostly health-related expenditures. Employees must use the amount set aside in the flexible spending account each year or lose it.

Individually Designed Network and Benefit Plans

Individually designed network and benefit plans require a defined contribution from the employer, usually in an amount equal to the amount that would otherwise have been spent for medical expense insurance.

FIGURE 8.7 Personal Health Spending Accounts

A ***medical savings account (MSA)*** can be funded by employers or employees, but not both, and is available only to employers with fewer than 50 employees or to self-employed individuals. (MSAs included in consumer-driven health plans are similar to the MSAs included under Medicare Advantage.)

A ***health reimbursement arrangement (HRA)*** is similar to an MSA, but accounts are funded only by employer contributions and plans are available to employers of any size. In addition, HRAs do not require fixed contributions by employers.

A ***health savings account (HSA)*** is similar to MSAs and HRAs, but includes (1) no restrictions on employer size; (2) no restrictions on source of contributions (both the employer and the employee can contribute to the account); (3) a higher maximum annual tax-deductible contribution (100 percent of the deductible for the accompanying medical expense policy); and (4) lower minimum deductibles for the accompanying medical expense policy ($1,000 for individual coverage and $2,000 for family coverage). Like MSAs and HRAs, HSAs allow withdrawals for non-medical purposes (subject to income taxes and penalties) and accounts are portable.

Employees design their own insurance coverage, including provider networks, benefit packages, and copayment levels, and use the money set aside by the employer to pay plan premiums. Informational software and services to help employees make selections are provided by the plan. The monthly premiums individuals pay for their insurance coverage are based on their selections and can change from month to month. Employees bear the financial risk if personalized premiums exceed the fixed contribution from the employer.

Customized Package Plans

Under a customized package plan, an employer contributes a fixed amount for health care coverage for each employee. The employee, using Internet-based medical information tools, chooses from a predetermined set of network and benefit options and pays premiums with funds set aside by the employer. Premiums vary according to the network and benefit options the employee selects. Most customized package plans offer tiered network and benefit options based on charges, discounts, and, in some cases, quality of care and service. Different tiers require different premiums and cost-sharing requirements. For example, care delivered at a hospital would require a higher copayment than care delivered at a doctor's office or community health care center. Similarly, care delivered by a specialist would require a higher copayment than care delivered by a primary care provider.

Although package plans are similar to traditional multiple-plan offerings funded by fixed employer contributions, they typically offer a wider choice of plans. In addition, employers can cap their contributions for health care benefits and require employees to assume the financial risk for selecting richer benefits or broader networks.

Disability Income Coverage

When a person is unable to work because of disability, the financial effect on the individual's family is potentially much greater than if the individual had died. When a wage earner dies, the family is left without a source of income. When a wage earner is disabled, the family not only loses a source of income, but they also face additional expenses resulting from the disability. To help relieve the financial stress created by disability, insurance companies and government agencies offer income replacement benefits in the form of disability income coverage. The following sections describe the primary sources of disability income coverage—the government and private insurers—and the key features of individual and group disability income policies.

Government-Provided Disability Income Coverage

Government-sponsored programs in many countries provide disability income benefits as well as medical expense benefits to specified individuals. In the United States, workers who are disabled as a result of work-related accidents or illnesses are eligible to receive wage replacement benefits, as well as medical expense benefits, under state-mandated workers' compensation programs. In addition, workers who are under age 65 and who have paid a specified amount of Social Security tax for a prescribed number of quarter-year periods are eligible to receive ***Social Security Disability Income (SSDI)*** benefit payments if they become disabled as a result of nonwork-related accidents or illnesses. For purposes of SSDI, disability is defined as a person's inability to work at any occupation because of a physical or mental illness or injury. Such a disability must have lasted or be expected to last for at least one year, or it must be expected to lead to the person's death.

SSDI benefits are equal to the monthly benefits that would normally have become payable when the worker retired. SSDI benefit payments do not begin until the insured has been disabled for at least five months and, hence, begin approximately six months after the onset of disability. Benefit payments continue until (1) two months after the disability ends, (2) the insured worker dies, or (3) the insured worker reaches the age when Social Security retirement income benefits become payable.

The spouse and dependent children of a disabled worker also may receive income benefits while the worker is disabled. Their income benefits are equal to a percentage of the amount received by the disabled worker. Benefits, however, are subject to an overall family maximum benefit amount.

Disability Income Insurance

Private insurance companies also provide disability income coverage. In Chapter 5, we discussed disability income benefits added as riders to individual life insurance policies. In this section, we discuss stand-alone disability income policies issued to individuals and to groups.

Disability income insurance is classified as either short term or long term, depending on the length of the benefit period. The ***benefit period*** is the time during which the insurer will pay income benefits. Different criteria are used to classify the benefit period of individual and group coverages. Figure 8.8 explains the benefit periods found in various disability income policies.

To receive periodic income benefits under a disability income insurance policy, an insured person must meet the policy's definition of disabled. In addition, the insured generally must be disabled for a certain period of time—the elimination period—before benefits become payable.

In this section, we describe typical definitions of disability, the elimination period, benefit amounts, and supplemental disability benefits.

Definitions of Total Disability

The definitions of total disability included in individual and group disability income policies typically are based on the insured's occupation or the nature of the insured's disability.

Any Occupation Definition

At one time, disability income policies defined total disability as a disability that prevented the insured from performing the duties of *any occupation*. Because most people would never qualify for disability income benefits under these terms, the "any occupation" definition is rarely used in individual disability income policies. However, it is used to determine eligibility for Social Security disability benefits.

Own Previous Occupation Definition

As an alternative to the "any occupation" definition, some policies define total disability as any disability that prevents the insured from performing the essential duties of the insured's *own previous occupa-*

FIGURE 8.8 Disability Income Policies' Benefit Periods

Individual Disability Income Benefit Periods

Individual disability income coverage is seldom offered with a maximum benefit period of less than one year.

- *Short-term individual disability income coverage* provides a maximum benefit period of from one to five years.
- *Long-term individual disability income coverage* provides a maximum benefit period of five years or more. The maximum benefit period provided by individual long-term coverage for illnesses commonly extends until the insured reaches age 65; for accidents, benefits often are provided for the insured's lifetime.

Group Disability Income Benefit Periods

Group disability income coverage generally specifies shorter benefit periods than those included in individual policies.

- *Short-term group disability income coverage* provides a maximum benefit period of one year or less; such coverage commonly specifies a maximum period of 13, 26, or 52 weeks.
- *Long-term group disability income coverage* provides a maximum benefit period of more than one year. Many policies extend the maximum benefit period to the insured's normal retirement age or to age 70.

tion. Under the terms of this definition, benefits are payable even if the insured is gainfully employed in another occupation. The "own previous occupation" definition of total disability typically is included in policies sold to members of certain professional occupations and is used more often in individual policies than in group policies.

Example: Rene Taylor, a surgeon, is insured under a disability income policy that includes an "own previous occupation" definition of total disability. Dr. Taylor was injured in an accident and lost the use of her hand. Although her accident prevents her from performing surgery, Dr. Taylor has begun working as a medical researcher.

Analysis: Because Dr. Taylor's accident prevents her from performing surgery, she will never be able to work in her "own previous occupation." Therefore, the insurer will pay Dr. Taylor the policy's full disability income benefit until the end of the policy's benefit period, even though she is working at another occupation.

Current Usual Definition

Most disability income policies issued today use a two-part definition of total disability. For an initial specified period, usually two to five years, an insured is considered totally disabled if the insured's disability satisfies the "own previous occupation" definition. At the end of the initial period, the insured is considered totally disabled only if the disability prevents participation in any occupation for which the insured is reasonably fitted by education, training, or experience, which is known as the "current usual" definition of total disability.

Example: Suppose Dr. Taylor from our previous example is insured under a disability income policy that includes a "current usual" definition of total disability and specifies a two-year initial disability period. Dr. Taylor was unemployed for two years after her accident before accepting the position as medical researcher.

Analysis: Because Dr. Taylor's injury prevented her from performing surgery, she met the policy's initial definition of total disability and, thus, was eligible to receive disability income benefits for up to two years. At the end of the two-year period, Dr. Taylor no longer qualified for disability income benefits because her disability did not prevent her from working at an occupation for which she is reasonably fitted by her education and training.

Some policies that apply the "current usual" definition of total disability also state that total disability no longer exists if the insured is working in any gainful occupation. Thus, no disability income benefits are payable if the insured voluntarily returns to work at any occupation.

Presumptive Disabilities

Certain conditions, if present, automatically cause an insured to be considered totally disabled. Such a condition is defined as a ***presumptive disability***. Presumptive disabilities include total and permanent blindness, loss of the use of any two limbs, and loss of speech or hearing. An insured who is presumptively disabled is eligible to receive the full income benefit amount provided under the policy, even if the insured resumes full-time employment in a former occupation.

Income Loss

One type of disability income coverage that has gained popularity in the upper-income, professional market is ***income protection insurance***, which provides benefits based on the extent of the insured's actual loss of earnings from disability rather than on the insured's inability to perform work-related duties. The definition of total disability included in income protection policies specifies that an insured is disabled if the disability results in a loss of income. Income protection policies typically specify (1) a maximum benefit amount that will be paid when an insured is completely unable to work and (2) a method of determining the amount of lost income when the disabled insured is working but is earning less than the amount previously earned.

> **Example:** Mitchell Reiner, a professional tennis player, is insured under an income protection policy. Mr. Reiner injured his knee in an accident and was forced to retire from active competition. Later, he was hired as a coach at a local university. However, his current income is significantly less than his previous income.
>
> **Analysis:** Under the terms of an income protection policy, Mr. Reiner received the maximum benefit specified by the policy during the period when he was unemployed. After that, he became eligible for a policy benefit based on the difference between his income as a professional athlete and his salary as a coach. These partial payments will continue until the end of the policy's maximum benefit period.

Elimination Period

In addition to meeting the definition of total disability, an insured must satisfy an elimination period to be eligible to receive disability benefits. An ***elimination period,*** often referred to as a *waiting period*, is the specific amount of time that an insured must be disabled before becoming eligible to receive policy benefits. Like the deductible amount included in medical expense policies, the elimination period is designed to reduce the cost of coverage by eliminating processing and claims costs for disabilities that last for only a very short time. This expense savings is reflected in the cost of the coverage; the longer the elimination period, the lower the cost for otherwise equivalent income coverage.

The length of the elimination period in individual disability income policies is typically from 30 days to 6 months for both short-term and long-term coverage. The length of the elimination period in group disability income policies is related to the length of the maximum benefit period. Most group short-term policies specify no elimination period for disabilities caused by accidents and an elimination period of 1 week for disabilities caused by illness. Most group long-term policies specify an elimination period of 13 or 26 weeks and coordinate this period with short-term benefit periods so that short-term coverage ends at the same time that long-term benefits become payable.

Benefit Amounts

As a general rule, the benefit amount available through disability income coverage is not intended to fully replace an individual's predisability earnings. Instead, benefits are limited to an amount that is lower than the individual's regular earnings when not disabled. Without such a restriction, a disabled insured could receive as much income during disability as he received when working and would have no incentive to return to work or minimize the period of disability. Disability amounts, however, should not be so low that a disabled insured suffers a drastic reduction in income and lifestyle.

The method an insurer uses to determine the amount of disability income benefits that will be paid to a disabled insured depends on whether the coverage is provided by an individual or a group policy.

Individual Disability Income Benefit Amounts

Individual disability income policies usually specify a flat benefit amount that the insurer will pay to an insured who becomes totally disabled according to the terms of the policy. The specified benefit amount is based on the amount of the insured's income when the policy was purchased.

Although the benefit amount that is paid to a disabled insured is not limited by any other income benefits the insured receives during the disability, it is limited by the maximum amount of disability income coverage that a particular applicant can purchase. When determining the maximum amount of disability income coverage available to an applicant, the insurer considers the following factors:

- The amount of the applicant's usual income earned from employment, before taxes
- The amount of the applicant's unearned income, such as dividends and interest, that will continue during a disability
- Additional sources of income available to the applicant during a disability, such as disability income benefits provided through group disability income coverage and government-sponsored disability income programs
- The applicant's current income tax bracket, because the applicant's usual earned income is taxable income, whereas disability income benefits provided under an individual policy usually are not taxable income

In general, the maximum benefit amount an individual disability income policy will provide is 50 to 70 percent of the insured's usual pre-tax earnings at the time of the application for the policy. Note that the amount of an insured's disability income benefit will be lower than the amount of after-tax income the insured earned before becoming disabled. If the insured pays premiums for the coverage, benefits are not taxable as income to the insured when they are received.

Group Disability Income Benefit Amounts

Insurers typically use an income benefit formula to determine the amount of the periodic benefit payable to a disabled insured under a group disability income insurance policy. This formula usually expresses the disability income benefit amount as a stated percentage of the insured's pre-disability earnings.

The specified percentage of earnings varies from policy to policy. The percentage included in group short-term disability income policies is typically from 90 to 100 percent of pre-disability income. The percentage included in group long-term disability income policies is lower, and typically ranges from 50 to 70 percent of pre-disability earnings. Unlike the benefit under individual disability income policies, the benefit under group disability income policies typically is reduced by the amount of any duplicate disability income benefits the insured receives from other sources, such as payments received from Social Security.

Exclusions

Disability income insurance policies often specify that income benefits will not be paid to a disabled insured if the insured's disability results from certain causes. The causes of disability that typically are excluded from coverage include the following:

- Injuries or illnesses that result from war, declared or undeclared, or any act of war
- Intentionally self-inflicted injuries
- Injuries received as a result of active participation in a riot
- Occupation-related disabilities or illnesses for which the insured is entitled to receive disability income benefits under some government program, such as workers' compensation

Supplemental Disability Benefits

In addition to disability income coverage issued to individuals and groups, insurers offer several types of supplemental and specialized disability coverage. These additional benefits may be included automatically with the basic coverage or may be available on an optional basis for an additional premium amount. Supplemental disability coverage for individuals and group members is designed to augment the benefits included in disability income policies. For example, most group disability income policies limit benefit amounts to a specified percentage of an insured employee's earnings. Supplemental coverage, which typically is purchased by the employee under a separate policy, usually increases the benefit amount. Therefore, an employee covered by a group disability income policy that provides 60 percent income replacement benefits could increase benefits to 80 percent of earnings by purchasing supplemental coverage. These individually purchased supplements, sometimes referred to as *buy-up options*, are becoming increasingly popular as employers reduce benefit levels in an effort to control costs. For tax purposes, benefits received under coverage that is paid for by the employer are considered to be taxable income for the employee. Benefits received under coverage paid for by the employee are not taxable to the employee.

Specialized coverages are designed to provide additional benefits not offered under standard disability income policies. Individual and group coverage options provide benefits for partial disability or allow insureds to increase benefit levels to reflect increases in earnings or cost of living. Business coverage options protect businesses against financial loss if an owner, partner, or key person becomes unable to work because of a disability. These specialized coverages are described in Figure 8.9.

FIGURE 8.9 Specialized Types of Disability Coverage

Specialized Disability Coverage Options for Individuals and Groups

- ***Partial disability coverage***—a coverage option designed to provide income replacement benefits to an insured whose disability prevents him either from performing some of the duties of his usual occupation or from engaging in that occupation on a full-time basis.
- ***Future purchase option***—a coverage option that grants the insured the right to increase the benefit amount under a disability income insurance policy in accordance with increases in earnings.
- ***Cost-of-living adjustment (COLA)***—a coverage option that allows benefit amounts to increase with increases in the cost of living.

Specialized Disability Coverage Options for Businesses

- ***Key person disability coverage***—a coverage option that provides benefit payments to a small business if an insured owner, partner, or other key person becomes disabled.
- ***Disability buyout coverage***—a coverage option that provides benefits designed to fund the buyout of a disabled partner's or owner's interest in a business.
- ***Business overhead expense coverage***—a coverage option that provides benefits designed to pay a disabled insured's share of the business' overhead expenses. Policies typically define overhead expenses as usual and necessary business expenses, including rent, mortgage payments, electric and gas utilities, employee salaries, and other expenses required to keep the business open.

Key Terms

health insurance
medical expense coverage
disability income coverage
indemnity benefits
basic medical expense coverage
hospital expenses
surgical expenses
physician expenses
first-dollar coverage
major medical expense coverage
supplemental major medical policy
comprehensive major medical policy
usual, customary, and reasonable (UCR) fee
deductible
coinsurance
calendar-year deductible
stop-loss provision
dental expense coverage
prescription drug coverage
vision care coverage
dread disease coverage
critical illness (CI) coverage
long-term care (LTC) insurance coverage
Medicare
Medicare Part A
Medicare Part B
Medicare Advantage
Medigap policy
Medicare SELECT plan
Medicaid
managed care
network
health maintenance organization (HMO)
copayment
preferred provider organization (PPO)
third-party administrator (TPA)
point-of-service (POS) product
managed indemnity plan
medically necessary services
medically appropriate services
utilization management
utilization review (UR)
prospective review
concurrent review
retrospective review
case management
disease management
capitation payment
consumer-driven health plan
medical savings account (MSA)
health reimbursement arrangement (HRA)
health savings account (HSA)
Social Security Disability Income (SSDI)
benefit period
presumptive disability
income protection insurance
elimination period
partial disability coverage
future purchase option
cost-of-living adjustment (COLA)
key person disability coverage
disability buyout coverage
business overhead expense coverage

Endnotes

1. "Research Studies," Health Insurance Association of America, http://www.hiaa.org/research/research_studies.cfm (11 December 2003).
2. Bruce W. Clark, "Negotiating Successful Managed Care Contracts," *Healthcare Financial Management* (August 1995): 28. © 1995, Healthcare Financial Management Association.
3. Mark A. Schuster, M.D., Elizabeth A. McGlynn, and Robert H. Brook, M.D., "Why the Quality of U.S. Health Care Must Be Improved," National Coalition on Health Care, October 1997, http://www.nchc.org/emerge/quality.html (1 March 2000).
4. Jon R. Gabel, Anthony T. Lo Sasso, and Thomas Rice, "Consumer-Driven Health Plans: Are They More Than Talk Now?" *Health Affairs* (20 November 2002), http://content.healthaffairs.org/cgi/reprint/hlthaff.w2.395v1.pdf (23 February 2004).

chapter

9

Health Insurance Policy Provisions and Pricing

outline

objectives

After reading this chapter, you should be able to

- Identify and describe the provisions that typically are included in individual and group health insurance policies
- Describe four ways in which health insurance pricing differs from life insurance pricing
- Explain how insurers calculate net premium rates for individual and group health insurance policies

In Chapter 8, we noted that health insurance consists of two types of coverage: medical expense coverage, which provides benefits for the treatment of illnesses and injuries, and disability income coverage, which provides income replacement benefits for insureds who are unable to work because of illness or injury. In this chapter, we provide an overview of the ways in which individual and group traditional medical expense policies and disability income policies offered by insurance companies are structured and priced.

Health Insurance Policies

A health insurance policy is a legally enforceable contract between an insurance company and the person or entity that purchases the policy, under which the insurer promises to provide protection against the risk of financial loss resulting from the insured person's sickness, injury, or disability. The contract is formed when an applicant submits a completed application and the policy's initial premium to the insurer and the insurer issues the policy. When the policy is issued, the applicant becomes the policyowner, unless the applicant names another person as the policyowner. In the case of group policies, the owner of the policy is referred to as the group policyholder.

As is the case with life insurance contracts, the parties to an individual health insurance contract are the insurance company and an individual policyowner. Under most individual health insurance policies, the policyowner is also the insured. The parties to a group health insurance contract are the insurance company and the group policyholder. The insured group members are not parties to the contract and are not given individual policies. Instead, a master policy is issued to the group policyholder, and each insured group member is given a certificate or benefit booklet that provides information about the group health insurance coverage and the insureds' rights under the policy.

The contents of health insurance policies are outlined in Figure 9.1. Within the framework outlined in Figure 9.1, individual and group applicants have some freedom to customize the coverage provided by the policy to ensure that it meets their needs. For example, applicants for individual medical expense policies generally are given options from which they can choose the benefit levels provided by the contract, the terms under which coverage can be renewed, the length of time they must wait before benefits are payable, and the maximum length of benefit periods. Applicants for individual medical expense coverage also can add coverage for family

FIGURE 9.1 Contents of Health Insurance Policies

- Description of coverage provided
- Maximum benefit amounts (if any)
- Expense participation, or cost-sharing, requirements
- Length of time before benefits are payable
- Maximum benefit periods (if any)
- Premium amounts and their due dates

members and dependents. Applicants for disability income coverage may be able to purchase supplemental benefits. However, disability income policies generally do not provide coverage for dependents.

Because group policies generally are large policies, group policyholders have even greater flexibility than individual policyowners have in designing the coverage they wish to provide for group members. In addition, group policyholders can choose to purchase both medical expense and disability income coverage under one group health insurance policy or purchase separate medical expense and disability income policies. Group policyholders also can choose to purchase all of their health insurance coverage from a single insurer, or they can purchase coverage from more than one provider.

Health Insurance Policy Provisions

The specific rights and responsibilities of the insurer and the owner of a health insurance policy are described in provisions included in the policy. The following sections describe the provisions typically included in individual and group health insurance policies. The provisions apply to both medical expense and disability policies unless otherwise noted.

Individual Health Insurance Policy Provisions

In Chapter 6, we described the provisions included in individual life insurance policies. Some of these provisions—such as the incontestability, grace period, and reinstatement provisions—also are included in individual health insurance policies, although their details often are different. Other provisions are unique to individual health insurance policies.

Incontestability Provision

All individual health insurance policies include an incontestability provision that, like the incontestability provision in individual life insurance policies, limits the time during which the insurer has the right to avoid the contract due to misrepresentations made in the application.

Contestabililty of Individual Medical Expense Policies

The incontestability provision included in individual medical expense policies is called the ***time limit on certain defenses provision.*** It states that after the policy has been in force for a specified period—usually two or three years—the insurer cannot use a material misrepresentation in the application to contest the policy or deny a claim unless the misrepresentation was fraudulent. The following example shows the wording typically used in a time limit on certain defenses provision.

> **Incontestability.**
>
> After coverage on a covered person has been in force during the lifetime of that person for two years, only fraudulent misstatements in the application shall be used to void the coverage on that person.
>
> No claim for a covered charge that is incurred after those two years will be denied because of a pre-existing condition, unless that pre-existing condition was excluded from coverage, by name or specific description, on the date that charge was incurred.
>
> This provision does not have any effect on nor does it bar any other defenses under this policy.

The word *defenses* refers to any reasons that the insurer may use to deny liability under the policy. Thus, the provision specifically notes that the insurer retains the right to deny a claim on the basis of another policy provision. For example, the insurer may deny a claim on the basis that the expenses are specifically excluded from coverage.

Contestability of Individual Disability Income Policies

The incontestability provision included in most individual disability income policies states that after the policy has been in force for a stated period—usually one or two years—the insurer cannot contest the policy's validity on the grounds of material misrepresentation in the application. Note that this incontestability provision (1) does not include a reference to fraudulent misstatements and (2) specifies a shorter time limit than is included in a medical expense policy.

Grace Period Provision

Like individual life insurance policies, individual health insurance policies include a grace period provision that allows the policyowner to pay a renewal premium within a stated period following the premium due date. Coverage remains in force during the grace period. If the premium is not paid by the end of the grace period, the policy lapses and all coverage ends.

Unlike the grace period provision in individual life insurance policies, however, the grace period in individual health insurance policies varies in length, depending on how frequently renewal premiums are payable. For example, the grace period for policies that require monthly renewal premiums typically is 10 days, although some insurers provide a 31-day grace period even when premiums are payable monthly. Policies that require payment of premiums less often than monthly typically contain a 31-day grace period.

Reinstatement Provision

Both individual life and individual health insurance policies also include a reinstatement provision, which states that if certain conditions are met, the insurer will reinstate to in-force status a policy that has lapsed for nonpayment of premiums. To reinstate an individual health insurance policy, the policyowner generally must complete a reinstatement application, pay any overdue premiums, and satisfy any other requirements specified in the provision.

The insurer has the right to decline to reinstate the policy on the basis of statements in the application. If the insurer does not complete its evaluation within a stated number of days after receiving a reinstatement application—in most states, 45 days—or if the insurer accepts an overdue premium without a reinstatement application, then the policy usually is considered to be automatically reinstated.

Coverage under a reinstated individual health insurance policy is limited to accidents that occur after the date of reinstatement and to illnesses that begin more than 10 days after the date of reinstatement. Thus, the insurer can protect against antiselection by excluding from coverage those losses that occur after the policy lapses and before it is reinstated. As we discussed in Chapter 2, antiselection is the tendency of those individuals who believe they have a greater-than-average likelihood of loss to seek insurance protection to a greater extent than do those who believe they have an average or a less-than-average likelihood of loss.

Pre-Existing Conditions Provision

Most individual health insurance policies include a ***pre-existing conditions provision*** stating that until the insured has been covered under the policy for a certain period—typically two years after the policy issue date—the insurer will not pay benefits for a pre-existing condition. After that point, the insurer will pay benefits for a pre-existing condition unless it has been specifically excluded. A sample pre-existing conditions provision is shown below.

> **Pre-existing conditions.**
>
> Benefits for a charge that results from a person's pre-existing condition, as defined in this policy, will be provided only if that charge is a covered charge and is incurred by that person after coverage for that person has been in force for two years. However, if a condition is excluded from coverage by name or specific description, no benefits will be provided for any charges that result from that condition even after those two years.

In an individual health insurance policy, a pre-existing condition usually is defined as any injury or illness that (1) occurred or manifested itself within a specified period before the policy was issued and (2) was not disclosed on the application. The second part of this two-part definition is especially important. A condition that is disclosed on the application is never considered pre-existing for purposes of this exclusion. The insurer has the opportunity to evaluate a disclosed condition and, thus, specifically can exclude the condition from the policy's coverage. If the insurer does not exclude a disclosed condition from the policy's coverage, then the policy will cover that condition after the specified exclusion period. Any specific exclusions, however, remain in effect throughout the life of the policy.

> **Example:** Mark Spellman was treated for a back injury one year before he applied for an individual medical expense insurance policy. Six months before completing the application, Mr. Spellman was diagnosed with, and treated for, allergies. When he completed the application, Mr. Spellman disclosed that he had been treated for allergies, but inadvertently omitted the fact that he had been treated for the back injury. When evaluating Mr. Spellman's application, the insurer decided not to exclude allergies from the policy's coverage.
>
> **Analysis:** Because Mr. Spellman did not disclose that he had been treated for a back injury, that condition is considered a pre-existing condition and the insurer has the right to exclude the condition from coverage for two years after the policy issue date. Thus, if Mr. Spellman has continuing problems related to the back injury and submits claims related to his back injury during the first two years after the policy was issued, the insurer can deny benefits because of the pre-existing conditions provision. In contrast, Mr. Spellman's allergies are not considered a

pre-existing condition because that condition was disclosed on the application and the insurer did not specifically exclude the condition from coverage. Thus, expenses incurred for treatment of allergies will be covered throughout the life of the policy.

In most jurisdictions, two years is the maximum period during which an insurer is permitted to exclude coverage for pre-existing conditions. Insurers, however, are permitted to specify a shorter exclusion period because a shorter exclusion period is more favorable to the insured.

In 1996, the United States passed the ***Health Insurance Portability and Accountability Act (HIPAA),*** a federal law that imposes requirements on group and individual health insurance plans, health insurers, and managed care organizations and that is designed to improve the availability and portability of health insurance benefits. HIPAA prohibits insurers from including a pre-existing conditions provision in individual medical expense insurance policies issued to specified individuals.

When an applicant fails to disclose a condition on the application for insurance, the insurer must determine whether the misrepresentation is material. If the insurer decides that the misrepresentation is not material, then it will apply the policy's pre-existing conditions provision. If the insurer determines that nondisclosure constitutes a material misrepresentation—or, in the case of medical expense coverage, a fraudulent misrepresentation—the insurer can apply the policy's incontestability provision and use the misrepresentation as grounds to avoid the policy.

Renewal Provision

One provision that is unique to individual health insurance policies is the ***renewal provision*** that describes (1) the circumstances under which the insurer has the right to cancel or refuse to renew the coverage and (2) the insurer's right to increase the policy's premium rate. Individual health insurance policies can be divided into five classes based on the type of renewal provision included in the policy. These renewal classes—which include noncancellable, guaranteed renewable, conditionally renewable, optionally renewable, and cancellable—are described in Figure 9.2.

The type of renewal provision included in a policy affects the premium rate for the policy. For example, noncancellable policies, which include guarantees not available in policies in other classifications, generally have higher premiums than do policies in the other classifications.

The number and types of renewal provisions insurers can use in individual health insurance policies depend on legal requirements and regulations. For example, in the United States, HIPAA requires insurers to renew or continue an individual medical expense insurance policy in force at the option of the policyowner. As a result, individual medical expense policies issued in the United States must be either noncancellable or guaranteed renewable policies.

FIGURE 9.2 Renewal Classes for Individual Health Insurance Policies

A ***noncancellable policy*** is guaranteed to be renewable until the insured reaches the limiting age stated in the contract. Most individual noncancellable policies are guaranteed until the insured reaches age 60 or 65. The premium rate specified in the policy also is guaranteed; the insurer cannot increase the premium rate for a noncancellable policy under any circumstances.

A ***guaranteed renewable policy*** must be renewed at the policyowner's option—as long as premium payments are made—at least until the insured attains the age limit specified in the contract. The insurer has the right to increase the premium rate for such a policy only if it increases the premium rate for an entire class of policies. A ***class of policies*** consists of all policies of a particular type (for example, all major medical expense policies) or all policies issued to a particular group of insureds (for example, all policies issued to insureds who are a particular age or who fall into a specific risk category).

A ***conditionally renewable policy*** grants the insurer a limited right to refuse to renew an individual health insurance policy at the end of a premium payment period. The insurer may refuse to renew a policy only if its decision is based on one or more specific reasons stated in the policy, such as the age of the insured. The reasons cannot be related to the insured's health. A conditionally renewable policy also gives the insurer the right to increase the premium rate for any class of conditionally renewable policies.

An ***optionally renewable policy*** grants the insurer the right to refuse to renew the policy for any reason on certain dates specified in the contract—usually either the policy anniversary date or any premium due date. The insurer also is allowed to add coverage limitations and to increase the premium rate for a class of optionally renewable policies.

A ***cancellable policy*** grants the insurer the right to terminate the policy at any time, for any reason, simply by notifying the policyowner that the policy is cancelled and by refunding any advance premium that has been paid for the policy.

Claims Provisions

Individual health insurance policies typically include provisions that define both the insured's obligation to provide timely notification of loss to the insurer and the insurer's obligation to make prompt benefit payments to the insured. In Canada, for example, the policy usually requires the insured to notify the insurer of a claim in writing within 30 days from the date the claim arose and to furnish the insurer with proof of the loss within 90 days from the date the claim arose. The insurer must pay benefits within 60 days of receipt of proof of loss for a medical expense claim and within 30 days of receipt of proof of loss for a disability income claim. Policies issued in the United States contain similar requirements.

Legal Actions Provision

Individual health insurance policies typically include a ***legal actions provision***, which limits the time during which a claimant who disagrees with an insurer's claim decision has the right to sue the insurer to collect the amount the claimant believes is owed under the policy. The length of the time period varies from jurisdiction to jurisdiction, but it typically ranges from one to three years after the claimant provides the insurer with proof of the loss.

Overinsurance Provision

To prevent a person who is covered under more than one health insurance policy from profiting from an illness or injury, many individual medical expense and disability income insurance policies contain an ***overinsurance provision*** stating that the benefits payable under the policy will be reduced if the person is overinsured. An ***overinsured person*** is one who is entitled to receive either (1) more in medical expense benefits than the actual costs incurred for treatment or (2) a greater income amount during disability than the amount that would have been earned from working.

An overinsurance provision takes effect only if the insurer was not notified of existing coverage at the time of application. In cases of overinsurance, the insurer reduces the amount of the benefits that would otherwise be payable under the policy and refunds any premium amount paid for the excess coverage.

Change of Occupation Provision (Disability Policies Only)

Because occupation has a direct effect on an insured's risk of illness or injury, many individual disability income insurance policies include a ***change of occupation provision*** that permits the insurer to adjust the policy's premium rate or the amount of benefits payable under the policy if the insured changes occupation. The insurer generally reduces the premium rate if the insured changes to a less hazardous occupation. The insurer generally reduces the maximum benefit amount payable under the policy if the insured changes to a more hazardous occupation. Because the benefit payable under a disability income insurance policy is based on the insured's income at the time of application, most insurers also adjust the maximum benefit amount if a change of occupation results in a significantly different income.

Physical Examination Provision (Disability Policies Only)

Both individual and group disability income insurance policies usually include a ***physical examination provision*** stating that the insurer has the right to have an insured who has submitted a disability income claim examined by a doctor of the insurer's choice, at the insurer's expense. Such an examination allows the insurer to verify the validity of disability income claims. The provision also usually grants the insurer the right to require that a disabled insured undergo medical examinations at regular intervals so that the insurer can verify that the insured is still disabled.

Group Health Insurance Policy Provisions

In Chapter 7, we described the eligibility, incontestability, grace period, and termination provisions often included in group life and health insurance policies. In this section, we describe additional provisions that insurers include in group health insurance policies—pre-existing conditions provision, coordination of benefits provision, and conversion provision. The pre-existing conditions provision applies to both medical expense and disability policies, whereas the coordination of benefits and conversion provisions apply only to medical expense policies.

Pre-Existing Conditions Provision

Like individual health insurance policies, many group health insurance policies include a pre-existing conditions provision stating that benefits are not payable for pre-existing conditions until the insured has been covered under the policy for a specified period of time. Group health insurance policies define a pre-existing condition in various ways. Group policies usually also specify that a condition will no longer be considered

"It appears we all have group insurance."

pre-existing—and thus the condition will be eligible for coverage—if the insured (1) has not received treatment for that condition for a specified period of time following the effective date of coverage or (2) has been covered under the policy for a specified number of consecutive months, such as 12 months.

Most insurers will waive the requirements of a group pre-existing conditions provision for any group member who was eligible for coverage when the policy became effective if (1) the group was previously covered by a group medical expense insurance policy issued by another insurer and (2) the group member was covered by that prior policy. Thus, if a group policyholder decides to switch insurance carriers, the pre-existing conditions provision in the new carrier's policy typically will not apply to group members who were covered under the earlier plan.

In the United States, HIPAA imposes a number of restrictions on the pre-existing conditions provision included in group medical expense insurance plans. These restrictions are described in Insight 9.1.

Coordination of Benefits Provision (Medical Expense Policies Only)

In the United States, many people are eligible for coverage under more than one group medical expense plan. For example, spouses who both work typically are eligible for coverage under their own employers' group policy and under their spouses' group policy. To prevent duplication of benefit payments, group medical expense insurance policies typically include a coordination of benefits provision. The ***coordination of benefits (COB) provision*** is designed to prevent a group member who is insured under more than one group medical expense insurance policy from receiving benefit amounts that are greater than the amount of medical expenses the insured actually incurs. The COB provision prevents duplicate benefit payments by defining the group medical expense plan that is the primary provider of benefits and the plan that is the secondary provider.

Under the terms of most COB provisions, when an insured requires medical care, the plan described as the primary provider is responsible for paying the full benefit amounts promised under the plan. To determine this amount, the primary provider first calculates the amount of the insured individual's total ***allowable expenses***—those expenses that the insured incurred and that are covered under a medical expense insurance policy. The primary provider then calculates the amount of any expense participation, or cost-sharing, features specified in the plan, including deductible and coinsurance amounts. The difference between the amount of allowable expenses and the deductible and coinsurance amounts is the amount payable by the primary provider.

INSIGHT 9.1 HIPAA Pre-Existing Conditions Requirements for Group Medical Expense Insurance Plans

The Health Insurance Portability and Accountability Act (HIPAA) of 1996 imposes a number of requirements on group medical expense plans in the United States. HIPAA's pre-existing conditions requirements are designed to allow group insureds who have a pre-existing condition to change jobs without losing coverage for the condition. HIPAA places the following limits on the pre-existing conditions exclusion that group medical expense plans may include:

- HIPAA defines a pre-existing condition as a physical or mental condition for which medical advice, diagnosis, care, or treatment was recommended or received within the six-month period preceding the date an individual enrolls in a group plan. The enrollment date is either the date the individual becomes covered under the group health plan or, if earlier, the first day of the waiting period for enrollment. Note that the maximum look-back period for purposes of defining a pre-existing condition under HIPAA is six months.
- The period during which a pre-existing condition is excluded from coverage ordinarily may not exceed 12 months after the enrollment date (18 months for late enrollees).
- The length of the pre-existing conditions exclusion period must be reduced by the total amount of the individual's creditable coverage, which includes coverage under a group medical expense plan, medical expense insurance policy, or benefits program provided by the federal or state government. An individual is credited with a period of creditable coverage only if that period was not followed by a break in coverage of 63 days or more. A waiting period under an employer-sponsored group medical expense benefits plan does not constitute a break in coverage.
- Pregnancy may not be treated as a pre-existing condition. In addition, pre-existing conditions cannot be imposed on newborn or adopted children under age 18 if the child is covered within 30 days of birth or adoption.

Source: Adapted from Academy for Healthcare Management, *Managed Healthcare: An Introduction,* 2nd ed. (Washington, DC: Academy for Healthcare Management, © 2001), 11-11.

After the primary provider has paid the full benefit allowed under the plan, the insured can submit the claim to the secondary plan along with a description of the benefit amounts the primary plan paid. The plan described as the secondary provider can determine the amount of the claim it is responsible for paying in a number of ways. The most common approach is to first calculate the amount of the insured's total allowable expenses the plan would have paid if it had been defined as the primary provider. The secondary provider then compares this amount to the amount paid by the primary provider. If payment of the full amount would result in benefit payments from both plans in excess of the total amount of allowable expenses, the secondary provider will pay only the difference between the allowable expenses incurred and the amount already paid by the primary provider.

Example: Sandra Polk is covered by two group medical expense insurance plans. Both plans include a coordination of benefits provision. Each plan specifies a $100 deductible and a 20 percent coinsurance requirement. In May, Ms. Polk incurred $5,100 in allowable medical expenses for treatment of an injury. Ms. Polk submitted a claim for her expenses to the plan designated as her primary provider. Ms. Polk then submitted the claim, along with a description of the benefit paid by the primary provider, to her secondary plan.

Analysis: The primary provider determined that Ms. Polk was eligible to receive the following benefit:

$5,100	Total allowable expenses
– 100	Deductible
$5,000	
– 1,000	Coinsurance ($5,000 × 0.20)
$4,000	Amount payable by insurer

Because the secondary plan contains the same deductible and coinsurance features, the secondary provider would normally pay Ms. Polk $4,000 in benefits. However, under the COB provision, the secondary provider will pay Ms. Polk only $1,100—the difference between the total allowable expenses ($5,100) and the amount paid by the primary provider ($4,000). Ms. Polk will incur no out-of-pocket costs.

Some group medical expense insurance policies include a special form of COB provision, generally called a nonduplication of benefits provision, that limits the amount payable if the plan is defined as the secondary provider. A ***nonduplication of benefits provision*** is a COB provision that limits the amount payable by the secondary plan to the difference, if any, between the amount paid by the primary plan and the amount that would have been payable by the secondary plan had that plan been the primary plan.

Example: Let's return to our earlier example in which Sandra Polk is covered under two group medical expense plans. In this case, however, assume that the plan designated as Ms. Polk's secondary plan contains a nonduplication of benefits provision.

Analysis: As in our earlier example, Ms. Polk's primary plan would have paid a $4,000 policy benefit. Under the nonduplication of benefit provision, the secondary plan would pay no benefit because the amount paid by the primary provider ($4,000) and the amount the secondary provider would have paid ($4,000) were the same.

Most COB provisions include rules for determining which plan is the primary plan. For example, most COB provisions state that when an insured is also covered by another group plan that does not include a COB provision, the plan without a COB provision will be the primary provider of benefits. In addition, if spouses are covered by two separate plans, the primary plan for each spouse is the one provided by that spouse's employer.

Example: Janet and Franklin Pratt are married and have a young daughter, Sharon. Both Janet and Franklin work full time for employers that provide group medical expense coverage to employees and their spouses and dependents.

Analysis: In this case, if only one plan includes a COB provision, then the plan without the COB provision will be considered the primary payer of benefits for both Janet and Franklin. If both plans include COB provisions, then Janet's primary provider is the plan provided by her employer and her secondary plan is the plan provided by Franklin's employer. Franklin's primary provider is the plan provided by his employer and his secondary plan is the plan provided by Janet's employer.

If an individual is covered as a dependent under more than one group plan, the plan that will be the primary provider can be determined in two ways. One method—the birthday rule or earlier birthday method—states that the plan covering the employee whose birthday falls earlier in the calendar year will be considered the primary provider of benefits for a dependent. Note that the employees' actual ages are not a factor in determining the primary provider under this method. The second method states that the primary provider of benefits for a dependent is the plan that provides benefits for a male employee rather than a female employee.

Example: Let's look again at the health insurance plans covering Janet and Franklin Pratt and their daughter, Sharon. Assume that Janet's birthday is on March 14 and Franklin's birthday is on August 2.

Analysis: According to the birthday rule, the plan provided by Janet's employer would be considered the primary provider of benefits for Sharon because Janet's birthday falls earlier in the year than Franklin's birthday. Under the second method, because Franklin is the male parent, the plan provided by Franklin's employer would be considered the primary provider of benefits for Sharon.

In some states in the United States, insurers are required by law to use the birthday rule. In other states, if only one plan has adopted the birthday rule or if neither plan has adopted the birthday rule, then the plan that provides benefits to a dependent of a male will be primary.

Conversion Provision (Medical Expense Policies Only)

The continuation of terminated employees' group health coverage is a critical issue associated with employer-sponsored plans in the United States. Congress responded to the need for standardized continuation of group health care benefits through passage of the Consolidated Omnibus Budget Reconciliation Act (COBRA) of 1985. COBRA mandates that employees and their dependents who become ineligible for group medical expense coverage as a result of a specified qualifying event be allowed to continue their group coverage for a specified period following termination of their group coverage. Qualifying events under COBRA include termination of employment, reduced work hours, and death or divorce of the covered employee. COBRA allows up to 18 months of continued coverage for employees and up to 36 months of continued coverage for spouses and dependents following the employee's death or a divorce or legal separation from the employee. A person who elects to continue group coverage under COBRA is responsible for paying the full cost of continued coverage.

In addition, the laws of most states in the United States require group medical expense insurance policies to include a conversion provision. A ***conversion provision*** grants an insured group member who is leaving the group a limited right to purchase an individual medical expense insurance policy without presenting evidence of insurability. The right is limited in that the insurer can refuse to issue the individual policy if the coverage would result in the insured group member becoming overinsured. For example, an employee who is changing jobs and will be eligible for group medical expense insurance from his new employer would probably be overinsured if he were also issued an individual medical expense insurance policy.

Requirements regarding the specific coverages that a conversion policy must provide vary from jurisdiction to jurisdiction. However, the benefits provided by individual policies generally are more restrictive than those provided by group policies. In addition, an insured group member who elects to convert group coverage to an individual medical expense insurance policy generally will be charged a higher premium rate for the individual policy than he paid for group coverage.

Pricing Health Insurance

In Chapter 6, we defined pricing and described how insurance companies price individual life insurance policies. In Chapter 7, we described the principles insurers apply in pricing group life insurance policies and explained that these principles also apply to group health insurance policies. Individual and group health insurance pricing differs from life insurance pricing with respect to four important factors, which are set forth in Figure 9.3.

In spite of these differences, the fundamental principles insurers use to price individual and group health insurance products (medical expense and disability) are the same as the principles insurers use to price life insurance products. To provide the funds it will need to pay health insurance claims as they come due and cover expenses, an insurance company must collect premiums from the people to whom it provides health insurance coverage.

Just as insurers use mortality rates to calculate life insurance premium rates, they use morbidity rates to calculate health insurance premium rates. ***Morbidity rates*** describe the incidence of sickness and accidents occurring among given groups of people. To predict morbidity rates,

FIGURE 9.3 Differences Between Life Insurance and Health Insurance Pricing

Amounts Payable

The amount of a life insurance claim generally is specified in the policy. The amount of a health insurance claim is often much less definite. For example, the amount of a medical expense claim depends on the severity of the illness or injury and can range from a fairly small amount to a very large amount.

Frequency of Claims

Life insurance pays only one claim for each person insured under the policy. Health insurance is likely to pay multiple claims for each person covered by the policy.

Effects of Environmental Factors

Most life insurance benefits are unaffected by changes in the environment. Health insurance benefits can be dramatically affected by economic conditions, medical practices, inflation, and technological and medical advances.

Location

Life insurance premiums for specific age groups generally do not vary from one area to another within a particular state or region. Because of variations in medical costs in different areas, certain health insurance premiums must be calculated separately for different geographic areas.

insurers typically consult ***morbidity tables***, which are charts displaying morbidity rates for individuals in different age groups.

The insurance company uses the information about morbidity rates to calculate its predicted ***claim costs***—the costs that it will incur to provide the policy benefits. The insurer must estimate its claim costs for each type of benefit provided.

Insurers calculate claim costs by multiplying the frequency of the expected claim—that is, the number of claims for a particular benefit that the insurer expects to receive during a particular time period—by the average amount of each claim, as shown below.

Claim Costs	=	**Frequency of expected claim**	×	**Average amount of each claim**

The following example shows how an insurer would calculate claim costs for hospital room and board benefits.

Example: The Hathaway Insurance Company expects to receive 100 claims for hospital room and board during the coming year from insureds living in a particular geographic area. Hathaway expects that the average amount of each claim will be $2,500.

Analysis: Hathaway's claim costs for hospital room and board in the particular area will be equal to $250,000 (100 claims × $2,500 per claim).

The insurer uses its projected claim costs to calculate the net annual premium rates that will be sufficient to pay the promised health insurance benefits. The insurer then adds a loading factor that it estimates will be sufficient to cover all of its expenses and unforeseen contingencies. Because the risk is more uncertain for health insurance than for life insurance, insurance companies usually include in their loading for health insurance premiums a greater amount for unforeseen contingencies than they include in their loading for life insurance premiums. The net annual premium rate plus the loading equals the gross annual premium rate that the insurer will charge for a policy.

Insurers generally calculate health insurance premium rates on an annual basis. If premiums are payable more frequently than annually, then the insurer will add a small amount to the gross annual premium to cover the additional expenses incurred in collecting premiums on this more frequent basis.

A number of states require gross premiums for health insurance policies to be reasonable. As a measure of reasonableness, insurers generally are required to calculate the anticipated loss ratio for a group of similar policies, and this loss ratio typically must be at least a minimum stated percentage. The ***loss ratio*** is the ratio of benefits an insurer paid out for a block of policies to the premiums the insurer received for those policies. It can be calculated using the following equation:

Loss Ratio = Benefits Paid ÷ Premiums Received

The loss ratio measures the extent to which an insurer is paying out more or less in benefits than it receives in premiums. Some insurers substitute incurred claims for benefits paid and earned premiums for premiums received in loss ratio calculations. A loss ratio of 1.00 indicates that the insurer paid the same amount in benefits as it received in premiums. A loss ratio smaller than one—for example, 0.75—indicates that the insurer received more in premiums than it paid in benefits. A loss ratio of greater than one—for example 1.25—indicates that benefits exceeded premiums. A very low loss ratio may indicate that the insurer is overcharging for the coverage. Note that even if the loss ratio for a block of policies remains level over time, the amount of premiums required for those policies will increase if policy benefit costs increase.

Premium Payments

To establish a valid health insurance contract, the applicant typically submits the initial premium for the contract along with the application for insurance. The owner of the policy must then pay periodic renewal premiums to keep the policy's coverage in force. How often and in what manner renewal premiums are to be paid depend on the terms of the contract.

Paying Individual Health Insurance Premiums

In our discussion of individual life insurance policies, we described various modes of paying renewal premiums. Most individual medical expense and disability insurance policies require monthly renewal premiums. These premiums can be paid in cash, by money order, or by check. An increasing number of insurers also allow policyowners to pay renewal premiums online by charging the premium amount against a credit card. Renewal premiums also can be paid using automatic premium payment techniques such as preauthorized check systems or electronic fund transfers. If a premium is not paid in cash, however, the insurer's acceptance of payment is contingent on the actual collection of the money.

Paying Group Health Insurance Premiums

For group medical expense and disability insurance plans, premiums can be paid by the group policyholder, the individuals insured under the group plan, or both. As we learned in Chapter 7, if the group policyholder pays all of the premiums without requiring the individual insureds to pay anything, the plan is said to be *noncontributory*. If individual insureds pay any part of the premium, the plan is said to be *contributory*. Individual insureds' contributions generally are paid to the group policyholder who then makes monthly premium payments to the insurer. Most employer-sponsored group health insurance plans collect premium amounts from employees through payroll deductions.

The way in which premiums are used to pay the group plan's claim costs and administrative expenses is known as the plan's ***funding mechanism.*** Funding mechanisms reflect risk management techniques (recall the discussion in Chapter 2) and can take a variety of forms. At one extreme is a ***fully insured plan*** under which the group policyholder makes periodic premium payments to the insurance company and the insurance company bears the responsibility for all claim payments. At the other extreme is a ***fully self-insured plan*** under which the group policyholder—usually an employer—takes complete responsibility for all claim payments and related expenses. Between these extremes are a number of alternative funding arrangements. In this section, we describe the methods most often used to fund group health insurance coverage.

Fully Insured Plans

Under fully insured plans, the insurer issues the group health insurance policy on a one-year renewable term basis. Premiums for coverage typically are guaranteed for 12 months, and each year's premium pays for just that year's coverage. At the end of the policy year, new premium rates are calculated, based on the sex and attained ages of the insured group members and the experience of the group. Most group long-term disability income insurance plans are fully insured.

The insurer bears all risk under a fully insured plan. If the dollar amount of the claims submitted exceeds the dollar amount of premiums collected, the insurer must absorb the loss. On the other hand, if the group experiences lower claim expenses than anticipated and the dollar amount of the claims submitted is less than the dollar amount of premiums collected, the insurer retains the difference as profit.

To enable employers to reduce the total cost of providing health insurance coverage for employees, insurers and employers have developed a number of alternatives to the traditional fully insured plan. Figure 9.4 explains three of these alternatives—retrospective rating arrangements, premium delay arrangements, and minimum premium plans—which

FIGURE 9.4 Alternative Funding Mechanisms

- A ***retrospective rating arrangement*** is a group health insurance funding mechanism under which the insurer agrees to charge the group policyholder a lower monthly premium than it would normally charge based on the group's prior claim experience, and the policyholder agrees to pay an additional amount if, at the end of the policy year, the group's claim experience has been unfavorable.
- A ***premium delay arrangement*** is a group health insurance funding mechanism that allows the group policyholder to postpone paying monthly group insurance premiums for a stated period of time beyond the expiration of the policy's grace period.
- A ***minimum premium plan (MPP)*** is a group health insurance funding mechanism under which the group policyholder deposits into a special account funds that are sufficient to pay a stated amount of expected claims, and the insurer administers the plan and pays claims from that special account until the funds are exhausted. Thereafter, the insurer is responsible for paying claims from its own funds, and it charges the group policyholder a premium for the coverage it provides.

modify the manner in which premiums are paid. The employer, however, must still pay premiums for the group insurance policy and the insurer remains responsible for paying all covered claims.

Self-Insured Plans

Under a self-insured plan, the employer assumes some or all of the risk of paying claims and the risk that claims may be excessive. For example, many employers fully self-insure short-term disability income coverage for their employees by means of a salary continuation plan. A ***salary continuation plan*** typically provides 100 percent of the insured employee's salary, beginning on the first day of the employee's absence due to illness or injury and continuing for some specified time. Most group medical expense insurance plans, on the other hand, are partially self-insured. Under this arrangement, the employer is financially responsible for paying a certain level of claims, and the risk for claims above that level is transferred to a traditional health insurance provider. For example, an employer might self-insure the plan's basic medical expense benefits and purchase supplemental major medical insurance coverage from an insurance company.

Many employers believe that self-insuring can help them better control increasing health care costs by allowing them to avoid some of the costs that are built into traditional insurance premium rates. For example, a self-insured employer can avoid paying agent commissions, state premium taxes, and the insurer's overhead expenses. Another benefit of self-insurance is an improved cash flow because the employer retains the money it would have paid in premiums and can earn interest on that money.

For U.S. companies, a final advantage of self-insuring health insurance coverage is the fact that self-insured plans are exempt from state laws that apply to insurance policies. Employers, therefore, have more freedom in designing their group health insurance plans. For example, many state insurance laws require health insurance policies to include certain coverages. The cost of those mandated coverages must be reflected in any plan an insurer offers in those states. A self-insured plan is not subject to these state insurance laws, and thus an employer offering a self-insured plan does not have to include state-mandated coverages. Many self-insured plans in the United States, however, are subject to federal regulation under the Employer Retirement Income Security Act (ERISA), which we will discuss in Chapter 13.

Stop-Loss Coverage

An employer that self-insures may not have the financial resources to pay all of the claims if the group experiences several catastrophic medical claims in one year. ***Stop-loss insurance*** is insurance purchased by employers that self-insure group health insurance plans so that they can place a maximum dollar limit on their liability for paying claims. Under ***individual stop-loss coverage***, or *specific stop-loss coverage*, the stop-loss insurer pays a portion of each claim that exceeds a stated amount. Under ***aggregate stop-loss coverage***, the stop-loss insurer becomes responsible for paying claims when the employer's total claims exceed a stated dollar amount within a stated period of time.

Stop-loss coverage typically is provided under a contract entered into between the stop-loss carrier (the insurer) and the employer. The contract defines the relationship between the carrier and the employer and includes a schedule of benefit payments for which the carrier will reimburse the employer. The contract typically is for a 12-month period. Note that the stop-loss carrier does not make benefit payments directly to the insured group members; instead, the carrier reimburses the employer, which retains responsibility for making claim payments to insureds.

Plan Administration

Self-insured plans are administered by a variety of methods. Some groups that self-insure their plans are able to fully administer their own plans. For other groups, having an outside organization provide some or all of the administrative services for the plan is more cost-effective. These groups usually purchase an ***administrative services only (ASO) contract*** under which the self-insured group policyholder pays a fee in exchange for administrative services provided by an outside organization. These fees are not subject to state premium taxes. ASO contracts can be purchased from an insurance company or another organization, such as a third-party administrator.

Key Terms

time limit on certain defenses provision
pre-existing conditions provision
Health Insurance Portability and Accountability Act (HIPAA)
renewal provision
noncancellable policy
guaranteed renewable policy
class of policies
conditionally renewable policy
optionally renewable policy
cancellable policy
legal actions provision
overinsurance provision
overinsured person
change of occupation provision
physical examination provision
coordination of benefits (COB) provision
allowable expense
nonduplication of benefits provision
conversion provision
morbidity rate
morbidity table
claim costs
loss ratio
funding mechanism
fully insured plan
fully self-insured plan
retrospective rating arrangement
premium delay arrangement
minimum premium plan (MPP)
salary continuation plan
stop-loss insurance
individual stop-loss coverage
aggregate stop-loss coverage
administrative services only (ASO) contract

chapter

10

Property and Liability Insurance

outline

Personal Property Insurance

Homeowners Insurance

Automobile Insurance

Personal Liability Insurance

Commercial Property and Liability Insurance

objectives

After reading this chapter, you should be able to

- Distinguish between named-perils coverage and open-perils coverage.
- Distinguish among replacement cost insurance, actual cash value insurance, and agreed value insurance
- Describe the types of coverages available under a homeowners policy
- Explain how the amounts of property coverage are determined under a homeowners policy
- Name the four parts of an automobile insurance policy and what they cover
- Explain the limits of coverage under an automobile insurance policy
- Describe policy conditions found in a homeowners policy and those found in an automobile insurance policy
- List the factors taken into account when setting premiums for homeowners policies and automobile insurance policies
- Explain how umbrella liability insurance coverage works
- Describe two types of commercial package policies

A person can devote considerable energy to earning and accumulating assets only to have them depleted completely by an accident or natural disaster. Fire could destroy his home; he could cause a car accident in which he severely injures himself and others; or someone could be hurt while in his home. Property and liability insurance offers protection against the financial losses that result from such events.

Property insurance provides protection against financial loss from property damage and theft, and ***liability insurance*** provides protection against financial responsibility for harming others or their property. Historically, property insurance and liability insurance were provided under separate policies. Now, however, a ***package policy*** can provide two or more types of insurance—property and liability, for example—in one policy. Homeowners insurance and automobile insurance, which we discuss in this chapter, are both examples of package policies.

Property insurance and liability insurance are known as *personal property insurance* and *personal liability insurance* when they insure individuals and as *commercial property insurance* and *commercial liability insurance* when they insure businesses. We begin this chapter with a discussion of two package policies that combine personal property insurance and personal liability insurance—homeowners and automobile insurance. We then discuss personal liability insurance products and end with a brief overview of commercial property and liability insurance products.

Personal property and liability insurance premiums paid by an individual are not tax deductible. However, a business may deduct premiums for commercial coverages. Claims paid under property insurance policies for loss to real or personal property may result in capital gains taxes if the policy proceeds exceed the insured's basis in his property. However, taxes on the gain can be postponed under certain conditions if the insured uses the policy proceeds to replace the damaged or lost property. Claims paid under liability insurance policies do not result in taxable income to the payee.

Personal Property Insurance

Personal property insurance can insure real property and/or personal property. Real property is land and whatever is affixed to it. Personal property is all property other than real property. In general terms, real property is immovable, and personal property is movable. Coverages for real property and personal property can be combined in one policy as they are in homeowners insurance, which covers the dwelling (real property) and its contents (personal property).

A property insurance policy is a contract between the insurer and the policyowner. Note that the policyowner and the insured property owner are almost always the same person under property and liability insurance products. The term *insured* is preferred to refer to this person.

The insured must have an insurable interest in the property that he insures, and the insurer will pay for only the insured's insurable interest. For example, if a homeowner with a mortgage insures his home, the policy typically will name both the homeowner and mortgage lender as insureds. In the event of a loss, a claim check would be made payable to both the insured and the mortgage lender, who would decide how to split the amount payable. Property owners are not allowed to profit by collecting policy proceeds for more than their interest in the property or for more than the property is worth.

The cause of a loss is known as a ***peril***. Typical property perils include fire, windstorm, hail, and collision. Property insurance policies describe covered perils in two ways: named-perils and open-perils. ***Named-perils*** protection covers losses caused only by specific perils named in the policy, subject to exclusions and limitations. ***Open-perils***, also known as *all-risks*, protection covers losses caused by all perils other than those excluded in the policy.

Property insurance policies can provide coverage on a replacement cost basis, actual cash value basis, or agreed value basis.

- ***Replacement cost insurance*** pays the insured the full cost of replacing the lost or damaged property, subject to a maximum amount. Because replacement cost insurance is an agreement to replace lost or damaged property with property of the same kind and quality at today's market prices, the cost may be higher than the property's original market value.

- ***Actual cash value insurance*** pays the insured an amount equal to the replacement cost minus an amount for depreciation.

- ***Agreed value insurance*** pays the insured an amount agreed upon by the insured and the insurer at the time of policy issue. Agreed value insurance is used when it is extremely difficult to determine the value of property after it is damaged or lost, such as with fine art.

In this section, we discuss the two most common types of personal property insurance—homeowners insurance and automobile insurance—both of which are sold as package policies that provide both property and liability coverage.

Homeowners Insurance

Homeowners insurance is a type of personal property insurance that protects an insured from financial losses resulting from damage to her home and/or its contents or resulting from being held liable for the losses of others. The insured under a homeowners policy includes

- The person named in the policy
- Residents of the household who are relatives of the insured
- Residents of the household who are under the age of 21 and in the care of any other person considered an insured
- Full-time students who were residents of the household prior to enrolling in school and who are under (1) 24 if an insured's relative or (2) 21 if not an insured's relative.

The coverages that can be provided by homeowners insurance are listed in Figure 10.1.

Although lenders typically require that homeowners insurance be obtained in conjunction with a mortgage, any person who owns a dwelling would be wise to purchase homeowners insurance if for no other reason than the peace of mind it offers. People who rent a house or an apartment also need coverage because the building owner's insurance does not cover renters' personal property.

Types of Homeowners Coverage

Some U.S. property insurance companies develop their own homeowners policies. Other companies use the standard homeowners policies of

FIGURE 10.1 Coverages under Homeowners Insurance

- Damage to the dwelling
- Damage to other structures on the property
- Damage to personal property and dwelling contents
- Theft
- Expenses arising from loss of use of the dwelling
- Personal liability
- Medical payments to others

the Insurance Services Office (ISO) or the American Association of Insurance Services (AAIS), which are advisory insurance organizations that develop various insurance policies for their member companies. Homeowners policies are similar whether they are developed by a company, the ISO, or the AAIS. In this section, we explain homeowners insurance using the standard ISO policy forms. Note that these homeowner policies are quite detailed in what is and is not covered.

The ISO has devised a series of six homeowners policy types—known as policy forms—for different situations and that offer different coverages. These forms are

- **Homeowners 2 Broad Form (HO-2).** Designed for owner-occupants of homes, this form provides coverage on buildings and personal property for a range of specifically named perils.

- **Homeowners 3 Special Form (HO-3).** Designed for owner-occupants of homes, this form provides coverage on buildings for all causes of loss not otherwise excluded and coverage on personal property for the same perils named in form HO-2.

- **Homeowners 4 Contents Broad Form (HO-4).** Designed for tenants, this form provides coverage on the personal property of the tenant of a residence for the same causes of loss covered in form HO-2.

- **Homeowners 5 Comprehensive Form (HO-5).** Designed for owner-occupants of homes, this form provides coverage on buildings and personal property for all causes of loss not otherwise excluded.

- **Homeowners 6 Unit-Owners Form (HO-6).** Designed for condominium and cooperative unit-owners, this form provides coverage for the personal property of the condominium unit owner-occupant as well as for certain building items in which the unit-owner has an insurable interest. The HO-6 covers the same specifically named perils as covered by form HO-2.

- **Homeowners 8 Modified Form (HO-8).** Designed to provide package coverage to the owner-occupants of homes that do not meet all the eligibility requirements applicable to other homeowners forms, the HO-8 provides limited named-perils coverage on buildings and personal property of owner-occupants of private homes. The HO-8 is particularly well suited for older residences for which market value is considerably less than the cost to rebuild them.[1]

HO-3 is the form most often used by owner-occupants of private homes.

Coverage under Homeowners Policies

Each of these homeowners policy forms has two coverage sections: Section I and Section II.

Section I

Section I of a homeowners policy describes property coverage, and the section is divided into four coverages:

- **Coverage A: Dwelling.** The home and any attached structures. The land itself is not insured.
- **Coverage B: Other structures.** Other structures that are set apart from the residence by a clear space. Examples include tree houses, garden sheds, and gazebos.
- **Coverage C: Personal property.** All personal property owned by the insured at any location in the world.
- **Coverage D: Loss of use.** Covers additional living expenses should the insured not be able to live in his residence due to repairs necessitated by a covered loss.

"Let's see now. 'Structural damage due to children eating property'.... Nope. Nothing here I'm afraid."

www.CartoonStock.com

Not all policy forms have all four coverages. For example, HO-4—commonly known as renters insurance—does not cover the dwelling or other structures.

Some of the coverages are open perils, while others are named perils. Two types of named perils—basic and broad—are found in the ISO homeowners policies. A ***basic form*** of named-perils coverage covers 10 named perils. A ***broad form*** of named-perils coverage covers the 10 named perils in a basic form plus 6 more perils. The types of perils covered under section I of each homeowners policy form are shown in Figure 10.2.

FIGURE 10.2 Types of Perils Covered under Section I of Each Homeowners Policy Form

	Type of Policy Form					
Coverage	**HO-2**	**HO-3**	**HO-4***	**HO-5**	**HO-6****	**HO-8**
A—Dwelling	Broad	Open perils	NA	Open perils	Broad	Basic
B—Other Structures	Broad	Open perils	NA	Open perils	NA	Basic
C—Personal Property	Broad	Broad	Broad	Open perils	Broad	Basic
D—Loss of Use	Broad	Open perils or broad***	Broad	Open perils	Broad	Basic

* Renter's insurance, for instances in which the insured does not own the dwelling.

** Condominium insurance, for instances in which the insured does not own the structure of the dwelling but owns appliances, fixtures, and improvements that are part of the building. Coverage B is included under Coverage A in an HO-6 policy for instances in which the insured owns other real property on the condominium property, such as a storage shed.

*** Depends on type of property damaged. If real property, open-perils coverage; if personal property, broad named-perils coverage.

Basic and broad named-perils are as follows:

Basic
Fire and lightning
Aircraft
Volcanic eruption
Vandalism and malicious mischief
Windstorm and hail
Vehicles
Theft
Explosion
Smoke
Riot or civil commotion

Broad
Basic perils *and*
Accidental discharge or overflow of water or steam
Falling objects
Freezing
Sudden and accidental tearing apart, cracking, burning, or bulging
Weight of ice, snow, or sleet
Sudden and accidental damage from artificially generated electrical current

Source: Excerpted and adapted from Karen L. Hamilton and Cheryl L. Ferguson, *Personal Risk Management and Property-Liability Insurance* (Malvern, PA: American Institute for Chartered Property Casualty Underwriters/Insurance Institute of America, 2002), 3.4. Used with permission.

All of the policy forms also have various miscellaneous additional coverages, which may include debris removal, unauthorized use of credit cards, and damage to grave markers. However, keep in mind that each homeowners policy names many specific exclusions from each of its coverages. In addition, all forms of homeowners policies contain the following general exclusions to section I property coverages:

- Enforcement of any ordinance or law that requires the repair, construction, or demolition of a structure, except as specifically covered under the additional coverages section of some policy forms
- Earth movement, for example, earthquakes, mud slides, and sink holes
- Water damage, including floods and sewer backups
- Power failure that occurs off the insured residence, such as a citywide power outage that leads to loss of the use of the dwelling due to lack of heat
- Neglect, which means failure to prevent further damage to an already damaged property
- War, including civil war, revolution, and rebellion
- Nuclear hazard, which means any nuclear reaction, radiation, or radioactive contamination
- Intentional loss, such as arson
- Government action, such as by exercise of eminent domain or condemnation

Some insurers may be willing to issue endorsements for a few typically excluded perils, such as ordinance or law and sewer backup. With other perils, such as flood, a person must purchase a separate, specialized policy to obtain coverage.

Section II

Section II of a homeowners policy has three coverage sections, all of which apply to all six ISO policy forms:

- **Coverage E: Personal liability coverage.** Protects the insured from liability for bodily injury and property damage whether the occurrence is in the insured's home or elsewhere. ***Bodily injury*** means bodily harm, illness, or disease. ***Property damage*** means damage to, destruction of, or loss of use of property. The insurer also agrees to defend the insured in any legal proceeding, and the cost of defense is in addition to the stated amount of coverage.

- **Coverage F: Medical payments payable to others.** Covers medical payments to others regardless of whether the insured is liable.
- **Additional coverages.** Covers various miscellaneous expenses, such as claim expenses and first aid expenses.

Coverages under Section II are subject to numerous exclusions, but many of those can be covered by endorsements or other policies. For example, a personal umbrella liability policy, which we discuss later in this chapter, can offer additional protection to an insured than that provided under Section II.

Amount of Coverage

The insured determines the Coverage A amount needed on the dwelling. The amount of insurance provided under Coverages B, C, and D are determined by applying a specified percentage to the Coverage A amount. The standard percentages are

- Coverage B: 10 percent
- Coverage C: 50 percent
- Coverage D: 30 percent

The amounts of insurance provided by Coverages B, C, and D are in addition to the amount provided under Coverage A.

Example: Gilda Holbeck insured her home for $150,000 under Coverage A. The property also contains a storage shed.

Analysis: Gilda's storage shed would be insured for $15,000 (10 percent of $150,000), her personal property for $75,000 (50 percent of $150,000), and she would have $45,000 (30 percent of $150,000) in coverage for loss of use of her dwelling.

Losses under Section I are subject to a deductible upon the occurrence of each covered loss. In addition, the insured must comply with the policy's insurance-to-value requirement, or he will bear a portion of the loss. The ***insurance-to-value requirement*** states that the insured must insure a certain percentage of the property's value—typically at least 80 percent—in order for any loss to be fully covered. The policy specifies whether the percentage is of replacement cost, actual cash value, or agreed value.

The amount of coverage for personal property under Coverage C is limited as to certain classes of property. For example, the insurer may pay only $200 for a loss of money, coins, and silverware. A homeowner could add an endorsement to the policy to increase the amount of coverage on specific items.

The typical limit on Coverage E—liability for bodily injury and property damage—is $100,000 per occurrence. The typical limit on Coverage F—medical payments payable to others—is $1,000 per occurrence.

Homeowners Policy Conditions

Policy provisions in a homeowners policy are referred to as *policy conditions*. Some conditions apply to both Section I and Section II. Other conditions apply to one section or the other. The following homeowners policy conditions apply to both Section I and Section II: policy period, fraud, liberalization, waiver or change of provision, cancellation, nonrenewal, assignment, subrogation, and death. These provisions are described in Figure 10.3.

Some of the more significant conditions that apply only to Section I include the insured's duties after loss, appraisal, other insurance and service agreements, insurer option, and mortgage clause.

- **Insured's Duties After Loss.** Among other actions, the insured must notify the insurer of a loss as soon as practicable, protect the property from further damage, and prepare an inventory of damaged property.

- **Appraisal.** Either the insurer or the insured can demand an appraisal of the damaged property if the parties do not agree on the amount of covered loss.

- **Other Insurance and Service Agreements.** If another policy more specifically covers a loss, the homeowners policy will not cover the loss. If the homeowners policy and another policy both cover the loss to the same degree, the amount of loss will be shared on a pro-rata basis. If a service agreement (for example, a home warranty) applies to a loss, the homeowners coverage will be secondary to that service agreement's coverage.

- **Insurer Option.** Rather than paying the insured cash in settlement of a loss, the insurer may repair or replace the damaged property if it notifies the insured of its intent to do so within 30 days of receiving the loss statement.

- **Mortgage Clause.** As mentioned earlier in this chapter, sometimes the mortgage lender is named as an insured. If so and a loss occurs,

FIGURE 10.3 Homeowners Policy Conditions that Apply to Sections I and II

Policy Period	The policy covers only property losses and bodily injury or property damage that occur during the policy period stated in the policy.
Fraud	The policy will be void if the insured at any time engages in fraud as defined by the policy.
Liberalization	If the insurer makes a change broadening coverage of the particular type and edition of policy held by a homeowner and no additional premium is required, the change shall apply automatically to the homeowner's policy.
Waiver or Change of Provision	For a waiver or change of a provision to be valid, the insurer must put it in writing. In addition, this condition states that the insurer does not waive its rights to deny coverage by asking the insured for an appraisal or examination of the property.
Cancellation	The insured can cancel the policy at any time by returning the policy and specifying the cancellation date in writing. The insurer can cancel the policy only for reasons permitted by law, such as nonpayment of premiums and material misrepresentation, and only by delivering to the insured written notice of cancellation within a certain period required by law. The insurer must refund any pre-paid premiums to the insured.
Nonrenewal	The insurer may choose not to renew the policy, but it must give the insured at least 30 days written notice of its intent not to do so. Some states require a longer notification period.
Assignment	Unlike life insurance, the insured cannot assign the homeowners policy without the insurer's prior written consent.
Subrogation	If an insured incurs a loss caused by a third party, the insured could recover twice—once from asserting a legal claim against the third party and again from her own insurer. This would be against public policy. ***Subrogation*** is the right of the insurer to enforce any claim the insured has against a third party resulting from a loss for which the insurer has paid. Basically, subrogation is the right of the insurer to recover its claim payment to its insured in such a case by "stepping into the shoes" of the insured with respect to her claim against the third party. For example, if a homeowner's neighbor damages the homeowner's fence and the insurer pays for the damage, the insurer has the right to seek restitution from the neighbor. Subrogation does not apply to certain coverages of Section II—medical payments to others and damage to property of others.
Death	In the event of the insured's death, the insurer will cover the deceased's legal representative as an insured under the policy.

the insurer will make a check payable to both the homeowner and the mortgage lender and will let them decide how the proceeds are to be split.

A few of the conditions that apply to only Section II coverage are limit of liability, insured's duties after an occurrence, and severability of insurance.

- **Limit of Liability.** This condition states how the insurer's maximum limit of liability is determined. The limit of liability for Coverage E—Personal Liability—is the total amount of coverage per occurrence. No matter how many insureds or injured parties are involved and regardless of the number of claims made, the insurer will pay policy proceeds only up to the limit stated in the policy. Thus, if the insured injures three people in one accident and the insured's policy has a total coverage amount of $100,000 under Coverage E, the insurer will pay up to a maximum of $100,000, even if each of the three injured parties claims damages that exceed $100,000 for a total exceeding $300,000. The coverage limit for Coverage F—Medical Payments to Others—is payable to each person, other than the insured, in any accident. Thus, if the insured injures three people in one accident and the insured's policy has a limit of $1,000 under Coverage F, each injured person can receive up to $1,000.

- **Insured's Duties After an Occurrence.** The insured must notify the insurer in writing about the occurrence and its circumstances in a timely fashion. The insured may not make any payments or incur any further liabilities other than for first aid to others.

- **Severability of Insurance.** Sometimes more than one insured is involved in a claim. For example, a neighbor may suffer damages and sue not only the homeowner, but also the homeowner's mother who lives in the home. The homeowner's policy will treat each insured as if she has separate coverage under the policy and will defend each insured in the suit. However, the insurer will pay no more than the stated coverage amount, as we discussed under the limit of liability condition.

Homeowners Insurance Premiums

The premium amount for homeowners insurance varies considerably depending on many factors, including the

- **Number of perils covered.** Typically, an open-perils policy will cover more perils than a named-perils policy and thus will have a higher premium than a named-perils policy.

- **Type of coverage.** A replacement cost policy typically will have a higher premium than an actual cash value policy.
- **Amount of coverage**. The higher the stated value of the premises and its contents, the higher the premium will be.
- **Type of construction.** The safety and durability of the construction affect the premium. For example, a policy insuring a brick home generally would have a lower premium than a policy insuring a home with wood siding.
- **Location.** Homes located in areas subject to natural hazards are more expensive to insure than are homes in low-risk areas. For example, homes along the Florida coast may have higher insurance premiums than do homes in New Mexico because the Florida homes have an increased risk of hurricane damage.
- **Deductible.** Generally, the higher the deductible, the lower the premium.
- **Evidence of smoke detectors and a security alarm system**. Many insurers allow discounts on premiums for loss prevention and reduction devices.

Automobile Insurance

Most countries and most states in the United States require people to have some form of automobile insurance if they own or drive a vehicle. ***Automobile insurance*** is a type of personal property insurance that protects an insured from financial losses arising from operation of a vehicle. Automobile insurance protects against property losses and liability.

Automobile Insurance Coverages

Automobile insurance policies provide four types of coverage:

- Part A: Liability
- Part B: Medical payments
- Part C: Uninsured or underinsured motorists
- Part D: Damage to the insured automobile

Each state in the United States that requires automobile insurance has its own legal requirements for each of these coverages, and each state sets minimum limits on the dollar amounts of coverage that an insured must have in force. Insurance agents who sell automobile insurance typically inform customers on the legally required coverages and limits.

Figure 10.4 is a sample of an automobile insurance policy's coverages.

Part A: Liability

As we mentioned, liability insurance protects the insured from financial loss when he is held legally responsible for bodily injury or property damage losses sustained by others. The bodily injury can be to passengers, persons in another vehicle, or bystanders. The property damage can be to another vehicle or any other property that is harmed.

The limits on liability coverage per event can be stated in one of two ways:

- Some policies state the liability limit in three figures, such as 100/300/50, with each figure representing a multiple of $1,000. The first figure is the maximum payable for bodily injury liability to one person. The second figure is the limit for bodily injury liability to all persons. The third figure is the limit for all property damage liability. Thus, if a policy's liability limit is 100/300/50, the insurer will pay a maximum of $100,000 for bodily injury liability to one person, $300,000 for bodily injury liability to all persons, and $50,000 for property damage liability.

FIGURE 10.4 Sample Automobile Insurance Coverages

Coverage Part	Limits	Premium
A. Liability	$ 500,000 each accident	$ 475
B. Medical payments	$ 5,000 each accident	$ 85
C. Uninsured motorists Property damage deductible: $250	$ 300,000 each accident	$ 95
D. Coverage for damage to your auto		
Collision Actual cash value less deductible of $500		$ 230
Comprehensive Actual cash value less deductible of $500		$ 65
Total annual policy premium		**$ 950**

Source: Adapted from Mary C. Bickley and David F. Johnson, *Intro to Financial Services* (Atlanta: LOMA, © 2001), 107. Used with permission; all rights reserved.

- Other policies state a single liability limit figure, such as $500,000. In this case, the insurer agrees to pay up to a total of $500,000 for all bodily injury and property damage liability losses incurred.

Insureds need to carefully consider their automobile insurance liability limits. Higher coverage requires a higher premium, but inadequate insurance coverage may force the insured to sell personal assets to cover the injured party's losses if an accident happens.

Part B: Medical Payments

The medical payments portion of automobile insurance is a form of accident insurance and provides medical expense reimbursement for bodily injury incurred by

- The insured driver whether in his covered vehicle or another vehicle
- Any passengers in the covered vehicle
- The insured and his insured family members who are injured while passengers in any vehicle or as pedestrians

This coverage applies even if the insured driver was not at fault.

The limits on medical payments coverage are stated in terms of an amount per person per accident, such as $5,000.

Part C: Uninsured Motorists Coverage

Almost all states require insurers to offer uninsured motorists coverage as an option on their automobile insurance policies. ***Uninsured motorists coverage*** covers an insured driver and her passengers for bodily injuries and, in some states, property damage incurred in an accident caused by a driver who, contrary to legal requirements, carries no liability insurance. This coverage comes into play when the insured's medical payments coverage is exhausted. For example, assume Frieda Handel's automobile policy has a medical payments limit of $5,000 and an uninsured motorists limit of $300,000. If Frieda incurs physical injury losses of $50,000 in an accident with an uninsured motorist, she would be covered for the first $5,000 under the medical payments portion of her policy and for the remaining $45,000 under the uninsured motorists portion.

The limits on uninsured motorists coverage can be stated in one of two ways—a single limit or two limits. For example, the single limit might be $300,000 for all bodily injury losses incurred. On the other hand, the limit might be stated as 100/300, which would provide up to $100,000 per injured person and up to $300,000 for injuries incurred by all persons.

A variation on uninsured motorists coverage is ***underinsured motorists coverage*** which protects the insured and his passengers when the other driver has coverage, but that coverage is inadequate to cover their injuries. Underinsured motorists coverage typically comes into play when the at-fault driver has only the legally required minimum liability coverage, but the injuries suffered by the other driver are greater than the minimum limit. In such a case, the driver who has underinsured motorists coverage can recover up to his own underinsured limit.

Part D: Physical Damage

Physical damage insurance covers losses the insured incurs due to damage to his covered automobile caused by collision or other perils. This coverage is divided into two portions:

- ***Collision insurance*** covers an insured for losses to his vehicle caused by a collision. The insurer will pay for losses regardless of whether the insured was at fault.

- ***Comprehensive insurance*** covers an insured for losses to his vehicle caused by perils other than collision, such as theft and hail.

Each portion of physical damage insurance carries its own limit and its own deductible. The deductible typically ranges from $100 to $500. The larger the deductible, the lower the premium charged for the coverage. Many people carry collision and comprehensive coverage when their vehicle is new and drop this coverage when the vehicle reaches a certain age and its value drops to a certain level.

Automobile Insurance Policy Provisions

Automobile insurance policies contain provisions similar to the following homeowners policy conditions: policy period, fraud, liberalization, subrogation, and assignment. Automobile insurance policies also include the provisions described in Figure 10.5.

Automobile Insurance Premiums

An insurer determines an automobile insurance premium based on a number of factors, as set forth in each state's insurance rating laws, including the

- **Rating territory.** The ***rating territory*** is the location where the vehicle is principally garaged and driven. For example, the premium will be higher in an urban area where more accidents and thefts occur than in a rural area.

FIGURE 10.5 Automobile Insurance Policy Provisions

Bankruptcy	The insurer must still fulfill its obligations under the policy if the insured is bankrupt.
Changes to the Policy	Changes to the policy will not be effective unless they are issued by the insurer in writing. If the conditions used to determine the premium are changed, the insurer may adjust the premium. Such changes include adding a vehicle or a driver to the coverage and changing the principal place where the vehicle is garaged.
Territorial Limits	The policy may place limits on the geographical area for which coverage is provided. For example, in the United States, policies generally cover accidents and losses occurring only in the United States and its territories and possessions, Puerto Rico, and Canada.
Termination	The insured may cancel the policy at any time for any reason by returning the policy to the insurer or giving advance written notice of the date cancellation is to be effective. Upon giving the proper notification as required by law, the insurer may cancel only for nonpayment of premiums, loss of an insured's driver's license, or a misrepresentation on the application. The insurer retains the right not to renew the policy upon the renewal date, subject to the insurer notifying the insured of the nonrenewal.
Two or More Policies	If the insured has purchased more that one policy from the insurer and the policies cover the same accident or loss, the insurer's limit of liability under the policies does not exceed the highest limit of liability under any one policy. It the insured has two or more policies in force with different insurers and the policies cover the same accident or loss, the insured is prevented from making a profit. In many cases, the claim will be prorated among the insurers.

- **Insured's driving record.** The more accidents and traffic violations a driver experiences, the higher his premium will be. If his experience becomes unacceptable to the insurer at any premium, his coverage will not be renewed.

- **Insured's characteristics, such as age.** Drivers between the ages of 16 and 25 are involved in more accidents than older individuals, so drivers in the 16-25 age bracket pay higher premiums than older individuals.

- **Type and age of automobile.** The more valuable and newer the automobile, the higher the premiums will be.

As noted in the preceding section, the deductibles selected by the insured also will affect the amount of the premium.

Personal Liability Insurance

As we discussed earlier, liability insurance protects the insured from financial loss when he is held legally responsible for bodily injury or property damage losses sustained by others. A person's automobile or homeowners insurance policies provide a certain amount of liability coverage. However, some people want or need more coverage than is provided by these policies. The following additional liability coverages are among those that are available:

- ***Professional liability insurance*** covers individuals who provide professional services, such as physicians and lawyers, from losses they incur as a result of being held responsible for losses of their clients. Medical malpractice insurance is a common example of professional liability insurance. Professional liability is regarded as a personal as opposed to a commercial risk, even though it arises from the conduct of business.

- ***Comprehensive personal liability insurance*** covers insureds from liability losses they incur that are not the result of practicing their profession or operating a vehicle. Homeowners insurance provides this type of coverage up to a limit, but some people desire the additional protection that a comprehensive personal liability insurance policy can provide.

- ***Umbrella liability insurance*** provides additional liability coverage over and above that provided by a homeowners, automobile, or comprehensive personal liability policy. To be covered under an umbrella policy, an insured must have the underlying basic policy. For example, an insured desiring umbrella automobile coverage must carry automobile liability insurance. With umbrella coverage, the types of risks insured against are broader and the limits are higher than those in the underlying policies. Figure 10.6 demonstrates how umbrella liability policies work.

Premiums for professional liability insurance vary considerably depending on the profession, but they can be extremely high. Premiums for comprehensive personal liability and umbrella coverages typically are relatively inexpensive.

FAST FACT

In some states, fraud costs insurers as much as $200 a year per automobile insurance policy.[2]

FIGURE 10.6 How Umbrella Liability Policies Work

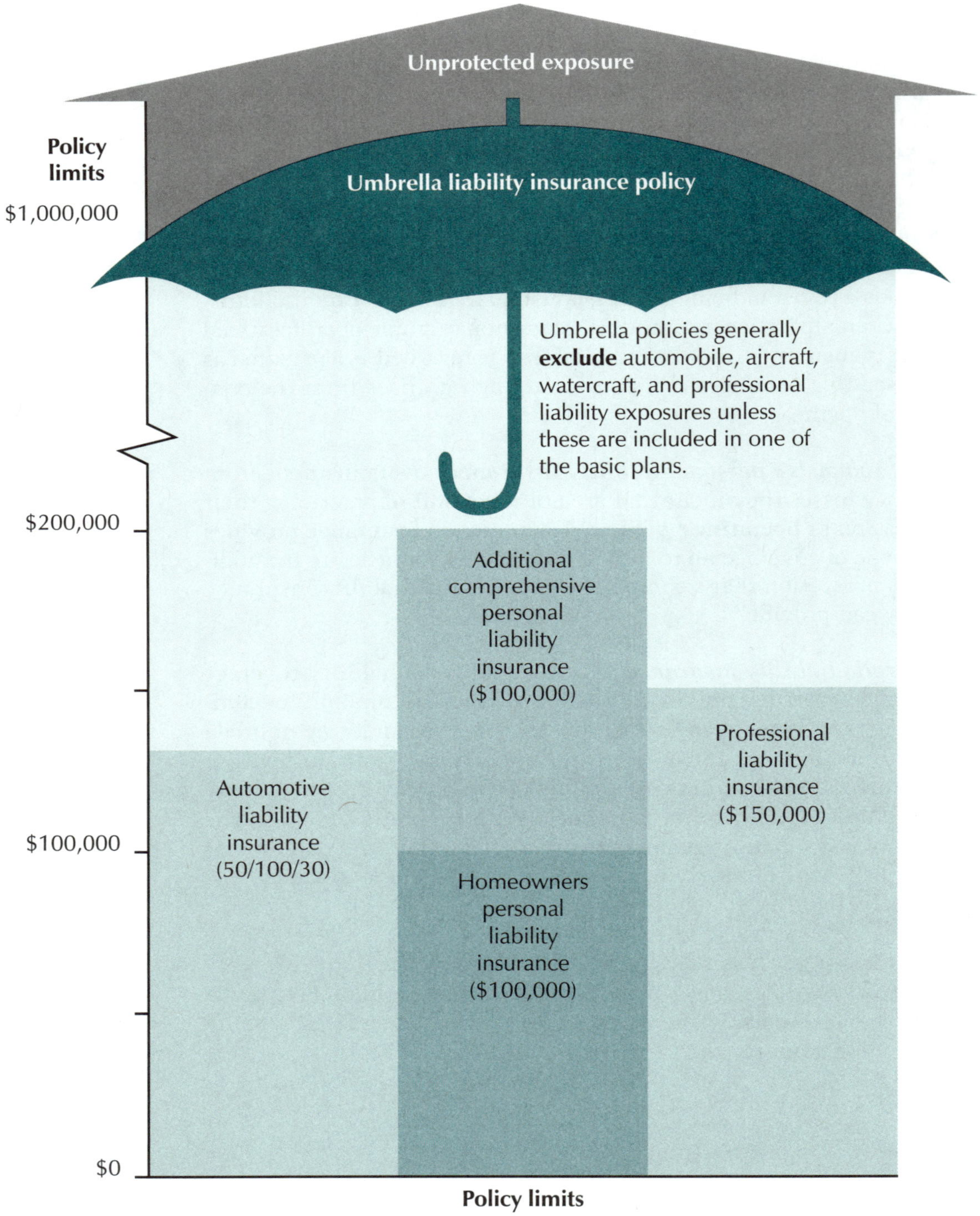

Source: Reprinted from E. Thomas Garman and Raymond E. Forgue, *Personal Finance,* Seventh Edition, 311. Copyright © 2003 by Houghton Mifflin Company. Used with permission.

Commercial Property and Liability Insurance

Although the focus of this text is on personal financial services and products, commercial property and liability insurance deserves mentioning because many people also have business needs for insurance. For example, a person who owns a small business will want to be sure that if he is sued as owner of that business, he will have adequate commercial property insurance and commercial liability insurance so that his personal assets are protected.

Numerous types of commercial property insurance and commercial liability insurance are available. Some of these types are listed in Figure 10.7.

Just as package policies are available to individuals, they are also available to businesses. The two most common types of commercial package policies, which provide most, but not all, of the insurance protection a business needs, are the commercial package policy (CPP) and the businessowners policy (BOP).

- The ***commercial package policy*** is designed for businesses of any size and type and gives the insured the option of selecting at least two of the following seven coverages:
  - Commercial property
  - Comprehensive general liability
  - Crime
  - Boiler and machinery
  - Inland marine
  - Automobile
  - Farm
- The ***businessowners policy*** is available to certain small- to medium-sized businesses and covers commercial real property, personal property, and liability.

Coverages not provided by these package policies, such as workers' compensation and excess and umbrella liability, must be purchased separately.

FIGURE 10.7 Some Types of Commercial Property Insurance and Commercial Liability Insurance

Property Coverages

- **Commercial property insurance** covers buildings, personal property in the business, and personal property of others in the care of the business.
- **Commercial automobile insurance** comes in three forms: business automobile coverage, which is similar to personal automobile coverage; garage coverage, which covers businesses that sell, service, park, or store automobiles; and motor carrier coverage, which covers businesses that provide transportation of people, goods, or both, as specified in the policy.
- **Business income insurance** covers losses resulting from the suspension of business operations, including loss of net income, expenses that continue during suspension of business operations, and extra expenses incurred to avoid or minimize business interruption.
- **Crime insurance** covers losses of money, securities, and tangible property resulting from the commission of certain specified crimes, such as burglary, robbery, theft, employee dishonesty, and forgery.
- **Boiler and machinery insurance** covers losses incurred to boilers and machinery as a result of boiler explosions, electrical malfunctions, and machinery breakdowns.
- **Inland marine insurance** covers property in transit over land and instruments of communications or transportation, such as tunnels and bridges.
- **Farm insurance** covers farm property and also can cover the farmowner's home and personal property.

Liability Coverages

- **Commercial liability insurance** covers bodily injury and property damage liability, personal and advertising injury liability (such as defamation), and medical payments.
- **Workers' compensation and employers liability insurance** covers liability resulting from employee injury or death.
- **Directors and officers (D&O) liability insurance** covers directors and officers of a corporation for their own liability resulting from failing to exercise the appropriate standard of care when discharging their corporate duties.
- **Excess and umbrella liability insurance** provides additional liability limits for underlying coverages.

Key Terms

property insurance
liability insurance
package policy
peril
named-perils
open-perils
replacement cost insurance
actual cash value insurance
agreed value insurance
homeowners insurance
basic form
broad form
bodily injury
property damage
insurance-to-value requirement
liberalization
subrogation
automobile insurance
uninsured motorists coverage
underinsured motorists coverage
physical damage insurance
collision insurance
comprehensive insurance
rating territory
professional liability insurance
comprehensive personal liability insurance
umbrella liability insurance
commercial package policy
businessowners policy

Endnotes

1. Karen L. Hamilton and Cheryl L. Ferguson, *Personal Risk Management and Property-Liability Insurance* (Malvern, PA: American Institute for Chartered Property Casualty Underwriters/Insurance Institute of America, 2002), 2-7–2-8.
2. "Facts and Statistics: Auto Insurance," Insurance Information Institute, http://www.iii.org/media/facts/statsbyissue/auto (10 December 2003).

chapter 11

Securities

outline

Product Characteristics

Securities

- Stocks
- Bonds
- Mutual Funds

Investment Accounts

- Brokerage Accounts
- Managed Accounts

objectives

After reading this chapter, you should be able to

- Explain the factors people consider when choosing among asset accumulation products
- Distinguish between common and preferred stock
- Describe the features of a bond
- Distinguish between convertible and callable bond features
- Explain the total return provided by stocks and bonds
- Compare how stocks and bonds are valued
- List three benefits of investing in mutual funds
- Describe four types and five common objectives of mutual funds
- Explain how to calculate a mutual fund's net asset value
- Describe mutual fund fees
- Describe brokerage accounts and managed accounts

People accumulate assets so that in the future they may fulfill their needs and desires. For example, they might save for emergencies, financial security, down payments, education, and vacations. People also save to replace any loss of income that occurs when they retire. Although some people still store their money somewhere in their house, most people invest their savings so that their assets will grow. In other words, most people apply the principle of the time value of money, which we discussed in Chapter 2. They put their money to work earning investment income in order to accumulate even more wealth.

www.CartoonStock.com

In this chapter, we discuss the characteristics that people consider when choosing among asset accumulation products. We then describe types of securities—stocks, bonds, and mutual funds—that are popular asset accumulation products. We conclude with a discussion of asset management products—brokerage accounts and managed accounts.

Product Characteristics

Consumers choose among asset accumulation products based on several factors, including the following:

- Safety of principal and income
- Types of risk
- Rate of return
- Liquidity
- Fees and expenses
- Taxation

The relative importance of these various factors depends on the person's ultimate objective in accumulating assets and his time line for doing so. For example, a person building an emergency fund that could be needed at any time probably would consider safety and liquidity to be more important than earning a high rate of return. Conversely, a person saving for retirement in 30 years probably would consider a high potential rate of return to be a more important factor than safety and liquidity, at least initially. An additional factor that influences many people in selecting among asset accumulation products is the person's individual risk tolerance, which we discussed along with the various types of risk in Chapter 2.

Figure 11.1 summarizes the degree of safety, primary types of risk, expected return, and relative liquidity that characterize various asset accumulation products that we discuss in this chapter and the next. Note that savings accounts, savings bonds, and certificates of deposit, which we discussed in Chapter 3, can serve as asset accumulation products in addition to cash management products. People evaluate the same characteristics we discuss here when evaluating these products.

Securities

FAST FACT

In the United States in 2001, 52 percent of households owned stock directly or indirectly, versus 37 percent in 1992.[1]

As we learned in Chapter 1, a security is an investment vehicle. The U.S. federal government does not insure securities as it does money in bank accounts. However, the Securities Investor Protection Corporation (SIPC) offers some protection to investors who buy their securities through a member broker-dealer. We discuss this organization in more detail later in this chapter.

FIGURE 11.1 Asset Accumulation Products and Their Characteristics

Product	Degree of Safety	Primary Types of Risk	Expected Return	Relative Liquidity
Savings accounts	Very high	Inflation risk	Very low	Very high
Certificates of deposit	High	Inflation risk Reinvestment risk	Low	Moderate
Savings bonds	High	Inflation risk	Low	Moderate
Treasury bills	High	Inflation risk	Low	High
Municipal bonds	Moderate	Default risk Inflation risk Interest rate risk	Moderate	Moderate
Corporate bonds	Moderate	Business risk Default risk Inflation risk Interest rate risk	Moderate	Moderate
High-yield (junk) bonds	Low	Business risk Default risk Inflation risk Interest rate risk	High	Moderate
Stock	Low	Business risk Market risk Political risk	High	Moderate
Fixed annuities	Moderate	Inflation risk Interest rate risk	Low to Moderate	Low to Moderate
Mutual funds and variable annuities	In general, mutual funds and variable annuities will exhibit characteristics of their underlying securities.			

Source: Herbert B. Mayo, *Investments: An Introduction*, 5th ed. (Fort Worth: Dryden Press, 1997), 821–822.

Stocks

A ***stock*** is an equity security representing a share of ownership in a corporation. A person who owns stock in a corporation is a ***shareholder***, or a *stockholder*, of that corporation. Shareholders are the owners of a company and typically share the profits of the organization, as well as the proceeds in the event the corporation is sold or liquidated.

Corporations typically issue stock to raise money to expand their operations. People buy stock as an investment because they believe they will earn a greater return by investing in stock than by putting their money in alternative financial products such as interest-earning checking accounts, savings accounts, and CDs. A stock's total return is the sum of the dividends received and the capital gains or losses realized. A stockholder can have a negative return if he sells the stock for a lower price than he paid for it.

As we explained in Chapter 2, capital gains—or appreciation—will result if a stockholder sells his stock for a higher price than he paid for it. In the United States, capital gains from the sale of stocks held for one year or less are classified as short-term capital gains and are taxable as ordinary income. Capital gains from the sale of stocks held for over a year are classified as long-term capital gains and are taxable at the capital gains rate, which, as we mentioned earlier, is lower than the ordinary income tax rate in most cases. Because appreciation in stock prices is not taxed until the investor actually sells the stock, the investor who holds a rising stock can reap the benefits of tax deferral.

As we learned in Chapter 2, a dividend is a company's distribution of earnings to shareholders. Not all stocks pay dividends because some companies choose to reinvest all their earnings in their operations. For companies that pay dividends, the corporation's board of directors decides when to pay a dividend and how much that dividend shall be. Some dividends are taxed at capital gains rates, and other dividends are taxed at ordinary income tax rates.

The primary advantage of stocks as investments is that historically they have provided a better return on investment than fixed income investments, such as bonds. The primary disadvantage of stocks is that they present the investor with a number of risks, including business risk, market risk, and political risk. In addition, the price of stocks fluctuates daily. This volatility, coupled with the fact that dividends are not guaranteed and the investor may lose some or his entire principal, may not appeal to conservative investors.

Common and Preferred Stock

Stock is classified as common or preferred stock. ***Common stock*** entitles the owner to vote in board of directors elections and on other important company matters and to receive dividends, if they are declared. ***Preferred stock*** typically does not carry the voting rights of common stock, but does carry a stated dividend rate that is paid before any payment of common stock dividends.

Preferred stock may be further classified as cumulative or noncumulative. ***Cumulative preferred stock*** requires the company to pay in full any unpaid scheduled dividends on its preferred stock before it may pay any dividends on its common stock.

Example: Zandor Corporation's board of directors voted not to pay dividends in the third and fourth quarters of 2004. In the first quarter of 2005, Zandor had unusually good profits and wanted to make a dividend distribution to common and preferred stockholders.

Analysis: In 2005, Zandor must pay its cumulative preferred stockholders the dividends they were scheduled to receive in the third and fourth quarters of 2004, as well as the first quarter of 2005 dividends, before Zandor may pay any dividends to common stockholders in 2005.

Noncumulative preferred stock does not require the company to pay in full any unpaid scheduled dividends on its preferred stock before it pays any dividends on its common stock.

Because preferred stock takes precedence over common stock in the distribution of dividends, preferred stock is generally less risky to the investor than common stock. However, because the price of preferred stock does not fluctuate as much as that of common stock in relation to the performance of the company, preferred stock typically does not appreciate as much as common stock.

Stock Value

Par value is the face value of a stock or bond. The company issuing a stock sets its par value, which is of little importance to a common stock investor. The par value is important to a preferred stockholder, though, because the amount of the dividend may be stated as a percentage of the par value of the preferred stock.

Stocks are typically valued by their ***market price***, which is the amount a willing buyer would pay a willing seller for one share of the stock. A stock does not have a fixed market price. As mentioned earlier, stock prices fluctuate continually in response to news of company performance, general market conditions, investor perceptions, and many other factors.

An investor can estimate the price he will pay or receive for a share of stock by referring to stock quotations found in newspapers, on the Internet, and from other sources. He will not know the exact price, though, until he receives a confirmation of his transaction. Sales commissions or fees charged by brokers are not included in the price. Figure 11.2 explains how to read a stock quotation.

Two means of valuing stock mentioned in stock quotations—dividend yield and price/earnings ratio—deserve further explanation, as they are two of the most popular measures of stock value. The ***dividend yield*** is the annual percentage return earned by dividends on a common or preferred stock. The dividend yield is determined by dividing the annual dividend per share by the current price per share. For example, if an

FIGURE 11.2 Stock Quotations

YTD % CHG	52-WEEK HI	LO	STOCK (SYM)	DIV	YLD %	PE	VOL 100s	CLOSE	NET CHG
			F						
34.8	26.70	15.20♣	FBL Fnl A **FFG**	.40	1.5	14	190	26.24	0.39
14.5	31.41	14.22	FMC **FMC**		...	38	2282	31.29	0.49
12.0	24.60	17.94♣	FMC Tech **FTI**		...	20	6279	22.89	0.84
3.4	58.60	48.61	FPL Gp Corp **FPLB**	4.00	7.3	...	272	55.17	0.27
5.9	68.08	53.55	FPL Gp **FPL**	2.40	3.8	13	10155	63.65	0.40
−17.4	32.45	16.79	FTI Cnsltng **FCN** s		...	14	3775	22.10	0.32
46.8	53.09	24.28	FactstRsch **FDS**	.24	.6	28	2266	41.50	−0.50
23.3	64.68	39.78	FairIsaac **FIC**	.08	.2	25	8358	52.63	−0.87
0.2	5.37	3.99	FairchldCp **FA**		...	dd	184	4.97	0.09
132.2	27	10.01	FrchldSemi **FCS**		...	...	25959	24.87	−0.64
98.7	178.50	46.71	FairfaxFnl **FFH** n	1.50p	...	5	131	153.01	0.01
13.8	27.60	19.07	FairmntHtlRt **FHR**	.06	.2	28	9567	26.81	0.05

YTD % CHG	52-WEEK HI	LO	STOCK (SYM)	DIV	YLD %	PE	VOL 100s	CLOSE	NET CHG
31.9	25.73	17.90	GettyRlty **GTY**	1.70	6.8	17	349	25	0.21
316.9	12.73	2.75	GiantInd **GI**		...	11	688	12.30	−0.18
17.7	30.79	22.15	Gildan A **GIL**		...	11	1050	27.56	−1.02
14.7	34.90	28	Gillette **G**	.65	1.9	26	30137	34.82	0.47
49.7	18.20	8.41♣	GlamisGld **GLG**		...	cc	13452	16.98	−0.81
−6.9	15.45	9.65	Glatfelter **GLT**	.36m	2.9	20	703	12.25	0.27
20.5	47.64	31.85	GSK ADS **GSK**	1.37e	3.0	...	19595	45.13	−0.85
8.9	20.83	14.87	Glenborough **GLB**	1.40m	7.2	88	1461	19.41	−0.09
25.6	23.49	16.83	GlimchRlty **GRT**	1.92	8.6	57	863	22.30	0.06
44.0	46.62	26	GlblPymts **GPN**	.16	.3	32	1576	46.08	0.38
20.9	6.79	4.61	GlblPwrEquip **GEG**		...	10	889	5.96	...
76.2	9.59	4.35	GlblTch **GAI**		...	...	200	8.35	0.05
−7.2	26.70	19.76	GlobSantaFe **GSF**	.20f	.9	34	25974	22.57	0.91
−6.0	15.52	9.52♣	GoldFields ADS **GFI**	.31e	2.4	19	19740	13.12	−0.58
37.0	18.50	9.39♣	Goldcp **GG**	.18	...	...	23929	17.43	−0.80

YTD %CHG
Stock price percentage change for the calendar year to date, adjusted for stock splits and dividends over 10%.

STOCK
The name of the stock.

DIV
Estimate of the cash dividends per share that will be paid annually.

PE
The price-earnings (P/E) ratio, which is the price per share divided by the earnings per share.

CLOSE
The closing price for the prior day.

YTD %CHG	52-WEEK HI	LO	STOCK	(SYM)	DIV	YLD %	PE	VOL 100s	CLOSE	NET CHG
14.7	34.90	28	Gilette	G	.65	1.9	26	30137	34.82	0.47

52 WEEK HI and LO
The highest and lowest prices at which the stock has traded during the past 52 weeks. The range between the numbers indicates how volatile the stock is. The greater the range, the greater the volatility.

(SYM)
The *ticker symbol*, which is the abbreviation of the name of the stock that investors use to identify stock when they give orders to buy or sell.

YLD %
The dividend yield, which is the amount of the annual dividend divided by the price per share.

VOL 100s
The number of shares (the "**s**" stands for shares) traded the previous day. The number reported is multiplied by 100 to get the actual number, unless a "**z**" appears before a number, which means that is the actual number.

NET CHG
The net change, which is the difference between the previous day's closing price and the closing price the day before that.

Source: *Wall Street Journal,* 5 December 2003, C4. Used with permission.

investor receives a $1 dividend on a stock with a current market price of $10 per share, the dividend yield is 10 percent. The dividend yield is a measure of the value of the stock, but it does not reflect total return, which cannot be determined until the stock is sold. When a security is sold, the capital gain or loss experienced by the seller is said to be realized. As long as an investor owns a security, the difference between the purchase price and the current market value is an unrealized gain or loss.

The ***price/earnings (P/E) ratio*** is the stock price per share divided by the earnings per share. In this case, *earnings* refers to the company's net income, which is its revenue minus its expenses. For example, if a stock quote says that a stock's P/E ratio is 15, this means that its price is 15 times its annual per share earnings. Investors use the P/E ratio to compare the relative value of various stocks, typically of companies in the same industry. Stable companies paying steady dividends tend to have lower P/E ratios than do rapidly growing companies. When a company's P/E ratio is lower than its peer companies, the stock of the company may be considered to be undervalued. The stock of companies with relatively high P/E ratios may be considered overvalued.

How Stocks Are Bought and Sold

When corporations first issue stock to the public, investment bankers sell the stock in an ***initial public offering (IPO)*** primarily to institutional investors such as mutual funds. Initial public offerings are made in the *primary market*, which is the market where stocks are first traded.

After stocks have been issued and sold through an initial public offering, subsequent trades are made on the secondary market. The secondary market is composed of exchanges and over-the-counter markets where already issued securities are bought and sold. A ***stock exchange*** is an organized marketplace where specific types of securities, such as common stocks and bonds, are bought and sold by members of the exchange. A stock exchange is housed in a physical facility where securities trading takes place. An ***over-the-counter market*** is an electronic communications network over which securities that are not bought and sold on an exchange are traded.

Typically, a person interested in buying or selling stock will open a brokerage account with a brokerage firm, which is a member of a stock exchange. The stockbroker in charge of the brokerage account is licensed by the government to trade stocks, and he places the order for the customer. Insight 11.1 describes how a stock transaction takes place. We discuss brokerage accounts in more detail later in this chapter.

INSIGHT 11.1 A Stock Transaction

Betsy Trippel receives a hot stock tip from her brother-in-law. She calls Fred Meyer, her broker, and asks that he buy 100 shares of Fudgnilla, Inc., which is listed on the New York Stock Exchange. Betsy is anxious to have the stock and asks Fred to explain how it will be purchased. Fred explains that each stock listed on the exchange has a specific spot on the actual floor of the facility where trading in that stock takes place. Individuals called floor traders are posted to these spots and are constantly receiving electronic messages instructing them to buy and sell that stock. Fred tells Betsy that he will call a particular floor trader and instruct him to buy 100 shares of Fudgnilla. The floor trader will use hand signals to indicate to other traders in the area his willingness to buy the stock. Hand signals also are used to negotiate the price with a willing seller. Fred assures Betsy that as soon as he receives confirmation from the floor that the purchase is complete, he will call her.

Source: Jeff Madura, *Personal Finance* (Boston: Addison Wesley, 2002), 302–303.

Bonds

A ***bond*** is a debt security whereby the entity that sells the bond promises to pay the owner of the bond a stated rate of interest over a specified period of time, at the end of which time the original amount of borrowed money must be repaid. The owner of the bond is known as the ***bondholder***. The entity that sells the bond to raise money is known as the ***bond issuer***. In the United States, corporations and various government entities issue bonds. Figure 11.3 describes some of the debt securities issued by government entities in the United States. In addition to bonds, these U.S. government issued debt securities include bills, which are statements of amounts owed, and notes, which are promises to pay specified amounts.

A bond is a loan that the bondholder makes to the bond issuer for a fixed ***term***, or period of time between when a bond is issued and when it matures. The ***maturity date*** is the specified date by which a bond must be redeemed. Most corporate bonds mature in 20 to 30 years, while most government bonds mature in 10 to 20 years.

Until the maturity date, the bond issuer must make interest payments, which are known as ***coupon payments***, to the bondholder. The bond issuer typically makes coupon payments semiannually at the ***coupon rate***, which is a fixed annual rate of interest set when the bond was issued and expressed as a percentage of the par value of the bond. Because they pay a fixed rate of interest, bonds also are known as *fixed-income securities*.

Governments cannot sell stocks—that is, ownership interests—so they must issue bonds to raise additional funds. Corporations in need of raising funds consider many factors when deciding whether to sell bonds or issue stock. Corporations may prefer to sell bonds than to issue stock because issuing stock tends to dilute, or lessen, the value of stock

FIGURE 11.3 U.S. Government Debt Securities

Treasuries

Debt securities issued by the U.S. Treasury, which are exempt from state and local, but not federal, income taxes.

- **Treasury bill.** A short-term Treasury that matures in one year or less and that is issued in minimum denominations of $10,000, with $5,000 increments above $10,000.
- **Treasury note.** An intermediate-term Treasury that matures in 1 to 10 years and that is issued in denominations from $1,000 to $1,000,000 or more.
- **Treasury bond.** A long-term Treasury that matures in 10 years or longer and that is issued in denominations of $1,000.

Agency bonds

Short- and intermediate-term bonds issued by federal and state government agencies and government related institutions. The most popular agency bonds are those issued by mortgage associations—Government National Mortgage Association (Ginnie Maes or GNMAs), Federal Home Loan Mortgage Corporation (Freddie Macs or FHLMC), and Federal National Mortgage Association (Fannie Maes or FNMAs)—to raise funds to purchase pools of mortgages.

Municipal bonds

Bonds issued by a state or local government entity whose interest income is generally exempt from federal income taxes and from state and local income taxes if the bondholder resides in the state that issued the bond.

- **General obligation bonds.** Municipal bonds backed by the full faith and credit (which includes the taxing and further borrowing power) of the municipality that issued the bond.
- **Revenue bonds.** Municipal bonds issued to finance a specific public project, such as building a toll road, and backed only by the income generated by the completed project.

already held by shareholders. People buy bonds for the predictable income stream that coupon payments provide and because their value generally is less volatile than that of stocks.

A bond's total return is the sum of coupon payments received and the capital gain or loss incurred. Coupon payments are taxed as ordinary income in the year in which they are received or made available. As with stocks, capital gains from the sale of bonds held for one year or less are classified as short-term capital gains and are taxable as ordinary income. In general, capital gains from the sale of bonds held for over a year are treated as long-term capital gains and are taxable as capital gains.

The primary advantage of bonds as an investment vehicle is their safety. The rate of interest and the semiannual coupon payments are fixed and guaranteed at issue, and the eventual repayment of principal is guaranteed. However, bondholders face business and default risk and thus need to assure themselves of the financial soundness of the bond issuer before purchasing a bond. In addition, the fixed nature of payments may be unattractive to those who would prefer to see their investments grow with the company, as they can with stocks.

In addition, bond investors face inflation risk. Bonds are issued with coupon rates that exceed the current rate of inflation. Nonetheless, if inflation increases, the purchasing power of coupon payments decreases. The longer the term of the bond, the greater the effects of inflation will be.

Example: In 2003 when the inflation rate is 3 percent, Toby Ascot purchases a bond with a coupon rate of 6 percent.

Analysis: If in 2004 the inflation rate increases to 6 percent, Toby's coupon payments no longer exceed inflation and have less purchasing power.

Bonds also present interest rate risk, which can erode the value of the bond's principal, as we explain in the section on bond value.

Convertible and Callable Bonds

Bonds may be issued with various features. Two common features are a conversion option and a call option. A ***convertible bond*** gives the bondholder the right to convert the bond into shares of the issuing company's stock. The conversion terms are set when the bond is issued and include the date the conversion can be made and the number of shares the bondholder can receive. Typically, convertible bonds have a lower coupon rate than nonconvertible bonds.

A ***callable bond*** gives the bond issuer the right to call, or pay off, the bond before the maturity date. Bond issuers may want to call, or redeem, their bonds if interest rates go down. Just as a homeowner may refinance her mortgage if interest rates decrease, bond issuers may pay off their outstanding bonds and then issue more bonds at lower rates.

Typically, callable bonds specify that the bond cannot be called before a specified number of years. Nonetheless, callable bonds present bondholders with a greater reinvestment risk than noncallable bonds. Issuers generally compensate investors for this increased risk by paying bondholders a call premium, which is a price above the par value of the bond.

Bond Value

A bond's par value is the face value of the bond. Bonds typically are issued with par values of $1,000. However, most people do not hold a bond from the date of issue to the maturity date. Rather, most investors buy and sell bonds at market prices that fluctuate above and below the par value.

A bond's market price fluctuates with the market interest rate. If the market interest rate increases above the coupon rate at which a bond was issued, that bond's price will decrease and any sale of the bond will be at a discount. A ***discount*** is the amount by which a bond's current market price is less than its par value. The bond's price decreases because investors find the bond's coupon rate less attractive than the higher coupon rates available on newly issued bonds. Conversely, if the market interest rate decreases below the coupon rate at which a bond was issued, that bond's price will increase and any sale of the bond will be at a premium. A ***premium*** is the amount by which a bond's current market price exceeds its par value. The bond's price increases because investors find the bond's coupon rate more attractive than the lower coupon rates available on newly issued bonds.

Example: Roger Trulow bought a 20-year bond with a 5 percent coupon rate for its par value of $1,000.

Analysis: If, a month later, the market interest rate increased to 6 percent, Roger would not be able to sell his bond at par because investors could buy newly issued bonds with coupon rates of 6 percent. Thus, Roger would have to sell his bond at a discount—in other words, for a price less than par.

If instead the market interest rate decreased to 4 percent one month after Roger bought the bond, Roger would be able to sell his bond at a premium—for a price greater than par—because investors could not buy newly issued bonds with a 5 percent coupon rate.

Just as with stocks, an investor estimates the price he will pay or receive for a bond by referring to bond quotations found in daily newspapers and on the Internet. Figure 11.4 explains how to read a corporate bond quotation.

The current yield stated in the bond quotation is different from the yield to maturity. The ***yield to maturity*** is the rate of return a bondholder will earn if he holds the bond until maturity. As noted in Figure 11.4, the ***current yield*** is the coupon rate divided by the closing price of the bond. The current yield is the actual income rate of return you will receive based on the price you pay for the bond as opposed to the coupon rate, which is the stated rate of interest when the bond is issued.

How Bonds Are Bought and Sold

Corporate bonds are sold much the same way as stocks are, although bonds are more likely to be available through banks, in addition to stockbrokers. Treasuries, though, are sold at issue by Federal Reserve Banks directly to investors.

FIGURE 11.4 Corporate Bond Quotations

Corporate Bonds

Thursday, December 4, 2003

Forty most active fixed-coupon corporate bonds

COMPANY (TICKER)	COUPON	MATURITY	LAST PRICE	LAST YIELD	*EST SPREAD	UST†	EST $ VOL (000's)
Household Finance (HBC)	4.125	Dec 15, 2008	100.058	4.112	71	5	156,787
Alcan (AL)	5.200	Dec 08, 2003	100.287	5.162	n.a.	n.a.	139,100
Ford Motor Credit (F)	7.000	Oct 01, 2013	102.628	6.629	226	10	127,777
Time Warner (TWX)	6.875	May 01, 2012	111.661	5.146	78	10	112,163
Alcan (AL)	6.125	Dec 15, 2033	99.753	6.143	99	30	99,204

COMPANY (TICKER) The name of the bond or an abbreviation thereof, followed by the ticker symbol.

MATURITY The date on which the bond will mature.

LAST YIELD Current yield, which is the coupon rate divided by the closing price of the bond of the prior day.

UST Term of comparable U.S. Treasury note.

COMPANY (TICKER)	COUPON	MATURITY	LAST PRICE	LAST YIELD	EST SPREAD	UST	EST $ VOL (000'S)
Ford Motor Credit (F)	7.000	Oct 1, 2013	102.628	6.629	226	10	127,777

COUPON The coupon interest rate.

LAST PRICE The previous day's closing price.

EST SPREAD The difference between the yield of the bond and the yield of the most recently issued Treasury note/bond with a comparable maturity, expressed in basis points.

EST $ VOL (000's) The value of the previous day's trading, stated in thousands of dollars.

Source: *Wall Street Journal,* 13 December 2003, C4. Used with permission.

Corporate bonds typically are issued and sold in increments of $1,000 or more. This high cost prevents many people from investing in bonds at issue. Bond mutual funds, which we discuss in the next section, give individuals interested in bonds an affordable way to invest in them.

Mutual Funds

As we discussed in Chapter 1, a mutual fund company is an investment company that operates a number of mutual funds. A mutual fund is a financial product that pools the funds of investors and uses these funds to buy a large number of securities to create a diversified portfolio of financial investments. The mutual fund company issues shares in the fund to the investors, which it stands ready to buy back at any time. Each share represents a proportional interest in the fund's underlying securities. A mutual fund share is also a security because it represents an ownership share in the portfolio of securities held by the mutual fund company.

Mutual funds are popular investment vehicles. In the United States, mutual funds hold over $6 trillion in assets, while worldwide the total is over $11 trillion in assets.[2] People invest in mutual funds because these funds offer an affordable means of reaping the benefits of professional fund management and diversification otherwise available only to wealthy individuals and institutional investors.

- **Affordability.** The minimum required investment in mutual funds can be quite low (approximately $500), and 11 percent of mutual funds have no minimum investment requirement.[3]
- **Professional management.** Each mutual fund has a fund manager who researches securities and chooses those that best match the fund's objective.
- **Diversification.** Fund managers invest in a variety of securities such that losses incurred by one security may be offset by gains in another. Thus, the average investor achieves more investment diversification by investing in mutual funds than typically is economically possible by investing in individual securities.

Example: Sharon Ledlow has $1,000 to invest.

Analysis: Sharon can buy 10 shares of 10 individual stocks priced at $10 each, not taking into account commissions, or she can invest in a mutual fund and own a proportional share of hundreds of stocks.

Another advantage of mutual funds is their liquidity. Mutual fund companies are required by law to *redeem*, or buy back, shares at any time they are requested to do so by a shareholder. In addition, most mutual funds allow shareholders to *exchange*, or transfer, money from one fund to another within the same fund family. A ***mutual fund family*** is a group of mutual funds managed by the same mutual fund company.

FAST FACT

The first mutual funds were established in Boston in 1924.[4]

The total return of a mutual fund investment is a combination of the income earned by the fund and capital gains or losses realized when a shareholder sells his shares, less fees and commissions. The income earned by a mutual fund has two components.

- A mutual fund is continually receiving interest and dividends from the securities it holds, which in turn must be distributed to shareholders as dividends in the same year the income is received by the fund.
- A mutual fund also is continually selling securities, which may produce capital gains that must be distributed to shareholders in the same year they are received by the fund.

Mutual funds typically give shareholders a choice of receiving dividends, as well as capital gains from the sale of securities within the fund, as cash payments or reinvesting them to buy more mutual fund shares. Whichever method of receipt a shareholder selects, he will be taxed in the year the distribution of income earned by the fund is made. He will be taxed on any capital gains from selling his mutual fund shares in the year in which he sells them.

Mutual funds do not guarantee a specified rate of return, and the value of a mutual fund can fluctuate considerably as the values of its underlying securities rise and fall. In addition, some funds charge fees that not only make them expensive to purchase but also reduce the fund's rate of return. Many mutual funds do not outperform the market as a whole. Further, shareholders have no control over the timing of purchases and sales of the underlying securities. Thus, shareholders face tax liabilities even in years in which the fund loses value.

A mutual fund's risk depends on the type of assets the fund holds and its investment objective.

Types of Mutual Funds

Consumers have a wide variety of mutual funds from which to choose. In the United States in 2002, investors could select from over 8,000 mutual funds.[5] Typically, investors categorize mutual funds by the nature of the fund's assets and by investment objectives.

Fund Assets

The major categories of mutual funds based on the nature of the assets in which their funds are invested are as follows:

- A ***stock fund***, also called an *equity fund*, is a mutual fund whose assets are invested primarily in stocks.
- A ***bond fund*** is a mutual fund whose assets are invested primarily in bonds.

- A ***hybrid fund*** is a mutual fund whose assets are invested in a mixture of stocks, bonds, and other securities.
- A money market fund, as we learned in Chapter 3, is a mutual fund whose assets are invested in short-term, low-risk securities.

Examples of mutual funds categorized by the type of assets in which they invest are shown in Figure 11.5.

The relative popularity of these funds shifts as economic conditions change. For example and as illustrated in Figure 11.6, between 1999 and 2002 in the United States, the amount invested in stock mutual funds decreased substantially as the performance of the stock market deteriorated.[6]

Mutual Fund Objectives

An investor selects a mutual fund with an investment objective that matches his own objectives, risk tolerance, and time horizon. Examples of mutual funds categorized by objectives are as follows:

FIGURE 11.5 Categories of Mutual Funds Based on Type of Assets

Stock Funds

Stock funds are categorized primarily by the type of companies in which they invest and/or the type of result they expect to incur.

- A **blue chip stock fund** invests in common stock of well-managed, generally large, nationally known companies that produce quality products and services and have a record of growth and dividend payments.
- A **large capitalization (large-cap) fund** invests in relatively large companies, typically those that have outstanding shares valued at $2 billion or more.
- A **mid-size capitalization (mid-cap) fund** invests in relatively medium-sized companies that typically are better established than small-cap companies but have less growth potential.
- A **small capitalization (small-cap) fund** invests in relatively small companies, typically those that are believed to have above-average growth potential.
- A **sector fund** invests in companies in a particular industry, for example, technology or financial services.
- An **index fund** is designed to provide returns similar to what an individual would receive if he invested in a specific market index. An ***index*** is a statistical measurement system that tracks the performance of a group of similar investments. An index fund will contain many, but not all, of the stocks in the index it is attempting to mimic. Bond index funds are also available.
- An **international fund** invests in securities issued by companies outside the country where the fund is offered for sale. International bond funds are also available.
- A **global fund** invests in securities issued by companies from around the world, including the country where the fund is offered for sale. Global bond funds are also available.

(continued on next page)

FIGURE 11.5 *(continued)* Categories of Mutual Funds Based on Type of Assets

Bond Funds

Bond funds generally are classified as taxable bond funds and tax-free bond funds depending on the type of bonds in which they invest. Each type of bond fund can be further divided by maturities—short term, medium term, or long term.

Taxable bond funds:

- A **corporate bond fund** invests in bonds issued by corporations.
- A **high-yield (junk) bond fund** invests in bonds issued by corporations that are prone to default risk but pay relatively high interest rates.

Tax-exempt bond funds:

- A **state municipal bond fund** invests in municipal bonds issued by a single state. These funds' income typically is exempt from federal tax and exempt from state income tax for residents of the issuing state.
- A **national municipal bond fund** invests in municipal bonds issued by various states. These funds' income is exempt from federal tax and sometimes exempt from state income tax.

Hybrid Funds

Hybrid funds determine the mix of securities they will own depending on their objectives.

- An **asset allocation fund** invests in various asset classes—stocks, bonds, and money market instruments—and seeks to maintain precise weightings in these classes.
- A **flexible portfolio** may invest up to 100 percent in a particular type of security, but may change weightings at any time in response to market conditions.

Money Market Funds

Money market funds seek to preserve capital while earning income from investment in highly liquid, low-risk, short-term debt securities. These funds are categorized as taxable and tax-exempt.

- A **taxable money market fund** invests in federal government debt securities, certificates of deposit from large banks, and other short-term securities.
- A **tax-exempt money market fund** invests in short-term securities that are issued by tax-exempt entities, such as state and municipal authorities.

- A ***conservative fund*** has the objective of preservation of capital. Money market funds are examples of conservative funds.
- A ***growth fund*** has the objective of long-term capital appreciation. Such funds provide long-term growth in the value of the fund and very little current dividend income. Growth funds typically are stock funds that hold common stocks of growing companies that tend to reinvest most of their earnings in the company rather than declare dividends. Growth funds generally take greater risks and experience greater volatility than other fund types in order to achieve greater returns.

FIGURE 11.6 How Mutual Funds Are Invested (Year-End 1999 and 2002)

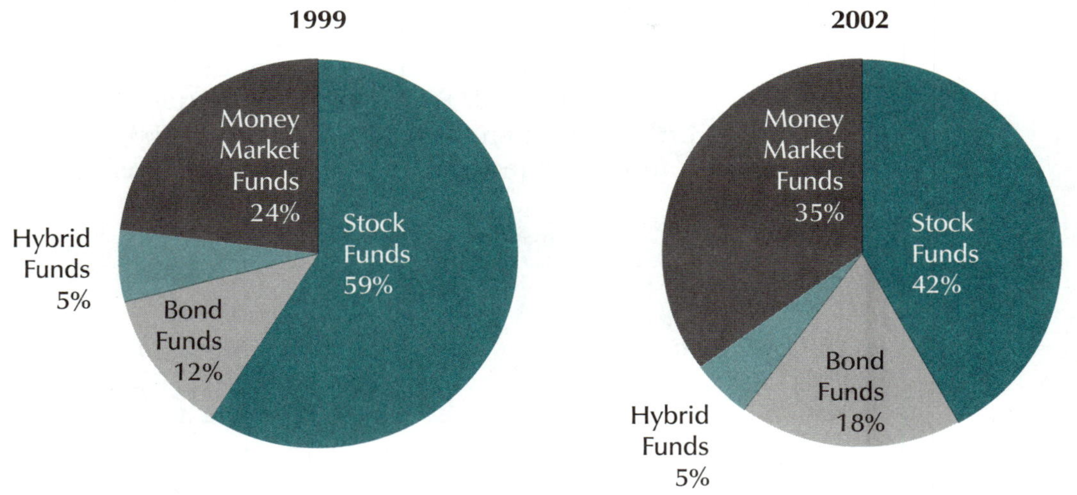

Source: Data from Investment Company Institute, *2003 Mutual Fund Fact Book*, 43rd ed., (Washington, DC: Investment Company Institute, 2003), 107, http://www.ici.org/stats/mf/2003_factbook.pdf (15 June 2003).

- An ***income fund*** has the objective of maximizing current income. Such funds emphasize high current dividend or interest income rather than capital gains. Income funds typically hold all types of bonds and/or stocks of companies with a consistent record of paying dividends. Examples of income funds include corporate bond funds and municipal bond funds.

- A ***growth and income fund*** has the objective of long-term capital gains and some current income. Such funds aim for capital appreciation that exceeds that of income funds and dividend and interest income that exceeds that of growth funds. Growth and income mutual funds typically are hybrid funds that hold a variety of stocks and bonds, but they can be stock funds that hold stocks that exhibit growth and pay dividends.

- A ***balanced fund*** has the objective of preservation of capital with moderate income and growth in value. Such funds emphasize safety of principal with some dividend income and some long-term capital appreciation. Balanced mutual funds typically are hybrid funds that hold blue-chip growth stocks and high-quality bonds.

- A ***value fund*** has the objective of long-term capital appreciation and invests in companies whose stock appears to be valued at less than it is worth.

Mutual Fund Value

By law, mutual funds must determine their net asset value each business day. The ***net asset value (NAV)*** is the value of one share in a mutual fund. The NAV is calculated by subtracting the fund's liabilities from the value of the fund's assets and then dividing the result by the total number of shares in the fund. For example, if Mutual Fund Z's asset portfolio is worth $10 million, its liabilities are $500,000, and its shareholders own 1 million shares, the NAV is $9.50, calculated as shown:

$$\frac{\$10{,}000{,}000 - \$500{,}000}{1{,}000{,}000}$$

A fund's market price, or offering price, is its NAV plus any front-end sales charge, which we explain in the section on fees. If the fund has no front-end sales charge, the market price is the same as the NAV.

As with stocks and bonds, an investor can estimate the price he will pay or receive for a mutual fund share by referring to mutual fund quotations. Figure 11.7 explains how to read a mutual fund quotation.

Typically, the performance of a mutual fund is judged by its total return, which—as we mentioned earlier—is the distributions the fund pays (interest, dividends, and capital gains or losses from the sale of securities within the fund) plus the change in the fund's value. Total return is shown as a percentage of the initial investment when reported in mutual fund quotations.

Mutual Fund Fees

Mutual funds charge shareholders various fees, which are required by law to be fully and clearly disclosed to prospective purchasers. These fees fall into two categories: shareholder fees and annual fund operating expenses. Whereas not all mutual funds charge shareholder fees, all mutual funds charge annual operating expenses.

Shareholder Fees

Mutual funds charge shareholder fees directly to an investor's account as compensation for a specific transaction. Shareholder fees typically are categorized by when they are charged.

A ***front-end load***, also known as a *sales charge*, is a fee a mutual fund charges when the investor buys shares. The front-end load is typically a marketing fee that compensates an investment professional—a bank, broker, agent, or financial planner—for his advice.

A ***back-end load***, also called a *deferred sales charge*, is a fee a mutual fund charges when an investor sells shares. A back-end load is a percentage of the redemption value or of the initial investment. This fee dissuades investors from redeeming their mutual fund shares. A common

FIGURE 11.7 Mutual Fund Quotations

MUTUAL FUNDS

FUND	NAV	NET CHG	YTD %RET	3-YR %RET
American Funds Cl A				
BalA p	16.81	0.08	18.8	7.9
AmcpA p	16.40	0.02	26.2	0.0
AMutlA p	23.46v	−0.11	18.7	5.0
BondA p	13.37	0.03	10.7	8.8

FUND	NAV	NET CHG	YTD %RET	3-YR %RET
TxMgdIntV	19.21	0.01	33.9	3.0
BerwynInc	11.65	0.05	14.1	13.3
Bishop Street Funds				
EquityInst	9.16	0.05	22.1	−12.4
HighGrdInst	10.53	0.02	2.3	7.6

FUND	NAV	NET CHG	YTD %RET	3-YR %RET
AcornB t	21.24	−0.07	40.4	10.9
FedSecB t	10.66	0.02	0.3	5.7
GrStkB t	10.76	0.05	21.2	NS
GrwIncB t	14.59	0.09	12.8	−3.4
HYOppsB t	4.60	0.01	22.6	4.8

FUND	NAV	NET CHG	YTD %RET	3-YR %RET
InLHorSA	10.93	0.02	17.6	−0.5
IntGvt p	11.29	0.02	0.3	5.1
IntHorSA	10.91	0.02	13.6	1.6
IntlEq p	12.86	−0.03	27.9	−5.2
LgHorSA	9.22	0.02	21.0	−4.3

FUND
The mutual fund company's name followed by the funds in its family. An "**r**" after the name means that it charges a back-end load, a "**p**" means that it charges a 12b-1 fee, and a "**t**" means that it charges both.

NAV
The fund's net asset value (NAV) expressed in dollar amounts.

NET CHG
The change in NAV from the previous trading day.

YTD % RET
Year-to-date return.

3-YR % RET
Three year return annualized.

FUND	NAV	NET CHG	YTD %RET	3-YR %RET
American Funds CL A				
BalA p	16.81	0.08	18.8	7.9
AmcpA p	16.40	0.02	26.2	0.0
AMutlA p	23.46v	-0.11	18.7	5.0
BondA p	13.37	0.03	10.7	8.8

Source: *Wall Street Journal,* 13 December 2003, C4. Used with permission.

type of back-end load is a ***contingent deferred sales charge***, which is charged only if the investor does not hold the shares a specified number of years after purchase. Typically, the charge will decrease each year that the investor holds the shares.

Some funds also charge the following additional shareholder fees:

- A load on reinvested dividends when dividends are used to purchase additional shares. Funds created after April 2000 are prohibited from charging this load.

- A ***redemption fee***, which is a fee for redeeming shares that is expressed as a dollar amount or as a percentage of the redemption price.

- An ***exchange fee***, which is a fee for transferring money from one mutual fund to another within the same fund family. However, many funds offer free transfer privileges.

- An ***account maintenance fee***, which is a fee to cover the costs of certain mutual fund accounts, such as those that carry a low balance.

Annual Operating Expenses

Mutual funds incur annual operating expenses that they must recoup from investors. These operating expenses are not deducted from investors' accounts but are deducted from fund assets before distribution of earnings to investors. A fund's ***expense ratio*** is the total annual operating expenses as a percentage of the fund's average net assets, and the mutual fund must disclose this expense ratio to investors.

Mutual fund annual operating expense charges may include:

- A ***management fee***, which is a fee paid to the fund's investment adviser who manages the fund's assets and selects its portfolio of securities.

- A ***12b-1 fee***, which is a fee that covers marketing and distribution expenses. By law this fee cannot exceed 0.75 percent of the fund's average net assets per year.

- Other expenses of the fund, such as the provision of customer service. This fee cannot exceed 0.25 percent of the fund's average net assets per year.

A mutual fund that charges a load—front-end or back-end—or a 12b-1 fee greater than 25 basis points, or both, is known as a ***load fund***. A mutual fund that does not charge a load or a 12b-1 fee greater than 25 basis points is known as a ***no-load fund***. A ***basis point*** is one-hundredth of a percent (0.01 percent). Thus, a fund may call itself "no-load" even if it assesses a 12b-1 fee of 0.25 percent or less. In addition, no-load funds can incur annual operating expenses other than 12b-1 fees.

Share Classes

Many mutual funds offer investors a choice in how they pay fees and expenses. These mutual funds offer various share classes, the names and definitions of which may differ depending on the fund. Each class invests in the same investment portfolio and has the same investment objective, but each class differs in the services and distribution arrangements it offers. Therefore, each share class has a different fee structure. The typical share classes are

- Class A, which generally has a front-end load and no, or a low, 12b-1 fee

- Class B, which generally has a contingent deferred sales charge and a 12b-1 fee
- Class C, which generally may have a higher 12b-1 fee than the other share classes but no front-end or back-end load[7]

Effect of Fees on Return

Mutual fund fees reduce the total return on the fund. However, just because a fund is no-load does not mean that it will produce a higher return. Some no-load funds have high annual operating fees that, in the long run, might exceed the total fees and expenses paid for a load fund. In addition, some load funds outperform no-load funds. Thus, investors must determine how valuable paying for investment advice is to them when selecting a mutual fund.

How Mutual Funds Are Bought and Sold

Mutual fund no-load shares may be purchased directly from the mutual fund company. Mutual fund shares purchased through investment advisers such as brokers, financial planners, bank representatives, or insurance agents are more likely to be load funds.

Investment Accounts

Some people buy securities directly from the companies or government agencies that issue the securities. Other people who engage in a high volume of security trading may prefer to establish an account with a brokerage firm or a managed account.

Brokerage Accounts

As we mentioned in Chapter 1, a person may choose between a full-service brokerage firm and a discount brokerage firm. Both types of firms execute their customers' orders to buy and sell securities, but only the full-service firm offers personalized investment advice. Full-service firms best serve investors who require assistance from the broker in selecting securities that are consistent with their risk tolerance and investment objectives.

A third option for an investor is to open an online brokerage account with an Internet brokerage firm. Many discount firms and some full-service firms now offer online brokerage accounts as well. These Internet accounts offer convenient access to placing orders and reviewing the account, and commission charges are lower than those associated with traditional accounts from full-service and discount firms.

The U.S. federal government does not insure brokerage accounts. However, as we mentioned earlier in the chapter, the Securities Investor Protection Corporation (SIPC) does offer brokerage account holders some protection. This organization is not a government agency or regulatory authority. Instead, the SIPC is a nonprofit, membership corporation funded by its member securities broker-dealers that protects customers of member broker-dealers registered with the SEC. The SIPC covers investors' accounts up to $500,000, including $100,000 held in cash, in the event of the firm's financial failure. Investment losses are not protected.

In the remainder of this section, we discuss the types of brokerage accounts and the fees brokerage firms charge for their services.

Types of Accounts

An investor can open several types of brokerage accounts.

- A ***cash account*** is a brokerage account in which all transactions are settled on a cash basis within three days after the investor places a buy or sell order. A cash account typically requires the investor to make a low initial deposit of approximately $50.

- A ***margin account*** is a brokerage account in which the investor is allowed to borrow money from the brokerage firm to buy securities. A margin account requires the investor to make a substantial deposit, which may be in cash or securities. Insight 11.2 describes how margin accounts are structured so that only the investor's funds, rather than those of the broker, are at risk of a loss.

- A ***discretionary account*** is a brokerage account in which the investor gives the broker discretionary authority to buy and sell securities for the account without the investor's prior consent.

As we discussed in Chapter 3, brokerage firms also offer asset management accounts (AMAs), which typically combine at least a checking account, money market fund, and a brokerage account. An investor with an AMA would select a cash account, margin account, or discretionary account to be the brokerage account portion of his AMA.

Commissions and Fees

Brokerage firms typically charge commissions for making trades. A ***commission*** is a fee paid to a brokerage firm in exchange for executing a buy or sell order. The commission may be a percentage of the entire transaction (the total price of the securities bought or sold), a flat fee per transaction, or a combination of both. Firms that charge a percentage of the transaction typically establish a commission schedule under which the commission percentage rate decreases as the value of the transaction increases.

INSIGHT 11.2 Operations of a Margin Account

Brokerage firms and the Board of Governors of the Federal Reserve System (the Fed) set a minimum initial margin requirement for opening margin accounts. The Fed's requirement is 50 percent of the value of the securities to be purchased. A brokerage firm's minimum may be more than, but not less than, the Fed's.

If the value of an investment made with borrowed funds falls to the point that the investor's equity in the investment is less than a certain percentage of the investment's current value, referred to as the maintenance margin requirement, the investor will get a margin call from his broker. A margin call is notification that the investor must deposit more cash or securities in the account. The Fed sets this maintenance margin level at 25 percent of the market value of the investment, and a brokerage firm's maintenance margin level again may be more than but not less than the Fed's. If the investor cannot meet the margin call, the broker will sell the securities at whatever price he can get.

Example: Rachel Turner bought 100 shares of stock priced at $40 on margin. Her broker's initial margin requirement is 50 percent, so Rachel has borrowed $2,000 and her equity in the stock is $2,000 ((100 shares x $40) × .50). A year later, the stock price drops to $25 per share, and the current market value of Rachel's investment is $2,500.

Analysis: Rachel still owes the broker $2,000, so her equity interest has dropped to $500, which is only 20 percent of the current value of the investment. The broker's maintenance margin requirement is 25 percent, so the broker will make a margin call requiring Rachel to deposit enough cash or securities to bring the equity up to the required level of 25 percent of the current value of the investment.

Example: Fred Lavoy opened a cash account with a full-service brokerage firm and placed an order to buy 100 shares of ToysInc, which is currently selling at $5 per share, and placed an order to sell 200 shares of GamesInc, which is currently selling at $10 per share. The brokerage firm's commission schedule is

- 3.0 percent on a transaction of less than $1,000
- 2.5 percent on a transaction of between $1,000 and $5,000
- 2.0 percent on a transaction of over $5,000

Analysis: On the ToysInc transaction, Fred will pay $15 in commissions ((100 × $5) × .03 = $15). On the GamesInc Transaction, Fred will pay $50 in commissions ((200 × $10) × .025 = $50).

Discount brokerage firms charge lower commissions than full-service brokerage firms—sometimes more than 50 percent less. Full-service and discount brokerages that offer Internet trading have lower commission rates for such trades than for those made by phone. Internet brokerage firms typically charge the lowest commission rates of all.

Many full-service brokerage firms, in lieu of charging a commission per trade, charge a maintenance fee. The fee can be a percentage of assets under management or a set amount.

Managed Accounts

A ***managed account***, also known as a *separately managed account*, is a customized portfolio of securities that is actively managed by an investment adviser, who provides the account holder with personalized advice on selection, diversification, and taxation of assets. The investment adviser has a particular objective—for example, current income or long-term growth—in mind for the performance of the account. The investment adviser's job is to continually monitor the performance of the holdings to assure that objective is being met.

With a managed account, the investment adviser typically is responsible for hundreds of accounts, which generally have the same objective and therefore hold the same securities. However, each account holder owns the individual securities in his account and may customize his account by requesting that certain securities be added or dropped from the typical mix. Generally, managed accounts hold between 30 and 70 types of securities, thus offering the opportunity for broad diversification.

Because the managed account holder owns the individual stocks, he can control the tax consequences of purchases and sales. For example, the account holder can instruct his investment adviser to hold a certain stock for over a year so that he has long-term rather than short-term capital gains.

Many financial planners and other financial advisers can assist their clients in opening managed accounts with a brokerage firm or an independent investment adviser. Typically, a minimum initial deposit (such as $100,000) is required to open a managed account. Investment advisers charge annual fees that cover advice, management, and the costs of all trades conducted during the course of the year, rather than commissions.

Key Terms

stock
shareholder
common stock
preferred stock
cumulative preferred stock
noncumulative preferred stock
par value
market price
dividend yield
price/earnings (P/E) ratio
initial public offering (IPO)
stock exchange
over-the-counter market
bond
bondholder
bond issuer

term
maturity date
coupon payment
coupon rate
convertible bond
callable bond
discount
premium
yield to maturity
current yield
mutual fund family
stock fund
bond fund
hybrid fund
index
conservative fund
growth fund
income fund
growth and income fund
balanced fund
value fund
net asset value (NAV)
front-end load
back-end load
contingent-deferred sales charge
redemption fee
exchange fee
account maintenance fee
expense ratio
management fee
12b-1 fee
load fund
no-load fund
basis point
cash account
margin account
discretionary account
commission
managed account

Endnotes

1. "Stat Bank," *Journal of Financial Planning* (July 2003), 21.
2. Investment Company Institute, *2003 Mutual Fund Fact Book*, 43rd ed., (Washington, DC: Investment Company Institute, 2003), 100, http://www.ici.org/stats/mf/2003_factbook.pdf (15 June 2003).
3. Investment Company Institute, 13.
4. Investment Company Institute, inside front cover.
5. Investment Company Institute, 23.
6. In the United States in 1999, $6.846 trillion was invested in mutual funds. Of this total, $4.042 trillion was invested in stock funds, $812 billion in bond funds, $379 billion in hybrid funds, and $1.613 trillion in money market funds. In the United States in 2002, $6.392 trillion was invested in mutual funds. Of this total, $2.667 trillion was invested in stock funds, $1.125 trillion in bond funds, $327 billion in hybrid funds, and $2.272 trillion in money market funds. Investment Company Institute, 2003 *Mutual Fund Fact Book* 43rd ed. (Washington, D.C.: Investment Company Institute, 2003), 107, http://www.ici.org/stats/mf/2003_factbook.pdf. (15 June 2003).
7. "Frequently Asked Questions about Mutual Fund Fees," Investment Company Institute, http://www.ici.org/funds/inv/bro_mf_fees_faq.html (19 November 2003).

chapter

12

Individual Annuities

outline

Types of Annuity Contracts

- Immediate and Deferred Annuities
- Single-Premium and Flexible-Premium Annuities
- Fixed and Variable Annuities

The Annuity Contract

- Annuity Contract Provisions for the Accumulation Period
- Enhanced Variable Annuity Benefits
- Distributions

Financial Design of Annuities

- Factors Affecting Periodic Income Payments
- Annuity Fees and Charges
- Annuity Share Classes

objectives

After reading this chapter, you should be able to

- Define the term *annuity contract*
- Distinguish among an annuity contract owner, annuitant, and payee
- Distinguish between immediate annuity contracts and deferred annuity contracts, single- and flexible-premium annuity contracts, and fixed and variable annuity contracts
- Explain important contractual provisions of an individual annuity
- Identify and distinguish among the types of payout options available under annuity contracts
- List the factors that affect the value of an annuity's periodic income payments and describe the effect of each factor
- List and explain the fees and charges typically paid by annuity contract owners

In the most general terms, an annuity is a series of periodic payments. Almost everyone makes and receives periodic payments; for example, monthly rent or mortgage payments constitute an annuity, as do salaries paid on a regular, periodic basis. In this text, we will use the terms *annuity* and *annuity contract* interchangeably.

An ***annuity contract*** is a legally enforceable written agreement between an insurance company and a contract owner under which the insurer grants a named person the right to receive a series of periodic payments in exchange for a premium or a series of premiums. The parties to the annuity contract are the insurance company and the ***contract owner***, who is the person or entity who exercises all rights and privileges of an annuity contract. The annuity contract specifies the ***annuitant***, whose lifetime is used to determine the amount of benefits payable under an annuity contract. The ***payee*** is the person or entity designated to receive the periodic income payments under an annuity contract. In most cases, the contract owner, the annuitant, and the payee are the same person. ***Periodic income payments*** are the monthly, quarterly, semiannually, or yearly annuity payments made to the payee.

Annuity contracts are the only financial products that can guarantee a payout that a recipient cannot outlive. Whereas life insurance protects against the financial consequences of premature death, certain annuities that offer a payout for life can protect against the financial consequences of outliving one's financial resources. With these annuities, some of the financial risk of "living too long" is transferred to the insurance company. However, annuities may not provide sufficient protection against inflation and catastrophic events.

Annuities represent the largest portion of the premium receipts of U.S. life insurance companies. The popularity of annuities is partly the result of favorable federal income tax treatment, which allows for tax-deferred investment earnings. This feature makes annuities a popular asset accumulation product. An annuity can be either an asset accumulation or an asset distribution product, or both, depending on the type of annuity. We discuss this concept further in the section explaining immediate and deferred annuities. Note, though, that the majority of annuity contracts are used as asset accumulation products.

In some countries, such as Argentina, companies that issue life insurance policies and annuity contracts must be different legal entities. In the United States, annuities are considered life insurance products, and only life insurance companies may issue annuities. Thus, annuities must comply with state insurance laws and regulations. In the United States, variable annuities, like variable life insurance policies, also are considered securities and must comply with federal securities laws in addition to state

FAST FACT

Annuities represented 53 percent of premium receipts of U.S. life insurers in 2002.[1]

insurance laws. In other countries, such as Argentina, variable annuities are not considered securities, and they are not subject to securities regulation. Many types of financial institutions, including depository institutions and broker-dealers, may market and distribute annuities.

In this chapter, we discuss the types of individual annuity contracts, typical annuity contract provisions, and the financial design of annuity contracts.

Types of Annuity Contracts

Annuity contracts can be classified as individual or group annuities.

- An ***individual annuity*** is an annuity contract purchased by an individual.
- A ***group annuity*** is an annuity contract established through a retirement plan that covers a group of people.

Annuity contracts also can be qualified or nonqualified.

- A ***qualified annuity*** is an annuity contract purchased to fund or distribute funds from a qualified plan. A ***qualified plan*** technically is a retirement plan that receives favorable income tax treatment by meeting the requirements imposed by U.S. federal tax law and ERISA. However, a broader, less formal usage of *qualified plan* includes other tax-advantaged savings plans such as IRAs, which we discuss in Chapter 13.
- A ***nonqualified annuity*** is an annuity that is not part of a qualified plan.

Under current U.S. federal tax laws, qualified annuities are taxed in accordance with the tax laws that apply to the qualified plan that they fund. For example, as we will discuss in Chapter 13, if an annuity is used to fund a traditional IRA, premiums will be tax deductible up to the limit allowed for the traditional IRA; but if the annuity is used to fund a Roth IRA, premiums are not tax deductible. Premiums for a nonqualified annuity are not tax deductible, but investment earnings are tax deferred.[2] The investment earnings of nonqualified annuities become subject to taxation when contract owners take funds out of the annuity.

Annuity contracts can be categorized in a number of other ways, including according to

- How the annuity contract is used and when periodic income payments begin

- How often premiums are paid
- How annuity premiums are invested

As we will explain, all of the categories overlap one another. Figure 12.1 illustrates major classifications of annuities.

Immediate and Deferred Annuities

As we have mentioned, people use annuity contracts to (1) accumulate savings and/or (2) distribute their savings as a periodic income. Immediate annuities can be used only to distribute funds as a periodic income over a specified period of time. Deferred annuities are used primarily to accumulate savings, but they also give the contract owner the right to receive periodic income payments at some point in the future. Exercising the right to receive a periodic income payment from a deferred annuity is called *annuitization*. Presently, many deferred annuity contracts are not annuitized.

Immediate and deferred annuities are distinguishable by when periodic income payments begin, as illustrated in Figure 12.2.

Immediate Annuities

An ***immediate annuity*** provides periodic income payments that generally are scheduled to begin one annuity period after the contract's issue date. The ***annuity period*** is the time span between the payments in the series of periodic income payments. An annuity that provides for a series of annual periodic income payments has an annuity period of one year and is referred to as an *annual annuity*. An annuity contract that provides for an annuity period of one month is referred to as a *monthly annuity*. Periodic income payments also may be made quarterly or semiannually.

FIGURE 12.1 Major Classifications of Annuity Contracts

	Immediate Annuity	Deferred Annuity
Fixed	Single-premium	Single-premium OR Flexible-premium
Variable	Single-premium	Single-premium OR Flexible-premium

FIGURE 12.2 Immediate vs. Deferred Annuities

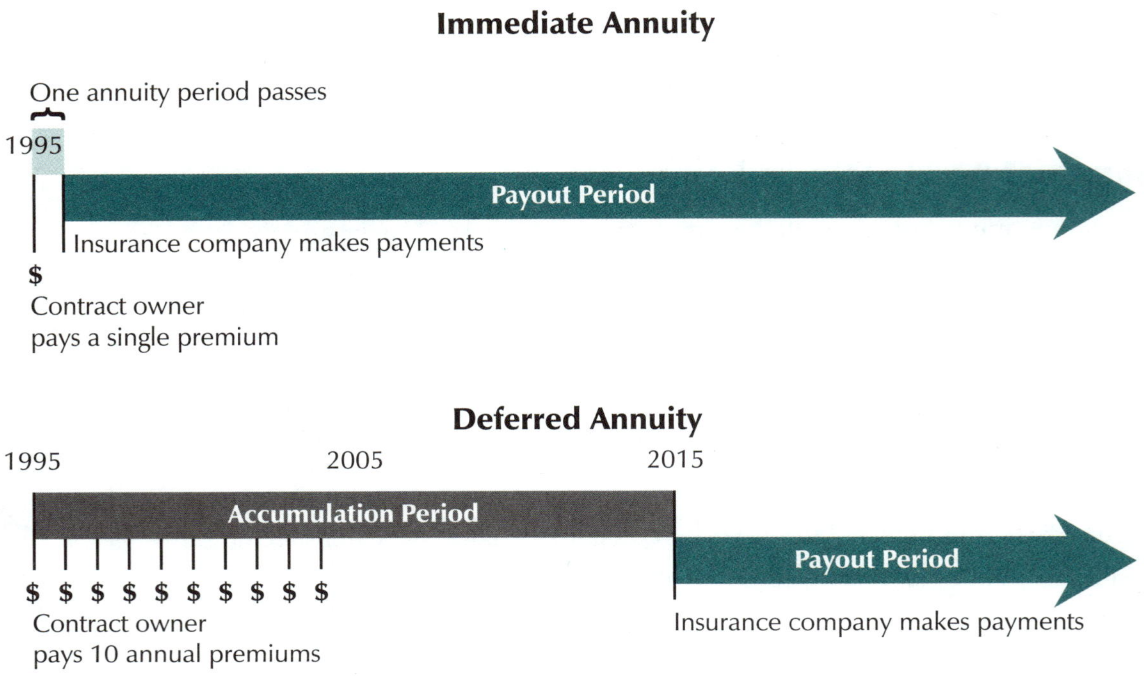

Source: Adapted from Mary C. Bickley and David F. Johnson, *Intro to Financial Services* (Atlanta: LOMA, © 2001), 81. Used with permission; all rights reserved.

Deferred Annuities

Under a ***deferred annuity***, periodic income payments are scheduled to begin more than one annuity period after the contract's issue date. The time period between the issue date and the date that the contract's periodic income payments begin is the ***accumulation period***. The ***payout period***, also known as the *annuitization period*, is the time period when periodic income payments are payable to the payee.

Deferred annuities give the contract owner the options of (1) continuing the annuity's accumulation period for many years, subject to certain restrictions associated with qualified plans, (2) withdrawing funds from the annuity during the accumulation period, or (3) annuitizing the contract so that the payout period begins and the payee receives periodic income payments.

The date on which the insurer begins to make the periodic income payments is known as the ***annuity date*** or the *income date*. ***Payout options***, also known as *settlement options*, of an annuity contract are the choices a contract owner has as to how the insurer will distribute annuity benefits during the payout period. An annuity in the payout period, whether purchased as an immediate annuity or purchased as a deferred annuity and allowed to annuitize, is commonly called a ***payout annuity***.

Figure 12.3 compares immediate annuity contracts and deferred annuity contracts.

Single-Premium and Flexible-Premium Annuities

Annuity contracts also can be categorized by how often premiums are paid.

- A ***single-premium annuity*** is funded by only one lump-sum premium payment from the contract owner to the insurance company. All immediate annuities are single-premium annuities.
- A ***flexible-premium annuity*** allows the contract owner to alter the amount and frequency of premium payments, within specified limits. Every annuity funded with flexible premiums is a deferred annuity.

Despite the many potential varieties of annuities, three configurations of annuity features are particularly common: the single-premium immediate annuity, the single-premium deferred annuity, and the flexible-premium deferred annuity. These types of annuities are described in Figure 12.4.

FIGURE 12.3 Comparison of Immediate and Deferred Annuity Contracts

	Type of Contract	
	Immediate Annuity Contract	**Deferred Annuity Contract**
Purpose	To convert a lump sum into an income stream.	To provide a means for the contract owner to accumulate funds until a future point in time.
Premium structure	Purchased with a single premium.	Can be purchased with a single premium or a series of premiums.
Accumulation period	No accumulation period. The periodic income payments typically begin no later than one year after the annuity is purchased.	Accumulation period usually lasts for years but is generally at least more than one annuity period after the annuity contract is issued.

Source: Adapted from John P. Burger, Kristen L. Falk, and Patsy Leeuwenburg, *Annuity Principles and Products,* 2nd ed. (Atlanta: LOMA, © 2003), 9. Used with permission; all rights reserved.

FIGURE 12.4 Popular Types of Annuities

A ***single-premium immediate annuity (SPIA) contract*** is an immediate annuity contract that is purchased with a lump-sum premium payment on the contract's issue date.

Example: Roger Draper, age 65, might use his retirement savings of $75,000 to purchase an immediate annuity that will provide monthly income payments beginning one month after the contract is purchased.

A deferred annuity that is purchased with a single premium payment is a ***single-premium deferred annuity (SPDA) contract***. Under an SPDA, the insurer holds the single-premium payment at interest until a date specified by the contract owner for periodic income payments to begin. During the first contract year of an SPDA, most insurers will accept additional premiums, known as ***window premiums***.

Example: Belinda Argus, upon changing jobs at age 45, might use a lump-sum distribution from a retirement plan as a single premium to purchase a deferred annuity that would not begin making payments until she retires. If Ms. Argus retires at age 65, her annuity contract would have a 20-year accumulation period.

Under a ***flexible-premium deferred annuity (FPDA) contract***, the contract owner typically must pay an initial premium of some minimum amount and then may make additional payments at any future times, usually subject to some smaller minimum amount. The contract owner may choose not to pay any premium in a given year. The only requirement is that any premium amount paid must meet the stated minimum.

Example: Maria Montoya elected to purchase an annuity with planned monthly premiums of $100. She paid the initial premium of $1,000 and paid $100 per month for three months before experiencing a financial emergency. Six months later, after she resolved the emergency, Ms. Montoya began making annuity premium payments of $150 per month.

Fixed and Variable Annuities

People who purchase annuities have different purposes in mind for the funds they place in an annuity. Annuity purchasers also have different tolerances for assuming financial risk when they place money in annuities. Thus, the returns paid under deferred or immediate annuity contracts can be either fixed or variable. The distinction relies upon the presence or absence of guarantees concerning the contract's (1) principal sum, which for annuities is the amount of premiums paid, and (2) interest rate.

Fixed Annuities

A ***fixed annuity*** is an annuity contract in which the insurer guarantees that the contract's accumulation value will experience no loss of the investment principal and will earn interest at a current rate no lower than the contract's minimum guaranteed interest rate. The ***accumulation value*** is the value paid for the deferred annuity plus interest earned, less the amount of any withdrawals or fees. The periodic income payments under a fixed annuity contract also are fixed in amount. As compared to a variable annuity, a fixed annuity provides more guarantees from the insurer to the contract owner, and consequently is viewed as a more conservative financial product. However, a fixed annuity contract owner still faces interest rate risk and inflation risk.

When an insurer receives fixed annuity premiums, the insurer invests them through its general account. As we discussed in Chapter 5, the general account is the undivided investment account in which an insurer maintains funds that support contractual obligations for guaranteed insurance products, such as whole life insurance and fixed annuities. Although the insurer guarantees a minimum rate of interest on a fixed annuity, the insurer has no guarantee itself that the funds held in the general account will earn that minimum rate of interest. Regardless of the investment performance of its general account, the insurer must pay the amounts guaranteed by the fixed annuity. Thus, the insurer bears the investment risk of a fixed annuity. Figure 12.5 describes how interest rates operate in fixed deferred annuities.

FIGURE 12.5 Fixed Annuities: Guaranteed and Current Interest Rates

Fixed deferred annuities specify a ***minimum guaranteed interest rate***—the lowest interest rate that the insurer will ever credit on a fixed annuity contract's accumulation value. The minimum guaranteed interest rate is guaranteed for the life of the contract. A fixed annuity contract further provides that a current interest rate will be declared at the discretion of the company. The ***current interest rate***, also known as the *credited rate*, in fixed annuity contracts is the interest rate that the insurer actually pays on the accumulation value for a given period. The current interest rate is equal to or higher than the minimum guaranteed interest rate. The difference between the minimum guaranteed interest rate and the current interest rate is known as the ***excess interest rate***, as shown in the following equation:

Current (Credited) Interest Rate – Minimum Guaranteed Interest Rate = Excess Interest Rate

Example: Ivan Petrenko purchased from the Nova Insurance Company a fixed annuity with a minimum guaranteed interest rate of 4.0 percent and a current interest rate of 5.25 percent. Three years later, the market interest rate was 3.75 percent, and Nova declared a new current interest rate of 4.0 percent.

Analysis: For the first three years Mr. Petrenko owned his annuity, the excess interest rate was 1.25 percent (5.25 percent – 4.0 percent). When the market interest rate dropped to 3.75 percent, Nova lowered the current interest rate, but could not lower it below 4.0 percent, the minimum guaranteed interest rate. At this time, the excess interest rate for Mr. Petrenko's annuity becomes 0.0 percent.

(continued on next page)

FIGURE 12.5 *(continued)* **Fixed Annuities: Guaranteed and Current Interest Rates**

This arrangement permits the company to declare a rate of interest that will limit the incentive for contract owners to move their money in search of a higher interest rate. For example, if the market interest rate in our example increased to 7 percent, Nova Insurance Company could increase its current interest rate, thus dissuading contract owners from taking their funds out of the annuity and putting them in a higher interest investment vehicle.

Some fixed annuity contracts contain a ***bailout provision***, also known as an *escape clause* or *cash-out provision*, which enables the contract owner to surrender the annuity contract, usually without surrender charges, if the current interest rate falls below a stated level—typically 1 percentage point below the initial current interest rate.

Fixed deferred annuity contracts contain payout schedules that guarantee that the payee will be able to obtain at least a minimum level of periodic income payments per dollar of premium or $1,000 of premium annuitized. Upon actual annuitization of a contract, however, the insurer typically provides periodic income payments on the basis of rates that are more favorable to the annuitant than those stated in the contract.

Hybrid types of annuity products such as equity-indexed annuities and market value adjusted annuities have been introduced into the fixed annuity market. Figure 12.6 explains these hybrid annuities.

Variable Annuities

A ***variable annuity*** is an annuity contract under which the amount of the accumulation value and periodic income payments fluctuate in accordance with the performance of one or more specified investment funds. Variable annuities do not guarantee principal or interest. Variable annuities offer some protection against inflation risk, but they are affected by market risk.

Because the variable annuity does not offer interest rate or principal guarantees, the variable annuity contract owner bears the investment risk. Thus, variable annuities, like variable life insurance policies, are securities and must comply with U.S. federal securities laws.

Subaccounts

Variable annuity premiums are maintained in a separate account, which, as we discussed in Chapter 5, is an investment account maintained separately from the insurer's general account to isolate and help manage the funds placed in variable insurance products, such as variable life insurance and variable annuities. As we also discussed, the insurer's separate account includes a number of subaccounts, which are alternative investment funds within an insurer's separate account. A variable annuity

FIGURE 12.6 Hybrid Annuities

Equity-Indexed Annuity

An ***equity-indexed annuity (EIA)*** is a type of annuity that offers certain principal and earnings guarantees, but also offers the possibility of additional earnings by linking the contract to a published index. As we learned in Chapter 11, an index is a statistical measurement system that tracks the performance of a group of similar investments. EIAs typically are classified as fixed annuities because of the guarantees they offer. However, like variable annuities, EIAs offer the potential for higher returns depending on investment performance.

Market Value Adjusted Annuities

A ***market value adjusted (MVA) annuity***, also known as a *modified guaranteed annuity*, is an annuity that offers multiple guarantee periods and multiple fixed rates. Rather than being "locked in" with fixed earnings for the life of the contract, contract owners can move or withdraw premium deposits at certain times stipulated in the contract to take advantage of prevailing market rates.

To be issued as fixed annuities in the United States, EIAs and MVA annuities must meet certain regulatory guidelines. Those EIAs and MVA annuities that do not meet these regulatory requirements are considered variable products and must be registered as securities.

contract owner may allocate premiums among a choice of subaccounts. A variable annuity subaccount portfolio can be viewed as a rough equivalent of a mutual fund. The subaccount portfolio may consist of stocks, bonds, or other assets. Insight 12.1 describes variable annuity subaccounts.

After the variable annuity has been issued, the contract owner may (1) transfer money among subaccounts, (2) change the percentage of money allocated to specific subaccounts, and (3) change the subaccounts in which future premiums are invested.

Typically, variable annuities offer a wide variety of variable subaccounts. In addition, contract owners usually can place a portion of premiums in a ***fixed subaccount***, which is a subaccount that guarantees payment of a fixed rate of interest for a specified period of time. Unlike money invested in variable subaccounts, money invested in the fixed subaccount is held in the insurer's general account.

Accumulation Units

Premiums paid for a variable deferred annuity purchase ***accumulation units***, which represent ownership shares in selected subaccounts of the separate account held during the accumulation period. The number of accumulation units that a given premium will purchase depends on the value of the subaccount when the premium is paid. Thus, if the value of the subaccount investments is low, the value of each accumulation unit also will be low. When accumulation unit values are low, more accumulation units can be purchased for a given amount of premium than when the value of the units is high.

INSIGHT 12.1 Variable Annuity Subaccounts

At the time a variable annuity contract owner purchases her annuity, she must select at least one subaccount in which to invest her premiums. If the contract owner chooses more than one subaccount, she must specify what percentage of premiums she wishes to invest in each subaccount. The insurer will distribute the initial premium payment and any additional premiums to the specified subaccounts in the percentages indicated. For example, suppose that Trisha Hart chooses to invest her premium payments in four subaccounts as indicated below:

20 percent to Subaccount A
10 percent to Subaccount B
50 percent to Subaccount C
20 percent to Subaccount D

If Ms. Hart makes an initial premium payment of $5,000, the insurer would invest $1,000 in Subaccount A, $500 in Subaccount B, $2,500 in Subaccount C, and $1,000 in Subaccount D. During the accumulation period, a variable annuity contract's accumulation value will fluctuate directly with the investment performance of the chosen subaccounts.

Example: Gus Howard purchased a variable deferred annuity and selected Subaccount A as the investment vehicle for his annuity. Gus paid a premium of $600 in each of three months. Over a three-month period, the value of an accumulation unit in Subaccount A varied, as did the number of accumulation units purchased.

Month	Premium ÷	Price per accumulation unit =	Number of accumulation units
January	$600	$2.00	300
February	$600	$3.00	200
March	$600	$2.50	240
Total	**$1800**		**740**

Analysis: In January, the $600 premium purchased 300 accumulation units at a price of $2.00 each; in February, the $600 premium purchased 200 accumulation units at $3.00 each; in March, the $600 premium purchased 240 accumulation units at $2.50 each. Over the three-month period, the $1,800 that Gus paid in premiums purchased a total of 740 accumulation units.

As a contract owner pays premiums throughout the accumulation period, his total number of accumulation units gradually increases. The value of a contract owner's investment in a variable annuity subaccount depends on both the number of accumulation units held and the current value of an accumulation unit. Insight 12.2 illustrates how changes in the value of an accumulation unit affect the value of a contract owner's investment in a variable annuity subaccount.

In Insight 12.2, the number of accumulation units remains constant, but the value of the subaccount fluctuates. This fluctuation results from changes in the value of an accumulation unit, in turn resulting from changes in the market value of the underlying investments. Through the valuation mechanism, market performance affects the value of the contract owner's investment in a variable annuity. Keep in mind that increasing or decreasing the number of accumulation units held in a variable subaccount also can change the value of the contract owner's investment.

Annuity Units

At the beginning of the payout period, the variable annuity contract owner typically has the option of receiving periodic income payments that

- Are fixed in amount from a fixed subaccount
- Fluctuate to directly reflect the investment experience of specified variable subaccounts
- Are based on the results of some combination of fixed and variable subaccounts, so that a portion of the periodic income payments would be stable and another portion would fluctuate

INSIGHT 12.2 Calculating Subaccount Values During the Accumulation Period

In the table below, the value of 100 accumulation units in a variable annuity subaccount is equal to $600 when the current value of an accumulation unit is $6.00. If the value of an accumulation unit drops to $4.00, the value of the annuity investment will drop to $400. However, if the value of an accumulation unit rises to $8.00, then the value of the annuity investment will increase to $800.

Date	Number of Accumulation Units	Accumulation Unit Value	Subaccount Value
January 2004	100	$6.00	$600
January 2005	100	$4.00	$400
January 2006	100	$8.00	$800

If the contract owner selects the variable payout option, the insurer pays to the payee a series of payments that vary throughout the payout period. Under this option, the accumulation value of the annuity remains in the separate account. When the contract annuitizes, the annuity's accumulation units are used to purchase annuity units. ***Annuity units*** are shares in the subaccounts of an insurer's separate account that determine the size of future periodic income payments under a variable annuity contract after the contract has annuitized. The calculation of the number of annuity units that can be purchased for each dollar applied depends on a number of factors, including the current value of the accumulation units and the payout option elected, and is beyond the scope of this text.

A variable contract owner who has selected a variable payout option will receive periodic income payments that vary depending upon the total number of annuity units he has purchased and the current value of each annuity unit at the time each periodic income payment is calculated. Note that the total number of annuity units remains the same throughout the payout period; the value of an annuity unit varies depending on the investment experience of the subaccounts. Insight 12.3 illustrates how annuity unit values affect the size of periodic income payments.

INSIGHT 12.3 Annuity Unit Values and Periodic Income Payments

Assume Todd Lovett has 1,000 annuity units in Subaccount A of his variable deferred annuity contract.

If the value of an annuity unit in Subaccount A is $5.00 on the date the insurer makes its first monthly periodic income payment to Todd, the periodic income payment will be $5,000.00.

1,000 annuity units	×	$5.00 per annuity unit	=	$5,000.00 periodic income payment

However, if the value of an annuity unit in Subaccount A falls to $4.75 on the date the insurer makes its next monthly periodic income payment to Todd, the payment will be only $4,750.00.

1,000 annuity units	×	$4.75 per annuity unit	=	$4,750.00 periodic income payment

On the other hand, if the value of an annuity unit in Subaccount A increases to $5.25 on this date, then the monthly periodic income payment the insurer makes to Todd will be $5,250.00.

1,000 annuity units	×	$5.25 per annuity unit	=	$5,250.00 periodic income payment

Source: Adapted from Nicholas L. Desoutter, *Annuity Systems and Administration,* (Atlanta: LOMA, © 2001), 155. Used with permission; all rights reserved.

The Annuity Contract

As we mentioned earlier, an annuity is a contract between an insurance company and a contract owner. Annuity contracts typically are required by law to contain certain contract provisions, many of which are identical or similar to life insurance policy provisions that we discussed in Chapter 6. Figure 12.7 sets forth typical annuity contract provisions.

FIGURE 12.7 Annuity Contract Provisions

- A **free-look provision** gives the contract owner a specified period, usually 10 days, within which to return the annuity contract and receive a full refund of all premiums paid.
- An **entire contract provision** states that the entire contract consists of the annuity contract, the application if it is attached to the contract, and any attached riders. The entire contract provision in an annuity is generally the same as the one in a life insurance policy, except that the application for an annuity contract is not necessarily required to be included as part of the annuity contract.
- An **incontestability provision** in an annuity contract typically states that, after the annuity contract becomes effective, the insurer may not contest the validity of the contract. This provision is much more restrictive to the insurer than its counterpart in life insurance policies. Contracts that include certain supplementary benefits—such as waiver of premium for disability—limit the time, typically to a maximum of two years, during which the issuer may contest the validity of the coverage provided by the supplementary benefit based on a material misrepresentation in the application.
- A **misstatement of age or sex provision** states that if the annuitant's age or sex was misstated on the application for the annuity, then the annuity benefits payable will be those that the premiums paid would have purchased for the correct age or sex.
- A **dividend provision** is required in participating annuities and describes the contract owner's right to receive dividends, if any, and the dividend options available.
- An **assignment provision** in an annuity contract grants the contract owner the right to temporarily or permanently transfer ownership of the contract to another entity, who is called the assignee. Some annuity contracts, however, do not allow assignment.
- A **nonforfeiture provision** states the benefit amounts that the insurer will pay under a deferred annuity contract if premium payments stop or the contract is surrendered during the accumulation period.

Annuity Contract Provisions for the Accumulation Period

Annuities have a number of features that give contract owners varying degrees of access to their accumulation values. These features are the surrender, withdrawal, loan, and death benefit provisions.

- The nonforfeiture provision discussed in Figure 12.7 is commonly referred to as the *surrender provision*. The ***surrender value*** of an annuity is the amount that the contract owner is entitled to receive if the contract is terminated during its accumulation period. The surrender value is equal to the deferred annuity's accumulation value, less any surrender charges. A ***surrender charge***, also known as the *contingent deferred sales charge* for a variable annuity, is a fee sometimes charged to an annuity contract owner when he withdraws a portion or all of the contract's accumulation value.

Surrender Value of a Deferred Annuity	=	Accumulation Value	–	Surrender Charge

- A ***withdrawal***, also known as a *partial surrender*, is the payment of a portion of an annuity's accumulation value to the contract owner during the accumulation period. Most deferred annuities allow the contract owner to withdraw without charge a stated maximum percentage of the accumulation value each year. If the contract owner withdraws more than that stated percentage in one year, then the insurer generally imposes a surrender charge. Withdrawals of less than a stated minimum amount typically are not permitted. A withdrawal permanently reduces the annuity's accumulation value.

- Although loans generally are not available under nonqualified annuities, many qualified annuity contracts include a provision that allows the contract owner to obtain a loan against the annuity's accumulation value. (Note, though, that annuities that fund IRAs do not allow loans.) An important distinction exists between a loan and a withdrawal. Annuity loans are not withdrawals, because the contract owner must repay the loan and pay interest that is then credited to the accumulation value. In contrast to a loan, a withdrawal is a permanent reduction in value.

- A ***death benefit***, also known as a *survivor benefit*, is an annuity contract feature that states that if the contract owner dies during the accumulation period, a named beneficiary will receive a benefit of at least as much as the accumulation value at the time of the contract owner's death.

Note that in the event of a surrender of or withdrawal from a nonqualified or qualified annuity before the contract owner reaches age 59½, the U.S. federal government imposes a tax penalty unless certain exceptions apply.

Enhanced Variable Annuity Benefits

Some people are reluctant to deposit funds into a variable annuity because they fear losing their money as a result of market fluctuations. Insurers have responded to these concerns by designing enhanced benefits for variable annuity contracts. A variable annuity contract may contain none, some, or all of these features, the most common of which are described in Figure 12.8 and include the guaranteed minimum accumulation benefit, guaranteed minimum withdrawal benefit, guaranteed minimum death benefit, and guaranteed minimum income benefit. Many variations of these benefits exist.

Distributions

When an annuity reaches the payout period, all provisions relating to the policy's accumulated value—including the withdrawal and death benefit provisions—become inoperable; the terms of the payout option provision govern the parties' rights and obligations under the contract. As we mentioned earlier in this chapter, payout options of an annuity con-

FIGURE 12.8 Enhanced Variable Annuity Benefits

- The ***guaranteed minimum accumulation benefit (GMAB)*** is a variable annuity contract feature that guarantees a return of principal if the contract remains in force for a specified period of time.
- The ***guaranteed minimum withdrawal benefit (GMWB)*** is a variable annuity contract feature that guarantees that up to a certain percentage of the amount paid into the contract will be available for withdrawals annually, even if subaccount investments perform poorly.
- The ***guaranteed minimum death benefit (GMDB)*** is a variable annuity contract feature that guarantees that if the contract owner dies before periodic income payments begin, the beneficiary will receive at least the amount that was deposited into the annuity contract, less any withdrawals, even if poor investment performance causes the contract's accumulation value to be less than the premiums paid.
- The ***guaranteed minimum income benefit (GMIB)*** is a variable annuity contract feature that guarantees that variable periodic income payments will not fall below a certain amount—usually a specified percentage of the first payment—even if investments drop in value as a result of poor performance.

tract are the choices a contract owner has as to how the insurer will distribute the accumulation value. In the case of an immediate annuity, the applicant chooses the payout option when he applies for the annuity. However, in the case of a deferred annuity, the contract owner chooses the payout option just prior to the beginning of the payout period. Contract owners may have the accumulation value of their annuity distributed in a single payment, known as a ***lump-sum distribution***. Figure 12.9 sets forth some typical annuity payout options over time, all of which can be paid on a fixed basis if the annuity is fixed, or on a fixed or variable basis if the annuity is variable.

Because some annuity contract owners want the security of knowing that they can get to their money in case of an emergency, some insurers have added a commutation right to payout options. A ***commutation right*** states that the owner of a payout annuity can withdraw all or part of the contract's remaining periodic income payments in a lump sum. However, if a contract owner chooses to exercise the commutation right, the withdrawal will reduce the amount of any future periodic income payments.

Financial Design of Annuities

An annuity contract owner pays a premium or premiums to the insurer. The insurer invests the premiums from a large group of contract owners, and then uses the premiums and investment earnings to provide the benefits promised under the annuity contract. In this section, we discuss the factors that affect periodic income payments, annuity fees and charges, and annuity share classes.

Factors Affecting Periodic Income Payments

An insurer uses a combination of factors to calculate the benefits that it will pay under an annuity contract. Every calculation of contract values under an annuity, however, is based on the following basic mathematical principle:

> A sum of money, known as the *principal*, that is invested for a certain time period at a stated interest rate can be paid out in a series of periodic income payments over a stated period of time.

This principle contains four variables:

1. **The amount of principal invested**. Premiums increase principal. Withdrawals and surrenders decrease principal.

FIGURE 12.9 Typical Annuity Payout Options Over Time

Payout Option	Characteristics of Periodic Income Payments and Any Guarantees
Period certain annuity *(Annuity certain)*	Guarantees a specified number of periodic income payments, whether the annuitant lives or dies. **Example:** Elizabeth Hirose is a 50-year-old office manager who plans to retire at age 60. She will not begin receiving pension benefits from her employer-sponsored pension plan until she reaches age 65. Thus, she wants to purchase an annuity that will provide her periodic income payments during the 5-year period following her retirement before she begins receiving her pension benefits. **Analysis:** Elizabeth wants to begin receiving periodic income payments in 10 years, when she retires at age 60. Thus, she purchases a 10-year deferred annuity. Elizabeth wants to receive periodic income payments only until she will begin to receive her pension benefits. Elizabeth therefore elects a payout option under which periodic income payments are paid as a 5-year annuity certain.
Life annuity	Covers only one life and guarantees periodic income payments for as long as the annuitant lives, regardless of how long that is. When the annuitant dies, no further income is payable. Makes no guarantee as to either the minimum cumulative amount or minimum duration of periodic income payments.
Life annuity with period certain	Guarantees a periodic income payment so long as the annuitant lives and at least until the end of a specified period. Payments are guaranteed to continue until (1) the death of the annuitant or (2) the end of a specified period, whichever occurs last. **Example:** Jamal Kahn purchased a life income annuity with a 10-year period certain. He named himself as the annuitant and the payee. He named his wife Alana as contingent payee. Jamal died 7 years after periodic income payments began. **Analysis:** Alana will receive the periodic income payments for the remaining 3 years of the 10-year period certain. After the expiration of the 10-year period certain, no more periodic income payments will be made. Had Jamal lived 15 years after annuity benefits began, he would have received periodic income payments throughout his life, but Alana would have received no periodic income payments after his death.
Fixed amount annuity	Guarantees to pay periodic income payments of a specified minimum dollar amount for as long a period as the annuity's accumulation value will provide regardless of when the annuitant dies.

(continued on next page)

FIGURE 12.9 *(continued)* Typical Annuity Payout Options Over Time

Payout Option	Characteristics of Periodic Income Payments and Any Guarantees
Life with refund annuity *(Refund annuity)*	Guarantees a periodic income payment for the lifetime of the annuitant and guarantees a refund will be paid if the annuitant dies before the annuity premiums paid are recovered. **Example:** Ansar Larouch paid a single premium of $120,000 for a life with refund annuity that would provide an annual periodic income payment of $10,000 during his lifetime. He named his wife Irene as the contingent payee. Ansar died 7 years after periodic income payments began; at the time of his death, he had received benefits totaling $70,000. **Analysis:** Irene will be entitled to a refund of $50,000, which is the difference between the $120,000 purchase price and the $70,000 paid in benefits during Ansar's lifetime. Had Ansar lived for 15 years after periodic income payments began, he would have received more in benefits than he paid for the annuity (15 years x $10,000 per year = $150,000). In that case, Irene would not have received a refund payment following Ansar's death.
Joint and survivor annuity	Covers two or more lives and pays periodic income payments until all annuitants die. The terms of the annuity contract determine whether the amount of each periodic income payment will remain the same after the first annuitant dies or decrease by a stated amount following the death of the first annuitant.

2. **The time period over which the principal grows at interest**. For annuity contracts, this time period is the accumulation period. The pattern of premium payments over time affects the length of time that the principal earns interest. The longer the time period, the larger will be the interest earnings.

3. **The interest rate that represents investment earnings**. Some annuity contracts earn interest at a stated rate. Other annuity contracts, however, earn investment income that may not carry a stated interest rate. In all cases, though, an interest rate can be used to represent the investment earnings.

4. **The number and timing of periodic income payments**. The number of periodic income payments is determined by the frequency of payments and the total length of the payout period. For all types of life annuities, the number and timing of periodic income payments also depends upon mortality experience. The longer the annuitant is expected to live, all other factors being equal, the smaller the peri-

odic income payments will be. Similarly, the shorter the time period the annuitant is expected to live, all other factors being equal, the larger the periodic income payments will be.

Figure 12.10 summarizes the relationships among the important factors that affect periodic income payments in annuities.

Annuity Fees and Charges

Although our discussion to this point has greatly simplified the financial design of annuities, it is accurate to the extent that it considers investment earnings and funding the amount of periodic income payments. Insurers also must incorporate their expenses into the financial designs of their annuities, and they do so using one or more of the following fees and charges, some of which are similar to those charged for mutual funds:

- A front-end load is an amount charged to the contract owner at the time she pays for the product. The front-end load compensates the insurer for sales commissions and other expenses associated with acquiring the business.

> **Example**. The Easton Insurance Company's fixed deferred annuity has a 2.5 percent front-end load. If Gary Nielsen purchases a fixed deferred annuity from Easton for $50,000, Easton will deduct 2.5 percent of the $50,000 and invest the remainder on behalf of Mr. Nielsen's accumulation account.

FIGURE 12.10 Factors Affecting Periodic Income Payments

In an annuity contract, if, while keeping all other factors unchanged, we increase the following value:	Then the value of the contract's periodic income payments will
Principal	Increase
Time (accumulation period)	Increase
Investment earnings or interest rate	Increase
Number of periodic income payments	Decrease

Analysis: The amount of the front-end load would be calculated as 2.5 percent multiplied by $50,000, or $1,250. Thus, Mr. Nielsen's annuity accumulation value in the beginning of Year 1 would be calculated as $50,000 minus $1,250, equaling $48,750.

- A back-end load, also known as a *surrender charge*, is an amount charged to the contract owner when she withdraws money from the product. In variable annuities, a back-end load is known as a *contingent deferred sales charge (CDSC)*. The back-end load/CDSC is expressed as a percentage of the withdrawal and typically decreases over time. Eventually the contract owner can withdraw funds with no load being incurred.

- A ***periodic fee***, also known as a *maintenance fee*, is an amount payable at predetermined intervals, for example, every year or every month. A periodic fee typically compensates the insurer for its administrative expenses. This fee can be either a flat amount or a percentage of the customer's account value.

- Insurers also might impose a ***service fee***, which is a one-time fee for a specific service.

Variable annuities charge the following additional fees:

- A ***mortality and expense risk (M&E) charge*** to cover three guarantees, which are the contract benefits:

  - Any guaranteed death benefit payable to the designated beneficiary

  - The fixed payout options which guarantee that a certain amount will be paid for the life of the annuitant

  - The guarantee that contract expenses will increase no more than the maximums stated in the contract

  The M&E charge is generally expressed as a percentage of the accumulation value.

- An ***investment management fee*** to cover the professional investment management services. The investment management fee is usually expressed as a percentage of the accumulation value.

Note that contracts typically do not have both a front-end load and a back-end load, as both loads are charged to offset commission costs. Figure 12.11 summarizes the fees and charges associated with annuities.

FIGURE 12.11 Expense Charges for Annuities

	Formula	Insurer Deducts from	Purpose
Front-end load	Stated percentage	Premium	• Covers commission expenses • Covers issue expenses
Back-end load/ contingent deferred sales charge	Stated percentage	Withdrawal amount	• Covers commission expenses • Covers issue expenses • Discourages withdrawals • Can provide some protection of market value of investments
Periodic fee	• Stated flat amount per period • Stated percentage of account value per period	Account balance	Offsets general administrative expenses
Service fee	Stated flat amount per transaction	Transaction amount	Offsets specific administrative expenses
Mortality and expense risk charge (variable only)	Stated percentage	Account balance	Covers guaranteed contract benefits
Investment management fee (variable only)	Stated percentage	Account balance	Covers professional investment management services

Source: Adapted from Susan Conant, *Product Design for Life Insurance and Annuities* (Atlanta: LOMA, 2001), 166. Used with permission; all rights reserved.

Recall that we discussed bundled and unbundled product designs in Chapter 5. A bundled product structure is a design in which an insurer presents a product to customers as a package of benefits provided in exchange for a given payment. In other words, the insurer does not reveal separately the investment earnings, cost of benefits, and operating expenses. In contrast, an unbundled product structure is a design in which an insurer explicitly discloses various expense and benefit charges and specifies the rate of investment return being credited to contract owners. Most fixed deferred annuities are unbundled products, but they are not required to be unbundled. In the United States, all variable annuities must disclose specific, unbundled expense charges.

Annuity Share Classes

Just as with mutual funds, many issuers of variable annuities offer potential contract owners a choice of how they pay fees and expenses. These variable annuity issuers offer various share classes, each of which differs in the services and distribution arrangements it offers. Therefore, each share class has a different fee structure. The names and definitions of share classes may differ depending on the insurer, but the typical share classes are

- A Shares—front-end load
- B Shares—back-end load
- C Shares—no load
- L Shares—short contingent deferred sales load

Key Terms

annuity contract
contract owner
annuitant
payee
periodic income payment
individual annuity
group annuity
qualified annuity
qualified plan
nonqualified annuity
immediate annuity
annuity period
deferred annuity
accumulation period
payout period
annuity date
payout options
payout annuity
single-premium annuity
flexible-premium annuity
single-premium immediate annuity (SPIA) contract
single-premium deferred annuity (SPDA) contract
window premium
flexible-premium deferred annuity (FPDA) contract
fixed annuity
accumulation value
minimum guaranteed interest rate
current interest rate
excess interest rate
bailout provision
variable annuity

equity-indexed annuity (EIA)
market value adjusted (MVA) annuity
fixed subaccount
accumulation unit
annuity unit
surrender value
surrender charge
withdrawal
death benefit
guaranteed minimum accumulation benefit (GMAB)
guaranteed minimum withdrawal benefit (GMWB)
guaranteed minimum death benefit (GMDB)
guaranteed minimum income benefit (GMIB)
lump-sum distribution
commutation right
period certain annuity
life annuity
life annuity with period certain
fixed amount annuity
life with refund annuity
joint and survivor annuity
periodic fee
service fee
mortality and expense risk (M&E) charge
investment management fee

Endnotes

1. ACLI, *Life Insurers Fact Book: 2003* (Washington, DC: American Council of Life Insurers, 2003), 53.
2. Note that the investment earnings are not tax deferred if the nonnatural person rule applies. The nonnatural person rule states that interest credited each year is currently taxable if the owner of a deferred annuity is a nonnatural person (for example, a corporation, partnership, or trust) not acting as an agent for a natural person, and if any premiums were paid after February 28, 1986.

chapter 13

Tax-Advantaged Savings Plans

outline

objectives

After reading this chapter, you should be able to

- Explain the tax advantages of certain individual and private retirement plans
- Distinguish between a traditional IRA and a Roth IRA
- Explain the purpose of the Employee Retirement Income Security Act (ERISA)
- Identify the four broad types of employer-sponsored retirement plans
- Distinguish among SEP, SIMPLE, and Keogh plans

As we discussed in Chapters 1 and 2, governments use tax policies to encourage people to act or refrain from acting in certain ways. For example, governments have created a number of savings plans that offer tax incentives for people to accumulate assets for certain worthy purposes and in some cases to take orderly distributions of such assets. Insight 13.1 describes one such U.S. savings plan—the section 529 plan—that encourages people to save for higher education.

We begin this chapter with a discussion of the tax advantages of these government-created plans. We then discuss retirement savings plans, which constitute the majority of tax-advantaged savings plans. Although the types of plans we discuss in this chapter are those found in the United States, similar plans in other countries afford the same basic tax advantages.[1]

Taxation of Tax-Advantaged Savings Plans

Government-established, tax-advantaged savings plans are accounts that people (or organizations in the case of group plans) open at financial institutions. A person deposits money into the account and uses the money to purchase certain asset accumulation products that enjoy tax advantages by virtue of being held in this savings plan or account. For example, an individual can open an IRA with his bank and then invest in mutual funds, annuities, stocks and bonds, and other financial products. The financial products are taxed according to the tax laws that apply to the saving plan.

Tax-advantaged savings plans generally offer tax deferral on investment earnings. With tax deferral, income earned by the investments in the plan is not subject to income tax in the year it is earned. Instead, this investment income is taxed when it is withdrawn from the plan. Deferring taxes on investment earnings can increase considerably the rate at which the assets accumulate because earnings that would otherwise have been taxed are left in the plan to earn more interest.

Some types of tax-advantaged savings plans offer an exclusion or deduction for contributions made to the plan in addition to tax deferral. Contributions excluded from income reduce the amount of gross income actually reported to the Internal Revenue Service. Deductible contributions are reported but subtracted from income. The effect of these exclusions and deductions is basically the same—less taxable income upon which to be taxed currently. Payment of federal income taxes on amounts excluded or deducted are then deferred until funds are withdrawn from the savings plan. Just as with investment earnings, contributions to the plan that otherwise would have been taxed are instead placed in the plan to earn interest.

INSIGHT 13.1 Section 529 Plans

A ***section 529 plan***—named after the section of the Internal Revenue Code that describes it—is a tax-advantaged savings plan designed to fund a student's higher education. The 50 states and the District of Columbia typically sponsor these plans, set the contribution limits, and determine the rules by which the plans operate. Privately sponsored plans are now permissible under law, but we will limit our discussion to state-sponsored plans.

The states contract with financial institutions to manage the assets of 529 plans. A few 529 plans are open only to residents of the sponsoring state, but most are open to residents of any state. However, residents of other states who purchase the plan may forfeit state tax advantages.

Section 529 plans come in two forms, and some people choose to hold both:

- A **prepaid tuition plan** is designed to prepay a student's tuition. The owner makes contributions of an amount specified by the plan and dependent on the age of the student. The plan sponsor pools the funds paid into the plan and is able to make long-term investments, the earnings on which are designed to meet or exceed tuition inflation. The plan sponsor thus is able to offer the contributor a tuition guarantee. Funding is based on the cost of tuition at a public university in the state sponsoring the plan. The money generally may be used for tuition at a private or out-of-state university, but some states' plans pay a smaller amount when the money is not used for an in-state, public college or university.
- A **college savings plan** is designed to allow the account owner to contribute the amount of his choosing, subject to certain minimums and maximums, to an investment account to pay a student's qualified higher education expenses. The account typically holds mutual funds, which invest in various types of securities and provide variable returns.

Contributions to 529 plans are not eligible for federal tax deductions, but earnings grow tax free. Withdrawals are free from federal income tax as long as they are used for qualified education expenses. However, the tax law creating this tax-free status is scheduled to expire in 2011 unless Congress takes further action. A 10 percent tax penalty is imposed on any distributions not made for educational purposes.

State tax treatment of 529 plans differs from state to state. However, in most states, withdrawals from 529 plans are free from state taxes. In addition, contributions may be partially deductible from state taxable income for some or all taxpayers of the state offering the plan, but not for out-of-state participants.

The 529 plans offered by the various states all differ somewhat from each other, but they typically have the following features in common:

- Plan owners authorize all withdrawals and are not required to transfer the money directly to the designated student.
- If a designated student does not go to a university, another student can be selected to receive the plan benefits.
- The plans do not set an age limit for the student to start his university education.
- Most plans offer the choice of colleges or universities—public and private, in state or out of state.

Example: David Johanson's taxable income in 2004 was $40,000, and his income tax rate was 25 percent.

Analysis: If David had no tax deduction, his tax liability would be 25 percent of $40,000, or $10,000. However, if David made a deductible contribution of $3,000 to a tax-advantaged plan, he could reduce his taxable income by $3,000 to $37,000, and his tax liability would be 25 percent of $37,000, or $9,250. Therefore, his deductible contribution would save him $750 in taxes in the year of his contribution.

A further potential advantage of exclusions, deductions, and deferrals stems from the fact that the individual reduces the amount of his taxable income during his working years when his income, and therefore income tax rate, is generally expected to be higher than it will be when he retires. Withdrawals from the qualified plan then are made during the individual's retirement years, when his income, and therefore income tax rate, may be lower than it was during his working years. As a result, the withdrawals presumably will be taxed at a lower rate than the tax rate that would have been applied on those amounts during the individual's working years.

Figure 13.1 summarizes the taxation of some of the tax-advantaged savings plans that we discuss in this chapter. In the United States, an additional tax benefit is provided to owners of certain tax-advantaged savings plans, including traditional and Roth IRAs. Eligible taxpayers can receive a tax credit of up to $1,000 per person for contributions to these plans.

FIGURE 13.1 The Tax Advantages of U.S. Savings Plans

Contributions excluded from employee's income and tax-deferred earnings
401(k)
SEP
SIMPLE
Keogh

Deductible contributions and tax-deferred earnings
Traditional IRA

Nondeductible contributions but tax-free earnings
Roth IRA
Section 529 plan

Keep in mind, though, that funds accumulated in a tax-advantaged plan may be subject to partial or full income taxation at ordinary income tax rates upon distribution from the plan, depending on the type of plan and whether contributions were deductible. However, paying taxes later rather than sooner may be preferable because of the advantages of compounding earnings on deferred funds and the possibility of a lower tax rate when distributions are made. Each person must carefully examine his own circumstances, though, to determine whether a tax-advantaged savings plan is the best choice for him.

Tax-Advantaged Retirement Savings Plans

The vast majority of these government-created savings plans are aimed at strengthening the second and third pillars of retirement funding we discussed in Chapter 1—individual savings and employer-sponsored savings. Recognition of the importance of retirement savings is being seen worldwide and is driven in many countries by the following factors:

- The increase in average life expectancy because of better health care, nutrition, and other factors
- Concern that government-provided retirement income benefit programs may be unable to provide present levels of benefits to future retirees
- The aging of baby boomers (those people born between 1946 and 1964), who, in some countries, represent the largest segment of the population in terms of age category
- The decline in the number of families supporting their elders, due in part to the slowing of the birth rate, which is the number of babies born per 1,000 of population in a given year

In this section, we discuss retirement savings plans held by individuals, employers, and the self-employed.

Individual Retirement Savings Plans

As mentioned earlier, people typically open individual retirement savings plans with financial institutions and choose from among many investment vehicles to fund the plan. Note, though, that investment choices may be limited to those offered by the financial institution. Insight 13.2 explains how an individual retirement savings plan is opened using an individual retirement arrangement (IRA), which we discuss later in this section, as an example.

INSIGHT 13.2 Opening a Tax-Advantaged Savings Plan

Sabrina Long decides it is time to begin saving for her retirement. She wants to open an IRA but is unsure how to do so. Her financial adviser tells her she can contact a bank, brokerage firm, mutual fund company, or insurance company, all of which can open an IRA for her and offer products that fund IRAs.

Sabrina opts for the brokerage firm and calls her broker, Dan DePalma. Dan tells Sabrina that she needs to fill out a certain form to open the IRA. When the IRA is open, it is similar to any account at a broker-dealer or bank—it is empty until Sabrina places funds in it. Dan informs Sabrina that the funds she places in the IRA can be used to purchase several different types of investments. She can purchase individual stocks and bonds, mutual funds, annuities, etc. Sabrina elects to purchase shares of three different mutual funds.

Sabrina begins to receive monthly statements from her brokerage firm. The statement is entitled "IRA account," and it details the performance of her holdings in the three mutual funds over the past month.

In the United States, the most popular type of individual retirement savings plan that qualifies to receive favorable federal income tax treatment is the individual retirement arrangement (IRA). Later in this chapter, we discuss several other plans—SEPs, SIMPLEs, and Keoghs—that are available to individuals if they are self-employed. Federal laws (1) define which individuals may establish each type of qualified plan, (2) place limits on the amounts a taxpayer may contribute to each type of qualified plan and deduct from income, and (3) establish rules for the taxation of plan withdrawals. In Insight 13.3, we discuss individual retirement savings plans in Canada.

An ***individual retirement arrangement (IRA)*** is a retirement savings plan that allows a person with taxable compensation to deposit a stated amount of that compensation into a savings arrangement that meets certain requirements specified in the federal tax laws and, thus, receives favorable federal tax treatment. An individual retirement arrangement may take one of two forms:

- An ***individual retirement account*** is an individual retirement arrangement that takes the form of a trust or custodial account set up in the United States for the exclusive benefit of a taxpayer and his beneficiaries. The trustee or custodian must be a bank, a federally insured credit union, a savings and loan association, or an entity approved by the IRS to act as trustee or custodian. We discuss trusts in Chapter 14. A ***custodial account*** is an account set up at a depository institution or other financial institution for a minor or other person who lacks legal capacity.

- An ***individual retirement annuity*** is an individual retirement arrangement that takes the form of an individual annuity issued by an insurance company.

INSIGHT 13.3 Canadian Individual Tax-Advantaged Retirement Savings Plans

In Canada, any gainfully employed person, including a person who is covered by an employer-sponsored registered pension plan, may establish a qualified retirement account known as a ***registered retirement savings plan (RRSP)***. The person who establishes an account that qualifies as an RRSP can deduct from his gross taxable income the amount of his annual contribution to the RRSP, which is generally a stated percentage of his annual earned income, subject to a stated maximum. The permitted contribution amount varies depending on whether the person is covered by a registered pension plan. A person who is not covered by a registered pension plan may deduct a larger contribution amount than can an individual who does participate in a registered pension plan.

The investment income earned on the funds in an RRSP is not taxed until the funds are withdrawn. Individuals who establish RRSP accounts must begin withdrawing the accumulated funds by the time they reach age 69.

The financial services industry uses the acronym *IRA* to refer to individual retirement arrangements as a whole, as well as to individual retirement accounts and individual retirement annuities. In this text, we use the term *IRA* to refer to individual retirement arrangements in general unless we specify otherwise.

The tax treatment of an IRA varies depending on whether it is a traditional IRA or a Roth IRA. Both types may be either an individual retirement account or an individual retirement annuity.

A ***traditional IRA***, also known as a *regular IRA*, is an IRA in which contributions may be deductible and investment earnings are tax deferred until the funds are withdrawn. The following is a summary of the current federal tax treatment of a traditional IRA:

- Anyone who is less than age 70½ and who has taxable compensation may contribute up to a certain maximum amount or 100 percent of his taxable compensation, whichever is less, per year into a traditional IRA. The maximum amount that can be contributed by persons under 50 is $3,000 in 2004, $4,000 in 2005 through 2007, and $5,000 in 2008 through 2010. The maximum amount that can be contributed by persons 50 and older is $3,500 in 2004, $4,500 in 2005, $5,000 in 2006 and 2007, and $6,000 in 2008 through 2010.

- Certain individuals may deduct IRA contributions from their current taxable income. However, if a person or his spouse was an active participant in a qualified employer-sponsored retirement plan at any time during the year for which contributions were made, the deduction may be reduced or eliminated depending on the person's income level and tax filing status. (We discuss qualified employer-sponsored retirement plans later in the chapter.)

- Taxation of investment earnings is deferred until funds are withdrawn. With only a few exceptions, however, penalties are imposed on withdrawals made before the taxpayer attains age 59½.

- A taxpayer must begin making annual withdrawals of at least a specified minimum amount, referred to as *minimum required distributions*, by April 1 of the calendar year after he reaches age 70½, and after that time he may not make additional contributions to his traditional IRA. A penalty is imposed for failure to adhere to the minimum required distribution requirements.

Example: Stephen Jacovich worked for a small hardware store that did not provide a pension plan for its employees. For 20 years, beginning when he was 50, Stephen deposited the maximum contribution allowed by law each year into a traditional IRA. At age 72, Stephen retired from the hardware store and began making monthly withdrawals from his IRA.

Analysis: Stephen was permitted to deduct from his taxable compensation the annual contributions to his IRA. He was required to stop making contributions to the IRA when he was 70½. Stephen was required to pay taxes on both the principal and the investment earnings when he withdrew the money from the IRA. Stephen also had to pay a penalty because he did not begin making withdrawals from his IRA by April 1 of the calendar year after which he turned 70½.

A ***Roth IRA*** is an IRA that provides for nondeductible contributions annually, but tax-free qualified withdrawals. In other words, contributions are not taxed when they are withdrawn because they were taxed previously. In addition, all investment earnings accumulate and are distributed on a tax-free basis, rather than on a tax-deferred basis as occurs with a traditional IRA. To qualify for tax-free withdrawals, the taxpayer must (1) have held the Roth IRA for at least five years and (2) be over age 59½ or be a qualified first-time homebuyer. Just as with a traditional IRA, federal tax laws impose limits on the amount of contributions a taxpayer may make to a Roth IRA. Unlike traditional IRAs, Roth IRAs are not subject to minimum distribution requirements.

Example: Kathleen O'Brien established a Roth IRA when she was 22 years old and contributed $2,000 per year to the IRA. When she was 28 years old, Kathleen decided to purchase a home as a qualified first-time homebuyer and withdrew $10,000 from her Roth IRA.

Analysis: Kathleen was not permitted to deduct her annual IRA contributions from her taxable compensation. When she makes qualified withdrawals from her Roth IRA, she pays no taxes, regardless of the amount of investment earnings included in the withdrawal. The $10,000 withdrawal Kathleen took to purchase a home is a qualified withdrawal because the Roth IRA had been held for at least five years and Kathleen was a qualified first-time homebuyer.

Figure 13.2 compares traditional IRAs and Roth IRAs.

Employer-Sponsored Retirement Plans

The U.S. government encourages employers and unions to establish retirement plans for their employees and members, in exchange for which they and their employees and members receive favorable income tax treat-

FIGURE 13.2 A Comparison of Traditional IRAs and Roth IRAs

	Traditional IRA	Roth IRA
Taxable compensation requirement	Yes	Yes
Contribution limits	Yes	Yes
Contributions deductible from taxable income	Yes (deductible amount determined by participation in qualified employer-sponsored retirement plan, income, and filing status)	No
Investment earnings tax-deferred	Yes	Yes (tax free after five years)
Contributions taxable at withdrawal	Yes	No
Investment earnings taxable at withdrawal	Yes	No (after five years)
Tax penalty for early withdrawal	Yes (penalties may be waived under certain conditions)	Yes (penalties may be waived under certain conditions)
Maximum age for withdrawals to begin	Yes (April 1 of calendar year following age 70½)	No

Source: Adapted from John P. Burger, Kristen L. Falk, and Patsy Leeuwenburg, *Annuity Principles and Products,* 2nd ed. (Atlanta: LOMA, © 2003), 79. Used with permission; all rights reserved.

ment. A ***plan sponsor*** is an employer or union that establishes a retirement plan for its employees or members, and a ***plan participant*** is a member of a covered group who is eligible to participate in a retirement plan and who actually chooses to take part in the plan or whose participation is automatic.

Retirement plans can be contributory or noncontributory. As with group life insurance, a contributory plan is a plan under which participants must contribute all or a portion of the cost, and a noncontributory plan is a plan under which participants are not required to contribute any part of the cost.

An employer-sponsored retirement plan is a type of employee benefit plan. In the United States, the ***Employee Retirement Income Security Act (ERISA)*** is a federal law designed to ensure that private employee benefit plans meet certain requirements in order to protect the covered employees. In this section and the next chapter, we limit our discussion to retirement plans sponsored by private employers rather than the government.

ERISA contains provisions for determining if a retirement plan is qualified or nonqualified. As we noted in Chapter 12, qualified plans must meet specific requirements, which are set forth in Figure 13.3.

Some employers may not want to establish qualified plans because they do not wish to comply with the applicable government regulations. For example, some employers set up nonqualifying pension plans because they do not want to comply with the stringent record-keeping requirements of a qualified plan. We limit our discussion in this chapter and the next to qualified plans.

Tax Treatment of Employer-Sponsored Retirement Plans

ERISA also amended the federal tax laws as those laws apply to qualified retirement plans. Although tax laws tend to be amended frequently, we can make the following generalizations about the federal income tax treatment of contributions to and earnings from a qualified retirement plan:

- Within stated limits, the contributions that an employer makes to a qualified plan are considered a business expense and are deductible from the employer's current taxable income.

- The contributions an employer makes to a qualified plan on behalf of a plan participant are *not* considered current taxable income to the participant. Instead, a plan participant's payment of income taxes on the employer's contributions is deferred until she actually receives benefits from the plan.

- Depending upon the plan, a participant can make tax-deductible contributions, nondeductible contributions, a combination of both,

FIGURE 13.3 Qualified Plan Requirements

Participation	An employer cannot require an employee to complete a period of service of more than one year or reach age 21 in order for the employee to participate in a qualified plan. Thus, the minimum age requirement for participation in the plan cannot be more than 21; and employees who meet the age requirement must be eligible to participate after completing one year of employment. However, if an employee will be fully vested in the plan after two years of service, the plan can impose a minimum service requirement of two years.
Vesting	***Vesting*** is a retirement plan participant's right to keep all or part of her accrued benefit even if she retires early or terminates employment before retirement. A plan participant's right to receive benefits funded by employer contributions must vest within a specified period after the participant becomes eligible to join the plan. A plan participant's right to receive benefits funded by his own contributions must vest immediately.
Nondiscrimination	The plan cannot discriminate in favor of highly paid employees.
Distribution	The plan must contain specific provisions regarding when benefits will begin to be paid and what, if any, benefits will be payable upon the death of the plan participant.
Investments	As is true for individual retirement arrangement contributions, group retirement plan contributions can be placed in a variety of investments. However, to ensure the safety of retirement benefits, a variety of regulations govern these investments.
Reporting	The plan sponsor is required to provide periodic reports about the plan's provisions and performance to governmental agencies and to plan participants.

or pre-tax contributions. If a participant has made nondeductible contributions to a qualified plan, the portion of the payments representing that part of the principal is not taxed again when the participant receives benefit payments. However, when she receives benefit payments, a participant pays income tax on the value of any deductible amounts or pre-tax amounts contributed to the plan. We explain pre-tax contributions in Insight 13.4.

- The investment earnings on plan contributions—whether the contributions are made by the employer or the employee—are allowed to accrue on a tax-deferred basis. As in the case of employer contributions, plan participants pay income taxes on these investment earnings only when they actually receive benefits from the plan.

Types of Employer-Sponsored Retirement Plans

The specific provisions of any given retirement plan govern the operation of the plan, but we can identify the following four broad types of employer-sponsored retirement plans:

- A ***savings plan*** is a retirement plan to which a plan sponsor may make contributions on behalf of a plan participant if the participant makes contributions to the plan. Note that the term *savings plan* is the same term used to describe the entire category of tax-advantaged savings plans we are discussing in this chapter. Here, though, *savings plan* is the term used to describe one particular type of retirement plan.

  A savings plan accumulates retirement savings on behalf of participants, but usually does not undertake to provide a monthly income benefit at retirement. The amount of an employee's contributions to a savings plan is subject to statutory limitations. If the plan has an employer match, the amount of an employer's contribution usually is equal to the amount contributed by the employee or is a percentage of that amount, subject to a specified maximum. Employee contributions to most types of savings plans are not tax deductible. Insight 13.4 describes a special type of savings plan—the 401(k)—that provides a tax incentive to employees to participate in the plan. Insight 13.5 describes a group RRSP, which is a popular savings plan found in Canada.

- A ***profit sharing plan*** is a retirement plan funded primarily by cash contributions from the employer's profits. Because employer contributions to such plans are based upon profits, and profits can fluctuate, the amount of contributions varies from year to year. If conditions warrant, the employer may not make any contribution in some years. A profit sharing plan accumulates retirement assets on behalf of participants, but does not promise to provide a monthly retirement income.

- A ***stock bonus plan*** is a retirement plan into which a corporate plan sponsor makes contributions in the form of the corporation's stock. A stock option plan is regarded as a type of stock bonus plan. Contributions to a stock bonus plan are not dependent upon corporate profits. The value of the stock shares, however, fluctuates with the fortunes of the issuing corporation. Stock bonus plans accumulate retirement assets on behalf of participants, but do not promise to provide a monthly retirement income.

INSIGHT 13.4 401(k) Plans

A ***401(k)*** plan is a special type of savings plan that allows employees to make pre-tax contributions to the plan. In other words, when an employee contributes to a 401(k) plan, the amount of her contribution is not included in her current gross taxable income. Instead, the employee's contributions will be taxed when she withdraws funds from her 401(k) plan. To participate in a 401(k) plan, an employee must enter into a salary reduction arrangement that permits the employer to deduct the amount of the employee's contributions from her salary. An employee under age 50 can contribute $13,000 in 2004, $14,000 in 2005, and $15,000 in 2006 through 2010. This dollar limit is subject to cost-of-living adjustments beginning in 2007, which means that the limit may be increased to keep up with inflation. Employees age 50 and older may be eligible to contribute additional amounts called *catch up contributions*.

Example: Ivan Major has become eligible to participate in a 401(k) plan. Ivan earns $30,000 a year, and he has decided to contribute $2,000 a year to the plan.

Analysis: Ivan can contribute to his 401(k) plan on a pre-tax basis. As a result, his $2,000 plan contribution will reduce the amount of his gross taxable income to $28,000.

A 403(b) plan is similar to a 401(k) plan but is available only to employees of public schools and colleges, churches, nonprofit hospitals, and other nonprofit institutions. A 457 plan is similar to a 401(k) plan but is available only to state and local government employees. Unlike 401(k) and 403(b) plans, which typically are qualified plans, 457 plans may be qualified or non-qualified.

INSIGHT 13.5 Canadian Group Retirement Savings Plan

In Insight 13.3, we discussed Registered Retirement Savings Plans (RRSPs) established by individuals in Canada. A ***group RRSP*** is an employer-sponsored registered retirement savings plan in which an account is established for each participating employee. Employees and employers are permitted to make plan contributions within specified limits, and any employer contributions are treated as if they were made by the employee. All funds deposited into an individual's account are immediately vested with the employee. For income tax purposes, the employee can deduct the amount of all contributions—employer and employee—from his current taxable income.

- A pension plan, as we discussed in Chapter 1, is a retirement plan that accumulates assets and provides a retirement income for people participating in the plan. In a pension plan, the plan sponsor undertakes to provide covered individuals with a lifetime monthly income benefit that begins at their retirement.

In Chapter 14, we will discuss private retirement plans in more detail.

Retirement Savings Plans for Small Businesses and the Self-Employed

Small employers, including self-employed individuals, may prefer to set up certain retirement plans without becoming involved in more complex private retirement plans. The plans are eligible for tax advantages, but they do not have to comply with ERISA to the extent that most large private retirement plans must comply. A self-employed individual is considered both the employer and the employee under these plans, which are simplified employee pensions, savings incentive match plans for employees, and Keogh plans.

Simplified Employee Pensions

A ***simplified employee pension (SEP)*** is a written plan that allows an employer to make contributions to individual retirement arrangements established by each participating employee. Note that the employee—not the employer—establishes and owns the IRA into which the employer deposits its contributions. Because the employee owns the SEP IRA, the employee is immediately vested in all amounts that are deposited into the SEP IRA. Contributions to a SEP cannot exceed the lesser of 25 percent of the employee's compensation or $41,000 in 2004. This dollar limit is subject to cost-of-living adjustments thereafter.

Although employers can no longer establish SEP plans that allow for employee pre-tax contributions, employees may still make pre-tax contributions to existing plans established prior to 1997. The employer's contributions to SEP IRAs are tax deductible as a business expense from the employer's taxable income, subject to the legislatively defined maximums. The amount of an employer's contribution is excluded from the employee's taxable income. A self-employed person can deduct contributions made to his own plan. Earnings on all contributions are tax deferred. Withdrawals are allowed without penalty only after age 59½, and withdrawals of contributions and investment earnings are taxable as income.

Savings Incentive Match Plans for Employees (SIMPLE Plans)

Small business owners and self-employed persons may choose to establish a savings incentive match plan for employees (SIMPLE) IRA or a savings incentive match plan for employees (SIMPLE) 401(k). A ***savings incentive match plan for employees (SIMPLE) IRA*** is a written agreement (salary reduction agreement) between an employer with 100 or fewer employees and its employees that allows eligible employees (including self-employed individuals) to choose to

- Reduce compensation by a certain percentage each pay period and

- Have the employer contribute the amount of the salary reduction to a SIMPLE IRA on the employee's behalf

For 2004, the maximum salary reduction contribution that an employer can make on behalf of an employee is $9,000. This amount increases to $10,000 in 2005 and is subject to cost-of-living adjustments in subsequent years. The limits for employees age 50 and older are $10,500 for 2004, $12,000 for 2005, $12,500 for 2006, and are subject to cost-of-living adjustments in subsequent years.

The employer must also make either

- Matching contributions—if the employee chooses to make salary reduction contributions—in an amount equal to the employee's salary reduction contributions to a maximum of 3 percent of the employee's annual compensation or

- Nonelective contributions—whether or not the employee chooses to make salary reduction contributions—in an amount equal to 2 percent of the employee's annual compensation

All contributions to a SIMPLE IRA account must be fully vested in the employee. Generally, withdrawals from a SIMPLE IRA must comply with the same requirements imposed on withdrawals from other types of IRAs.

A ***savings incentive match plan for employees (SIMPLE) 401(k)*** is a special arrangement whereby an employer with 100 or fewer employees can establish a simplified 401(k) retirement savings plan for employees. The SIMPLE 401(k) functions in much the same way as a regular 401(k) plan—both the employer and the employee can make contributions to the plan up to a specified maximum.

Under the SIMPLE IRA and the SIMPLE 401(k), the employee's and employer's contributions are excluded from the employee's current income, the employer's contributions are tax deductible to the employer as a business expense, and investment earnings accumulate on a tax-deferred basis. Withdrawals of contributions and investment earnings from a SIMPLE IRA and SIMPLE 401(k) are taxable as income.

Keogh Plans

A ***Keogh plan***, also known as an *HR 10 plan*, is a qualified retirement plan set up by a small business or self-employed individual to which such a business or individual can make annual tax-deductible contributions, subject to certain limits and conditions. Keogh plans can be either defined benefit plans or defined contribution plans. We will explain these types of plans in Chapter 14.

The maximum annual contribution allowed under a defined contribution Keogh plan in 2004 is the lesser of 100 percent of an employee's annual income or $41,000, subject to cost-of-living adjustments in subsequent years. The maximum annual contribution allowed under a defined benefit Keogh plan is determined by an IRS formula. The defined benefit version of the Keogh is more expensive and complicated to establish and administer than the defined contribution version.

Contributions to a Keogh plan are tax deductible for a small business and a self-employed individual, contributions are excluded from the employee's current income, and earnings are tax deferred. Withdrawals of contributions and investment earnings from a Keogh account are taxable as income. Withdrawals may begin as early as age 59½ and must begin by age 70½.

Key Terms

section 529 plan
individual retirement arrangement (IRA)
individual retirement account
custodial account
individual retirement annuity
registered retirement savings plan (RRSP)
traditional IRA
Roth IRA
plan sponsor
plan participant
Employee Retirement Income Security Act (ERISA)
vesting
savings plan
profit sharing plan
stock bonus plan
401(k) plan
group RRSP
simplified employee pension (SEP)
savings incentive match plan for employees (SIMPLE) IRA
savings incentive match plan for employees (SIMPLE) 401(k)
Keogh plan

Endnote

1. While this text was being written, U.S. federal legislation was proposed to revise the system of savings plans available in the United States. If any of these bills become law, the plans described in this text may be outdated. However, these plans are still instructional of how governments worldwide may provide tax benefits for those who meet certain requirements.

chapter

14

Employer-Sponsored Retirement Plans

outline

objectives

After reading this chapter, you should be able to

- Define the terms *coverage*, *eligibility requirements*, and *participation* for employer-sponsored retirement plans
- Discuss the documentation for and administration of an employer-sponsored retirement plan
- Discuss the important differences between a defined benefit formula and a defined contribution formula
- Define and distinguish among normal retirement age, early retirement, and late retirement
- Explain retirement plan in-service distributions, distributions upon leaving employment, and distributions upon retirement
- Distinguish between allocated and unallocated investment arrangements for employer-sponsored retirement plans
- List and describe the various employer-sponsored retirement plan funding vehicles provided by insurance companies

In Chapter 1, we introduced the concept of the three pillars of retirement funding—the government, personal savings, and employers—and discussed the government's role in replacing income upon a person's retirement. In Chapter 12, we described individual annuity products and noted that people can use such products to fund their retirement years. In Chapter 13, we described tax-advantaged savings plans that also can be used as asset accumulation vehicles for retirement. In this chapter, we address the third pillar of retirement funding—private employer-sponsored retirement plans. Although the same types of groups that we discussed in Chapter 7 as being eligible for group life insurance also are eligible for retirement plans, we limit our discussion in this chapter to retirement plans offered by employers as an employee benefit. We also limit our discussion to retirement plans provided by private employers.

When establishing a retirement plan for employees, employers usually ensure that the plan will qualify for favorable tax treatment by meeting applicable regulatory requirements. In Chapter 13, we examined the various regulations that apply to retirement plans and the benefits that plan sponsors and plan participants obtain through meeting such requirements. In this chapter, we discuss the characteristics of employer-sponsored retirement plans. We also discuss retirement benefits and describe how financial institutions participate in the administration of these retirement plans and the investment of the plans' assets.

Characteristics of Employer-Sponsored Retirement Plans

All types of employer-sponsored retirement plans in the United States have some characteristics in common. For example, these retirement plans must maintain similar documentation. All employer-sponsored retirement plans are established by plan sponsors and accumulate assets on behalf of plan participants. As we mentioned in Chapter 13, a plan sponsor is an employer or union that establishes a retirement plan for its employees or members, and a plan participant is an employee or member who is covered by an employer's or union's retirement plan. In this chapter, we will sometimes use the term *employer* to refer to a plan sponsor and the term *employee* to refer to a plan participant.

Plan participants are distinguished from plan beneficiaries. Retirement ***plan beneficiaries*** are all individuals who receive benefits under retirement plans. Plan beneficiaries include current and former plan participants; plan beneficiaries also can include dependents, spouses, and survivors of plan participants.

In this section, we describe common elements of employer-sponsored retirement plans: plan coverage, eligibility, and participation; plan funding; plan documentation; and plan administration.

Plan Coverage, Eligibility, and Participation

An employer-sponsored retirement plan must specify (1) which members of a group are covered by the plan, (2) which group members are eligible to participate in the plan, and (3) how an eligible group member participates in the plan. Participants in employer-sponsored retirement plans are members of the covered group who are eligible to participate in the plan and who actually choose to take part in the plan or whose participation is automatic.

Coverage

Coverage refers to the specification of characteristics of the group members intended to benefit from an employee benefit plan. The covered group typically is specified in terms of job class, location of the work site, salary, and/or occupation. For example, a plan may cover all non-union employees.

Eligibility

Eligibility requirements are conditions that a covered person must satisfy in order to participate in an employee benefit plan. The most common eligibility requirement is a ***service requirement*** that states a minimum required length of service a group member must have to be eligible for participation in the plan. Some plans also have an ***age requirement*** that states a minimum age a group member must be to be eligible to participate in the plan.

For example, a plan's eligibility provision can specify that it covers all non-union employees, provided they are at least 21 years old and have at least one full year of service. Eligibility requirements are limited by regulation in some jurisdictions. In the United States, for example, the setting of a maximum age for participation is not permitted.

Participation

Participation refers to the inclusion of a person as a plan participant in an employee benefit plan. Employer-sponsored retirement plans typically specify a start date, which is the date that participation becomes effective. The start date typically is the first day of the month or the first day of the calendar year following the person's completion of the eligibility requirements.

Participation in an employer-sponsored retirement plan can be automatic or voluntary.

- If participation in an employer-sponsored retirement plan is *automatic*, all eligible group members are automatically enrolled as participants.

- If participation in an employer-sponsored retirement plan is *voluntary*, eligible group members have a choice between participating or not participating in the plan. When plan participation is voluntary, not all covered employees who are eligible for participation in the plan are necessarily plan participants.

Plan Funding

An employer-sponsored retirement plan might be noncontributory—funded entirely by the plan sponsor—or it might be contributory—requiring plan participants to make contributions to fund the plan. Typically, noncontributory plans are automatic, and contributory plans are voluntary.

Plan Documentation

A ***plan document*** is a detailed legal agreement establishing the existence of an employer-sponsored retirement plan and specifying the rights and obligations of various parties to the plan. The plan sponsor must keep in its office at least one copy of the complete plan document for disclosure purposes. The document must be available for inspection upon request.

Regulations for qualified plans in the United States also require the plan sponsor to provide to each plan participant a document known as a summary plan description. A ***summary plan description*** is a written disclosure document that accurately summarizes the provisions of a plan document. Figure 14.1 specifies information that must be disclosed in a summary plan description.

Plan Administration

The plan sponsor names a ***plan administrator***, who is the party responsible for handling the administrative aspects of an employer-sponsored retirement plan and ensuring the plan complies with applicable regulatory requirements. The plan administrator typically is someone in the human resources department of the plan sponsor. The plan administrator may receive assistance in administering the plan from a plan trustee,

FIGURE 14.1 Disclosures in a Summary Plan Description

The contents of a summary plan description reflect the contents of the plan document and must specify

- The name and address of the plan administrator
- The names and addresses of plan trustees, if any
- The plan's source of financing
- The identity of any organization through which plan benefits are provided
- The plan's eligibility requirements
- The plan's provisions regarding vesting of plan benefits
- The circumstances that may result in disqualification, ineligibility, or denial or loss of plan benefits
- The procedures to be followed in presenting claims for plan benefits
- The remedies available for appealing claims that are denied
- The ending date of the plan year
- Whether the plan's records are kept on a calendar-year, policy-year, or fiscal-year basis

Source: Adapted from Harriett E. Jones and Monica R. Maxwell, *Regulatory Compliance: Insurance and Annuity Products,* 2nd ed. (Atlanta: LOMA, © 2002), 267. Used with permission; all rights reserved.

an insurance company or other financial institution, or a third-party administrator. As we learned in Chapter 8, a third-party administrator is an organization other than an insurance company that provides administrative services to the sponsors of group benefit plans.

The responsibilities of a plan administrator for an employer-sponsored plan may include maintaining accurate employment records on all participants, determining the amount and directing the distribution of benefit payments, preparing and filing required reports, and assuring compliance with regulatory requirements. In the course of administering a plan, the plan administrator also may hire various professionals, such as accountants, actuaries, and attorneys.

Retirement Benefits

A plan document must describe how retirement benefits will be calculated, when participants may receive benefits, and how benefits may be distributed.

Benefit Formulas

An employer-sponsored retirement plan's ***benefit formula*** describes the calculation of the plan sponsor's financial obligation to plan participants. This benefit formula can take the form of a promise to (1) pay a specified benefit to participants or their beneficiaries or (2) contribute a specified amount to the plan on behalf of participants. These two main types of benefit formulas are known respectively as *defined benefit* and *defined contribution* formulas. A retirement plan structured according to a defined benefit formula is referred to as a ***defined benefit plan***. Similarly, a retirement plan structured according to a defined contribution formula is referred to as a ***defined contribution plan***. Most defined benefit plans have automatic participation, whereas most defined contribution plans have voluntary participation.

Defined Benefit Formulas

A ***defined benefit formula*** specifies the amount of retirement benefit a plan sponsor promises to provide to each plan participant. A defined benefit formula does not specify the amount a plan sponsor is obligated to spend to fund a retirement benefit. All defined benefit plans are pension plans, and these are the only retirement plans that provide a specific and guaranteed lifetime income benefit at retirement. Defined benefit formulas can take several forms, as set forth in Figure 14.2.

To the plan participants, the defined benefit formula has the advantage of providing a benefit amount that is reasonably determinable in advance. To the plan sponsor, one drawback of the defined benefit formula is that the plan sponsor cannot predict the dollar amount of its obligation to the plan for any given year in the future. This drawback carries with it the difficulty of trying to fund the plan and invest its assets over the long term. Another drawback is that regulatory reporting requirements for defined benefit plans in the United States are particularly costly and administratively burdensome.

Another advantage of defined benefit plans in the United States is that these plans offer plan participants a benefit insurance program through the ***Pension Benefit Guaranty Corporation (PBGC)***—a federal agency that guarantees the payment of part or all of retirement benefits for participants in defined benefit retirement plans when those plans become financially unable to pay benefits. The plan sponsor is required to pay a premium every year to participate in this insurance program.

Defined Contribution Formulas

A ***defined contribution formula*** specifies the level of contributions to the plan but not the benefits to be paid. The benefit that a participant will receive is not determined in advance of the participant's retirement

FIGURE 14.2 Defined Benefit Formulas

Flat amount

Every plan participant receives the same benefit amount upon retirement, such as $600 per month.

Flat amount per year of service

Plan participants receive a flat amount for each year of service with the employer. For example, if the flat amount is $20 per month for each year of service, a plan participant who has been employed for 20 years at retirement will receive a retirement benefit of $400 per month.

Flat percentage of earnings

Each plan participant will receive a specified percentage of earnings as a retirement benefit, regardless of years of service. The formula must specify the exact percentage and define the earnings that will be counted. The percentage specified usually ranges from 20 to 40 percent. *Earnings* may be defined as the average of the final five years' (or some other period) earnings (referred to as *final average pay*) or a career average of earnings. As an example, suppose a plan specifies that each plan participant will receive 30 percent of final average pay as a retirement benefit. Then, a plan participant with a final average pay of $6,000 per month at retirement would receive a monthly retirement benefit of $1,800.

Percentage of earnings per year of service

Plan participants receive a retirement benefit equal to a specified percentage of earnings for each year of their participation in the pension plan. The percentage specified usually is much lower than under the flat percentage of earnings formula. Earnings may be the final average pay or a career average of earnings. As a greatly simplified example, suppose a plan provides that participants will receive 1 percent of their final average earnings for each year employed with the plan sponsor. A participant who has been employed for 20 years and who has a final average pay of $6,000 per month at the time of retirement will receive a monthly benefit of $1,200, calculated as 1 percent x $6,000 final average pay x 20 years.

Cash balance

The benefit is defined as a cash amount instead of a monthly benefit. An account is created for each plan participant, and this account grows in two ways: (1) a guaranteed percentage of salary is added to the account each year, and (2) the account grows at a guaranteed percentage each year. The benefit at retirement is based on the cash balance account at that time. Although this description sounds more like that of a defined contribution plan, it is a defined benefit plan because the employer rather than the employee bears the investment risk.

Negotiated contribution plans

These plans are usually the result of collective bargaining and include multiple employers. Each employer's contributions on behalf of plan participants are determined by earnings, hours of work, or a measure of productivity for each plan participant they employ. However, all contributions are made to a group account. Each plan participant then receives benefits according to a published scale of benefits, such as a flat monthly benefit for each year of service.

Source: Dan M. McGill et al., *Fundamentals of Private Pensions,* 7th ed. (Philadelphia: University of Pennsylvania Press, 1996).

as it is under a defined benefit formula but depends on the investment performance of the funds in the plan. Defined contribution formulas can take several forms, as described in Figure 14.3, and the investment allocation is directed by the plan participants rather than by the plan sponsor under all these formulas except the target benefit formula.

In defined contribution plans, plan administrators must keep an individual record for each plan participant. A participant's account is potentially increased by the amounts of (1) contributions, (2) investment earnings, and, in some cases, (3) forfeitures of non-vested contributions that arise when other non-vested participants leave the plan. ***Forfeitures*** are the account balances abandoned by plan participants who leave the

FIGURE 14.3 Defined Contribution Formulas

Money purchase plans	The plan sponsor makes periodic contributions according to a stated formula. For example, annual contributions may be set at 5 percent of an employee's annual salary. For a plan participant earning $30,000 in a given year, the plan sponsor would contribute $1,500 to the plan for that year.
Target benefit plans	The plan sponsor uses a benefit formula to calculate a target benefit. The plan sponsor contributes a level annual amount that, along with investment earnings, would result in achieving the target benefit. No guarantee exists, however, that the target benefit will be achieved.
Savings plans	Recall from Chapter 13 that a savings plan is a retirement plan to which a plan sponsor may make contributions on behalf of a plan participant if the participant makes contributions to the plan. A savings plan specifies a range of contribution levels, and each employee determines his contribution level. The plan also specifies the level of contributions to be made by the plan sponsor and whether plan sponsor's contributions will be based on a participant's total contributions or a portion thereof.
Profit sharing plans	As we learned in Chapter 13, a profit sharing plan is a retirement plan funded primarily by cash contributions from the employer's profits. A profit sharing plan is not required to have a definite predetermined contribution formula. Contributions just must be recurring and substantial.
Stock bonus plans	In Chapter 13, we defined a stock bonus plan as a retirement plan into which a corporate plan sponsor makes contributions in the form of the corporation's stock. Typical formulas for stock bonus plans require that the employer contribute a specified percentage of payroll or profits but not less than a specified dollar amount per year.

Source: Dan M. McGill et al., *Fundamentals of Private Pensions,* 7th ed. (Philadelphia: University of Pennsylvania Press, 1996).

FIGURE 14.4 Sources of Increases and Decreases to Defined Contribution Accounts

TYPE OF EVENT	CAUSES THE ACCOUNT TO . . . Increase	Decrease
• Contributions	↑	
• Investment earnings	↑	
• Forfeitures by other participants	↑	
• General administrative expenses		↓
• Investment management costs		↓
• Investment losses		↓

plan before they have a right to keep those benefits. In some defined contribution plans, these forfeited account balances are distributed among the remaining plan participants; in other cases, however, forfeitures are applied to offset plan expenses or future contributions from the plan sponsor. Note that each participant's account may be charged for a share of the plan's operating expenses, including general administrative expenses, investment costs, certain legal fees, and certain plan start-up expenses.

Figure 14.4 summarizes the effects of various events on the accounts of participants in defined contribution plans.

Under a defined contribution formula, the plan sponsor's contribution amount can reasonably be estimated in advance, which is a benefit for plan sponsors. For the participant, a drawback of this formula is that the amount of the retirement benefit cannot be accurately predicted very far in advance of the retirement date. However, many participants value the fact that they may control the investment of their assets in a defined contribution plan.

Comparison of Benefit Formulas

Because a defined contribution formula provides greater flexibility and predictability for the plan sponsor, most plans designed since the early 1970s have employed a defined contribution formula. The table in Figure 14.5 contrasts the important differences between defined benefit and defined contribution formulas.

FIGURE 14.5 Differences Between Defined Benefit and Defined Contribution Formulas

	Retirement Benefit Formula	
Plan Design Element	**Defined Benefit Formula**	**Defined Contribution Formula**
Amount of sponsor's future contributions	Uncertain, not specified, and can only be estimated	Specified and amount is reasonably certain
Amount of future retirement benefit	Specified and amount is reasonably certain	Uncertain, not specified, and can only be estimated

Retirement Ages

Some retirement plans, mainly defined benefit plans, specify rules for determining the date when a plan participant can elect to begin receiving benefits. These rules usually set forth (1) a specified minimum retirement age and (2) a minimum number of years of service. (In the United States, additional requirements are permitted, but are rare.)

Participants can retire at the normal retirement age, or they can take early retirement or late retirement.

- The ***normal retirement age*** is the earliest age at which participants in a retirement plan can retire with full benefits. Age 65 is traditionally the normal retirement age.

- ***Early retirement*** is a retirement plan participant's retirement before the normal retirement age, subject to a minimum age requirement and a minimum service requirement and resulting in a reduced retirement income benefit. Age 50 or 55 is typically the early retirement age.

- ***Late retirement*** is a retirement plan participant's retirement from employment later than the normal retirement age. A participant who worked past normal retirement age would continue to receive employer contributions or accrue benefits until actual retirement. A participant might elect late retirement because of entrance into the retirement plan at a late age—for example, older than 55. Late retirement can allow the participant to meet a minimum service requirement or otherwise to qualify for a larger benefit than he would have been eligible to receive at normal retirement age.

Distribution of Benefits

Employer-sponsored retirement plans are designed to hold participants' funds until participants retire. However, sometimes participants desire to take money out of the plan during their working years, and sometimes participants' employment is terminated before retirement. In this section, we describe in-service distributions, distributions upon leaving employment, and distributions upon retirement

In-Service Distributions

Whether a participant can take funds out of his retirement plan while he is still employed depends on the type of plan. Pension plans will lose their tax advantages if they allow in-service distributions. Thus, participants may not withdraw funds from pension plans while they are still employed. Profit sharing plans and stock bonus plans may be designed to allow in-service withdrawals subject to certain restrictions concerning years of participation.

All types of employer-sponsored retirement plans may allow participants to borrow from their retirement account, although most defined benefit plans do not. If a plan allows loans, the following conditions must be met:

- The term of the loan must be no longer than five years, unless the loan is used to buy a primary residence.
- Repayments must be made at least quarterly and in substantially equal amounts.
- The amount of the loan must not exceed a certain dollar limit.

Distributions Upon Leaving Employment

As we mentioned in Chapter 13, *vesting* can be defined as the participant's right to keep all or part of her accrued benefit even if she retires early or terminates employment before retirement. A participant's right to vested benefits is nonforfeitable. Qualified retirement plans in the United States must provide for a participant's immediate vesting in any values funded by her own contributions.

A retirement plan participant may have no vesting, partial vesting, or full vesting in benefits funded by employer contributions. The formula or timetable that determines when a retirement plan participant obtains a nonforfeitable right to values or benefits is known as a ***vesting schedule***. The two types of minimum vesting schedules for qualified retirement plans, other than 401(k) plans, in the United States are the

- ***Graded vesting schedule,*** which provides a retirement plan participant with a nonforfeitable right to employer-funded benefits or account values according to a schedule of gradual increases, with full vesting for qualified plans being achieved no later than the completion of seven full years of employment.

- ***Cliff vesting schedule,*** which provides a retirement plan participant with a nonforfeitable right to all employer-funded plan benefits or account values upon attaining five full years of employment; before completing five full years of employment, though, the participant has no employer-funded vested benefits at all.

U.S. federal tax laws require that an accelerated vesting schedule be applied to employer-funded contributions to 401(k) plans. A graded vesting schedule for 401(k) plans must provide for full vesting of employer-funded contributions no later than the completion of six years of employment. A cliff vesting schedule for 401(k) plans must provide for full vesting of employer-funded contributions no later than the completion of three years of employment.

Vested retirement benefits are said to be ***portable*** if they can be moved from one retirement plan to another employer-sponsored or individual retirement plan when the participating individual leaves employment with the plan sponsor. A qualified retirement plan in the United States may provide portable benefits, but portability is not required. For registered plans in Canada, vested benefits must be portable.

A person can roll over lump-sum distributions from certain retirement plans. A ***rollover*** is a tax-free movement of cash or other assets

"He specializes in retirement account rollovers."

disbursed from one retirement plan into another retirement plan. So long as funds are transferred directly from the original plan to the new plan and not paid to the plan participant, income taxes on the rollover amount are deferred until money is disbursed by the new plan. Subject to certain restrictions, current tax laws in the United States allow for the types of rollovers shown in Figure 14.6.

If a participant takes the entire amount of his account or the value of his defined benefit plan benefits in cash and he does not roll it over, income taxes will be due and in some circumstances (withdrawal under age 59½) penalty taxes also will be due.

Distributions Upon Retirement

Employer-sponsored retirement plans specify how benefits are distributed upon retirement, which is known as the ***normal form of benefit***. Typically in defined benefit plans, the single life annuity is designated as the normal form of benefit for single participants. However, defined benefit plans are required by law in the United States to provide a type of joint and survivor benefit for married participants. Defined contribution plans often have a lump-sum payment as the normal form of benefit.

Employer-sponsored retirement plans usually permit retiring participants to elect a form of benefit other than the normal form of benefit. Married participants in defined benefit plans must obtain spousal consent before selecting anything other than a joint and survivor form of annuity. The other forms of benefits from which a participant may choose are

- Other types of annuities

FIGURE 14.6 Allowable Types of Rollovers

- From an employer-sponsored qualified plan to a traditional IRA
- From an employer-sponsored qualified plan to another employer-sponsored qualified plan
- From a traditional IRA to another traditional IRA
- From a traditional IRA to an employer-sponsored qualified plan
- From a traditional IRA to a Roth IRA
- From a SEP plan, SIMPLE IRA, or Roth IRA to a Roth IRA

Rollovers from Roth IRAs to traditional IRAs or to employer-sponsored qualified plans are not allowed.

- Installment payments for a specified amount until the funds are depleted or a specified period

- Lump-sum distributions, which may be rolled over

Investment Arrangements for Retirement Plans

A qualified retirement plan sponsor must choose a funding vehicle for the plan. A ***funding vehicle***, also known as an *investment vehicle* or *funding instrument*, is an arrangement for investing a retirement plan's assets. The funding vehicle must be a trust, group insurance contract, or custodial account. We limit our discussion in this section to trusts and group insurance contracts, which are the most common funding vehicles.

Funding vehicles for retirement plans can be classified according to whether they are allocated or unallocated.

- An ***allocated funding vehicle*** is one in which all of the plan sponsor's contributions are credited to individual participants in a manner that gives the participants a legally enforceable claim to the benefits related to those contributions. In practice, life insurance companies are the only financial institutions that can provide for individual allocation of assets.

- An ***unallocated funding vehicle*** is one in which some or all contributions are pooled together and not assigned to individual participants until each participant begins to collect benefits. Under an unallocated investment contract, the plan sponsor's contributions are credited to a pooled account. Any type of financial institution can provide unallocated investment contracts.

A defined benefit plan would be more likely to use an unallocated funding vehicle. A defined contribution plan could use either, but typically uses an allocated funding vehicle.

Trusts

Most employer-sponsored retirement plans use a trust agreement to facilitate investment arrangements. A ***trust*** is a legal arrangement whereby one person or entity who creates the trust, known as the *grantor*, gives legal title to property, known as the *res*, to another person or entity, known as the *trustee*, for the benefit of a third person or entity, known as the *trust beneficiary*. With a retirement plan trust, the grantor is the plan sponsor, and the res is the plan's assets. The trustee is typically the plan sponsor in the case of a small company or a bank or trust company in the case of a larger company. The trust beneficiaries are the plan participants.

A retirement plan trust typically holds the retirement plan's assets, invests the assets, and distributes benefits according to the plan's provisions and the terms of the trust agreement. The trust may invest the plan's assets in a wide variety of instruments, including deposit accounts, certificates of deposit, money market instruments, stocks, and bonds. Mutual funds have been increasingly popular investments for retirement plan assets.

The trustee has a legal obligation to manage the property and invest its assets solely for the benefit of the trust beneficiaries. Thus, a trustee is an example of a fiduciary. A ***fiduciary*** is a person or other legal entity who holds a special position of trust or confidence when handling the business affairs of another and who must put the other's interest above his or her own. In general, a fiduciary must fulfill specified duties for the plan participants, including a duty to manage the assets wisely and a duty to refrain from misusing the funds for personal gain. Plan fiduciaries also must meet detailed standards of care and, above all, must act solely for the benefit of plan participants. A plan fiduciary can be held personally liable for the amount of any losses that result from a failure to carry out a fiduciary duty, and may, in some cases, be subject to criminal penalties for failing to carry out fiduciary duties.

Group Insurance Contracts

The most common insurance company products that serve as funding vehicles for employer-sponsored retirement plans are deposit administration contracts, immediate participation guarantee contracts, separate account contracts and riders, guaranteed investment contracts, group annuity contracts, group deferred annuity contracts, and individual policy pension trusts.

Deposit Administration Contracts

Though no longer offered by most insurance companies, deposit administration contracts are still in force. A ***deposit administration contract*** is a type of retirement plan funding vehicle in which a plan sponsor deposits assets with an insurer and the assets are placed in the insurer's general investment account. Upon a plan participant's retirement, the insurer applies funds from the general account to provide an immediate annuity for the retiree. The insurer usually guarantees the plan assets against investment loss within limits and guarantees a minimum investment return. If investment return exceeds the guarantee, the insurance company may pay a dividend. Further, the insurer usually guarantees, in advance, the price of the immediate annuity to be purchased at a plan participant's retirement. When the immediate annuity is purchased, the insurance company also guarantees the amount of the periodic annuity benefit to be paid.

A deposit administration contract is an unallocated type of group annuity contract. Deposit administration contracts are suited for use with defined benefit plans.

Immediate Participation Guarantee Contracts

When a plan sponsor enters into an ***immediate participation guarantee (IPG) contract***, plan assets are held in an investment account in the name of the plan sponsor and deposited in the general account of the insurer. Under an IPG contract, the plan assets fully experience the actual monetary gains or losses from investing and paying benefits from the plan's assets. Typically, IPG contracts neither guarantee a minimum investment return nor provide guarantees against investment loss. Some IPG contracts, however, guarantee the principal.

When a plan participant retires and a retirement income benefit becomes payable, the plan sponsor may either (1) withdraw funds from the IPG account to purchase an immediate annuity for that retiree or (2) direct that the monthly retirement benefit be paid directly from the IPG account to the retiree.

An IPG is an unallocated investment vehicle. IPGs are typically used for defined benefit plans, but they can be used for defined contribution plans.

Separate Account Contracts or Riders

Under a ***separate account contract or rider***, the insurance company invests the plan assets in the insurance company's separate account investment subaccounts. (We first discussed separate account subaccounts in Chapter 12.) A separate account rider is generally used as an addition to a deposit administration or an immediate participation guarantee contract.

Separate account contracts and riders usually do not make any guarantees regarding investment returns or even preservation of the invested principal. At the time of a plan participant's retirement, the plan sponsor is permitted to purchase an immediate annuity from the insurer. However, the plan sponsor is not required to purchase such an annuity. The monthly benefits also may be paid directly from one of the separate accounts such as a money market separate account.

For a separate account contract or rider, the insurance company keeps records of plan assets under an administrative account set up in the name of the plan sponsor. Then, the plan sponsor has the option of investing the plan assets in a selection of the insurer's separate account subaccounts. The insurer follows a different stated investment strategy for each separate account subaccount, and the plan sponsor chooses the subaccounts in which the plan contributions are to be placed. Notice that this arrangement is similar to mutual funds.

For example, suppose the Roster Insurance Company has issued a separate account contract to the Largo Corporation. Last year, Roster received a plan contribution of $2.5 million for Largo's investment account. Largo directed Roster to invest the money in the separate account subaccounts as follows:

Reliable Fund A	Common stock	30%	$750,000
Reliable Fund B	Corporate bonds	30%	$750,000
Reliable Fund C	Government bonds	20%	$500,000
Reliable Fund D	Real estate	20%	$500,000

Thus, in defined benefit plans, the plan sponsor chooses not only the type of investments used for the plan, but also the level of risk it is willing to bear. In defined contribution plans, the plan sponsor still chooses the types of investment funds offered but because contributions are invested based on participants' directions, the participants decide the level of risk they are willing to bear.

A separate account contract or rider is an unallocated investment vehicle for defined benefit plans and defined contribution plans. A coordinating service package that includes allocation services is used to accommodate the individual participant record-keeping requirements of defined contribution plans.

Guaranteed Investment Contracts (GICs)

Under a basic ***guaranteed investment contract (GIC)***, also called a *guaranteed interest contract* or a *guaranteed income contract*, the plan sponsor makes a single deposit for the insurer to hold for a specified period of time, such as five years. GICs generally have a specified maturity date and guarantee the repayment at the maturity date of the amounts deposited under the contract, plus the amount of credited interest, less withdrawals. Some GICs allow the sponsor to make monthly contributions rather than a single up-front deposit.

The GIC guarantees that the insurer will pay at least a stated minimum interest rate during the contract period. The plan sponsor can choose for interest earned to be (1) accumulated until the GIC expires or (2) paid annually. When the GIC expires, the account balance—with any accumulated interest—is returned to the plan sponsor. Some GICs provide for ongoing contributions and automatically renew at maturity.

Under an optional arrangement for benefit payments to plan participants, the plan sponsor can choose to have the principal and interest paid out in installments. Like separate account contracts, GICs permit but do not require the plan sponsor to purchase an immediate annuity at the time of a plan participant's retirement. GICs are unallocated investment vehicles used primarily for defined benefit plans. A coordinating service package that includes allocation services is used to accommodate the individual record-keeping requirements of defined contribution plans.

Group Annuity Contracts

Although IPGs, separate account contracts and riders, and GICs sometimes are also referred to as *group annuity contracts*, defined contribution plans often use a type of contract that is called a group annuity contract. A ***group annuity contract*** operates much like an immediate participation guarantee contract with a separate account rider. The contract itself is unallocated but the insurance company typically also offers a coordinating service package that includes allocation services in order to accommodate the individual participant record-keeping requirements of defined contribution plans.

Group Deferred Annuity Contracts

A ***group deferred annuity contract*** is a retirement plan funding vehicle that provides plan participants with annuities upon retirement. Under a group deferred annuity, the insurer usually issues a master contract to plan trustees for the benefit of plan participants. Plan participants hold individual certificates as evidence of their promised annuity benefits. Each year, the sponsor uses the contributions made on behalf of each plan participant to purchase a single-premium deferred annuity.

When a plan participant retires, group deferred annuities provide the retirement benefit payments promised under the plan. The total benefit amount paid to a retiree is equal to the sum of the deferred annuities purchased each year. Group deferred annuities are a type of allocated funding vehicle.

Individual Policy Pension Trusts

An ***individual policy pension trust***, also known as a *412(i) plan*, is a type of allocated funding vehicle that is typically used for small pension plans. Under this arrangement, plan trustees purchase individual life insurance or individual annuity contracts for each participant in the plan annually. Note that this arrangement uses individual, not group, annuities. An individual policy pension trust is one instance in which a defined benefit plan uses an allocated funding vehicle.

Figure 14.7 summarizes our discussion of insurance company contracts for retirement plan funding.

FIGURE 14.7 Features of Insurance Contracts Used for Retirement Plan Funding

TYPE	Principal guaranteed	Interest guaranteed	Purchase of annuity(ies) at guaranteed rates	Allocated	Unallocated
Deposit administration contract	✓	✓	✓		✓
Immediate participation guarantee contract	Some		✓		✓
Separate account contract or rider			Some		✓*
Guaranteed investment contract	✓	✓	Some		✓*
Group annuity contract			Some		✓*
Group deferred annuity contract	✓	✓	✓	✓	
Individual policy pension trust	**	**	**	✓	

* Defined contribution plans use a service agreement for allocations.
** Depends on the nature of the underlying life insurance policy or annuity contract.

Key Terms

plan beneficiary
coverage
eligibility requirement
service requirement
age requirement
participation
plan document
summary plan description
plan administrator
benefit formula
defined benefit plan
defined contribution plan
defined benefit formula
Pension Benefit Guaranty Corporation (PBGC)
defined contribution formula
forfeiture
normal retirement age
early retirement
late retirement
vesting schedule
graded vesting schedule
cliff vesting schedule
portable
rollover
normal form of benefit
funding vehicle
allocated funding vehicle
unallocated funding vehicle
trust
fiduciary
deposit administration contract
immediate participation guarantee (IPG) contract
separate account contract or rider
guaranteed investment contract (GIC)
group annuity contract
group deferred annuity contract
individual policy pension trust

Glossary

12b-1 fee. A mutual fund fee that covers marketing and distribution expenses. [11]

401(k) plan. In the United States, a special type of savings plan that allows employees to make pre-tax contributions to the plan. [13]

412(i) plan. *See* **individual policy pension trust**.

accelerated death benefit. A supplemental life insurance policy benefit that provides that a policyowner may elect to receive all or part of the policy's death benefit before the insured's death if certain conditions are met. Also known as a *living benefit*. [5]

accidental death and dismemberment (AD&D) benefit. An accidental death benefit that provides an additional benefit for dismemberment as the result of an accident. [5]

accidental death benefit. A supplemental life insurance policy benefit that provides a death benefit in addition to the policy's basic death benefit if the insured's death occurs as the result of an accident. [5]

account maintenance fee. A mutual fund fee to cover the costs of certain accounts, such as those that carry a low balance. [11]

accumulation at interest dividend option. A dividend option in which the insurer retains the policy dividends on deposit to accumulate at interest. [6]

accumulation period. The time period between the issue date and the date that the annuity contract's periodic income payments begin. [12]

accumulation unit. An ownership share in a selected subaccount of a separate account held during the accumulation period of a variable deferred annuity. [12]

accumulation value. The value paid for the deferred annuity plus interest earned, less the amount of any withdrawals or fees. [12]

acquisition. A transaction in which one corporation purchases a controlling interest in another corporation, typically resulting in a parent/subsidiary relationship between formerly independent corporations; after the transaction, both corporations survive. [1]

actively-at-work provision. A group insurance policy provision that states that to be eligible for coverage an employee must be actively at work—rather than ill or on leave—on the day the coverage is to take effect. [7]

actual cash value insurance. Property insurance that pays the insured an amount equal to the replacement cost minus an amount for depreciation. [10]

actuarial assumptions. The estimated values on which an insurer bases its product pricing calculations. [6]

actuary. A technical expert in insurance, annuities, and financial instruments who applies mathematical knowledge to industry and company statistics and performs all of the calculations needed to ensure that an insurance company's products are financially sound. [6]

AD&D benefit. *See* **accidental death and dismemberment benefit**.

additional insured rider. *See* **second insured rider**.

additional term insurance dividend option. A dividend option in which the insurer uses the policy dividend as a net single premium to purchase one-year term insurance on the insured's life. [6]

adjustable rate CD. *See* **variable rate certificate of deposit**.

adjustable rate mortgage (ARM). A mortgage in which the interest rate fluctuates according to a benchmark rate specified in the mortgage agreement. Also known as a *variable rate mortgage*. [4]

adjusted balance method. A method used to calculate the amount of a credit card's outstanding balance in which any payments made during the current billing period are subtracted from the balance at the end of the previous billing period without adding new purchases to the balance. [4]

administrative services only (ASO) contract. A contract under which a self-insured group policyholder pays a fee in exchange for administrative services provided by an outside organization. [9]

adverse selection. *See* **antiselection.**

affiliates. Two companies that are under the common control of a holding company. [1]

age requirement. The minimum age for an employee benefit plan member to be eligible to participate in the plan. [14]

aggregate stop-loss coverage. A type of stop-loss insurance under which the stop-loss insurer becomes responsible for paying claims when the employer's total claims exceed a stated dollar amount within a stated period of time. [9]

agreed value insurance. Property insurance that pays the insured an amount agreed upon by the insured and the insurer at the time of policy issue. [10]

allocated funding vehicle. A funding vehicle in which all of the plan sponsor's contributions are credited to individual participants in a manner that gives the participants a legally enforceable claim to the benefits related to those contributions. [14]

allowable expense. An expense that an insured incurred and that is covered under a medical expense insurance policy. [9]

all-risks. *See* **open-perils**.

AMA. *See* **asset management account**.

amortization. The process of eliminating a debt through periodic payments. [4]

amortization period. The period of time during which a loan is paid off through periodic payments. [4]

annual percentage rate (APR). The total cost of credit expressed as a yearly rate of interest. [4]

annuitant. The person whose lifetime is used in determining the amount of benefits payable under an annuity contract. [12]

annuitization period. *See* **payout period**.

annuity certain. *See* **period certain annuity**.

annuity contract. A legally enforceable written agreement between an insurance company and a contract owner under which the insurer grants a named person the right to receive a series of periodic payments in exchange for a premium or a series of premiums. [12]

annuity date. The date on which the insurer begins to make the periodic income payments. Also known as the *income date*. [12]

annuity period. The time span between the payments in the series of periodic income payments. [12]

annuity unit. A share in a subaccount of an insurer's separate account that determine the size of future periodic income payments under a variable annuity after the contract has annuitized. [12]

antiselection. The tendency of individuals who believe they have a greater-than-average likelihood of loss to seek insurance protection to a greater extent than do those who believe they have an average or a less-than-average likelihood of loss. Also known as *adverse selection* or *selection against the insurer*. [2]

APL provision. *See* **automatic premium loan provision**.

applicant. The person or business that applies for an insurance policy. [2]

APR. *See* **annual percentage rate**.

ARM. *See* **adjustable rate mortgage**.

ASO contract. *See* **administrative services only contract**.

asset management account (AMA). An account that offers checking services as part of a package of financial services, including a money market deposit account or money market mutual fund, securities brokerage services (such as the buying and selling of mutual funds, stocks, and bonds), credit and debit cards, loans, and unified record keeping. Also known as a *sweep account*. [3]

assignment. An agreement under which one party transfers some or all of his ownership rights in a particular property, such as a life insurance policy, to another party. [6]

assignment provision. An individual life insurance policy or annuity contract provision that describes the duties of the insurer and the policyowner or contract owner when the policy is assigned. [6]

assuming company. *See* **reinsurer**.

ATM. *See* **automated teller machine**.

ATM card. *See* **debit card**.

automated teller machine (ATM). A computer terminal that allows electronic access to a person's account and various transactions, including cash withdrawals, 24 hours a day, 7 days a week. [3]

automatic dividend option. The dividend option that an insurer will apply if the policyowner does not choose an option. [6]

automatic nonforfeiture benefit. The specified nonforfeiture benefit that becomes effective automatically when a premium for a cash value life insurance policy is not paid by the end of the grace period and the policyowner has not elected another nonforfeiture option. [6]

automatic premium loan (APL) provision. A nonforfeiture provision that allows an insurer automatically to pay an overdue premium for a policyowner by making a loan against the policy's cash value as long as the cash value equals or exceeds the amount of the premium due. [6]

automobile insurance. A type of personal property insurance that protects an insured from financial losses arising from operation of a vehicle. [10]

average daily balance method. A method used to calculate the amount of a credit card's outstanding balance in which each day's balance during the billing period is added together and then the total is divided by the number of days in the billing period. Payments made during the billing period are taken into account when calculating the balances, and purchases may or may not be included. [4]

back-end load. 1) A fee a mutual fund charges when an investor sells shares. Also known as a *deferred sales charge.* [11] 2) An amount charged to an annuity contract owner when she withdraws money from the product. Also known as a *surrender charge*, and, for variable annuities, a *contingent deferred sales charge.* [12] *Contrast with* **front-end load.**

bailout provision. A provision in some fixed annuity contract that enables the contract owner to surrender the annuity contract, usually without surrender charges, if the current interest rate falls below a stated level—typically 1 percentage point below the initial current interest rate. Also known as an *escape clause* or *cash-out provision.* [12]

balanced fund. A mutual fund that has the objective of preservation of capital with moderate income and growth in value. [11]

balloon payment. A final debt payment that is much larger than the preceding payments. [4]

bancassurance company. *See* **bank insurance company**.

bank insurance company. A company that offers both banking and insurance services. Also known as a *bancassurance company.* [1]

bankruptcy. A state of insolvency that occurs when a court finds that the debts of a borrower exceed her assets, and her income is not sufficient to provide a reasonable expectation that the debts will be repaid in full in the future. [4]

basic form. A type of named-perils homeowners coverage that covers 10 named perils. [10]

basic medical expense coverage. A form of medical expense coverage that provides separate benefits for hospital, surgical, and physicians' expenses. [8]

basis point. One-hundredth of a percent (0.01 percent). [11]

beneficiary. The person or legal entity named to receive the life insurance policy benefits when the insured dies. [2]

benefit formula. A formula that describes the calculation of a plan sponsor's financial obligation to plan participants. [14]

benefit period. The time during which the insurer will pay income benefits under a disability income insurance policy. [8]

benefit schedule. A schedule found in a group life insurance policy that shows the amount of life insurance that the policy provides for each group insured. [7]

blended rating. A method of calculating group insurance premium rates that combines manual rating and experience rating. [7]

block of policies. A group of policies issued to insureds who are all the same age, the same sex, and in the same risk classification. [6]

bodily injury. Bodily harm, illness, or disease. [10]

bond. A debt security whereby the entity that sells the bond promises to pay the owner of the bond a stated rate of interest over a specified period of time, at the end of which time the original amount of borrowed money must be repaid. [11]

bond fund. A mutual fund whose assets are invested primarily in bonds. [11]

bondholder. The owner of a bond. [11]

bond issuer. The entity that sells the bond to raise money. [11]

broad form. A type of named-perils homeowners coverage that covers the 10 named perils in a basic form plus 6 more perils. [10]

broker. A middleman institution that matches buyers of securities with sellers of those securities. [1]

brokerage. *See* **securities broker/dealer**.

brokerage firm. *See* **securities broker-dealer**.

broker-dealer. *See* **securities broker-dealer**.

bundled product structure. A life insurance and annuity product design in which an insurer presents a product to customers as a package of benefits provided in exchange for a given payment. *Contrast with* **unbundled product structure**. [5]

business continuation plan. A plan designed to enable a business to continue operations upon the death of an owner or other person important to the business. [5]

business finance company. *See* **commercial finance company**.

business overhead expense coverage. A disability coverage option that provides benefits designed to pay a disabled insured's share of a business's overhead expenses. [8]

businessowners policy. A package commercial property and liability insurance policy that is available to certain small- to medium-sized businesses and covers commercial real property, personal property, and liability. [10]

business risk. The risk that the business itself will fail. [2]

buy-sell agreement. An agreement in which (1) one party agrees to purchase the financial interest that a second party has in a business following the second party's death and (2) the second party agrees to direct his estate to sell his interest in the business to the purchasing party. [5]

calendar-year deductible. A deductible that applies to the total of all allowable expenses an insured incurs during a given calendar year. [8]

callable bond. A bond that gives the bond issuer the right to call, or pay off, the bond before the maturity date. [11]

Canada Pension Plan (CPP). A Canadian federal program that provides a pension for wage earners who have contributed money into the plan during their working years. [1]

cancellable policy. An individual health insurance policy that grants the insurer the right to terminate the policy at any time, for any reason, simply by notifying the policyowner that the policy is cancelled and refunding any advance premium that has been paid for the policy. [9]

capital gains. Profits made when an asset is sold for a price that is higher than the price paid to purchase the asset. [2]

capital losses. Losses taken when an asset is sold for a price that is lower than the price paid to purchase the asset. [2]

capitation payment. A flat amount a provider receives each month for each patient under the provider's care, regardless of the number or cost of services provided. [8]

case management. A process by which a health plan (1) identifies plan members who require extensive, complex health care, (2) develops an appropriate treatment strategy based on medical necessity and appropriateness and the availability of alternative care solutions, and (3) coordinates and monitors patient care. [8]

cash account. A brokerage account in which all transactions are settled on a cash basis within three days after the investor places a buy or sell order. [11]

cash advance. Cash borrowed from the issuer of a credit card. [4]

cash advance limit. The maximum amount of cash available to a credit cardholder, which can be less than or equal to the credit limit. [4]

cash dividend option. A dividend option in which the insurer sends the policyowner a check in the amount of the policy dividend. [6]

cashier's check. A check issued on a financial institution's own account and backed by the creditworthiness of the institution. [3]

cash management. The allocation of readily available funds among various living expenses as well as among savings and investment opportunities. [1]

cash-out provision. *See* **bailout provision**.

cash payment nonforfeiture option. A nonforfeiture option that gives the policyowner the right to receive the net cash surrender value in a lump sum payment upon discontinuation of premium payments as a result of surrender or lapse. [6]

cash value. The savings element of a cash value life insurance policy. [5]

cash value life insurance. A type of life insurance that provides coverage throughout the insured's lifetime and contains a savings element. Also known as *permanent life insurance*. [5]

CD. *See* **certificate of deposit**.

cede. To obtain reinsurance on insurance business by transferring all or part of the risk to a reinsurer. [2]

ceding company. In a reinsurance transaction, the insurance company that purchases reinsurance from another insurer. [2]

certificate holder. *See* **group insured**.

certificate of deposit (CD). An interest-earning time deposit held in a depository institution for a specified period of time. [3]

certificate of insurance. A document that a group policyholder delivers to each group insured that describes the coverage provided and the group insured's rights under the contract. [7]

change of occupation provision. A provision in individual disability income insurance policies that permits the insurer to adjust the policy's premium rate or the amount of benefits payable under the policy if the insured changes occupation. [9]

change of ownership provision. An individual life insurance policy provision that specifies a simple, direct method of transferring all the policy's ownership rights. [6]

check. A signed, written order by which the owner of an account instructs the financial institution to pay a stated sum from the account to another party. [3]

check card. *See* **debit card**.

checking account. A demand deposit account that allows the account owner to write checks for specified amounts against funds he has deposited into the account. [3]

children's insurance rider. A supplemental life insurance policy benefit that provides term coverage on the insured's children. [5]

CI coverage. *See* **critical illness coverage**.

claim. A request for payment under the terms of an insurance policy. [2]

claim costs. The costs an insurer incurs to provide policy benefits. [9]

class of policies. All policies of a particular type or all policies issued to a particular group of insureds. [9]

cliff vesting schedule. A type of minimum vesting schedule that provides a retirement plan participant with a nonforfeitable right to all employer-funded plan benefits or account values upon attaining five full years of employment; before completing five full years of employment, though, the participant has no vested benefits at all. The period is three years for 401(k) plans. [14]

closing costs. Fees that a borrower incurs in taking out a mortgage. [4]

COB provision. *See* **coordination of benefits provision**.

coinsurance. A specified percentage of all allowable expenses that remain after the deductible has been paid under a medical expense insurance policy and that must be paid by the insured. [8]

COLA. *See* **cost-of-living adjustment**.

collateral. Property that serves as security for the repayment of a loan. [4]

collision insurance. Physical damage insurance that covers an insured for losses to his vehicle caused by a collision regardless of whether the insured was at fault. [10]

commercial bank. A depository institution that accepts deposits from people, businesses, and government agencies and uses these deposits to make loans to people, businesses, and government agencies. [1]

commercial finance company. A finance company that extends loans and leases equipment to businesses. Also known as a *business finance company*. [1]

commercial package policy. A package commercial property and liability insurance policy that is designed for businesses of any size and type and that gives the insured the option of selecting at least two of the following seven coverages: commercial property, comprehensive general liability, crime, boiler and machinery, inland marine, automobile, and farm. [10]

commission. A fee paid to a brokerage firm in exchange for executing a buy or sell order. [11]

common stock. A type of stock that entitles the owner to vote in board of directors elections and on other important company matters and to receive dividends, if they are declared. [11]

commutation right. An annuity contract provision that states that the owner of a payout annuity can withdraw all or part of the contract's remaining periodic income payments in a lump sum. [12]

compounding. The process of determining a future value when compound interest is applied. [2]

compound interest. Interest payable both on the principal and on all accumulated interest. *Contrast with* **simple interest**. [2]

comprehensive insurance. Physical damage insurance that covers an insured for losses to his vehicle caused by perils other than collision, such as theft and hail. [10]

comprehensive major medical policy. A single policy that combines coverages provided by both a supplemental major medical policy and an underlying basic medical expense policy. [8]

comprehensive personal liability insurance. Liability insurance that covers insureds from liability losses they incur that are not the result of practicing their profession or operating a vehicle. [10]

concurrent review. A review of treatment plans and services that takes place while a patient is in the hospital or receiving ongoing treatment. [8]

conditionally renewable policy. An individual health insurance policy that grants the insurer a limited right to refuse to renew the policy at the end of a premium payment period, as long as the reason for refusal is stated in the policy and is not related to the insured's health, and to increase the premium rate for any class of conditionally renewable policies. [9]

conservative fund. A mutual fund that has the objective of preservation of capital. [11]

consolidation. The combination of financial services institutions within or across sectors. [1]

consumer-driven health plan. An employer-sponsored health benefit plan that gives individuals freedom to choose health care providers and benefits, but also requires them to assume financial risk for their choices. [8]

consumer finance company. A finance company that makes loans to people so that they can buy items such as furniture and appliances, make home improvements, and pay off small debts. [1]

contingent beneficiary. The party designated to receive the proceeds of a life insurance policy following the insured's death if the primary beneficiary dies before the insured. Also known as a *secondary beneficiary*. [6]

contingent deferred sales charge. 1) A type of back-end load on a mutual fund that is charged only if the investor does not hold the shares a specified number of years after purchase. [11] 2) *See* **surrender charge**.

continuous-premium whole life policy. A type of whole life insurance policy for which premiums are payable until the insured's death. Also known as a *straight life insurance policy* or an *ordinary life insurance policy*. [5]

contract of indemnity. An insurance policy under which the amount of the policy benefit payable for a covered loss is based on the actual amount of financial loss as determined at the time of loss. [2]

contract owner. The person or entity who exercises all rights and privileges of an annuity contract. [12]

contribution. A payment from any source to fund an employee benefit plan's benefits. [7]

contributory plan. An employee benefit plan under which participating employees must contribute all or a portion of the cost to be covered under the plan. *Contrast with* **noncontributory plan**. [7]

conventional mortgage. A mortgage in which the interest rate, term, and periodic payment amount are all fixed in advance. [4]

convergence. The movement toward a single financial institution being able to serve a consumer's banking, insurance, and securities needs. [1]

conversion privilege. A group life insurance policy provision that allows a group insured whose coverage terminates for certain reasons to convert the group life coverage to an individual life insurance policy. [7]

conversion provision. A provision in group medical expense insurance policies that grants an insured group member who is leaving the group a limited right to purchase an individual medical expense insurance policy without presenting evidence of insurability. [9]

convertible bond. A bond that gives the bondholder the right to convert the bond into shares of the issuing company's stock. [11]

convertible term insurance policy. A term life insurance policy that gives the policyowner the right to convert the term policy to a cash value life insurance policy without providing evidence of insurability. [5]

coordination of benefits (COB) provision. A provision in group medical expense insurance policies that prevents a group member who is insured under more than one group medical expense insurance policy from receiving benefit amounts that are greater than the amount of medical expenses the insured actually incurs. [9]

copayment. A specified, fixed amount health plan members must pay for specified services at the time the services are received. [8]

co-signer. A person who agrees to repay a loan if the borrower defaults on that loan, but who has no ownership rights to the property being financed by the loan. [4]

cost of benefits. The value of all contractually required benefits that a product promises to pay. [6]

cost-of-living adjustment (COLA). A coverage option that allows benefit amounts to increase with increases in the cost of living. [8]

coupon payment. An interest payment made on a bond. [11]

coupon rate. A fixed annual rate of interest set when a bond is issued and expressed as a percentage of the par value of the bond. [11]

coverage. The specification of characteristics of the group members intended to benefit from an employee benefit plan. [14]

CPP. *See* **Canada Pension Plan**.

credit. 1) The financial service that enables people to purchase now by giving a promise to pay in the future. [1] 2) A reduction from tax liability. [2]

credit card. A plastic card that entitles the cardholder to access an open-end line of credit. [4]

credited rate. *See* **current interest rate**.

credit life insurance. A type of term life insurance designed to pay the balance due on a loan other than a mortgage if the borrower dies before the loan is repaid. [5]

credit limit. The maximum amount of credit available to a credit cardholder. [4]

credit report. A document that provides information on a person's credit repayment history and on the amount of unused credit the person may have available from other sources. [4]

credit union. A nonprofit depository institution that does business only with its depositors—called members—who traditionally shared a common bond, such as an employer or their industry. [1]

critical illness benefit. *See* **dread disease benefit**.

critical illness (CI) coverage. Insurance that pays a lump-sum benefit if an insured is diagnosed with a critical illness while the policy is in force. [8]

cumulative preferred stock. A type of preferred stock that requires the company to pay in full any unpaid scheduled dividends on its preferred stock before it may pay any dividends on its common stock. [11]

current interest rate. The interest rate in fixed annuity contracts that the insurer actually pays on the accumulation value for a given period. Also known as the *credited rate*. [12]

current yield. The coupon rate divided by the closing price of the bond. [11]

custodial account. An account set up at a depository institution or other financial institution for a minor or other person who lacks legal capacity. [13]

DD benefit. *See* **dread disease benefit**.

dealer. An institution that holds an inventory of securities and is always ready to buy and sell securities from its own account. [1]

death benefit. 1) The amount of money actually paid by an insurer to the beneficiary when the insured dies. Also known as the *policy proceeds*. [5] 2) An annuity contract feature that states that if the contract owner dies during the accumulation period, a named beneficiary will receive a benefit of at least as much as the accumulation value at the time of the contract owner's death. Also known as a *survivor benefit*. [12]

debit card. A plastic card with coded account information that allows an account holder to access his funds in an account electronically. Also known as an *ATM card* and a *check card*. [3]

debit insurance. *See* **monthly debit ordinary insurance**.

decreasing term life insurance. Term life insurance that provides a face amount that decreases in amount over the policy term. [5]

deductible. A flat dollar amount of allowable expenses that the insured must pay before the insurer will begin making benefit payments under a medical expense insurance policy. [8]

deduction. An expense that is subtracted from adjusted gross income in computing taxable income. A deduction is technically an expense subtracted from adjusted gross income. However, in this text, we use the term *deduction* also to refer to what is technically called an *adjustment to income* because this terminology is commonly used in the financial services industry. Both deductions and adjustments to income are expenses that are subtracted from income in computing taxable income. [2]

default risk. The risk that a borrower will not make scheduled payments of principal and interest to the lender. [2]

deferral. A postponement of payment of taxes from the current year to a later year. [2]

deferred annuity. An annuity contract in which periodic income payments are scheduled to begin more than one annuity period after the contract's issue date. [12]

deferred compensation plan. A plan established by an employer to provide income benefits to an employee at a date later than the income was earned, such as after the employee's retirement, if the employee does not voluntarily terminate employment before that date. [5]

deferred sales charge. *See* **back-end load**.

defined benefit formula. A benefit formula that specifies the amount of retirement benefit a plan sponsor promises to provide to each plan participant. [14]

defined benefit plan. A retirement plan structured according to a defined benefit formula. [14]

defined contribution formula. A benefit formula that specifies the level of contributions to the plan but not the benefits to be paid. [14]

defined contribution plan. A retirement plan structured according to a defined contribution formula. [14]

deflation. A decrease in the average level of prices for goods and services. *Contrast with* **inflation**. [2]

demand deposit account. An account under which the financial institution must give the account holder access to his funds upon the account holder's demand. [3]

demutualization. The reorganization of a mutual insurance company as a stock insurance company. [1]

dental expense coverage. Insurance that provides benefits for routine dental examinations, preventive work, and dental procedures needed to treat tooth decay and diseases of the teeth and jaw. [8]

deposit administration contract. A type of retirement plan funding vehicle in which a plan sponsor deposits assets with an insurer and the assets are placed in the insurer's general investment account. Upon a plan participant's retirement, the insurer applies funds from the general account to provide an immediate annuity for the retiree. [14]

depository institution. A financial institution that specializes in accepting deposits and making loans. In the United States, depository institutions include commercial banks, savings and loan associations, savings banks, and credit unions. [1]

disability buyout coverage. A disability coverage option that provides benefits designed to fund the buyout of a disabled partner's or owner's interest in a business. [8]

disability income benefit. A supplemental life insurance policy benefit that provides a monthly income benefit if the insured becomes totally disabled while the policy is in force. Typically, the amount of the monthly disability income benefit is a stated dollar amount—such as $10—per $1,000 of life coverage. [5]

disability income coverage. Health insurance coverage that provides income replacement benefits to an insured who is unable to work because of illness or injury. [8]

discount. The amount by which a bond's current market price is less than its par value. [11]

discretionary account. A brokerage account in which the investor gives the broker discretionary authority to buy and sell securities for the account without the investor's prior consent. [11]

disease management. A coordinated system of preventive, diagnostic, and therapeutic measures intended to provide cost-effective, quality health care for a patient population that has or is at risk for a specific chronic illness or medical condition. [8]

diversification. The process of investing in a number of financial instruments to minimize the impact of the risk associated with any one investment or type of investment. [2]

dividend. A distribution of a business' earnings to its shareholders. [2]

dividend options. The ways in which a life insurance policyowner may receive policy dividends or the ways in which a participating annuity contract owner may receive dividends. [6]

dividend yield. The annual percentage return earned by dividends on a common or preferred stock. [11]

divisible surplus. The amount of surplus available for distribution to owners of participating policies. [6]

double indemnity benefit. A supplemental life insurance benefit term for when the amount of the accidental death benefit is equal to the face amount of the life insurance policy. [5]

down payment. A portion of the purchase price paid by a borrower at the time of purchase. [4]

dread disease (DD) benefit. An accelerated death benefit under which the insurer agrees to pay a portion of the policy's face amount to a policyowner if the insured suffers from one of a number of specified diseases. Also known as a *critical illness benefit*. [5]

dread disease coverage. Insurance that provides benefits for medical expenses incurred by an insured who has contracted a specified disease. [8]

early retirement. A retirement plan participant's retirement before the normal retirement age, subject to a minimum age requirement and a minimum service requirement and resulting in a reduced retirement income benefit. [14]

economies of scale. The economic principle that holds that as production volume increases, the cost per unit of production decreases. [1]

economies of scope. The economic principle that holds that as the types of products sold through one outlet increase, the cost per unit of production will be lower than if each product were sold separately. [1]

effective interest rate. The interest rate that includes the effects of compounding, or stated simply, the interest rate that is actually paid or earned. *Contrast with* **nominal interest rate**. [2]

EFT. *See* **electronic funds transfer**.

EIA. *See* **equity-indexed annuity**.

electronic funds transfer (EFT). The transfer of funds electronically among accounts. [3]

eligibility requirement. A condition that a covered person must satisfy in order to participate in an employee benefit plan. [14]

elimination period. The specific amount of time that an insured must be disabled before becoming eligible to receive disability income insurance policy benefits. Also known as a *waiting period*. [8]

employee benefit. An item of nonwage compensation. [5]

Employee Retirement Income Security Act (ERISA). In the United States, a federal law designed to ensure that private employee benefit plans meet certain requirements in order to protect the covered employees. [13]

endorsement. *See* **rider**.

endowment insurance. A type of life insurance that provides a policy benefit payable either when the insured dies or on a stated date if the insured is still alive on that date. [5]

enrollment period. A specified time, usually 31 days, during which a new group member who is eligible for group insurance coverage may first enroll for that coverage, usually without having to provide evidence of insurability. [7]

entire contract provision. A provision in a life insurance policy or annuity contract that defines which documents constitute the entire contract between the insurer and the policyowner or contract owner. [6]

equity. An ownership interest. [4]

equity fund. *See* **stock fund**.

equity-indexed annuity (EIA). A type of annuity that offers certain principal and earnings guarantees, but also offers the possibility of additional earnings by linking the contract to a published index. [12]

ERISA. *See* **Employee Retirement Income Security Act**.

escape clause. *See* **bailout provision**.

ethics. A system of accepted standards of conduct and moral judgment that combines the elements of honesty, integrity, and fair treatment. [1]

evidence of insurability. Proof that an insurance underwriter requires to determine that a proposed insured meets the insurer's health and lifestyle requirements and is an insurable risk. [5]

excess interest rate. The difference between the minimum guaranteed interest rate and the current interest rate. [12]

exchange fee. A mutual fund fee for transferring money from one mutual fund to another within the same fund family. [11]

exclusion. 1) Funds received that are not taxed. [2] 2) An insurance policy provision that describes circumstances under which the insurer will not pay benefits that otherwise would be payable. [6]

expense ratio. The total annual operating expenses as a percentage of the mutual fund's average net assets. [11]

experience rating. A method of calculating group insurance premium rates by which the insurer bases the premium rate on the particular group's prior claims and expense experience. [7]

extended term insurance nonforfeiture option. A nonforfeiture option that allows the owner of a policy with a cash value to discontinue premium payments and to use the policy's net cash surrender value as a net single premium to purchase term insurance for the full face amount of the original policy for as long as the net cash surrender value can provide. [6]

face amount. The monetary amount of life insurance benefits applied for by the applicant. [5]

family income insurance. A plan of decreasing term life insurance that provides a stated monthly income benefit amount to the insured's beneficiary—typically the surviving spouse—if the insured dies during the term of coverage. [5]

family policy. A type of life insurance policy that covers all the members of a family under one contract. The primary insured is issued a whole life insurance policy, and the insured's spouse and children receive term life insurance coverage. [5]

FDIC. *See* **Federal Deposit Insurance Corporation**.

Federal Deposit Insurance Corporation (FDIC). A U.S. federal agency that insures deposits made in member depository institutions. [3]

fiduciary. A person or other legal entity who holds a special position of trust or confidence when handling the business affairs of another and who must put the other's interest above his or her own. [14]

finance charge. The total cost of credit paid by a borrower for a loan, expressed as a dollar amount. [4]

finance company. A financial institution that specializes in making short- and medium-term loans to businesses and to people. [1]

financial hazard. The likelihood that a person who purchases more insurance than he can afford may have an ulterior motive in doing so or that he may ultimately not be able to afford the premiums, resulting in the insured discontinuing his coverage. [2]

financial holding company. A holding company that conducts activities that are financial in nature or incidental to financial activities, such as insurance, banking, investment, and financial advisory services. [1]

financial institution. A business that owns primarily financial assets, such as stocks and bonds, rather than fixed assets, such as equipment and raw materials. [1]

financial intermediary. An organization that channels funds from those people, businesses, and governments who have a surplus of funds (savers) to those who have a shortage of funds (borrowers). [1]

financial planner. A professional who analyzes a customer's personal financial circumstances and goals and prepares a plan, usually in writing, to meet the customer's financial goals. [1]

financial planning. The process of consciously determining how to spend, finance, protect, accumulate, and distribute assets to meet financial goals. [1]

financial services industry. The industry consisting of financial institutions that offer products and services to help people, businesses, and governments meet their financial goals. [1]

first-dollar coverage. Coverage under which the insurer begins to reimburse the insured for eligible medical expenses without first requiring an out-of-pocket contribution from the insured. [8]

first-to-die life insurance. *See* **joint whole life insurance**.

fixed amount annuity. An annuity payout option that guarantees to pay periodic income payments of a specified minimum dollar amount for as long a period as the annuity's accumulation value will provide regardless of when the annuitant dies. [12]

fixed amount option. A life insurance settlement option under which the insurer pays equal installments of a preselected amount until the policy proceeds, plus the interest earned, are exhausted. [6]

fixed annuity. An annuity contract in which the insurer guarantees that the contract's accumulation value will experience no loss of the investment principal and will earn interest at a current rate no lower than the contract's minimum guaranteed interest rate. [12]

fixed interest rate. An interest rate that does not change over the stated repayment schedule of the loan. [4]

fixed period option. A life insurance settlement option under which the insurer pays the policy proceeds and interest in a series of annual or more frequent installments for a preselected period. [6]

fixed subaccount. A subaccount that guarantees payment of a fixed rate of interest for a specified period of time. [12]

flexible-premium annuity. An annuity contract that allows the contract owner to alter the amount and frequency of premium payments, within specified limits. [12]

flexible-premium deferred annuity (FPDA) contract. A deferred annuity contract for which the contract owner typically must pay an initial premium of some minimum amount and then may make additional payments at any future times, usually subject to some smaller minimum amount. [12]

flexible variable life. *See* **variable universal life insurance**.

foreclosure. The legal proceeding by which a lender acquires the title to a mortgaged property from a borrower in default of its loan terms. [4]

forfeiture. An account balance abandoned by a plan participant who leaves the plan before he has a right to keep that benefit. [14]

FPDA. *See* **flexible-premium deferred annuity contract**.

fraternal benefit society. An organization formed to provide social and insurance benefits to its members. [1]

free-examination provision. *See* **free-look provision**.

free-look provision. A provision in a life insurance policy or annuity contract that allows the policyowner a specified period, usually at least 10 days, following policy delivery within which to cancel the policy and receive a refund of all premiums paid. Also known as a *free-examination provision*. [6]

front-end load. 1) A fee a mutual fund charges when the investor buys shares. Also known as a *sales charge.* [11] 2) An amount charged to an annuity contract owner at the time she pays for the product. [12] *Contrast with* **back-end load**.

fully insured plan. A group insurance plan under which the group policyholder makes periodic premium payments to the insurance company and the insurance company bears the responsibility for all claim payments. [9]

fully self-insured plan. A group insurance plan under which the group policyholder—usually an employer—takes complete responsibility for all claim payments and related expenses. [9]

funding instrument. *See* **funding vehicle**.

funding mechanism. The way in which premiums are used to pay a group health insurance plan's claim costs and administrative expenses. [9]

funding vehicle. An arrangement for investing a retirement plan's assets. Also known as an *investment vehicle* or *funding instrument*. [14]

future purchase option. A disability coverage option that grants the insured the right to increase the benefit amount under a disability income insurance policy in accordance with increases in earnings. [8]

future value. The value at the end of a given period of time of a sum of money invested at a specified interest rate. *Contrast with* **present value**. [2]

general account. An undivided investment account in which an insurer maintains funds that support contractual obligations for guaranteed insurance products such as whole life insurance or fixed annuities. *Contrast with* **separate account**. [5]

general insurance company. *See* **property/casualty insurance company**.

GI benefit. *See* **guaranteed insurability benefit**.

GIC. *See* **guaranteed investment contract**.

GIO. *See* **guaranteed insurability option**.

GLB Act. *See* **Gramm-Leach-Bliley Act**.

GMAB. *See* **guaranteed minimum accumulation benefit**.

GMDB. *See* **guaranteed minimum death benefit**.

GMIB. *See* **guaranteed minimum income benefit**.

GMWB. *See* **guaranteed minimum withdrawal benefit**.

grace period. 1) A period of time between the date of a purchase and the date the lender begins to charge interest during which no interest accrues. [4] 2) A length of time following each premium due date within which the premium due may be paid without loss of coverage. [6]

grace period provision. A provision in an insurance policy that specifies a length of time following each premium due date within which the premium due may be paid without loss of coverage. [6]

graded vesting schedule. The type of minimum vesting schedule for qualified retirement plans in the United States that provides a retirement plan participant with a nonforfeitable right to employer-funded benefits or account values according to a schedule of gradual increases, with full vesting for qualified plans being achieved no later than the completion of seven full years of employment (six years for 401(k) plans). [14]

graduated interest rates. *See* **tiered interest rates**.

Gramm-Leach-Bliley (GLB) Act. United States federal legislation that removed many of the regulatory barriers that prevented affiliations among different types of financial institutions. [1]

gross premium. The lump sum amount of money the insurer actually charges for a policy. [5]

group annuity. An annuity contract established through a retirement plan that covers a group of people. [12]

group annuity contract. A type of retirement plan funding vehicle that operates much like an immediate participation contract with a separate account rider. The contract itself is unallocated but the insurance company typically also offers a coordinating service package that includes allocation services in order to accommodate the individual participant record-keeping requirements of defined contribution plans. [14]

group creditor life insurance. Life insurance issued to a creditor, such as a bank, to insure the lives of the creditor's current and future borrowers. [7]

group deferred annuity contract. A type of retirement plan funding vehicle that provides plan participants with annuities upon retirement. The insurer usually issues a master contract to plan trustees for the benefit of plan participants. Plan participants hold individual certificates as evidence of their promised annuity benefits. Each year, the sponsor uses the contributions made on behalf of each plan participant to purchase a single-premium deferred annuity. [14]

group insured. A group member insured by a group insurance policy. Also known as a *certificate holder* and, in Canada, as a *group life insured*. [7]

group life insurance policy. An insurance policy that is issued to a party that is purchasing life insurance coverage for a specific group of people. Also known as a *master group insurance contract*. [5]

group life insured. *See* **group insured**.

group RRSP. In Canada, an employer-sponsored registered retirement savings plan in which an account is established for each participating employee. [13]

growth and income fund. A mutual fund that has the objective of long-term capital gains and some current income. [11]

growth fund. A mutual fund that has the objective of long-term capital appreciation. [11]

guaranteed income contract. *See* **guaranteed investment contract**.

guaranteed insurability (GI) benefit. A supplemental life insurance policy benefit that gives the policyowner the right to purchase additional insurance of the same type as the basic life insurance policy for an additional premium amount on specified option dates or upon specified events (for example, marriage of the insured or birth of the insured's child) during the life of the policy without providing evidence of the insured's insurability. Also known as the *guaranteed insurability option (GIO)*. [5]

guaranteed insurability option (GIO). *See* **guaranteed insurability benefit**.

guaranteed interest contract. *See* **guaranteed investment contract**.

guaranteed investment contract (GIC). A type of retirement plan funding vehicle in which the plan sponsor makes a single deposit for the insurer to hold for a specified period of time, such as five years. GICs generally have a specified maturity date and guarantee the repayment at the maturity date of the amounts deposited under the contract, plus the amount of credited interest, less withdrawals. Also known as a *guaranteed interest contract* or a *guaranteed income contract*. [14]

guaranteed minimum accumulation benefit (GMAB). A variable annuity contract feature that guarantees a return of principal if the contract remains in force for a specified period of time. [12]

guaranteed minimum death benefit (GMDB). A variable annuity contract feature that guarantees that if the contract owner dies before periodic income payments begin, the beneficiary will receive at least the amount that was deposited into the annuity contract, less any withdrawals, even if poor investment performance causes the contract's accumulation value to be less than the premiums paid. [12]

guaranteed minimum income benefit (GMIB). A variable annuity contract feature that guarantees that variable periodic income payments will not fall below a certain amount—usually a specified percentage of the first payment—even if investments drop in value as a result of poor performance. [12]

guaranteed minimum withdrawal benefit (GMWB). A variable annuity contract feature that guarantees that up to a certain percentage of the amount paid into the contract will be available for withdrawals, even if subaccount investments perform poorly. [12]

guaranteed renewable policy. An individual health insurance policy that must be renewed at the policyowner's option at least until the insured attains the age limit specified in the contract, but for which the insurer can increase the premium rate if it increases the premium rate for an entire class of policies. [9]

health insurance. Insurance that provides protection against the risk of financial loss that may result from illness, injury, or disability. [8]

Health Insurance Portability and Accountability Act (HIPAA). A 1996 U.S. federal law that imposes requirements on group and individual health insurance plans, health insurers, and managed care organizations and that is designed to improve the availability and portability of health insurance benefits. [9]

health maintenance organization (HMO). A health care financing and delivery system that provides comprehensive health care services to plan members—often referred to as *subscribers*—in a particular geographic area; it typically requires subscribers to gain access to services through a primary care provider and use in-network providers. [8]

health reimbursement arrangement (HRA). A personal health spending account that is similar to a medical savings account, but can be funded only by employer contributions and that is available to employers of any size; HRAs do not require fixed contributions by employers. [8]

health savings account (HSA). A personal health spending account that is similar to medical savings accounts and health reimbursement arrangements, but includes (1) no restrictions on employer size, (2) no restrictions on source of contributions, (3) a higher maximum annual tax-deductible contribution, and (4) lower minimum deductibles for the accompanying medical expense policy. [8]

HIPAA. *See* **Health Insurance Portability and Accountability Act**.

HMO. *See* **health maintenance organization**.

holding company. A company in a holding company system that owns and controls another company (or companies). Also known as a *parent company*. [1]

holding company system. A corporate ownership structure in which one company—known as the holding company—owns and controls another company (or companies)—known as a subsidiary of the holding company. [1]

home-equity installment loan. A second mortgage in which the borrower receives a specified amount of the equity and then repays this loan with fixed or variable periodic payments of principal and interest over a fixed period. [4]

home-equity line of credit. An agreement giving the borrower a line of credit equal to a specified amount of the borrower's equity. [4]

homeowners insurance. A type of personal property insurance that protects an insured from financial losses resulting from damage to her home and/or its contents or resulting from being held liable for the losses of others. [10]

home service distribution system. A method of selling and servicing insurance policies through commissioned sales agents who sell a range of products and provide specified policyowner services, including the collection of renewal premiums, within a specified geographic area. [5]

hospital expenses. Charges for specific inpatient and outpatient hospital services, including room and board, medications, laboratory services, and other fees associated with a hospital stay. [8]

HR 10 plan. *See* **Keogh plan**.

HRA. *See* **health reimbursement arrangement**.

HSA. *See* **health savings account**.

hybrid fund. A mutual fund whose assets are invested in a mixture of stocks, bonds, and other securities. [11]

immediate annuity. An annuity contract that provides periodic income payments that generally are scheduled to begin one annuity period after the contract's issue date. [12]

immediate participation guarantee (IPG) contract. A type of retirement plan funding vehicle in which plan assets are held in an investment account in the name of the plan sponsor and deposited in the general account of the insurer. Under an IPG contract, the plan assets fully experience the actual monetary gains or losses from investing and paying benefits from the plan's assets. [14]

income date. *See* **annuity date**.

income fund. A mutual fund that has the objective of maximizing current income. [11]

income protection insurance. A type of disability income coverage that provides benefits based on the extent of the insured's actual loss of earnings from disability rather than on the insured's inability to perform work-related duties. [8]

incontestability provision. A provision in a life or health insurance policy that limits the time within which an insurer has the right to avoid the contract due to misrepresentation in the application for the policy. An incontestability provision in an annuity contract typically states that after the annuity contract becomes effective, the insurer may not contest the validity of the contract. [6]

increasing term life insurance. A type of term life insurance that provides a face amount that starts at one amount and increases by some specified amount or percentage at stated intervals over the policy term. [5]

indemnity benefits. Contractual benefits that are based on the actual amount of financial loss. Also known as *reimbursement benefit*. [8]

index. A statistical measurement system that tracks the performance of a group of similar investments. [11]

individual annuity. An annuity contract purchased by an individual. [12]

individual life insurance policy. An insurance policy that is issued to insure the life of a named person. [5]

individual policy pension trust. A type of allocated retirement plan funding vehicle typically used for a small group pension plan under the terms of which plan trustees purchase individual life insurance policies or individual annuity contracts for each participant in the plan annually. Note that this arrangement uses individual, not group, annuities. Also known as a *412(i) plan*. [14]

individual retirement account. In the United States, an individual retirement arrangement that takes the form of a trust or custodial account set up for the exclusive benefit of a taxpayer and his beneficiaries. [13]

individual retirement annuity. In the United States, an individual retirement arrangement that takes the form of an individual annuity issued by an insurance company. [13]

individual retirement arrangement (IRA). In the United States, a retirement savings plan that allows a person with taxable compensation to deposit a stated amount of that compensation into a tax-deferred savings arrangement that meets certain requirements specified in the federal tax laws and, thus, receives favorable federal tax treatment. [13]

individual stop-loss coverage. A type of stop-loss insurance under which the stop-loss insurer pays a portion of each claim that exceeds a stated amount. Also known as *specific stop-loss coverage*. [9]

inflation. A rise in the average price level of goods and services in an economy. *Contrast with* **deflation**. [2]

inflation rate. The percentage increase in the prices for goods and services during a specific period. [2]

inflation risk. The risk that the real value of the returns on an investment will be less than anticipated because of higher-than-expected inflation. Also known as *purchasing power risk*. [2]

initial public offering (IPO). The initial offering of a stock to the public. [11]

installment credit. A credit arrangement that requires the borrower to make periodic repayments on the loan amount according to a prearranged schedule. [4]

insurable interest. The interest a person has in the risk that is insured such that the person will suffer a genuine economic loss if the event insured against occurs. [2]

insurance. A mechanism for transferring the risk of financial loss from a person or entity to an insurance company. [1]

insurance company. A financial institution that provides protection against the risk of financial loss caused by specified events. [1]

insurance-to-value requirement. A property insurance policy provision that requires the insured to insure a certain percentage of the property's value—typically at least 80 percent—in order for any loss to be fully covered. [10]

insured. The person whose life, health, or property is insured under an insurance policy. [2]

interest. A fee an institution or a person pays for the use of someone else's money. [2]

interest option. A life insurance settlement option under which the insurer invests the policy proceeds for the policy beneficiary or policy payee and the interest earned is paid out annually, semiannually, quarterly, or monthly. [6]

interest rate. Interest stated as a percent of the principal. [2]

interest-rate cap. A loan provision that sets a maximum limit on the interest rate that will be charged on an adjustable rate mortgage, even if the benchmark interest rate exceeds that cap in the future. [4]

interest rate risk. The risk that the value of an investment will decline in the future because of changes in the market interest rate. [2]

intermediation. The transfer of funds from savers to borrowers through the services of a financial intermediary. [1]

investment management fee. A variable annuity fee that covers the professional investment management services. [12]

investment vehicle. *See* **funding vehicle**.

IPG. *See* **immediate participation guarantee contract**.

IPO. *See* **initial public offering**.

IRA. *See* **individual retirement arrangement**.

irrevocable beneficiary. A life insurance policy beneficiary who has a vested interest in the policy proceeds even during the insured's lifetime because the policyowner has the right to change the beneficiary designation only after obtaining the beneficiary's consent. [6]

joint and survivor annuity. An annuity payout option that covers two or more lives and pays periodic income payments until all annuitants die. [12]

joint whole life insurance. A type of whole life insurance that has the same features and benefits as individual whole life insurance, except that it insures two or more lives under the same policy. Also known as *first-to-die life insurance*. [5]

juvenile insurance policy. An insurance policy that is issued on the life of a child but is owned and paid for by an adult, usually the child's parent or legal guardian. [5]

Keogh plan. In the United States, a qualified retirement plan set up by a small business or self-employed individual to which annual tax-deductible contributions can be made, subject to certain limits and conditions. Also known as an *HR 10 plan*. [13]

key person. Any person or employee whose continued participation in a business is necessary to the success of the business and whose death would cause the business a significant financial loss. [5]

key person disability coverage. A disability coverage option that provides benefit payments to a small business if an insured owner, partner, or other key person becomes disabled. [8]

key person life insurance. Insurance that a business purchases on the life of a key person. [5]

lapse. The termination of an insurance policy due to nonpayment of a renewal premium by the end of the grace period. [6]

last survivor life insurance. A variation of joint whole life insurance under which the policy benefit is paid only after both people insured by the policy have died. Also known as *second-to-die life insurance*. [5]

late retirement. A retirement plan participant's retirement from employment later than the normal retirement age. [14]

law of large numbers. A principal that states that, typically, the more times we observe a particular event, the more likely our observed results will approximate the true probability that the event will occur. [2]

legal actions provision. A provision in individual health insurance policies that limits the time during which a claimant who disagrees with an insurer's claim decision has the right to sue the insurer to collect the amount the claimant believes is owed under the policy. [9]

level premium pricing system. A life insurance pricing system that allows the policyowner to pay the same premium amount each year the policy is in force. [6]

level term life insurance. Term life insurance that provides a face amount that remains the same over the policy term. [5]

liability insurance. Insurance that provides protection against financial responsibility for harming others or their property. [10]

liability risk. The risk of economic loss resulting from a person being held responsible for harming others or their property. [2]

liberalization. A homeowners policy condition that states that if the insurer makes a change broadening coverage of the particular type and edition of policy held by a homeowner and no additional premium is required, the change shall apply automatically to the homeowner's policy. [10]

lien. A legal claim on property for payment of a debt. [4]

life and health insurance company. An insurance company that insures a person against financial loss from death, disability, illness, and accident by providing life and health insurance and against the risk of outliving financial resources by issuing annuities. [1]

life annuity. An annuity payout option that covers only one life and guarantees periodic payments for as long as the annuitant lives, regardless of how long that is. [12]

life annuity with period certain. An annuity payout option that guarantees a periodic income payment so long as the annuitant lives and at least until the end of a specified period. [12]

life income option. A life insurance settlement option under which the insurer pays the policy proceeds in periodic installments over the payee's lifetime. [6]

life insurance. Insurance that provides protection against the economic loss caused by the death of the person whose life is insured. [5]

life with refund annuity. An annuity payout option that guarantees a periodic income payment for the lifetime of the annuitant and that pays a refund if the annuitant dies before the annuity premiums paid are recovered. Also known as a *refund annuity*. [12]

limited-payment whole life policy. A type of whole life insurance policy for which premiums are payable only until some stated period expires or until the insured's death, whichever occurs first. [5]

liquidity. The ease with which an asset can be converted into cash for an approximation of its true value. [2]

liquidity risk. The risk that an investor will not be able to sell an asset or investment quickly at its market value. [2]

living benefit. *See* **accelerated death benefit**.

load fund. A mutual fund that charges a load—front-end or back-end—or a 12b-1 fee greater than 25 basis points, or both. *Contrast with* **no-load fund**. [11]

loan-to-value ratio. A ratio of the amount of a mortgage loan to the value of the property. [4]

long-term care (LTC) insurance benefit. An accelerated death benefit under which the insurer agrees to pay a monthly benefit to the policyowner if the insured requires constant care for a medical condition. [5]

long-term care (LTC) insurance coverage. Insurance that provides benefits for medical and other services to insureds who, because of their advanced age or the effects of a serious illness or injury, need constant care in their own homes or in a qualified nursing facility. [8]

loss ratio. The ratio of benefits an insurer paid out for a block of policies to the premiums the insurer received for those policies. [9]

LTC insurance benefit. *See* **long-term care insurance benefit**.

LTC insurance coverage. *See* **long-term care insurance coverage**.

lump-sum distribution. Payment of the accumulation value of an annuity contract in a single payment. [12]

maintenance fee. *See* **periodic fee**.

major medical expense coverage. Coverage that provides substantial benefits for (1) basic hospital, surgical, and physician expenses, (2) additional medical services related to illnesses or injuries, and (3) preventive care. [8]

managed account. A customized portfolio of securities that is actively managed by an investment adviser, who provides the account holder with personalized advice on selection, diversification, and taxation of assets. Also known as a *separately managed account*. [11]

managed care. A method of integrating the financing and delivery of health care services within a system that manages the cost, accessibility, and quality of care. [8]

managed indemnity plan. A health care plan that is organized and administered like a traditional indemnity plan, but includes managed care techniques, such as precertification and utilization review, to control costs. [8]

management fee. A mutual fund fee paid to the fund's investment adviser who manages the fund's assets and selects its portfolio of securities. [11]

M&E charge. *See* **mortality and expense risk charge**.

manual rating. A method of calculating group insurance premium rates for broad classes of groups, especially for groups with no credible claims and expense experience, in which the insurer often uses its own past experience with incurred claims and expenses to develop manual rates. [7]

margin account. A brokerage account in which the investor is allowed to borrow money from the brokerage firm to buy securities. [11]

market price. The amount a willing buyer would pay a willing seller for one share of a stock. [11]

market risk. The possibility of losses or reduced returns simply because of the tendency of prices to move together. [2]

market value adjusted (MVA) annuity. An annuity that offers multiple guarantee periods and multiple fixed rates. Also known as a *modified guaranteed annuity*. [12]

master group insurance contract. *See* **group life insurance policy**.

material misrepresentation. A misrepresentation of the facts by an insurance applicant that is relevant to the insurer's evaluation of a proposed insured. [6]

maturity date. 1) The date on which the insurer will pay an endowment policy's face amount to the policyowner if the insured is still living. [5] 2) The specified date by which a bond must be redeemed. [11]

MDO insurance. *See* **monthly debit ordinary insurance**.

Medicaid. A joint federal and state program that provides basic medical expense and nursing home coverage to the low-income population and certain aged and disabled individuals. [8]

medical expense coverage. Health insurance coverage that provides benefits to pay for the treatment of an insured's illnesses and injuries. [8]

medical savings account (MSA). A type of personal health spending account that can be funded by employers or employees, but not both, and is available only to employers with fewer than 50 employees or to self-employed individuals. [8]

medically appropriate services. Diagnostic or treatment measures for which the expected health benefits exceed the expected risks by a margin wide enough to justify the measures.[1] [8]

medically necessary services. Services that are considered by the payor to be (1) consistent with the symptoms, diagnosis, and treatment of the member's condition, (2) in accordance with the standards of good medical practice, (3) not solely for the convenience of the member, member's family, physician, or other health care provider, and (4) furnished in the least intensive type of medical care setting required by the member's condition.[2] [8]

Medicare. A U.S. federal government program established under the Old Age, Survivors, Disability and Health Insurance (OASDHI) Act that provides medical expense benefits to elderly and disabled persons. [8]

Medicare Advantage. The component of Medicare that describes how and by whom covered services are delivered to enrollees. [8]

Medicare Part A. The component of Medicare that provides basic hospital insurance that covers that costs of inpatient hospital services, confinement in nursing facilities or other extended care facilities after hospitalization, home care services following hospitalization, and hospice care. Individuals who satisfy Medicare eligibility requirements are automatically enrolled in Medicare Part A. [8]

Medicare Part B. The component of Medicare that provides benefits to cover the costs of physicians' professional services and other services necessary for the diagnosis or treatment of illness or injury; eligible Medicare beneficiaries must enroll to receive benefits. [8]

Medicare SELECT plan. A managed care plan that supplements Medicare Part B (but not Part A) coverage. [8]

Medigap policy. An individual medical expense insurance policy sold by an insurance company to supplement Medicare Part A and Part B coverage. [8]

merger. A transaction in which one corporation absorbs another corporation, with the absorbed corporation ceasing to exist. [1]

minimum guaranteed interest rate. The lowest interest rate that the insurer will ever credit on a fixed annuity contract's accumulation value. [12]

minimum premium plan (MPP). A group health insurance funding mechanism under which the group policyholder deposits into a special account funds that are sufficient to pay a stated amount of expected claims, and the insurer administers the plan and pays claims from that special account until the funds are exhausted. Thereafter, the insurer is responsible for paying claims from its own funds, and it charges the group policyholder a premium for the coverage it provides. [9]

misrepresentation. A false or misleading statement. [6]

misstatement of age or sex provision. A life insurance policy or annuity contract provision that describes the action the insurer will take to adjust the amount of the benefits payable in the event that the age or sex of the insured or annuitant is incorrectly stated in the application. [6]

MMDA. *See* **money market deposit account**.

MMMF. *See* **money market mutual fund**.

modified guaranteed annuity. *See* **market value adjusted annuity**.

money market account. A category of interest-earning accounts that offers higher interest rates than most NOW accounts and savings accounts and allows a limited number of checks to be written on the account. [3]

money market deposit account (MMDA). A deposit account offered by a depository institution that invests amounts on deposit in short-term, low-risk investments and then pays an interest rate according to the performance of these investments. [3]

money market mutual fund (MMMF). A mutual fund that pools the funds of customers and uses the funds to invest in short-term, low-risk investments and then pays customers interest rates that fluctuate according to the performance of these investments. [3]

money order. A type of check issued by a financial institution, the U.S. Postal Service, and some retail stores that allows the party named on the order to receive the face amount in cash on demand. [3]

monthly debit ordinary (MDO) insurance. Whole life insurance that is marketed through the home service distribution system and is paid for by monthly premium payments. Also known as *debit insurance*. [5]

moral hazard. The likelihood that a person may act dishonestly in the insurance transaction. [2]

morale hazard. The likelihood that a person may act carelessly. [2]

morbidity rate. The incidence of sickness and accidents occurring among a given group of people. [9]

morbidity table. A chart that displays morbidity rates for individuals in different age groups. [9]

mortality. The incidence of death in a specified group of people. [6]

mortality and expense (M&E) risk charge. A variable annuity fee that covers three guarantees, which are the contract benefits: (1) any guaranteed death benefit payable to the designated beneficiary, (2) the fixed payout options which guarantee that a certain amount will be paid for the life of the annuitant, and (3) the guarantee that contract expenses will increase no more than the maximums stated in the contract. [12]

mortality rate. A percentage rate at which death occurs among a defined group of people of a specified age and sometimes of a specified gender. [6]

mortality table. A chart that shows the expected death rates among a particular group at each age—that is, how many people in each age group may be expected to die in a given year. [6]

mortgage. A real estate loan in which the property being financed is pledged as collateral for the loan. [4]

mortgage life insurance. A plan of decreasing term life insurance designed to provide a face amount that corresponds to the decreasing amount owed on a mortgage loan. [5]

mortgage refinancing. The process of obtaining a new mortgage and using some or all of the new mortgage loan to pay off the old mortgage. [4]

MPP. *See* **minimum premium plan**.

MSA. *See* **medical savings account**.

mutual fund. An investment vehicle that pools the funds of investors and uses these funds to buy a number of stocks, bonds, and other financial instruments to create a diversified portfolio of financial investments. Also known as a *unit trust*. [1]

mutual fund company. An investment company that operates a number of mutual funds. [1]

mutual fund family. A group of mutual funds managed by the same mutual fund company. [11]

mutual insurance company. An insurance company that is owned by its policyowners. [1]

MVA annuity. *See* **market value adjusted annuity.**

named-perils. A type of property policy coverage that covers losses caused only by specific perils named in the policy. [10]

National Credit Union Share Insurance Fund (NCUSIF). The insurance arm of the National Credit Union Administration that insures credit union accounts up to $100,000. [3]

NAV. *See* **net asset value**.

NCUSIF. *See* **National Credit Union Share Insurance Fund**.

negotiable order of withdrawal account. *See* **NOW account**.

net asset value (NAV). The value of one share in a mutual fund. [11]

net cash surrender value. The actual cash value available to a policyowner upon policy surrender or lapse; it equals the cash value shown in the policy increased by any cash values of paid-up additions, policy dividend accumulations, and advance premium payments and decreased by outstanding policy loans and any charges imposed on the surrender. [6]

net single premium. The lump sum of money the insurer needs to provide benefits for the policy. [6]

network. A group of physicians, hospitals, and ancillary services providers that a specific managed care plan has contracted with to deliver health care services to its members. [8]

no-load fund. A mutual fund that does not charge a load or a 12b-1 fee greater than 25 basis points. *Contrast with* **load fund**. [11]

nominal interest rate. An interest rate that is quoted without the effects of compounding. Also known as the *stated interest rate. Contrast with* **effective interest rate**. [2]

noncancellable policy. An individual health insurance policy that is guaranteed to be renewable until the insured reaches the limiting age stated in the contract and for which the premium rate is guaranteed; the insurer cannot increase the premium rate under any circumstances. [9]

noncontributory plan. An employee benefit plan under which participating employees are not required to contribute any part of the cost for coverage. *Contrast with* **contributory plan**. [7]

noncumulative preferred stock. A type of preferred stock that does not require the company to pay in full any unpaid scheduled dividends on its preferred stock before it may pay any dividends on its common stock. [11]

nonduplication of benefits provision. A type of coordination of benefits provision in group medical expense insurance policies that limits the amount payable by the secondary plan to the difference, if any, between the amount paid by the primary plan and the amount that would have been payable by the secondary plan had that plan been the primary plan. [9]

nonforfeiture provision. 1) A cash value life insurance policy provision that sets forth the options available to the owner of a cash value policy if the policy lapses or if the policyowner decides to surrender the policy. [6] 2) An annuity contract provision that states the benefit amounts that an insurer will pay under a deferred annuity contract if the premium payments stop or the contract is surrendered during the accumulation period. [12]

noninstallment credit. Any loan or credit arrangement that does not require the borrower to make a series of periodic payments on the loan or credit balance. [4]

non-interest-earning checking account. See **regular checking account**.

nonlife insurance company. See **property/casualty insurance company**.

nonparticipating policy. A form of life insurance policy under which the policyowner does not share in the insurance company's divisible surplus. *Contrast with* **participating policy**. [6]

nonqualified annuity. An annuity that is not part of a qualified plan. [12]

normal form of benefit. The manner in which a retirement plan specifies funds are to be distributed upon retirement. [14]

normal retirement age. The earliest age at which participants in a retirement plan can retire with full benefits. [14]

NOW account. A checking account that earns interest. Also known as a *negotiable order of withdrawal account*. [3]

OAS Act. *See* **Old Age Security Act**.

Old Age Security (OAS) Act. A federal universal public pension plan that provides a pension to virtually all Canadian residents who are age 65 or older, whether or not they have been employed. [1]

open-end credit. A credit arrangement that allows a person to borrow money repeatedly up to a prearranged limit and to make at least minimum payments, allowing the credit balance to continue to accrue interest. Also known as *revolving credit*. [4]

open-perils. A type of property policy coverage that covers losses caused by all perils other than those excluded in the policy. Also known as *all-risks*. [10]

opportunity cost. The alternative benefit that is given up when limited resources are used in choosing one alternative over another. [2]

Option 1 plan. *See* **Option A plan**.

Option 2 plan. *See* **Option B plan**.

optional insured rider. *See* **second insured rider**.

optionally renewable policy. An individual health insurance policy that grants the insurer the right to refuse to renew the policy for any reason on certain dates specified in the contract and to add coverage limitations and increase the premium rate if it does so for a class of optionally renewable policies. [9]

Option A plan. A universal life insurance policy that provides a level death benefit amount, which is always equal to the policy's face amount. Also known as an *Option 1 plan*. [5]

Option B plan. A universal life insurance policy that provides a death benefit amount that, at any given time, is equal to the policy's face amount plus the amount of the policy's cash value. Also known as an *Option 2 plan*. [5]

ordinary life insurance policy. *See* **continuous-premium whole life policy**.

overinsurance provision. A provision in individual health insurance policies that states that the benefits payable under the policy will be reduced if the person is overinsured. [9]

overinsured person. A person who is entitled to receive either (1) more in medical expense benefits than the actual costs incurred for treatment or (2) a greater income amount during disability than would have been earned from working. [9]

over-the-counter market. An electronic communications network over which securities that are not bought and sold on an exchange are traded. [11]

package policy. An insurance policy that provides two or more types of insurance—property and liability, for example—in one policy. [10]

paid-up additional insurance dividend option. A dividend option in which the insurer uses each policy dividend as a net single premium to purchase additional insurance on the insured's life; the paid-up additional insurance is issued on the same plan as the basic policy and in whatever face amount the policy dividend can provide at the insured's age at the time of purchase. [6]

paid-up additions option benefit. A supplemental life insurance policy benefit that allows the owner of a whole life insurance policy to purchase single-premium paid-up additions to the policy on stated dates, such as each policy anniversary, and thus to increase the amount of coverage provided under the basic policy. [5]

parent company. *See* **holding company**.

partial disability coverage. A disability coverage option designed to provide income replacement benefits to an insured whose disability prevents him either from performing some of the duties of his usual occupation or from engaging in that occupation on a full-time basis. [8]

partial surrender. *See* **withdrawal**.

participating policy. A form of life insurance policy under which the policyowner shares in the insurance company's divisible surplus. *Contrast with* **nonparticipating policy**. [6]

participation. The inclusion of a person as a plan participant in an employee benefit plan. [14]

par value. The face value of a stock or bond. [11]

payee. 1) The person or party who is to receive insurance policy proceeds in accordance with the terms of a settlement agreement. [6] 2) The person or entity designated to receive the periodic income payments under an annuity contract. [12]

payment cap. A loan provision that sets a maximum on the periodic payment amount on an adjustable rate mortgage. [4]

payout annuity. An annuity in the payout period, whether purchased as an immediate annuity or purchased as a deferred annuity and allowed to annuitize. [12]

payout options. The choices an annuity contract owner has as to how the insurer will distribute annuity benefits during the payout period. Also known as *settlement options*. [12]

payout period. The time period when periodic income payments are payable to the payee. Also known as the *annuitization period*. [12]

PBGC. *See* **Pension Benefit Guaranty Corporation**.

Pension Benefit Guaranty Corporation (PBGC). A federal agency that guarantees the payment of part or all or retirement benefits for participants in defined benefit retirement plans when those plans become financially unable to pay benefits. [14]

pension plan. A plan that accumulates assets and provides a retirement income benefit for people participating in the plan. [1]

P/E ratio. *See* **price/earnings ratio**.

peril. The cause of a loss. [10]

period certain annuity. An annuity payout option that guarantees a specified number of periodic payments, whether the annuitant lives or dies. Also known as *annuity certain*. [12]

periodic fee. An annuity fee that is an amount payable at predetermined intervals, for example, every year or every month. Also known as a *maintenance fee*. [12]

periodic income payments. The monthly, quarterly, semiannually, or yearly annuity payments made to the payee. [12]

periodic rate. The annual percentage rate divided by the number of billing periods per year. [4]

permanent life insurance. *See* **cash value life insurance**.

personal risk. The risk of economic loss associated with death, poor health, injury, and outliving one's economic resources. [2]

physical damage insurance. Insurance that covers losses the insured incurs due to damage to his covered automobile caused by collision or other perils. [10]

physical examination provision. A provision in individual and group disability income insurance policies that gives the insurer the right to have an insured who has submitted a disability income claim examined by a doctor of the insurer's choice, at the insurer's expense. [9]

physical hazard. A physical characteristic that may increase the likelihood of loss. [2]

physician expenses. Charges associated with physicians' visits both in and out of the hospital. [8]

plan administrator. The party responsible for handling the administrative aspects of a retirement plan and ensuring the plan complies with applicable regulatory requirements. [14]

plan beneficiary. An individual who receives benefits under a retirement plan. [14]

plan document. A detailed legal agreement establishing the existence of a retirement plan and specifying the rights and obligations of various parties to the plan. [14]

plan participant. A member of a covered group who is eligible to participate in a retirement plan and who actually chooses to take part in the plan or whose participation is automatic. [13]

plan sponsor. An employer or union that establishes a retirement plan for its employees or members. [13]

point. A fee charged at the time a mortgage is taken out that is equal to one percent of the loan amount. [4]

point-of-sale terminal. A computer terminal at a retail location that allows a person to use his debit card to take funds from his account and transfer them directly to the retailer's account. [3]

point-of-service (POS) product. A managed care option under which plan members in need of medical care can choose, at the point of service, whether to seek care in-network or out-of-network. [8]

policy. A written document that contains the terms of the agreement between the insurance company and the owner of the policy. [2]

policy anniversary. The anniversary of the date on which coverage under an insurance policy became effective. [5]

policy dividend. A policyowner's share of an insurance company's divisible surplus. [6]

policy dividends provision. A provision in a participating life insurance policy that describes the ways in which the policyowner may receive the policy dividends. [6]

policyholder. The employer or other type of organization that decides what kind of coverage to purchase for the group, negotiates the terms of and enters into a group insurance contract with the insurer, and usually administers part or all of the coverage. [7]

policy loan. A loan secured by a policy's cash value that an insurer makes to the owner of a cash value life insurance policy. [6]

policy loan provision. A cash value life insurance policy provision that specifies the terms on which a policyowner may obtain a policy loan. [6]

policyowner. The person or business that owns an individual insurance policy. [2]

policy proceeds. *See* **death benefit definition 1**.

policy term. The specified period of time during which a term life insurance policy provides coverage. [5]

policy withdrawal provision. A universal life insurance policy provision that permits the universal life policyowner to reduce the amount in the policy's cash value by withdrawing up to the amount of the cash value. [6]

political risk. The possibility of losses or reduced returns because of a change in laws, regulations, or taxes. [2]

portable. 1) The characteristic of group insurance coverage that can be continued when a group insured leaves the group [7] 2) The characteristic of vested retirement benefits that can be moved from one retirement plan to another employer-sponsored or individual retirement plan when the participating individual leaves employment with the plan sponsor. [14]

portfolio. A collection of various securities usually assembled by an investor for the purpose of meeting a defined set of financial goals. [2]

POS product. *See* **point-of-service product**.

PPO. *See* **preferred provider organization**.

pre-existing condition. An injury or sickness that occurred or manifested itself within a specified period—usually two years—before the policy was issued and that was not disclosed on the application for insurance. [5]

pre-existing conditions provision. A provision in individual and group health insurance policies that states that until the insured has been covered under the policy for a certain period, the insurer will not pay benefits for a pre-existing condition. [9]

preferred provider organization (PPO). A health care benefit arrangement that provides incentives for members to use network providers, but also provides at least some coverage for services rendered by non-network providers. [8]

preferred stock. A type of stock that typically does not carry the voting rights of common stock, but does carry a stated dividend rate that is paid before any payment of common stock dividends. [11]

premium. 1) A specified amount of money an insurance company charges for the insurance coverage. [2] 2) The amount by which a bond's current market price exceeds its par value. [11]

premium delay arrangement. A group health insurance funding mechanism that allows the group policyholder to postpone paying monthly group insurance premiums for a stated period of time beyond the expiration of the policy's grace period. [9]

premium payment mode. The frequency (monthly, quarterly, semiannually, or annually) at which renewal premiums are payable. [6]

premium reduction dividend option. A dividend option in which the insurer applies policy dividends toward the payment of renewal premiums. [6]

pre-need funeral insurance. Whole life insurance that provides funds to pay for the insured's funeral and burial. Also known as *pre-need insurance*. [5]

pre-need insurance. *See* **pre-need funeral insurance**.

prescription drug coverage. Insurance that provides benefits for the purchase of drugs and medicines that are prescribed by a physician and are not available over-the-counter. [8]

present value. The amount of money that must be invested today at a specified interest rate to accumulate a specified amount by a certain future date. *Contrast with* **future value**. [2]

presumptive disability. A condition that, if present, automatically causes an insured to be considered totally disabled; this includes total and permanent blindness, loss of the use of any two limbs, and loss of speech or hearing. [8]

previous balance method. A method used to calculate the amount of a credit card's outstanding balance in which the balance due on the account at the end of the previous billing period is used as the current billing period's outstanding balance without including payments or new purchases made in the current billing period. [4]

price/earnings (P/E) ratio. The stock price per share divided by the earnings per share. [11]

pricing. The process of determining the amount to charge a customer for a product. [6]

prime interest rate. The interest rate banks charge their best and most creditworthy customers. [4]

principal. A sum of money originally borrowed or lent. [2]

private mortgage insurance. A form of insurance that protects the lender by insuring the gap between the required down payment—typically 20 percent of the home purchase price—and the actual down payment made by the borrower. [4]

probationary period. An employee benefit plan provision that specifies the length of time—typically from one to six months—that a new group member must wait before becoming eligible to enroll in the plan. [7]

professional liability insurance. Liability insurance that covers individuals who provide professional services, such as physicians and lawyers, from losses they incur as a result of being held responsible for losses of their clients. [10]

profit sharing plan. A retirement plan funded primarily by cash contributions from the employer's profits. [13]

property/casualty insurance company. An insurance company that insures against financial loss from property damage and theft by providing property insurance, such as homeowners insurance and automobile insurance, and from being held responsible for harming others or their property by providing liability insurance. Also known as a *nonlife insurance company* and *general insurance company*. [1]

property damage. Damage to, destruction of, or loss of use of property. [10]

property damage risk. The risk of economic loss resulting from damage to or loss of a person's property. [2]

property insurance. Insurance that provides protection against financial loss from property damage and theft. [10]

prospective review. The review and possible authorization of proposed treatment plans for a patient before the treatment is implemented. [8]

purchasing power risk. *See* **inflation risk**.

pure risk. Risk that involves no possibility of gain; either a loss occurs or no loss occurs. [2]

QPP. *See* **Quebec Pension Plan**.

qualified annuity. An annuity contract purchased to fund or distribute funds from a qualified plan. [12]

qualified plan. In the United States, technically a retirement plan that receives favorable income tax treatment by meeting the requirements imposed by U.S. federal tax law and ERISA. However, a broader, less formal usage of *qualified plan* includes other tax-advantaged savings plans such as IRAs. [12]

Quebec Pension Plan (QPP). A Canadian provincial plan that functions in the same manner as the Canada Pension Plan except that the QPP applies only to wage earners in Quebec. [1]

rate of return. The profit that results from investing money, expressed as a percentage of the amount invested. [2]

rating territory. The location where a vehicle is principally garaged and driven. [10]

redemption fee. A mutual fund fee for redeeming shares that is expressed as a dollar amount or as a percentage of the redemption price. [11]

reduced paid-up insurance nonforfeiture option. A nonforfeiture option that allows the owner of a policy with a cash value to discontinue premium payments and to use the policy's net cash surrender value as a net single premium to purchase paid-up insurance of the same plan as the original policy. [6]

refund annuity. *See* **life with refund annuity**.

registered retirement savings plan (RRSP). In Canada, a qualified retirement account that may be established by a gainfully employed individual. [13]

regular checking account. A checking account that does not pay interest. Also known as a *non-interest-earning checking account*. [3]

regular IRA. *See* **traditional IRA**.

reimbursement benefits. *See* **indemnity benefits**.

reinstatement provision. A life and health insurance policy provision that describes the conditions a policyowner must meet for the insurer to reinstate—or put back into force—a policy that has either lapsed or, in the case of life policies, been continued under the extended term or reduced paid-up insurance nonforfeiture options. [6]

reinsurance. Insurance that one insurance company purchases from another insurance company. [2]

reinsurance company. *See* **reinsurer**.

reinsurer. An insurance company that accepts risks transferred from another insurer in a reinsurance transaction. Also known as a *reinsurance company* or *assuming company*. [2]

reinvestment risk. The risk that after the principal and interest on a loan or other investment have been returned, the lender or investor may have difficulty finding another investment that offers returns as high as the previous investment. [2]

renewable term insurance policy. A term life insurance policy that gives the policyowner the option to renew the coverage at the end of the policy term without presenting evidence of insurability. [5]

renewal provision. A provision in individual health insurance policies that describes (1) the circumstances under which the insurer has the right to cancel or refuse to renew the coverage and (2) the insurer's right to increase the policy's premium rate. [9]

replacement cost insurance. Property insurance that pays the insured the full cost of replacing the lost or damaged property, subject to a maximum amount. [10]

retention limit. A specified maximum amount of insurance that a ceding company is willing to carry at its own risk without transferring some of the risk to a reinsurer. [2]

retrocession. A transaction by which a reinsurer cedes risk to another reinsurer. [2]

retrocessionaire. The reinsurer that accepts the risk ceded by another reinsurer in a retrocession. [2]

retrospective rating arrangement. A group health insurance funding mechanism under which the insurer agrees to charge the group policyholder a lower monthly premium than it would normally charge based on the group's prior claim experience, and the policyholder agrees to pay an additional amount if, at the end of the policy year, the group's claim experience has been unfavorable. [9]

retrospective review. A review and evaluation of the treatment and services a plan member received. [8]

return. The compensation that results from investing or lending money. [2]

reverse mortgage. A special type of loan by means of which older people can convert the equity in their homes into cash. [4]

revocable beneficiary. A life insurance policy beneficiary whose right to the policy's proceeds can be cancelled or reduced by the policyowner at any time before the insured's death. [6]

revolving credit. *See* **open-end credit**.

rider. An amendment or addition to a contract that either expands or limits the benefits payable under or otherwise modifies the contract. Also known as an *endorsement*. [5]

risk. The possibility of an unexpected outcome, which is typically a loss. [2]

risk management. The practice of identifying, assessing, and dealing with risk. [2]

risk-return tradeoff. The concept that a direct relationship exists between the risk of an investment and the level of return the investment potentially will provide. [2]

risk tolerance. The degree to which a person is willing to accept financial risk. [2]

rollover. The tax-free movement of cash or other assets disbursed from one retirement plan into another retirement plan. [14]

Roth IRA. An individual retirement arrangement that provides for non-deductible contributions annually, but tax-free qualified withdrawals. [13]

RRSP. *See* **registered retirement savings plan**.

salary continuation plan. A short-term disability income insurance plan that typically provides 100 percent of the insured employee's salary, beginning on the first day of the employee's absence due to illness or injury and continuing for some specified time. [9]

sales charge. *See* **front-end load**.

sales finance company. A finance company owned by a retail company as a means of assisting customers in purchasing the retail company's goods. [1]

S&L. *See* **savings and loan association**.

savings account. A time deposit account that pays interest on deposited funds, typically from the day of deposit to the day of withdrawal. [3]

savings and loan association (S&L). A depository institution that principally pools the savings of people and makes residential mortgage loans. [1]

savings bank (SB). A depository institution similar to a savings and loan association in that it accepts deposits—primarily savings account deposits— mainly from people rather than businesses and makes primarily mortgage loans; but SBs are legally permissible only in certain states, primarily in the northeast. [1]

savings incentive match plan for employees (SIMPLE) 401(k). In the United States, a special arrangement whereby an employer with 100 or fewer employees can establish a simplified 401(k) retirement savings plan for employees. [13]

savings incentive match plan for employees (SIMPLE) IRA. In the United States, a written agreement (salary reduction agreement) between an employer with 100 or fewer employees and its employees that allows eligible employees (including self-employed individuals) to choose to reduce compensation by a certain percentage each pay period and have the employer contribute the amount of the salary reduction to a SIMPLE IRA on the employee's behalf. [13]

savings plan. A retirement plan to which a plan sponsor may make contributions on behalf of a plan participant if the participant makes contributions to the plan. [13]

SB. *See* **savings bank**.

secondary beneficiary. *See* **contingent beneficiary**.

second insured rider. A supplemental life insurance policy benefit that provides term insurance coverage on the life of a person other than the policy's insured. Also known as an *optional insured rider* or an *additional insured rider*. [5]

second mortgage. A mortgage loan secured by the borrower's equity in real estate that is already collateral for a first mortgage. [4]

second-to-die life insurance. *See* **last survivor life insurance**.

section 529 plan. A tax-advantaged savings plan designed to fund a student's higher education. [13]

secured loan. A loan backed by collateral. [4]

securities broker-dealer. An institution that specializes in the purchase and sale of investment instruments, such as stocks and bonds. Also known as a *broker-dealer*, *brokerage firm*, or *brokerage*. [1]

security. An investment instrument, such as a stock or bond. [1]

segregated account. *See* **separate account**.

selection against the insurer. *See* **antiselection**.

selection of risks. *See* **underwriting**.

self-insurance. A risk-management strategy by which a person or business accepts financial responsibility for losses associated with specific risks. [2]

SEP. *See* **simplified employee pension**.

separate account. An investment account maintained separately from an insurer's general account to isolate and help manage the funds placed in variable products. Also known as a *segregated account*. *Contrast with* **general account**. [5]

separate account contract or rider. A type of retirement plan funding vehicle in which the insurance company invests the plan assets in the insurance company's separate account investment subaccounts. [14]

separately managed account. *See* **managed account**.

series EE savings bond. A U.S. government bond purchased for 50 percent of its face value that earns interest at rates based on the yields of Treasury notes and bonds. [3]

series HH savings bond. A U.S. government bond that is purchased at face value not by paying cash but by exchanging series EE bonds. [3]

service. A primarily intangible activity that one party performs for another. [1]

service fee. A one-time annuity fee for a specific service. [12]

service requirement. The minimum required length of service for a group benefit plan member to be eligible to participate in the plan. [14]

settlement options. 1) The choices a life insurance policyowner or beneficiary has as to how the insurer will distribute the policy proceeds. [6] 2) *See* **payout options**.

settlement options provision. A life insurance policy provision that grants the policyowner or beneficiary several choices as to how the insurer will distribute a policy's proceeds. [6]

share draft account. A checking account that is offered by credit unions. [3]

shareholder. A person who owns stock in a corporation. Also known as a *stockholder*. [11]

SIMPLE 401(k). *See* **savings incentive match plan for employees 401(k)**.

simple interest. A type of interest that is calculated only on the original principal amount. *Contrast with* **compound interest**. [2]

SIMPLE IRA. *See* **savings incentive match plan for employees IRA**.

simplified employee pension (SEP). In the United States, a written plan that allows an employer to make contributions to individual retirement arrangements established by each participating employee. [13]

single-payment loan. A loan in which the borrower receives the entire principal at one time and agrees to pay the principal and any interest in a single payment on a specified future date. [4]

single-premium annuity. An annuity contract funded by only one lump-sum premium payment from the contract owner to the insurance company. [12]

single-premium deferred annuity (SPDA) contract. A deferred annuity contract that is purchased with a single premium payment. [12]

single-premium immediate annuity (SPIA) contract. An immediate annuity contract that is purchased with a lump-sum premium payment on the contract's issue date. [12]

single-premium whole life policy. A type of limited-payment whole life insurance policy that requires only one premium payment. [5]

smart card. A plastic card with a computer chip that is programmed to represent a certain amount of cash and to which money can be added when the stored value is depleted. [3]

social insurance program. A welfare plan established by law and administered by a government that provides the population with income security. [1]

Social Security. A U.S. federal program that provides specified benefits, including monthly retirement income benefits, to people who have contributed to the plan during their income-earning years. The program also provides a benefit to qualified disabled individuals, as well as to the surviving spouses and dependent children of qualified deceased workers. [1]

Social Security Disability Income (SSDI). A federal program that provides disability income benefits to U.S. workers who become disabled as a result of nonwork-related accidents or illnesses, who are under age 65, and who have paid a specified amount of Social Security tax for a prescribed number of quarter-year periods. [8]

SPDA. *See* **single-premium deferred annuity contract**.

specific stop-loss coverage. *See* **individual stop-loss coverage**.

speculative risk. Risk that involves three possible outcomes—loss, gain, or no change. [2]

SPIA. *See* **single-premium immediate annuity contract**.

split-dollar life insurance plan. An agreement under which a business provides individual life insurance policies for certain employees, who share in paying the cost of the policies. [5]

spouse and children's insurance rider. A supplemental life insurance policy benefit that provides term coverage on the insured's spouse and children. The coverage provided by such a rider is typically sold on the basis of coverage units unlike the coverage provided under a family income insurance policy. [5]

SSDI. *See* **Social Security Disability Income**.

stated interest rate. *See* **nominal interest rate**.

stock. An equity security representing a share of ownership in a corporation. [11]

stock bonus plan. A retirement plan into which a corporate plan sponsor makes contributions in the form of the corporation's stock. [13]

stock exchange. An organized marketplace where specific types of securities, such as common stocks and bonds, are bought and sold by members of the exchange. [11]

stock fund. A mutual fund whose assets are invested primarily in stocks. Also known as an *equity fund*. [11]

stockholder. *See* **shareholder**.

stock insurance company. An insurance company that is owned by the people and organizations that purchase shares of the company's stock. [1]

stop-loss insurance. Insurance purchased by employers that self-insure group health insurance plans so that they can place a maximum dollar limit on their liability for paying claims. [9]

stop-loss provision. A provision in a major medical expense policy that specifies that the policy will cover 100 percent of allowable medical expenses after the insured has paid a specified amount out-of-pocket to satisfy deductible and coinsurance requirements. [8]

stored-value card. A plastic card with a computer chip that is programmed to represent a certain amount of cash but requires the cardholder to get a new card when the stored value is expended. [3]

straight life insurance policy. *See* **continuous-premium whole life policy**.

subaccount. One of several alternative pools of investments to which a policyowner or contract owner allocates premiums paid and accumulated cash values or accumulation values. [5]

subrogation. The right of the insurer to enforce any claim the insured has against a third party resulting from a loss for which the insurer has paid. [10]

subsidiary. A company in a holding company system that is owned and controlled by the holding company. [1]

suicide exclusion provision. A life insurance policy provision that states that policy proceeds will not be paid if the insured dies as the result of suicide as defined within the policy within a specified period following the date of policy issue. [6]

summary plan description. A written disclosure document that accurately summarizes the provisions of a plan document. [14]

super NOW account. A high-interest NOW account that offers only limited check-writing privileges. [3]

supplemental major medical policy. A separate policy issued in conjunction with an underlying basic medical expense policy that is designed to provide payment for expenses that exceed the benefit levels of the underlying basic plan and, often, for expenses that are not covered by the underlying plan. [8]

surgical expenses. Charges for inpatient and outpatient surgical procedures. [8]

surrender charge. A fee sometimes charged to an annuity contract owner when he withdraws a portion or all of the contract's accumulation value. Also known as a *back-end load*, or, for variable annuities, a *contingent deferred sales charge.* [12]

surrender value. The amount that an annuity contract owner is entitled to receive if the contract is terminated during its accumulation period. [12]

survivor benefit. *See* **death benefit definition 2**.

survivor income plan. An employee benefit plan that provides periodic income payments to specified dependents who survive a covered group member. [7]

sweep account. *See* **asset management account**.

term. 1) The period of time during which a loan is outstanding and the interest rate is guaranteed. [4] 2) The period of time between when a bond is issued and when it matures. [11]

term life insurance. A type of life insurance that provides coverage only if the insured dies during the period specified in the policy. [5]

terminal illness (TI) benefit. An accelerated death benefit under which the insurer pays some or all of the policy's death benefit to a policyowner if the insured suffers from a terminal illness and has a physician-certified life expectancy of 12 months or less. [5]

third-party administrator (TPA). An organization other than an insurance company that provides administrative services to the sponsors of group benefit plans. [8]

thrift. Another term for a savings and loan association and savings bank, which were established to encourage the careful management of money and to help finance home building. [1]

TI benefit. *See* **terminal illness benefit**.

tiered interest rates. Interest rates that vary according to the amount on deposit in the account. Also known as *graduated interest rates*. [3]

time deposit account. An account into which funds are deposited with the expectation that they will remain on deposit for a period of time. [3]

time limit on certain defenses provision. A provision in individual medical expense insurance policies that states that after the policy has been in force for a specified period—usually two or three years—the insurer cannot use a material misrepresentation in the application to contest the policy or deny a claim unless the misrepresentation was fraudulent. [9]

time value of money. The concept that the value of a sum of money will change over time as the result of the effect of interest. [2]

TPA. *See* **third-party administrator**.

traditional IRA. An individual retirement arrangement in which contributions may be deductible and investment earnings are tax deferred until the funds are withdrawn. Also known as a *regular IRA*. [13]

traditional whole life insurance. *See* **whole life insurance**.

traveler's check. A check bought by a person from a financial institution, typically to use as a substitute for cash while traveling. [3]

trust. A legal arrangement whereby one person or entity who creates the trust, known as the *grantor*, gives legal title to property, known as the *res*, to another person or entity, known as the *trustee*, for the benefit of a third person or entity, known as the *trust beneficiary*. [14]

UCR fee. *See* **usual, customary, and reasonable fee**.

umbrella liability insurance. Liability insurance that provides additional liability coverage over and above that provided by a homeowners, automobile, or comprehensive personal liability policy. [10]

unallocated funding vehicle. A funding vehicle in which some or all contributions are pooled together and not assigned to individual participants until each participant begins to collect benefits. [14]

unbundled product structure. A life insurance and annuity product design in which an insurer explicitly discloses various expense and benefit charges to customers and specifies the rate of investment return being credited to customers. *Contrast with* **bundled product structure**. [5]

underinsured motorists coverage. Insurance that protects the insured and his passengers when the other driver has coverage, but that coverage is inadequate to cover their injuries. [10]

underwriting. The process of identifying and classifying the degree of risk represented by a proposed insured. Also known as *selection of risks*. [2]

uninsured motorists coverage. Insurance that covers an insured driver and her passengers for bodily injuries and, in some states, property damage incurred in an accident with a driver who, contrary to legal requirements, carries no liability insurance. [10]

unit trust. *See* **mutual fund**.

universal life insurance. A form of cash value life insurance characterized by flexible premiums, flexible face amounts and death benefit amounts, and unbundled product structures. [5]

unsecured loan. A loan not backed by collateral. [4]

UR. *See* **utilization review**.

usual, customary, and reasonable (UCR) fee. The amount that physicians within a particular geographic region commonly charge for a particular medical service. [8]

utilization management. A process designed to help ensure that plan members receive the most appropriate care from the most appropriate provider in the most appropriate and most cost-effective setting. [8]

utilization review (UR). A process managed care plans use to evaluate the medical necessity, appropriateness, and cost-effectiveness of health care services and treatment plans. [8]

valued contract. An insurance policy that specifies the amount of the benefit that will be payable when a covered loss occurs, regardless of the actual amount of the loss that was incurred. [2]

value fund. A mutual fund that has the objective of long-term capital appreciation and invests in companies whose stock appears to be valued at less than it is worth. [11]

variable annuity. An annuity contract under which the amount of the accumulation value and periodic income payments fluctuate in accordance with the performance of one or more specified investment funds. [12]

variable interest rate. An interest rate that fluctuates according to the rise and fall of interest rates in the marketplace. [4]

variable life (VL) insurance. A form of cash value life insurance in which premiums are fixed, but the face amount and other values may vary, reflecting the performance of the investment subaccounts selected by the policyowner. [5]

variable rate certificate of deposit. A certificate of deposit that pays an interest rate that rises and falls in accordance with a benchmark rate. Also known as an *adjustable rate CD*. [3]

variable rate mortgage. *See* **adjustable rate mortgage**.

variable universal life (VUL) insurance. A form of cash value life insurance that combines the premium and death benefit flexibility of universal life insurance with the investment flexibility and risk of variable life insurance. Also known as *flexible variable life*. [5]

vesting. A retirement plan participant's right to keep all or part of her accrued benefit even if she retires early or terminates employment before retirement. [13]

vesting schedule. The formula or timetable that determines when a retirement plan participant obtains a nonforfeitable right to values or benefits. [14]

vision care coverage. Insurance that provides benefits for expenses incurred in obtaining eye examinations and corrective lenses. [8]

waiting period. *See* **elimination period**.

waiver of premium for disability (WP) benefit. A supplemental life insurance policy benefit under which the insurer promises to give up its right to collect premiums that become due while the insured is disabled according to the policy or rider's definition of disability. [5]

waiver of premium for payor benefit. A supplemental life insurance policy benefit that provides that the insurance company will waive its right to collect a policy's premiums if the payor—the person responsible for paying premiums—dies or becomes totally disabled. [5]

whole life insurance. A type of cash value life insurance that remains in effect, if the premiums are current, until the insured dies. Also known as *traditional whole life insurance.* [5]

window premiums. Additional premiums accepted by most insurers during the first contract year of a single-premium deferred annuity contract. [12]

withdrawal. 1) The payment of a portion of the cash value of a universal life insurance policy to the policyowner while the policy is in force. [6] 2) The payment of a portion of an annuity's accumulation value to the contract owner during the accumulation period. Also known as a *partial surrender.* [12]

WP benefit. *See* **waiver of premium for disability benefit**.

yearly renewable term (YRT) insurance. One-year term life insurance that is renewable at the end of each policy year. [5]

yield to maturity. The rate of return a bondholder will earn if he holds a bond until maturity. [11]

YRT insurance. *See* **yearly renewable term insurance**.

---

1. Mark A. Schuster, M.D., Elizabeth A McGlynn, and Robert H. Brook, M.D., "Why the Quality of U.S. Health Care Must Be Improved," National Coalition on Health Care, October 1997, http://www.nchc.org/emerge/ quality.html (1 March 2000).
2. Adapted from Bruce W. Clark, "Negotiating Successful Managed Care Contracts," *Healthcare Financial Management* (August 1995): 28. © 1995, Healthcare Financial Management Association.

Index

Symbols

A

B

C

D

E

F

G

H

I

N

O

P

T

U

V

W

Y

IMPORTANT—READ CAREFULLY BEFORE REMOVING THE QUICK REVIEW CD FROM ITS JACKET. USE OF THE SOFTWARE PROGRAM ON THE ENCLOSED DISK IS SUBJECT TO THE TERMS OF THE LICENSE AGREEMENT PRINTED BELOW. BY REMOVING THE DISK FROM ITS JACKET, YOU INDICATE YOUR ACCEPTANCE OF THE FOLLOWING LOMA LICENSE AGREEMENT.

QUICK REVIEW CD LICENSE AGREEMENT

This Quick Review CD License Agreement (the "Agreement") is a legal agreement between You (either as an individual or a single entity) and LOMA (Life Office Management Association, Inc.) for the use of the Quick Review CD software ("the Software") accompanying this Agreement. By removing the disk from its jacket, You are agreeing to be bound by the terms of this Agreement.

Definition of in "Use"
The Software is in "use" on a computer when it is loaded into temporary memory (RAM) or installed into permanent memory (hard disk, CD-ROM, or other storage device) of that computer.

Grant of License

Rights of an Individual. If You are an individual, LOMA grants to You a nonexclusive license to use one copy of the Software on both your office computer and on your home computer provided that You are the only individual using the Software.

Rights of an Entity. If You are an entity, LOMA grants to You a nonexclusive license to use the Software in only one of the following two ways, with the selection to be yours:

- You may designate one individual within your organization to have the sole right to use the Software in the manner provided above under "Rights of an Individual."
- Alternatively, You may install one copy of the Software on a single computer and allow multiple members of your organization to use the Software on that one computer. If You wish to use the Software on another computer, You must deinstall it from the computer it is on before installing it on another computer.

Copyright

The Software is owned by LOMA and is protected by U.S. copyright laws and international treaty provisions. Therefore, You must treat the Software like any other copyrighted material (e.g., a book or musical recording) EXCEPT that You may either make one copy of the Software solely for backup or archival purposes or transfer the Software to a single hard disk provided You keep the original solely for backup or archival purposes. You may not copy the written material accompanying the Software. The instructional material (hereinafter "the Content") contained in the Software is also owned by LOMA and protected by U.S. copyright laws and international treaty provisions. It is illegal to make any copy whatsoever of the Content; to install the Software on a network, intranet, or Web site; to download the Content to another Computer or device EXCEPT as expressly allowed under "Grant of License" above; to print screens or otherwise cause the Content to be printed; or to in any other way reproduce the Content contained in or accompanying the Software.

Other Restrictions

You may not rent or lease the Software. You may not reverse engineer, decompile, or disassemble the Software or in any way duplicate the contents of the code and other elements therein.

Disclaimer of Warranty

LOMA MAKES NO WARRANTY EXPRESS OR IMPLIED INCLUDING, WITHOUT LIMITATION, NO WARRANTY OF MERCHANTABILITY OR FITNESS OR SUITABILITY FOR A PARTICULAR PURPOSE. UNDER NO CIRCUMSTANCES SHALL LOMA BE LIABLE TO YOU OR ANY THIRD PARTY FOR ANY INCIDENTAL OR CONSEQUENTIAL DAMAGES WHATSOEVER.

Limitation of Liability

You agree to indemnify and hold harmless LOMA, its employees, its agents, and their successors and assigns against any loss, liability, cost or expense (including reasonable attorneys' fees) asserted against or suffered or incurred by LOMA as a consequence of, or in the defense of, any claim arising from or based upon any alleged negligence, act or failure to act whatsoever of You, your employees, their successors, agents, heirs, and/or assigns with respect to the aforementioned Software.